The Basics of Explosives

Volume 1 of 2

" The Design & Function "

Edited by Paul F. Kisak

Contents

1 Explosive material   1
   1.1 History 1
   1.2 Applications 2
       1.2.1 Commercial 2
       1.2.2 Military 2
       1.2.3 Civilian 2
       1.2.4 Safety 2
   1.3 Types 2
       1.3.1 Chemical 2
       1.3.2 Exotic 3
   1.4 Properties of explosive materials 3
       1.4.1 Sensitivity 3
       1.4.2 Sensitivity to initiation 4
       1.4.3 Velocity of detonation 4
       1.4.4 Stability 4
       1.4.5 Power, performance, and strength 4
       1.4.6 Brisance 5
       1.4.7 Density 5
       1.4.8 Volatility 6
       1.4.9 Hygroscopicity and water resistance 6
       1.4.10 Toxicity 6
       1.4.11 Explosive train 6
       1.4.12 Volume of products of explosion 6
       1.4.13 Oxygen balance (OB% or Ω) 6
       1.4.14 Chemical composition 7
       1.4.15 Availability and cost 7
   1.5 Classification of explosive materials 7
       1.5.1 By sensitivity 7
       1.5.2 By velocity 9

		1.5.3	By composition	9
		1.5.4	By physical form	9
		1.5.5	Shipping label classifications	10
	1.6	Regulation		11
		1.6.1	Netherlands	11
		1.6.2	UK	11
		1.6.3	United States	11
	1.7	List of explosives		13
		1.7.1	Compounds	13
		1.7.2	Mixtures	13
		1.7.3	Elements	14
	1.8	See also		14
	1.9	References		14
	1.10	Further reading		15
	1.11	External links		15

2 Explosion 16

	2.1	Causes		17
		2.1.1	Natural	17
		2.1.2	Chemical	17
		2.1.3	Electrical and magnetic	17
		2.1.4	Mechanical and vapor	17
		2.1.5	Nuclear	17
	2.2	Properties of explosions		17
		2.2.1	Force	18
		2.2.2	Velocity	18
		2.2.3	Evolution of heat	18
		2.2.4	Initiation of reaction	18
		2.2.5	Fragmentation	18
	2.3	Notable explosions		18
		2.3.1	Chemical explosions	18
		2.3.2	Nuclear testing	18
		2.3.3	Use in war	19
		2.3.4	Volcanic eruptions	19
	2.4	Etymology		19
	2.5	See also		19
	2.6	References		19

3 Explosive weapon 20

	3.1	References	20
	3.2	External links	21

4 Fuel — 22

- 4.1 History — 22
- 4.2 Chemical — 22
  - 4.2.1 Solid fuel — 23
  - 4.2.2 Liquid fuels — 23
  - 4.2.3 Gaseous fuels — 24
  - 4.2.4 Biofuels — 24
  - 4.2.5 Fossil fuels — 24
- 4.3 Nuclear — 25
  - 4.3.1 Fission — 25
  - 4.3.2 Fusion — 26
- 4.4 World trade — 26
- 4.5 See also — 26
- 4.6 Footnotes — 27
- 4.7 References — 27
- 4.8 Further reading — 27

5 Oxidizing agent — 28

- 5.1 Electron acceptors — 28
  - 5.1.1 Mechanism — 28
- 5.2 Atom-transfer reagents — 29
  - 5.2.1 Common oxidizing agents (O-atom transfer agents) — 29
- 5.3 Dangerous materials definition — 29
- 5.4 Common oxidizing agents and their products — 30
- 5.5 See also — 30
- 5.6 References — 30

6 Explosive booster — 31

- 6.1 Gallery — 31

7 Explosive train — 32

- 7.1 Low explosive train — 32
- 7.2 High explosive train — 32
  - 7.2.1 Primary components — 32
  - 7.2.2 Secondary components — 32
  - 7.2.3 Tertiary components — 33
- 7.3 References — 33

8 Detonation velocity — 34
- 8.1 See also — 34
- 8.2 References — 34

9 Sensitivity (explosives) — 35
- 9.1 Explosive train — 35
- 9.2 Classifications — 35
- 9.3 References — 35

10 Use forms of explosives — 36
- 10.1 Pressings — 36
- 10.2 Castings — 36
- 10.3 Polymer bonded — 37
- 10.4 Putties, aka Plastic explosives — 37
- 10.5 Rubberized — 37
- 10.6 Extrudable — 37
- 10.7 Binary — 38
- 10.8 Blasting agents — 38
- 10.9 Slurries and gels — 38
- 10.10 Dynamites — 38
- 10.11 References — 38

11 Combustibility — 40
- 11.1 Code Definitions — 40
- 11.2 Fire testing — 41
- 11.3 Relevance in construction — 41
- 11.4 Combustible dust — 41
- 11.5 Related matters — 41
  - 11.5.1 The chemistry underlying the fire testing and resulting code classifications — 41
- 11.6 References — 42
- 11.7 Notes — 42
- 11.8 See also — 42
- 11.9 External links — 42

12 Flammability — 43
- 12.1 Definitions — 44
- 12.2 Testing — 44
- 12.3 Categorization of building materials — 44
- 12.4 Important characteristics — 45
  - 12.4.1 Flash point — 45

- 12.4.2 Vapor pressure 45
- 12.5 Furniture flammability 45
- 12.6 Examples of flammable substances 45
- 12.7 Examples of nonflammable liquids 45
- 12.8 Classification of flammability 45
- 12.9 Codes 46
    - 12.9.1 Flammability 46
- 12.10 See also 46
- 12.11 References 46
- 12.12 External links 46

13 Deflagration 47
- 13.1 Applications 47
- 13.2 Oil/wax fire and water 47
- 13.3 Flame physics 47
- 13.4 Damaging events 48
- 13.5 See also 48
- 13.6 References 48

14 Detonation 49
- 14.1 Theories 49
- 14.2 Applications 50
- 14.3 In engines and firearms 50
- 14.4 Etymology 50
- 14.5 See also 50
- 14.6 References 50
- 14.7 External links 51

15 Brisance 52
- 15.1 See also 52
- 15.2 References 52

16 Pressure 53
- 16.1 Definition 53
    - 16.1.1 Formula 53
    - 16.1.2 Units 54
    - 16.1.3 Examples 55
    - 16.1.4 Scalar nature 56
- 16.2 Types 56
    - 16.2.1 Fluid pressure 56

16.2.2 Explosion or deflagration pressures 57
16.2.3 Negative pressures 57
16.2.4 Stagnation pressure 58
16.2.5 Surface pressure and surface tension 58
16.2.6 Pressure of an ideal gas 58
16.2.7 Vapor pressure 58
16.2.8 Liquid pressure 58
16.2.9 Direction of liquid pressure 59
16.2.10 Kinematic pressure 60
16.3 See also 60
16.4 Notes 60
16.5 References 60
16.6 External links 61

17 Blasting cap 62

17.1 Description 62
17.2 Types 62
17.2.1 Pyrotechnic fuse blasting cap 62
17.2.2 Solid pack electric blasting cap 63
17.2.3 Match or fusehead electric blasting cap 63
17.2.4 Exploding bridgewire detonator or blasting cap 63
17.2.5 Slapper detonator or blasting cap 63
17.2.6 Laser ordnance initiators 64
17.3 History 64
17.4 See also 64
17.5 References 64
17.6 External links 64

18 Percussion cap 65

18.1 History 66
18.1.1 Firing devices and fuze mechanisms 66
18.2 See also 67
18.3 References 67

19 Shock wave 68

19.1 Terminology 68
19.2 In supersonic flows 68
19.3 Normal shocks 69
19.4 Other shocks 69

        19.4.1 Oblique shocks 69
        19.4.2 Bow shocks 70
   19.5 Shock waves due to nonlinear steepening 70
   19.6 Analogies 70
   19.7 Phenomena types 70
        19.7.1 Moving shock 70
        19.7.2 Detonation wave 70
        19.7.3 Bow shock (detached shock) 71
        19.7.4 Attached shock 72
        19.7.5 In rapid granular flows 72
        19.7.6 In astrophysics 72
   19.8 Technological applications 73
        19.8.1 Recompression shock 73
        19.8.2 Pipe flow 73
        19.8.3 Combustion engines 73
        19.8.4 Memristors 73
   19.9 Shock capturing and detection 74
   19.10 See also 74
   19.11 References 74
   19.12 External links 75
   19.13 Further reading 75

20 Binary explosive   76
   20.1 See also 76
   20.2 External links 76

21 Improvised explosive device   77
   21.1 Background 77
   21.2 Historical use 78
        21.2.1 Afghanistan 78
        21.2.2 India 79
        21.2.3 Iraq 79
        21.2.4 United Kingdom/Republic of Ireland 80
        21.2.5 Lebanon 81
        21.2.6 Libya 81
        21.2.7 Nepal 81
        21.2.8 Russia 81
        21.2.9 Syria 81
        21.2.10 United States 81

21.2.11 Vietnam 82
21.3 Types 82
 21.3.1 By warhead 82
 21.3.2 By delivery mechanism 83
 21.3.3 By trigger mechanism 85
21.4 Counterefforts 85
 21.4.1 Detection and disarmament 86
21.5 See also 86
21.6 References 87
21.7 External links 88

22 Insensitive munition 90
22.1 Description 90
22.2 Insensitive high explosives 90
 22.2.1 Origin 91
 22.2.2 Use in nuclear weapons 91
22.3 See also 91
22.4 References 91
22.5 External links 91

23 Chemical explosive 92
23.1 Chemical explosive reaction 92
23.2 Sensitiser 92
23.3 Measurement of chemical explosive reaction 92
23.4 Balancing chemical explosion equations 93
23.5 Example of thermochemical calculations 93
23.6 References 94

24 Nuclear explosive 95
24.1 External links 95

25 Nuclear weapon 96
25.1 Types 97
 25.1.1 Fission weapons 97
 25.1.2 Fusion weapons 97
 25.1.3 Other types 99
25.2 Weapons delivery 99
25.3 Nuclear strategy 101
25.4 Governance, control, and law 102
 25.4.1 Disarmament 103

CONTENTS

- 25.4.2 United Nations ... 104
- 25.5 Controversy ... 104
  - 25.5.1 Ethics ... 104
  - 25.5.2 Notable nuclear weapons accidents ... 105
  - 25.5.3 Nuclear testing and fallout ... 105
- 25.6 Effects of nuclear explosions on human health ... 106
  - 25.6.1 Public opposition ... 107
- 25.7 Costs and technology spin-offs ... 107
- 25.8 Non-weapons uses ... 107
- 25.9 See also ... 108
  - 25.9.1 History ... 108
  - 25.9.2 More technical details ... 108
  - 25.9.3 Popular culture ... 108
  - 25.9.4 Proliferation and politics ... 108
- 25.10 Notes and references ... 108
- 25.11 Bibliography ... 111
- 25.12 External links ... 112

26 Chemical energy — 113
- 26.1 References ... 113

27 Explosives engineering — 114
- 27.1 Topics ... 114
- 27.2 Organizations ... 114
- 27.3 See also ... 114
- 27.4 References ... 114
- 27.5 External links ... 114

28 Explosives safety — 115
- 28.1 US Air Force ... 115
- 28.2 US Army ... 115
- 28.3 Net Explosives Weight (NEW) ... 115
- 28.4 Blast Wave Phenomena ... 116
- 28.5 Fragments ... 116
- 28.6 Thermal Hazards ... 116
- 28.7 Susan Test ... 117
- 28.8 Explosives Safety Specialist ... 117
- 28.9 See also ... 117
- 28.10 References ... 118

28.11 External links 118

29 Examples of Military Explosions   119

30 Strength (explosive)   122

31 Gurney equations   124
31.1 Underlying physics 124
    31.1.1 Definitions and units 124
    31.1.2 Gurney constant and detonation velocity 124
    31.1.3 Fragmenting versus nonfragmenting outer shells 124
    31.1.4 Effective charge volume for small diameter charges 125
    31.1.5 Anomalous predictions 125
31.2 Equations 125
    31.2.1 Cylindrical charge 125
    31.2.2 Spherical charge 126
    31.2.3 Symmetrical sandwich 126
    31.2.4 Asymmetrical sandwich 126
    31.2.5 Infinitely tamped sandwich 126
    31.2.6 Open-faced sandwich 127
    31.2.7 Imploding cylinder 127
    31.2.8 Imploding spherical 127
31.3 Applications 128
31.4 See also 128
31.5 References 128

32 Nitroglycerin   129
32.1 History 129
    32.1.1 Wartime production rates 130
32.2 Instability and desensitization 130
32.3 Detonation 130
32.4 Manufacturing 130
32.5 Use as an explosive and a propellant 131
32.6 Medical use 132
32.7 Industrial exposure 132
32.8 See also 133

- 32.9 References 133
- 32.10 External links 134

33 Acetone peroxide 135
- 33.1 History 135
- 33.2 Chemistry 135
- 33.3 Industrial uses 136
- 33.4 Use in improvised explosive devices 136
- 33.5 References 136
- 33.6 External links 137

34 Trinitrotoluene 138
- 34.1 History 138
- 34.2 Preparation 139
- 34.3 Applications 140
- 34.4 Explosive character 140
- 34.5 Energy content 141
- 34.6 Detection 141
- 34.7 Safety and toxicity 141
- 34.8 Ecological impact 141
  - 34.8.1 Aqueous solubility 142
  - 34.8.2 Soil adsorption 142
  - 34.8.3 Chemical breakdown 142
  - 34.8.4 Biodegradation 143
- 34.9 See also 143
- 34.10 References 143
- 34.11 External links 144

35 Nitrocellulose 145
- 35.1 Guncotton/Nitrocellulose 145
  - 35.1.1 Discovery 145
  - 35.1.2 Industrial production 145
- 35.2 Nitrate film 146
  - 35.2.1 Replacement filmstocks 147
- 35.3 Production 148
  - 35.3.1 Guncotton 148
  - 35.3.2 Nitrate film 148
- 35.4 Uses 148
- 35.5 Hazards 149

36 RDX — 153

- 36.1 Name ... 153
- 36.2 Usage ... 153
- 36.3 Chemistry ... 154
  - 36.3.1 Stability and explosive properties ... 154
- 36.4 History ... 154
  - 36.4.1 Germany ... 154
  - 36.4.2 UK ... 155
  - 36.4.3 Canada ... 155
  - 36.4.4 UK, US and Canadian production and development ... 155
  - 36.4.5 Military compositions ... 156
  - 36.4.6 Terrorism ... 156
- 36.5 Toxicity ... 157
- 36.6 Biodegradation ... 157
- 36.7 References ... 157
- 36.8 Bibliography ... 159
- 36.9 Further reading ... 159
- 36.10 External links ... 159

37 Pentaerythritol tetranitrate — 160

- 37.1 History ... 160
- 37.2 Properties ... 160
- 37.3 Production ... 160
- 37.4 Explosive use ... 161
  - 37.4.1 In mixtures ... 161
  - 37.4.2 Terrorist use ... 162
  - 37.4.3 Detection ... 162
- 37.5 Medical use ... 162
- 37.6 See also ... 163
- 37.7 References ... 163
- 37.8 Further reading ... 164
- 37.9 External links ... 164

38 HMX — 165

- 38.1 Production ... 165

(35.6 See also ... 149; 35.7 References ... 150; 35.8 External links ... 151)

CONTENTS

- 38.2 Applications ... 165
  - 38.2.1 Toxicity ... 165
- 38.3 Biodegradation ... 166
- 38.4 See also ... 166
- 38.5 Notes ... 166
- 38.6 References ... 166

39 C-4 (explosive) — 167

- 39.1 Characteristics and uses ... 167
  - 39.1.1 Composition ... 167
  - 39.1.2 Detonation ... 167
  - 39.1.3 Form ... 168
  - 39.1.4 Safety ... 168
- 39.2 Analysis ... 169
  - 39.2.1 Toxicity ... 169
  - 39.2.2 Investigation ... 169
- 39.3 History ... 170
  - 39.3.1 Development ... 170
  - 39.3.2 Vietnam War ... 170
- 39.4 Use in terrorism ... 170
- 39.5 See also ... 170
- 39.6 References ... 170
- 39.7 External links ... 172

40 Gunpowder — 173

- 40.1 History of gunpowder ... 173
  - 40.1.1 China ... 174
  - 40.1.2 Middle East ... 175
  - 40.1.3 Mainland Europe ... 176
  - 40.1.4 Britain and Ireland ... 179
  - 40.1.5 India ... 180
  - 40.1.6 Indonesia ... 181
- 40.2 Manufacturing technology ... 181
- 40.3 Composition and characteristics ... 182
- 40.4 Serpentine ... 183
- 40.5 Corning ... 183
- 40.6 Modern types ... 183
- 40.7 Other types of gunpowder ... 184
- 40.8 Sulfur-free gunpowder ... 184

40.9 Combustion characteristics 185
    40.9.1 Advantages 185
    40.9.2 Disadvantages 185
    40.9.3 Transportation 185
40.10 Other uses 186
40.11 See also 186
40.12 References 186
40.13 External links 190

41 Flash powder — 192

41.1 Mixtures 192
    41.1.1 Aluminium and chlorate 192
    41.1.2 Aluminium - nitrate with sulphur 192
    41.1.3 Aluminium and perchlorate 193
    41.1.4 Magnesium and nitrate 193
    41.1.5 Magnesium and PTFE 194
    41.1.6 Antimony trisulfide and chlorate 194
41.2 Safety and handling 194
41.3 See also 194
41.4 References 195
41.5 External links 195

42 Ammonal — 196

42.1 History 196
42.2 Proportions 196
42.3 See also 196
42.4 References 197

43 Armstrong's mixture — 198

43.1 Safety considerations 198
43.2 References 198

44 Sprengel explosive — 199

44.1 See also 199
44.2 References 199

45 ANFO — 200

45.1 Chemistry 200
45.2 Industrial use 201
45.3 In popular culture 201

- 45.4 Disasters 202
- 45.5 Malicious use 202
- 45.6 ANNM 202
- 45.7 References 203
- 45.8 External links 203

46 Cheddite 204
- 46.1 See also 204

47 Oxyliquit 205
- 47.1 Properties 205
- 47.2 History 205
- 47.3 Fiction 206
- 47.4 External links 206

48 Panclastite 207
- 48.1 References 207
- 48.2 External links 207
- 48.3 Text and image sources, contributors, and licenses 208
  - 48.3.1 Text 208
  - 48.3.2 Images 221
  - 48.3.3 Content license 229

Chapter 1

Explosive material

An **explosive material**, also called an **explosive**, is a reactive substance that contains a great amount of potential energy that can produce an explosion if released suddenly, usually accompanied by the production of light, heat, sound, and pressure. An **explosive charge** is a measured quantity of explosive material.

This potential energy stored in an explosive material may be

- chemical energy, such as nitroglycerin or grain dust
- pressurized gas, such as a gas cylinder or aerosol can.
- nuclear energy, such as in the fissile isotopes uranium-235 and plutonium-239

Explosive materials may be categorized by the speed at which they expand. Materials that detonate (the front of the chemical reaction moves faster through the material than the speed of sound) are said to be "high explosives" and materials that deflagrate are said to be "low explosives". Explosives may also be categorized by their sensitivity. Sensitive materials that can be initiated by a relatively small amount of heat or pressure are primary explosives and materials that are relatively insensitive are secondary or tertiary explosives.

A wide variety of chemicals can explode; a smaller number are manufactured specifically for the purpose of being used as explosives. The remainder are too dangerous, sensitive, toxic, expensive, unstable, or prone to decomposition or degradation over short time spans.

In contrast, some materials are merely combustible or flammable if they burn without exploding.

The distinction, however, is not razor-sharp. Certain materials -- dusts, powders, gasses, or volatile organic liquids -- may be simply combustible or flammable under ordinary conditions, but become explosive in specific situations or forms, such as dispersed airborne clouds, or confinement or sudden release.

1.1 History

Tet Offensive 1968. 12.7mm M2 machine gun at USMC Camp Carroll firing on advancing enemy troops as seen from LZ Betty 15 miles southeast.

See also: History of gunpowder

Though early thermal weapons, such as Greek fire, have existed since ancient times, the first widely used explosive in warfare and mining was black powder, invented in 9th century China. This material was sensitive to water, and it produced dark smoke. The first useful explosive stronger than black powder was nitroglycerin, developed in 1847. Since nitroglycerin is a liquid and highly unstable, it was replaced by nitrocellulose, TNT in 1863, smokeless powder, dynamite in 1867 and gelignite (the latter two invented by Alfred Nobel). World War I saw the adoption of TNT trinitrotoluene in artillery shells. World War II saw an extensive use of new explosives (see explosives used during

World War II). In turn, these have largely been replaced by more powerful explosives such as C-4 and PETN. However, C-4 and PETN react with metal and catch fire easily, yet unlike TNT, C-4 and PETN are waterproof and malleable.*[1]

1.2 Applications

1.2.1 Commercial

A video describing how to safely handle explosives in mines.

The largest commercial application of explosives is mining. Whether the mine is on the surface or is buried underground, the detonation or deflagration of either a high or low explosive in a confined space can be used to liberate a fairly specific sub-volume of a brittle material in a much larger volume of the same or similar material. Normally, ceramic explosives are used in mining. In mineral deposits containing large masses of native metal (usually copper), using explosives to "liberate" the ore typically doesn't work well.

In Materials Science and Engineering, explosives are used in cladding. A thin plate of some material is placed atop a thick layer of a different material, both layers typically of metal. Atop the thin layer is placed an explosive. At one end of the layer of explosive, the explosion is initiated. The two metallic layers are forced together at high speed and with great force. The explosion spreads from the initiation site throughout the explosive. Ideally, this produces a metallurgical bond between the two layers.

As the length of time the shock wave spends at any point is small, we can see mixing of the two metals and their surface chemistries, through some fraction of the depth, and they tend to be mixed in some way. It is possible that some fraction of the surface material from either layer eventually gets ejected when the end of material is reached. Hence, the mass of the now "welded" bilayer, may be less than the sum of the masses of the two initial layers.

There are applications where a shock wave, and electrostatics, can result in high velocity projectiles.

1.2.2 Military

Main article: Explosive weapons

1.2.3 Civilian

See also: Explosives engineering

1.2.4 Safety

Main article: Explosives safety

1.3 Types

1.3.1 Chemical

Main article: Chemical explosive

An explosion is a type of spontaneous chemical reaction

The international pictogram for explosive substances.

that, once initiated, is driven by both a large exothermic change (great release of heat) and a large positive entropy change (great quantities of gases are released) in going from reactants to products, thereby constituting a thermodynamically favorable process in addition to one that propagates very rapidly. Thus, explosives are substances that contain a large amount of energy stored in chemical bonds. The energetic stability of the gaseous products and hence their generation comes from the formation of strongly bonded species like carbon monoxide, carbon dioxide, and (di)nitrogen, which contain strong double and triple bonds having bond strengths of nearly 1 MJ/mole. Consequently, most commercial explosives are organic compounds containing -NO_2, -ONO_2 and -$NHNO_2$ groups that, when detonated, release gases like the aforementioned (e.g., nitroglycerin, TNT, HMX, PETN, nitrocellulose).*[2]

An explosive is classified as a low or high explosive according to its rate of burn: low explosives burn rapidly (or deflagrate), while high explosives detonate. While these definitions are distinct, the problem of precisely measuring rapid decomposition makes practical classification of explosives difficult.

Decomposition

The chemical decomposition of an explosive may take years, days, hours, or a fraction of a second. The slower processes of decomposition take place in storage and are of interest only from a stability standpoint. Of more interest are the two rapid forms of decomposition, deflagration and detonation.

Deflagration

Main article: Deflagration

In deflagration, decomposition of the explosive material is propagated by a flame front which moves slowly through the explosive material, in contrast to detonation. Deflagration is a characteristic of low explosive material.

Detonation

Main article: Detonation

This term is used to describe an explosive phenomenon whereby the decomposition is propagated by an explosive shock wave traversing the explosive material. The shock front is capable of passing through the high explosive material at great speeds, typically thousands of metres per second.

1.3.2 Exotic

In addition to chemical explosives, there are a number of more exotic explosive materials, and exotic methods of causing explosions. Examples include nuclear explosives, and abruptly heating a substance to a plasma state with a high-intensity laser or electric arc.

Laser- and arc-heating are used in laser detonators, exploding-bridgewire detonators, and exploding foil initiators, where a shock wave and then detonation in conventional chemical explosive material is created by laser- or electric-arc heating. Laser and electric energy are not currently used in practice to generate most of the required energy, but only to initiate reactions.

1.4 Properties of explosive materials

To determine the suitability of an explosive substance for a particular use, its physical properties must first be known. The usefulness of an explosive can only be appreciated when the properties and the factors affecting them are fully understood. Some of the more important characteristics are listed below:

1.4.1 Sensitivity

Main article: Sensitivity (explosives)

Sensitivity refers to the ease with which an explosive can be ignited or detonated, i.e., the amount and intensity of shock, friction, or heat that is required. When the term sensitivity is used, care must be taken to clarify what kind of sensitivity is under discussion. The relative sensitivity of a given explosive to impact may vary greatly from its sensitivity to friction or heat. Some of the test methods used to determine sensitivity relate to:

- **Impact** —Sensitivity is expressed in terms of the distance through which a standard weight must be dropped onto the material to cause it to explode.
- **Friction** —Sensitivity is expressed in terms of what occurs when a weighted pendulum scrapes across the material (it may snap, crackle, ignite, and/or explode).
- **Heat** —Sensitivity is expressed in terms of the temperature at which flashing or explosion of the material occurs.

Specific explosives (usually but not always highly sensitive on one or more of the three above axes) may be idiosyncratically sensitive to such factors as pressure drop, acceleration, the presence of sharp edges or rough surfaces, incompatible materials, or even -- in rare cases -- nuclear or electromagnetic radiation. These factors present special hazards that may rule out any practical utility.

Sensitivity is an important consideration in selecting an explosive for a particular purpose. The explosive in an armor-piercing projectile must be relatively insensitive, or the shock of impact would cause it to detonate before it penetrated to the point desired. The explosive lenses around nuclear charges are also designed to be highly insensitive, to minimize the risk of accidental detonation.

1.4.2 Sensitivity to initiation

The index of the capacity of an explosive to be initiated into detonation in a sustained manner. It is defined by the power of the detonator which is certain to prime the explosive to a sustained and continuous detonation. Reference is made to the Sellier-Bellot scale that consists of a series of 10 detonators, from n. 1 to n. 10, each of which corresponds to an increasing charge weight. In practice, most of the explosives on the market today are sensitive to an n. 8 detonator, where the charge corresponds to 2 grams of mercury fulminate.

1.4.3 Velocity of detonation

The velocity with which the reaction process propagates in the mass of the explosive. Most commercial mining explosives have detonation velocities ranging from 1800 m/s to 8000 m/s. Today, velocity of detonation can be measured with accuracy. Together with density it is an important element influencing the yield of the energy transmitted for both atmospheric over-pressure and ground acceleration. By definition, a "low explosive," such as gasoline, black powder, or smokeless gunpowder has a burn (detonation) rate of less than 3,300 feet per second (1,006 m/s). In contrast, a "high explosive," whether a primary, such as detonating cord, or a secondary, such as TNT or C-4 has a burn rate above that point.*[1]

1.4.4 Stability

Main article: Chemical stability

Stability is the ability of an explosive to be stored without deterioration.

The following factors affect the stability of an explosive:

- **Chemical constitution.** In the strictest technical sense, the word "stability" is a thermodynamic term referring to the energy of a substance relative to a reference state or to some other substance. However, in the context of explosives, stability commonly refers to ease of detonation, which is concerned with kinetics (i.e., rate of decomposition). It is perhaps best, then, to differentiate between the terms thermodynamically stable and kinetically stable by referring to the former as "inert." Contrarily, a kinetically unstable substance is said to be "labile." It is generally recognized that certain groups like nitro ($-NO_2$), nitrate ($-ONO_2$), and azide ($-N_3$), are intrinsically labile. Kinetically, there exists a low activation barrier to the decomposition reaction. Consequently, these compounds exhibit high sensitivity to flame or mechanical shock. The chemical bonding in these compounds is characterized as predominantly covalent and thus they are not thermodynamically stabilized by a high ionic-lattice energy. Furthermore, they generally have positive enthalpies of formation and there is little mechanistic hindrance to internal molecular rearrangement to yield the more thermodynamically stable (more strongly bonded) decomposition products. For example, in lead azide, $Pb(N_3)_2$, the nitrogen atoms are already bonded to one another, so decomposition into Pb and N_2^*[1] is relatively easy.

- **Temperature of storage.** The rate of decomposition of explosives increases at higher temperatures. All standard military explosives may be considered to have a high degree of stability at temperatures from -10 to $+35$ °C, but each has a high temperature at which its rate of decomposition rapidly accelerates and stability is reduced. As a rule of thumb, most explosives become dangerously unstable at temperatures above 70 °C.

- **Exposure to sunlight.** When exposed to the ultraviolet rays of sunlight, many explosive compounds containing nitrogen groups rapidly decompose, affecting their stability.

- **Electrical discharge.** Electrostatic or spark sensitivity to initiation is common in a number of explosives. Static or other electrical discharge may be sufficient to cause a reaction, even detonation, under some circumstances. As a result, safe handling of explosives and pyrotechnics usually requires proper electrical grounding of the operator.

1.4.5 Power, performance, and strength

Main articles: Power (physics) and Strength (explosive)

The term **power** or **performance** as applied to an explosive refers to its ability to do work. In practice it is defined as the explosive's ability to accomplish what is intended in the way of energy delivery (i.e., fragment projection, air blast, high-velocity jet, underwater shock and bubble energy, etc.). Explosive power or performance is evaluated by a tailored series of tests to assess the material for its intended use. Of the tests listed below, cylinder expansion and air blast tests are common to most testing programs, and the others support specific applications.

- **Cylinder expansion test.** A standard amount of explosive is loaded into a long hollow cylinder, usually of copper, and detonated at one end. Data is collected concerning the rate of radial expansion of the cylinder and the maximum cylinder wall velocity. This also establishes the Gurney energy or $2E$.

- **Cylinder fragmentation.** A standard steel cylinder is loaded with explosive and detonated in a sawdust pit. The fragments are collected and the size distribution analyzed.

- **Detonation pressure (Chapman-Jouguet condition).** Detonation pressure data derived from measurements of shock waves transmitted into water by the detonation of cylindrical explosive charges of a standard size.

- **Determination of critical diameter.** This test establishes the minimum physical size a charge of a specific explosive must be to sustain its own detonation wave. The procedure involves the detonation of a series of charges of different diameters until difficulty in detonation wave propagation is observed.

- **Infinite-diameter detonation velocity.** Detonation velocity is dependent on loading density (c), charge diameter, and grain size. The hydrodynamic theory of detonation used in predicting explosive phenomena does not include the diameter of the charge, and therefore a detonation velocity, for an imaginary charge of infinite diameter. This procedure requires the firing of a series of charges of the same density and physical structure, but different diameters, and the extrapolation of the resulting detonation velocities to predict the detonation velocity of a charge of infinite diameter.

- **Pressure versus scaled distance.** A charge of a specific size is detonated and its pressure effects measured at a standard distance. The values obtained are compared with those for TNT.

- **Impulse versus scaled distance.** A charge of a specific size is detonated and its impulse (the area under the pressure-time curve) measured as a function of distance. The results are tabulated and expressed as TNT equivalents.

- **Relative bubble energy (RBE).** A 5 to 50 kg charge is detonated in water and piezoelectric gauges measure peak pressure, time constant, impulse, and energy.

  The RBE may be defined as $K_x 3$
  $$RBE = K_s$$
  where K = the bubble expansion period for an experimental (x) or a standard (s) charge.

1.4.6 Brisance

Main article: Brisance

In addition to strength, explosives display a second characteristic, which is their shattering effect or brisance (from the French meaning to "break"), which is distinguished and separate from their total work capacity. This characteristic is of practical importance in determining the effectiveness of an explosion in fragmenting shells, bomb casings, grenades, and the like. The rapidity with which an explosive reaches its peak pressure (power) is a measure of its brisance. Brisance values are primarily employed in France and Russia.

The sand crush test is commonly employed to determine the relative brisance in comparison to TNT. No test is capable of directly comparing the explosive properties of two or more compounds; it is important to examine the data from several such tests (sand crush, trauzl, and so forth) in order to gauge relative brisance. True values for comparison require field experiments.

1.4.7 Density

Density of loading refers to the mass of an explosive per unit volume. Several methods of loading are available, including pellet loading, cast loading, and press loading, the choice being determined by the characteristics of the explosive. Dependent upon the method employed, an average density of the loaded charge can be obtained that is within 80–99% of the theoretical maximum density of the explosive. High load density can reduce sensitivity by making the mass more resistant to internal friction. However, if density is increased to the extent that individual crystals are crushed, the explosive may become more sensitive. Increased load density also permits the use of more explosive, thereby increasing the power of the warhead. It is possible to compress an explosive beyond a point of sensitivity, known also as *dead-pressing*, in which the material is no longer capable of being reliably initiated, if at all.

1.4.8 Volatility

Volatility is the readiness with which a substance vaporizes. Excessive volatility often results in the development of pressure within rounds of ammunition and separation of mixtures into their constituents. Volatility affects the chemical composition of the explosive such that a marked reduction in stability may occur, which results in an increase in the danger of handling.

1.4.9 Hygroscopicity and water resistance

The introduction of water into an explosive is highly undesirable since it reduces the sensitivity, strength, and velocity of detonation of the explosive. Hygroscopicity is used as a measure of a material's moisture-absorbing tendencies. Moisture affects explosives adversely by acting as an inert material that absorbs heat when vaporized, and by acting as a solvent medium that can cause undesired chemical reactions. Sensitivity, strength, and velocity of detonation are reduced by inert materials that reduce the continuity of the explosive mass. When the moisture content evaporates during detonation, cooling occurs, which reduces the temperature of reaction. Stability is also affected by the presence of moisture since moisture promotes decomposition of the explosive and, in addition, causes corrosion of the explosive's metal container.

Explosives considerably differ from one another as to their behavior in the presence of water. Gelatin dynamites containing nitroglycerine have a degree of water resistance. Explosives based on ammonium nitrate have little or no water resistance due to the reaction between ammonium nitrate and water, which liberates ammonia, nitrogen dioxide and hydrogen peroxide. In addition, ammonium nitrate is hygroscopic, susceptible to damp, hence the above concerns.

1.4.10 Toxicity

There are many types of explosives which are toxic to some extent. Manufacturing inputs can also be organic compounds or hazardous materials that require special handling due to risks (such as carcinogens). The decomposition products, residual solids or gases of some explosives can be toxic, whereas others are harmless, such as carbon dioxide and water. Examples of harmful by-products are:

- Heavy metals, such as lead, mercury and barium from primers (observed in high volume firing ranges).

- Nitric oxides from TNT.
- Perchlorates when used in large quantities.

"Green explosives" seek to reduce environment and health impacts. An example of such is the lead-free primary explosive copper(I) 5-nitrotetrazolate, an alternative to lead azide.*[3]

1.4.11 Explosive train

Main article: Explosive train

Explosive material may be incorporated in the explosive train of a device or system. An example is a pyrotechnic lead igniting a booster, which causes the main charge to detonate.

1.4.12 Volume of products of explosion

The most widely used explosives are condensed liquids or solids converted to gaseous products by explosive chemical reactions and the energy released by those reactions. The gaseous products of complete reaction are typically carbon dioxide, steam, and nitrogen.*[4] Gaseous volumes computed by the ideal gas law tend to be too large at high pressures characteristic of explosions.*[5] Ultimate volume expansion may be estimated at three orders of magnitude, or one liter per gram of explosive. Explosives with an oxygen deficit will generate soot or gases like carbon monoxide and hydrogen, which may react with surrounding materials such as atmospheric oxygen.*[4] Attempts to obtain more precise volume estimates must consider the possibility of such side reactions, condensation of steam, and aqueous solubility of gases like carbon dioxide.*[6]

1.4.13 Oxygen balance (OB% or Ω)

Main article: Oxygen balance

Oxygen balance is an expression that is used to indicate the degree to which an explosive can be oxidized. If an explosive molecule contains just enough oxygen to convert all of its carbon to carbon dioxide, all of its hydrogen to water, and all of its metal to metal oxide with no excess, the molecule is said to have a zero oxygen balance. The molecule is said to have a positive oxygen balance if it contains more oxygen than is needed and a negative oxygen balance if it contains less oxygen than is needed.*[7] The sensitivity, strength, and brisance of an explosive are all somewhat dependent upon oxygen balance and tend to approach their maxima as oxygen balance approaches zero.

1.4.14 Chemical composition

A chemical explosive may consist of either a chemically pure compound, such as nitroglycerin, or a mixture of a fuel and an oxidizer, such as black powder or grain dust and air.

Chemically pure compounds

Some chemical compounds are unstable in that, when shocked, they react, possibly to the point of detonation. Each molecule of the compound dissociates into two or more new molecules (generally gases) with the release of energy.

- **Nitroglycerin**: A highly unstable and sensitive liquid.
- **Acetone peroxide**: A very unstable white organic peroxide.
- **TNT**: Yellow insensitive crystals that can be melted and cast without detonation.
- **Nitrocellulose**: A nitrated polymer which can be a high or low explosive depending on nitration level and conditions.
- **RDX, PETN, HMX**: Very powerful explosives which can be used pure or in plastic explosives.
    - **C-4** (or Composition C-4): An RDX plastic explosive plasticized to be adhesive and malleable.

The above compositions may describe most of the explosive material, but a practical explosive will often include small percentages of other substances. For example, dynamite is a mixture of highly sensitive nitroglycerin with sawdust, powdered silica, or most commonly diatomaceous earth, which act as stabilizers. Plastics and polymers may be added to bind powders of explosive compounds; waxes may be incorporated to make them safer to handle; aluminium powder may be introduced to increase total energy and blast effects. Explosive compounds are also often "alloyed": HMX or RDX powders may be mixed (typically by melt-casting) with TNT to form Octol or Cyclotol.

Mixture of oxidizer and fuel

An oxidizer is a pure substance (molecule) that in a chemical reaction can contribute some atoms of one or more oxidizing elements, in which the fuel component of the explosive burns. On the simplest level, the oxidizer may itself be an oxidizing element, such as gaseous or liquid oxygen.

- **Black powder**: Potassium nitrate, charcoal and sulfur

- **Flash powder**: Fine metal powder (usually aluminium or magnesium) and a strong oxidizer (e.g. potassium chlorate or perchlorate).
- **Ammonal**: Ammonium nitrate and aluminium powder.
- **Armstrong's mixture**: Potassium chlorate and red phosphorus. This is a very sensitive mixture. It is a primary high explosive in which sulfur is substituted for some or all of the phosphorus to slightly decrease sensitivity.
- **Sprengel explosives**: A very general class incorporating any strong oxidizer and highly reactive fuel, although in practice the name was most commonly applied to mixtures of chlorates and nitroaromatics.
    - **ANFO**: Ammonium nitrate and fuel oil.
    - **Cheddites**: Chlorates or perchlorates and oil.
    - **Oxyliquits**: Mixtures of organic materials and liquid oxygen.
    - **Panclastites**: Mixtures of organic materials and dinitrogen tetroxide.

1.4.15 Availability and cost

The availability and cost of explosives are determined by the availability of the raw materials and the cost, complexity, and safety of the manufacturing operations.

1.5 Classification of explosive materials

1.5.1 By sensitivity

Primary explosive

A **primary explosive** is an explosive that is extremely sensitive to stimuli such as impact, friction, heat, static electricity, or electromagnetic radiation. A relatively small amount of energy is required for initiation. As a very general rule, primary explosives are considered to be those compounds that are more sensitive than PETN. As a practical measure, primary explosives are sufficiently sensitive that they can be reliably initiated with a blow from a hammer; however, PETN can also usually be initiated in this manner, so this is only a very broad guideline. Additionally, several compounds, such as nitrogen triiodide, are so sensitive that they cannot even be handled without detonating. Nitrogen triiodide is so sensitive that it can be reliably detonated by exposure to alpha radiation; it is the only explosive for which this is true.

Primary explosives are often used in detonators or to trigger larger charges of less sensitive secondary explosives. Primary explosives are commonly used in blasting caps and percussion caps to translate a physical shock signal. In other situations, different signals such as electrical/physical shock, or, in the case of laser detonation systems, light, are used to initiate an action, i.e., an explosion. A small quantity, usually milligrams, is sufficient to initiate a larger charge of explosive that is usually safer to handle.*[8]

Examples of primary high explosives are:

- Acetone peroxide
- Alkali metal ozonides
- Ammonium permanganate
- Ammonium chlorate
- Azidotetrazolates
- Azo-clathrates
- Benzoyl peroxide
- Benzvalene
- Chlorine oxides
- Copper(I) acetylide
- Copper(II) azide
- Cumene hydroperoxide
- Cyanogen azide
- Diacetyl peroxide
- 1-Diazidocarbamoyl-5-azidotetrazole
- Diazodinitrophenol
- Diazomethane
- Diethyl ether peroxide
- 4-Dimethylaminophenylpentazole
- Disulfur dinitride
- Ethyl azide
- Explosive antimony
- Fluorine perchlorate
- Fulminic acid
- Halogen azides:
    - Fluorine azide
    - Chlorine azide
    - Bromine azide
- Hexamethylene triperoxide diamine
- Hydrazoic acid
- Hypofluorous acid
- Lead azide
- Lead styphnate
- Lead picrate*[9]
- Manganese heptoxide
- Mercury(II) fulminate
- Mercury nitride
- Methyl ethyl ketone peroxide
- Nitrogen trihalides:
    - Nitrogen trichloride
    - Nitrogen tribromide
    - Nitrogen triiodide
- Nitroglycerin
- Nitronium perchlorate
- Nitrotetrazolate-N-oxides
- Octaazacubane
- Pentazenium hexafluoroarsenate
- Peroxy acids
- Peroxymonosulfuric acid
- Selenium tetraazide
- Silicon tetraazide
- Silver azide
- Silver acetylide
- Silver fulminate
- Silver nitride
- Sodium azide
- Tellurium tetraazide
- tert-Butyl hydroperoxide
- Tetraamine copper complexes
- Tetraazidomethane

1.5. CLASSIFICATION OF EXPLOSIVE MATERIALS

- Tetrazene explosive
- Tetranitratoxycarbon
- Tetrazoles
- Titanium tetraazide
- Triazidomethane
- Xenon dioxide
- Xenon oxytetrafluoride
- Xenon tetroxide
- Xenon trioxide

Secondary explosive

A **secondary explosive** is less sensitive than a primary explosive and requires substantially more energy to be initiated. Because they are less sensitive, they are usable in a wider variety of applications and are safer to handle and store. Secondary explosives are used in larger quantities in an explosive train and are usually initiated by a smaller quantity of a primary explosive.

Examples of secondary explosives include TNT and RDX.

Tertiary explosive

Tertiary explosives, also called **blasting agents**, are so insensitive to shock that they cannot be reliably detonated by practical quantities of primary explosive, and instead require an intermediate explosive booster of secondary explosive. These are often used for safety and the typically lower costs of material and handling. The largest consumers are large-scale mining and construction operations.

ANFO is an example of a tertiary explosive.

1.5.2 By velocity

Low explosives

Low explosives are compounds where the rate of decomposition proceeds through the material at less than the speed of sound. The decomposition is propagated by a flame front (deflagration) which travels much more slowly through the explosive material than a shock wave of a high explosive. Under normal conditions, low explosives undergo deflagration at rates that vary from a few centimetres per second to approximately 400 metres per second. It is possible for them to deflagrate very quickly, producing an effect similar to a detonation. This can happen under higher pressure or temperature, which usually occurs when ignited in a confined space.

A low explosive is usually a mixture of a combustible substance and an oxidant that decomposes rapidly (deflagration); however, they burn more slowly than a high explosive, which has an extremely fast burn rate.

Low explosives are normally employed as propellants. Included in this group are petroleum products such as propane and gasoline, gunpowder (both black and smokeless), and light pyrotechnics, such as flares and fireworks, but can replace high explosives in certain applications, see gas pressure blasting.

High explosives

High explosives (HE) are explosive materials that detonate, meaning that the explosive shock front passes through the material at a supersonic speed. High explosives detonate with explosive velocity ranging from 3 to 9 km/s. For instance, TNT has a detonation (burn) rate of approximately 5.8 km/s (19,000 feet per second), Detonating cord of 6.7 km/s (22,000 feet per second), and C-4 about 8.5 km/s (29,000 feet per second). They are normally employed in mining, demolition, and military applications. They can be divided into two explosives classes differentiated by sensitivity: primary explosive and secondary explosive. The term *high explosive* is in contrast with the term *low explosive*, which explodes (deflagrates) at a lower rate.

1.5.3 By composition

Priming composition

Priming compositions are primary explosives mixed with other compositions to control (lessen) the sensitivity of the mixture to the desired property.

For example, primary explosives are so sensitive that they need to be stored and shipped in a wet state to prevent accidental initiation.

1.5.4 By physical form

Main article: Use forms of explosives

Explosives are often characterized by the physical form that the explosives are produced or used in. These use forms are commonly categorized as:*[10]

- Pressings
- Castings

- Plastic or polymer bonded
- Putties (AKA plastic explosives)
- Rubberized
- Extrudable
- Binary
- Blasting agents
- Slurries and gels
- Dynamites

1.5.5 Shipping label classifications

Shipping labels and tags may include both United Nations and national markings.

United Nations markings include numbered Hazard Class and Division (HC/D) codes and alphabetic Compatibility Group codes. Though the two are related, they are separate and distinct. Any Compatibility Group designator can be assigned to any Hazard Class and Division. An example of this hybrid marking would be a consumer firework, which is labeled as 1.4G or 1.4S.

Examples of national markings would include United States Department of Transportation (U.S. DOT) codes.

United Nations Organization (UNO) Hazard Class and Division (HC/D)

Explosives warning sign

See also: HAZMAT Class 1 Explosives

The Hazard Class and Division (HC/D) is a numeric designator within a hazard class indicating the character, predominance of associated hazards, and potential for causing personnel casualties and property damage. It is an internationally accepted system that communicates using the minimum amount of markings the primary hazard associated with a substance.*[11]

Listed below are the Divisions for Class 1 (Explosives):

- **1.1** Mass Detonation Hazard. With HC/D 1.1, it is expected that if one item in a container or pallet inadvertently detonates, the explosion will sympathetically detonate the surrounding items. The explosion could propagate to all or the majority of the items stored together, causing a mass detonation. There will also be fragments from the item's casing and/or structures in the blast area.

- **1.2** Non-mass explosion, fragment-producing. HC/D 1.2 is further divided into three subdivisions, HC/D 1.2.1, 1.2.2 and 1.2.3, to account for the magnitude of the effects of an explosion.

- **1.3** Mass fire, minor blast or fragment hazard. Propellants and many pyrotechnic items fall into this category. If one item in a package or stack initiates, it will usually propagate to the other items, creating a mass fire.

- **1.4** Moderate fire, no blast or fragment. HC/D 1.4 items are listed in the table as explosives with no significant hazard. Most small arms and some pyrotechnic items fall into this category. If the energetic material in these items inadvertently initiates, most of the energy and fragments will be contained within the storage structure or the item containers themselves.

- **1.5** mass detonation hazard, very insensitive.

- **1.6** detonation hazard without mass detonation hazard, extremely insensitive.

To see an entire UNO Table, browse Paragraphs 3-8 and 3-9 of NAVSEA OP 5, Vol. 1, Chapter 3.

Class 1 Compatibility Group

Compatibility Group codes are used to indicate storage compatibility for HC/D Class 1 (explosive) materials. Letters are used to designate 13 compatibility groups as follows.

A: Primary explosive substance (1.1A).

B: An article containing a primary explosive substance and not containing two or more effective protective features. Some articles, such as detonator assemblies for blasting and primers, cap-type, are included. (1.1B, 1.2B, 1.4B).

C: Propellant explosive substance or other deflagrating explosive substance or article containing such explosive substance (1.1C, 1.2C, 1.3C, 1.4C). These are bulk propellants, propelling charges, and devices containing propellants with or without means of ignition. Examples include single-based propellant, double-based propellant, triple-based propellant, and composite propellants, solid propellant rocket motors and ammunition with inert projectiles.

D: Secondary detonating explosive substance or black powder or article containing a secondary detonating explosive substance, in each case without means of initiation and without a propelling charge, or article containing a primary explosive substance and containing two or more effective protective features. (1.1D, 1.2D, 1.4D, 1.5D).

E: Article containing a secondary detonating explosive substance without means of initiation, with a propelling charge (other than one containing flammable liquid, gel or hypergolic liquid) (1.1E, 1.2E, 1.4E).

F containing a secondary detonating explosive substance with its means of initiation, with a propelling charge (other than one containing flammable liquid, gel or hypergolic liquid) or without a propelling charge (1.1F, 1.2F, 1.3F, 1.4F).

G: Pyrotechnic substance or article containing a pyrotechnic substance, or article containing both an explosive substance and an illuminating, incendiary, tear-producing or smoke-producing substance (other than a water-activated article or one containing white phosphorus, phosphide or flammable liquid or gel or hypergolic liquid) (1.1G, 1.2G, 1.3G, 1.4G). Examples include Flares, signals, incendiary or illuminating ammunition and other smoke and tear producing devices.

H: Article containing both an explosive substance and white phosphorus (1.2H, 1.3H). These articles will spontaneously combust when exposed to the atmosphere.

J: Article containing both an explosive substance and flammable liquid or gel (1.1J, 1.2J, 1.3J). This excludes liquids or gels which are spontaneously flammable when exposed to water or the atmosphere, which belong in group H. Examples include liquid or gel filled incendiary ammunition, fuel-air explosive (FAE) devices, and flammable liquid fueled missiles.

K: Article containing both an explosive substance and a toxic chemical agent (1.2K, 1.3K)

L Explosive substance or article containing an explosive substance and presenting a special risk (e.g., due to water-activation or presence of hypergolic liquids, phosphides, or pyrophoric substances) needing isolation of each type (1.1L, 1.2L, 1.3L). Damaged or suspect ammunition of any group belongs in this group.

N: Articles containing only extremely insensitive detonating substances (1.6N).

S: Substance or article so packed or designed that any hazardous effects arising from accidental functioning are limited to the extent that they do not significantly hinder or prohibit fire fighting or other emergency response efforts in the immediate vicinity of the package (1.4S).

1.6 Regulation

The legality of possessing or using explosives varies by jurisdiction. Various countries around the world has enacted explosives law and require licenses to manufacture, distribute, store, use, possess explosives or ingredients.

1.6.1 Netherlands

In the Netherlands, the civil and commercial use of explosives is covered under the Wet explosieven voor civiel gebruik (explosives for civil use Act), in accordance with EU directive nr. 93/15/EEG*[12] (Dutch). The illegal use of explosives is covered under the Wet Wapens en Munitie (Weapons and Munition Act)*[13] (Dutch).

1.6.2 UK

Main article: Explosive Substances Act 1883

1.6.3 United States

During World War I, numerous laws were created to regulate war related industries and increase security within the United States. In 1917, the 65th United States Congress created many laws, including the *Espionage Act of 1917* and *Explosives Act of 1917*.

The *Explosives Act of 1917* (session 1, chapter 83, 40 Stat. 385) was signed on 6 October 1917 and went into effect on 16 November 1917. The legal summary is "An Act to prohibit the manufacture, distribution, storage, use, and possession in **time of war** of explosives, providing regulations for the safe manufacture, distribution, storage, use, and possession of the same, and for other purposes". This was the first federal regulation of licensing explosives purchases. The act was deactivated after World War I ended.*[14]

After the United States entered World War II, the Explosives Act of 1917 was reactivated. In 1947, the act was deactivated by President Truman.*[15]

The *Organized Crime Control Act of 1970* (Pub.L. 91–452) transferred many explosives regulations to the Bureau of Alcohol, Tobacco and Firearms (ATF) of the Department of Treasury. The bill became effective in 1971.*[16]

Currently, regulations are governed by Title 18 of the United States Code and Title 27 of the Code of Federal Regulations:

- "Importation, Manufacture, Distribution and Storage of Explosive Materials" (18 U.S.C. Chapter 40).*[17]

- "Commerce in Explosives" (27 C.F.R. Chapter II, Part 555).*[18]

State laws

- Alabama Code Title 8 Chapter 17 Article 9*[19]
- Alaska State Code Chapter 11.61.240 & 11.61.250*[20]
- Arizona State Code Title 13 Chapter 31 Articles 01 through 19
- Arkansas State Code Title 5 Chapter 73 Article 108
- California Penal Code Title 2 Division 5
- Colorado (Colorado statutes are copyrighted and require purchase before reading.)
- Connecticut Statutes Volume 9 Title 29 Chapters 343-355
- Delaware Code Title 16 Part VI Chapters 70 & 71
- Florida Statutes Title XXXIII Chapter 552
- Georgia Code Title 16 Chapter 7 Articles 64-97
- Hawaii Administrative Rules Title 12 Subtitle 8 Part 1 Chapter 58 AND Hawaii Revised Statutes
- Idaho
- Illinois Explosives Act 225 ILCS 210
- Indiana
- Iowa
- Kansas
- Kentucky
- Louisiana
- Maine
- Maryland
- Massachusetts
- Michigan Penal Code Chapter XXXIII Section 750.200 - 750.212a
- Minnesota
- Mississippi Code Title 45 Chapter 13 Article 3 Section 101 - 109
- Montana
- Nebraska
- Nevada
- New Hampshire
- New Jersey
- New Mexico
- New York. Health and safety regulations restrict the quantity of black powder a person may store and transport.*[21]
- North Carolina
- North Dakota
- Ohio
- Oklahoma
- Oregon
- Pennsylvania
- Rhode Island
- South Carolina
- South Dakota
- Tennessee
- Texas
- Utah
- Vermont
- Virginia
- Washington
- West Virginia
- Wisconsin Chapter 941 Subchapter 4-31
- Wyoming

1.7 List of explosives

1.7.1 Compounds

Acetylides

- CUA, DCA, AGA

Fulminates

- HF, AUF, HGF, PTF, KF, AGF

Nitro

- **MonoNitro:** NGA, NE, NM, NP, NS, NU
- **DiNitro:** DDNP, DNB, DNEU, DNN, DNP, DNPA, DNPH, DNR, DNPD, DNPA, DNC, DPS, DPA, EDNP, KDNBF, BEAF
- **TriNitro:** RDX, DATB, TATB, PBS, PBP, TNAL, TNAS, TNB, TNBA, TNC, MC, TNEF, TNOC, TNOF, TNP, TNT, TNN, TNPG, TNR, BTNEN, BTNEC, Tetryl, SA, API, TNS
- **OctaNitro:** ONC

Nitrates

- **Mononitrates:** AN, BAN, CAN, MAN, NAN, UN
- **Dinitrates:** DEGDN, EDDN, EDNA, EGDN, HDN, TEGDN, TAOM
- **Trinitrates:** BTTN, TMOTN, ETN, NG
- **Tetranitrates:** ETEN, PETN, TNOC
- **Pentanitrates:** XPN
- **Hexanitrates:** CHN, MHN

Amines

- **Tertiary Amines:** NTBR, NTCL, NTI, NTS, SEX, AGN
- **Diamines:** DSDN
- **Azides:** CNA, CYA, CLA, CUA, EA, FA, HA, PBA, AGA, NAA, SEA, SIA, TEA, TAM, TIA
- **Tetramines:** TZE, TZO
- **Pentamines:** PZ
- **Octamines:** OAC, ATA

Peroxides

- AP, CHP, DAP, DBP, DEP, HMTD, MEKP, TBHP

Oxides

- XOTF, XDIO, XTRO, XTEO

Yet To be sorted

- Benzvalene,
- Alkali metal ozonides,
- Ammonium chlorate,
- Ammonium perchlorate,
- Ammonium permaganate
- Azidotetrazolates
- Azoclathrates
- Chlorine oxides
- DMAPP
- Fluorine perchlore
- Hexafluro arsenate
- Hypofluorous acid
- Maganese heptoxide
- Mercury nitride
- Nitronium perchlorate
- Nitrotetrazolate-N-Oxides
- Peroxy acids
- Peroxymonosulfuric acid
- Tetramine copper complexes
- Tetrasulfur tetranitride

1.7.2 Mixtures

- Aluminum Orphorite, Amatex, Amatol, Armstrong's mixture, ANFO, ANNMAL
- Baranol, Baratol, Blackpowder, Blasting gelatin, Butyl Tetryl

- Composition A, Composition B, Composition C, Composition 1, Composition 2, Composition 3, Composition 4, Composition 5, Cyclotol
- Detonating cord, Dynamite
- Ednatol
- Flash powder
- Hydromite 600
- Schneiderite, Semtex
- Tannerit simply, Tannerite, Tovex, Tritonal

1.7.3 Elements

- Explosive Antimony
- Uranium-235
- Plutonium-239
- Alkaline Earth Metals

1.8 See also

- Binary explosive
- Blast injury
- Detection dog
- Explosive velocity
- Fireworks
- Flame speed
- Gunpowder
- Improvised explosive devices
- Insensitive munitions
- Largest artificial non-nuclear explosions
- Nuclear weapon
- Orica; largest supplier of commercial explosives
- Pyrotechnics
- Relative effectiveness factor

1.9 References

[1] Ankony, Robert C., *Lurps: A Ranger's Diary of Tet, Khe Sanh, A Shau, and Quang Tri*, revised ed., Rowman & Littlefield Publishing Group, Lanham, MD (2009), p.73.

[2] W. W. Porterfield, *Inorganic Chemistry: A Unified Approach*, 2nd ed., Academic Press, Inc., San Diego, pp. 479-480 (1993).

[3] "Green explosive is a friend of the Earth". New Scientist. 27 March 2006. Retrieved 12 November 2014.

[4] Zel'dovich, Yakov; Kompaneets, A.S. (1960). *Theory of Detonation*. Academic Press. pp. 208–210.

[5] Hougen, Olaf A.; Watson, Kenneth; Ragatz, Roland (1954). *Chemical Process Principles*. John Wiley & Sons. pp. 66–67.

[6] Anderson, H.V. (1955). *Chemical Calculations*. McGraw-Hill. p. 206.

[7] Meyer, Rudolf; Josef Köhler; Axel Homburg (2007). *Explosives, 6th Ed*. Wiley VCH. ISBN 3-527-31656-6.

[8] Primary Explosives. Globalsecurity.org. Retrieved on 2010-02-11.

[9] Sam Barros. "PowerLabs Lead Picrate Synthesis".

[10] Cooper, Paul W. (1996). "Chapter 4: Use forms of explosives". *Explosives Engineering*. Wiley-VCH. pp. 51–66. ISBN 0-471-18636-8.

[11] Table 12-4.—United Nations Organization Hazard Classes. Tpub.com. Retrieved on 2010-02-11.

[12] "wetten.nl - Wet- en regelgeving - Wet explosieven voor civiel gebruik - BWBR0006803".

[13] "wetten.nl - Wet- en regelgeving - Wet wapens en munitie - BWBR0008804".

[14] "1913 - 1919".

[15] "1940 - 1949".

[16] "1970 - 1979".

[17] "Federal Explosives Laws" (PDF). U.S. Department of Justice, Bureau of Alcohol, Tobacco, Firearms and Explosives. Retrieved 1 February 2016.

[18] http://www.atf.gov/content/library/codified-regulations ATF Regulations

[19] "ACASLogin".

[20] "Document - Folio Infobase".

[21] Special provisions relating to black powder

1.10 Further reading

U.S. Government

- *Explosives and Demolitions* FM 5-250; U.S. Department of the Army; 274 pages; 1992.

- *Military Explosives* TM 9-1300-214; U.S. Department of the Army; 355 pages; 1984.

- *Explosives and Blasting Procedures Manual*; U.S. Department of Interior; 128 pages; 1982.

- *Safety and Performance Tests for Qualification of Explosives*; Commander, Naval Ordnance Systems Command; NAVORD OD 44811. Washington, D.C.: GPO, 1972.

- *Weapons Systems Fundamentals*; Commander, Naval Ordnance Systems Command. NAVORD OP 3000, vol. 2, 1st rev. Washington, D.C.: GPO, 1971.

- *Elements of Armament Engineering - Part One*; Army Research Office. Washington, D.C.: U.S. Army Materiel Command, 1964.

- Hazardous Materials Transportation Placards; US-DOT.

Institute of Makers of Explosives

- *Safety in the Handling and Use of Explosives* SLP 17; Institute of Makers of Explosives; 66 pages; 1932 / 1935 / 1940.

- *History of the Explosives Industry in America*; Institute of Makers of Explosives; 37 pages; 1927.

- *Clearing Land of Stumps*; Institute of Makers of Explosives; 92 pages; 1917.

- *The Use of Explosives for Agricultural and Other Purposes*; Institute of Makers of Explosives; 190 pages; 1917.

- *The Use of Explosives in making Ditches*; Institute of Makers of Explosives; 80 pages; 1917.

Other Historical

- *Farmers' Hand Book of Explosives*; duPont; 113 page; 1920.

- *A Short Account of Explosives*; Arthur Marshall; 119 pages; 1917.

- *Historical Papers on Modern Explosives*; George MacDonald; 216 pages; 1912.

- *The Rise and Progress of the British Explosives Industry*; International Congress of Pure and Applied Chemistry; 450 pages; 1909.

- *Explosives and their Power*; M. Berthelot; 592 pages; 1892.

1.11 External links

- Class 1 Hazmat Placards
- Blaster Exchange - Explosives Industry Portal
- Explosives info
- Explosives GlobalSecurity.org
- Journal of Energetic Materials
- Military Explosives
- The Explosives and Weapons Forum
- UN Hazard Classification Code at GlobalSecurity.org
- Why high nitrogen density in explosives?
- YouTube video demonstrating blast wave in slow motion

Chapter 2

Explosion

"Bomb blast" redirects here. For the Bollywood movie, see Bomb Blast (1993 film).
"Explosions" redirects here. For the Ellie Goulding song, see Explosions (song). For the American post-rock band, see Explosions (band).
For other uses, see Explosion (disambiguation).

An **explosion** is a rapid increase in volume and

Black smoke from an explosion rising after a bomb detonation inside the outside Nahr al-Bared, Lebanon.

Detonation of 16 tons of explosives.

Detonation of a MICLIC to destroy a 1km in depth blast resistant minefield in Iraq.

Gasoline explosions, simulating bomb drops at an airshow.

release of energy in an extreme manner, usually with the generation of high temperatures and the release of gases. Supersonic explosions created by high explosives are known as detonations and travel via supersonic shock waves. Subsonic explosions are created by low explosives through a slower burning process known as deflagration. When caused by a man-made device such as an exploding rocket or firework, the audible component of an explosion is referred to as its "report" (which can also be used as a verb, e.g., "the rocket reported loudly upon impact".)

2.1 Causes

2.1.1 Natural

Explosions can occur in nature. Most natural explosions arise from volcanic processes of various sorts. Explosive volcanic eruptions occur when magma rising from below has much dissolved gas in it; the reduction of pressure as the magma rises causes the gas to bubble out of solution, resulting in a rapid increase in volume. Explosions also occur as a result of impact events and in phenomena such as hydrothermal explosions (also due to volcanic processes). Explosions can also occur outside of Earth in the universe in events such as supernova. Explosions frequently occur during bushfires in eucalyptus forests where the volatile oils in the tree tops suddenly combust.*[1]

Animal bodies can also be explosive, as some animals hold a large amount of flammable material such as animal fat. This, in rare cases, results in naturally exploding animals.

Astronomical

Among the largest known explosions in the universe are supernovae, which result when a star explodes from the sudden starting or stopping of nuclear fusion, and gamma ray bursts, whose nature is still in some dispute. Solar flares are an example of explosion common on the Sun, and presumably on most other stars as well. The energy source for solar flare activity comes from the tangling of magnetic field lines resulting from the rotation of the Sun's conductive plasma. Another type of large astronomical explosion occurs when a very large meteoroid or an asteroid impacts the surface of another object, such as a planet.

2.1.2 Chemical

Main article: Explosive material

The most common artificial explosives are chemical explosives, usually involving a rapid and violent oxidation reaction that produces large amounts of hot gas. Gunpowder was the first explosive to be discovered and put to use. Other notable early developments in chemical explosive technology were Frederick Augustus Abel's development of nitrocellulose in 1865 and Alfred Nobel's invention of dynamite in 1866. Chemical explosions (both intentional and accidental) are often initiated by an electric spark or flame. Accidental explosions may occur in fuel tanks, rocket engines, etc.

2.1.3 Electrical and magnetic

A high current electrical fault can create an 'electrical explosion' by forming a high energy electrical arc which rapidly vaporizes metal and insulation material. This arc flash hazard is a danger to persons working on energized switchgear. Also, excessive magnetic pressure within an ultra-strong electromagnet can cause a *magnetic explosion*.

2.1.4 Mechanical and vapor

Strictly a physical process, as opposed to chemical or nuclear, e.g., the bursting of a sealed or partially sealed container under internal pressure is often referred to as a 'mechanical explosion'. Examples include an overheated boiler or a simple tin can of beans tossed into a fire.

Boiling liquid expanding vapor explosions are one type of mechanical explosion that can occur when a vessel containing a pressurized liquid is ruptured, causing a rapid increase in volume as the liquid evaporates. Note that the contents of the container may cause a subsequent chemical explosion, the effects of which can be dramatically more serious, such as a propane tank in the midst of a fire. In such a case, to the effects of the mechanical explosion when the tank fails are added the effects from the explosion resulting from the released (initially liquid and then almost instantaneously gaseous) propane in the presence of an ignition source. For this reason, emergency workers often differentiate between the two events.

2.1.5 Nuclear

Main articles: Nuclear explosion and Effects of nuclear explosions

In addition to stellar nuclear explosions, a man-made nuclear weapon is a type of explosive weapon that derives its destructive force from nuclear fission or from a combination of fission and fusion. As a result, even a nuclear weapon with a small yield is significantly more powerful than the largest conventional explosives available, with a single weapon capable of completely destroying an entire city.

2.2 Properties of explosions

2.2.1 Force

Explosive force is released in a direction perpendicular to the surface of the explosive. If a grenade is in mid air during the explosion, the direction of the blast will be 360°. If the surface is cut or shaped, the explosive forces can be focused to produce a greater local effect; this is known as a shaped charge.

2.2.2 Velocity

The speed of the reaction is what distinguishes an explosive reaction from an ordinary combustion reaction. Unless the reaction occurs very rapidly, the thermally expanding gases will be moderately dissipated in the medium, with no large differential in pressure and there will be no explosion. Consider a wood fire. As the fire burns, there certainly is the evolution of heat and the formation of gases, but neither is liberated rapidly enough to build up a sudden substantial pressure differential and then cause an explosion. This can be likened to the difference between the energy discharge of a battery, which is slow, and that of a flash capacitor like that in a camera flash, which releases its energy all at once.

2.2.3 Evolution of heat

The generation of heat in large quantities accompanies most explosive chemical reactions. The exceptions are called entropic explosives and include organic peroxides such as acetone peroxide*[2] It is the rapid liberation of heat that causes the gaseous products of most explosive reactions to expand and generate high pressures. This rapid generation of high pressures of the released gas constitutes the explosion. The liberation of heat with insufficient rapidity will not cause an explosion. For example, although a unit mass of coal yields five times as much heat as a unit mass of nitroglycerin, the coal cannot be used as an explosive (except in the form of coal dust) because the rate at which it yields this heat is quite slow. In fact, a substance which burns less rapidly (*i.e.* slow combustion) may actually evolve more total heat than an explosive which detonates rapidly (*i.e.* fast combustion). In the former, slow combustion converts more of the internal energy (*i.e.* chemical potential) of the burning substance into heat released to the surroundings, while in the latter, fast combustion (*i.e.* detonation) instead converts more internal energy into work on the surroundings (*i.e.* less internal energy converted into heat); *c.f.* heat and work (thermodynamics) are equivalent forms of energy. See Heat of Combustion for a more thorough treatment of this topic.

When a chemical compound is formed from its constituents, heat may either be absorbed or released. The quantity of heat absorbed or given off during transformation is called the heat of formation. Heats of formations for solids and gases found in explosive reactions have been determined for a temperature of 25 °C and atmospheric pressure, and are normally given in units of kilojoules per gram-molecule. A positive value indicates that heat is absorbed during the formation of the compound from its elements; such a reaction is called an endothermic reaction. In explosive technology only materials that are exothermic—that have a net liberation of heat and have a negative heat of formation—are of interest. Reaction heat is measured under conditions either of constant pressure or constant volume. It is this heat of reaction that may be properly expressed as the "heat of explosion."

2.2.4 Initiation of reaction

A chemical explosive is a compound or mixture which, upon the application of heat or shock, decomposes or rearranges with extreme rapidity, yielding much gas and heat. Many substances not ordinarily classed as explosives may do one, or even two, of these things.

A reaction must be capable of being initiated by the application of shock, heat, or a catalyst (in the case of some explosive chemical reactions) to a small portion of the mass of the explosive material. A material in which the first three factors exist cannot be accepted as an explosive unless the reaction can be made to occur when needed.

2.2.5 Fragmentation

Fragmentation is the accumulation and projection of particles as the result of a high explosives detonation. Fragments could be part of a structure such as a magazine. High velocity, low angle fragments can travel hundreds or thousands of feet with enough energy to initiate other surrounding high explosive items, injure or kill personnel and damage vehicles or structures.

2.3 Notable explosions

Further information: List of the largest artificial non-nuclear explosions

2.3.1 Chemical explosions

2.3.2 Nuclear testing

- Trinity test

- Castle Bravo
- Tsar Bomba
- Atomic bombings of Hiroshima and Nagasaki

2.3.3 Use in war

- Artillery, mortars, and cannons
- Gunpowder and smokeless powder as a propellant in firearms and artillery
- Bombs
- Missiles, rockets, and torpedoes
- Atomic bombings of Hiroshima and Nagasaki
- Land mines, naval mines, and IEDs
- Satchel charges and sapping
- Hand grenades

2.3.4 Volcanic eruptions

Main article: Volcanic Explosivity Index

- Santorini
- Krakatoa
- Mount St. Helens
- Mount Tambora
- Mount Pinatubo
- Toba catastrophe theory
- Yellowstone Caldera

2.4 Etymology

Classical Latin *explōdere* means "to hiss a bad actor off the stage", "to drive an actor off the stage by making noise", from ex- ("out") + plaudere ("to clap; to applaud").. The modern meaning developed later:[3]

- Classical Latin: "to drive an actor off the stage by making noise" hence meaning to "to drive out" or "to reject"

In English:

- Around 1538: "drive out or off by clapping" (originally theatrical)
- Around 1660: "drive out with violence and sudden noise"
- Around 1790: "go off with a loud noise"
- Around 1882: first use as "bursting with destructive force"

2.5 See also

- Combustion
- Deflagration
- Detonation
- Dust explosion
- Explosion protection
- Explosive limit
- Fuel tank explosion
- Implosion (mechanical process): opposite of explosion
- Internal combustion engine
- Mushroom cloud
- Piston engine
- Plofkraak
- Standards for electrical equipment in potentially explosive environments
- Underwater explosion

2.6 References

[1] Kissane, Karen (2009-05-22). "Fire power equalled 1500 atomic bombs". *The Age*. Melbourne.

[2] Dubnikova, Faina; Kosloff, Ronnie; Almog, Joseph; Zeiri, Yehuda; Boese, Roland; Itzhaky, Harel; Alt, Aaron; Keinan, Ehud (2005-02-01). "Decomposition of Triacetone Triperoxide Is an Entropic Explosion". *Journal of the American Chemical Society*. **127** (4): 1146–1159. doi:10.1021/ja0464903. PMID 15669854.

[3] wikt:explode#Etymology

Chapter 3

Explosive weapon

An **explosive weapon** generally uses high explosive to project blast and/or fragmentation from a point of detonation.

Explosive weapons may be subdivided by their method of manufacture into explosive ordnance and improvised explosive devices (IEDs). Certain types of explosive ordnance and many improvised explosive devices are sometimes referred to under the generic term bomb.

When explosive weapons fail to function as designed they are often left as unexploded ordnance (UXO).

In the common practice of states, explosive weapons are generally the preserve of the military, for use in situations of armed conflict, and are rarely used for purposes of domestic policing. Certain types of explosive weapons may be categorised as light weapons (e.g. hand-held under-barrel and mounted grenade launchers, portable launchers of anti-tank missile and rocket systems; portable launchers of anti-aircraft missile systems (MANPADS); and mortars of calibres of less than 100 mm).*[1] Many explosive weapons, such as aircraft bombs, rockets systems, artillery and larger mortars, are categorised as heavy weapons.

Taken in combination, Amended Protocol II and Protocol V to the United Nations Convention on Certain Conventional Weapons establish a responsibility on the users of explosive weapons to record and retain information on their use of such weapons (including the location of use and the type and quantity of weapons used), to provide such information to parties in control of territory that may be affected by UXO, and to assist with the removal of this threat.

Certain types of explosive weapon have been subject to prohibition in international treaties. The Saint Petersburg Declaration of 1868 prohibits the use of certain explosive rifle projectiles. This prohibition has evolved into a ban on 'exploding bullets' under customary international humanitarian law binding on all States. The 1997 Mine Ban Treaty and the 2008 Convention on Cluster Munitions also prohibit types of explosive weapons, anti-personnel landmines and cluster munitions, for states parties to these treaties.

In armed conflict, the general rules of international humanitarian law governing the conduct of hostilities apply to the use of all types of explosive weapons as means or methods of warfare.

The Secretary-General of the United Nations has expressed increasing concern at "the humanitarian impact of explosive weapons, in particular when used in densely populated areas." *[2] The President of the International Committee of the Red Cross (ICRC), Jakob Kellenberger has noted that "ICRC's key operations in 2009 – in the Gaza Strip and in Sri Lanka – provided stark illustrations of the potentially devastating humanitarian consequences of military operations conducted in densely populated areas, especially when heavy or highly explosive weapons are used." *[3]

According to the British NGO Action on Armed Violence (AOAV), when explosive weapons are used in populated areas (towns, villages, residential neighbourhoods) the overwhelming majority (91% in 2012) of direct casualties are civilians.*[4]

Action on Armed Violence has also charted a dramatic rise in the use of suicide bombing and improvised explosive devices globally. Their data showed the number of civilians killed or injured by car and suicide bombs and other improvised explosive devices rising by 70 percent in the three years to 2013.*[5]

The International Network on Explosive Weapons (INEW), a partnership of NGOs, is calling for immediate action to prevent human suffering from the use of explosive weapons in populated areas.

3.1 References

[1] "1997 Report of the Panel of Governmental Experts on Small Arms". Retrieved 6 August 2012.

[2] Report of the Secretary-General on the protection of civilians in armed conflict, United Nations Security Council, 29 May 2009, S/2009/277, para 36.

[3] The 2009 Annual Report of the International Committee of the Red Cross, Message from the President, p.8.

[4] *An Explosive Situation: Monitoring Explosive Violence in 2012* (PDF). AOAV. 2013. p. 3.

[5] "Data shows 70 percent rise in civilian casualties from car bombs, suicide attacks – campaigners". Thomson Reuters Foundation. 2014.

3.2 External links

- The International Network on Explosive Weapons (INEW)
- Action on Armed Violence (AOAV) Explosive Violence Monitoring project
- United Nations Institute for Disarmament Research (UNIDIR) project on explosive weapons
- *Explosive Violence, The Problem of Explosive Weapons*, report by Richard Moyes (Landmine Action, 2009) on the humanitarian problems caused by the use of explosive weapons in populated areas
- Article 36 - civil society initiative on the humanitarian impact of weapons

Chapter 4

Fuel

A **fuel** is any material that can be made to react with other

Wood was one of the first fuels to be used by humans and is still the primary energy source in much of the world.

substances so that it releases chemical or nuclear energy as heat or to be used for work. The concept was originally applied solely to those materials capable of releasing chemical energy but has since also been applied to other sources of heat energy such as nuclear energy (via nuclear fission or nuclear fusion).

The heat energy released by reactions of fuels is converted into mechanical energy via a heat engine. Other times the heat itself is valued for warmth, cooking, or industrial processes, as well as the illumination that comes with combustion. Fuels are also used in the cells of organisms in a process known as cellular respiration, where organic molecules are oxidized to release usable energy. Hydrocarbons and related oxygen-containing molecules are by far the most common source of fuel used by humans, but other substances, including radioactive metals, are also utilized.

Fuels are contrasted with other substances or devices storing potential energy, such as those that directly release electrical energy (such as batteries and capacitors) or mechanical energy (such as flywheels, springs, compressed air, or water in a reservoir).

4.1 History

The first known use of fuel was the combustion of wood or sticks by *Homo erectus* near 2,000,000 (two million) years ago.*[1] Throughout most of human history fuels derived from plants or animal fat were only used by humans . Charcoal, a wood derivative, has been used since at least 6,000 BCE for melting metals. It was only supplanted by coke, derived from coal, as European forests started to become depleted around the 18th century. Charcoal briquettes are now commonly used as a fuel for barbecue cooking.*[2]

Coal was first used as a fuel around 1000 BCE in China. With the energy in the form of chemical energy that could be released through combustion.*[3] but the concept development of the steam engine in the United Kingdom in 1769, coal came into more common use as a power source. Coal was later used to drive ships and locomotives. By the 19th century, gas extracted from coal was being used for street lighting in London. In the 20th and 21st centuries, the primary use of coal is to generate electricity, providing 40% of the world's electrical power supply in 2005.*[4]

Fossil fuels were rapidly adopted during the industrial revolution, because they were more concentrated and flexible than traditional energy sources, such as water power. They have become a pivotal part of our contemporary society, with most countries in the world burning fossil fuels in order to produce power.

Currently the trend has been towards renewable fuels, such as biofuels like alcohols.

4.2 Chemical

Chemical fuels are substances that release energy by reacting with substances around them, most notably by the process of combustion. Most of the chemical energy released in combustion was not stored in the chemical bonds of the fuel, but in the weak double bond of molecular oxygen.*[5]

4.2. CHEMICAL

Chemical fuels are divided in two ways. First, by their physical properties, as a solid, liquid or gas. Secondly, on the basis of their occurrence: *primary (natural fuel)* and *secondary (artificial fuel)*. Thus, a general classification of chemical fuels is:

4.2.1 Solid fuel

Main article: Solid fuel
Solid fuel refers to various types of solid material that are

Coal is an important solid fuel.

used as fuel to produce energy and provide heating, usually released through combustion. Solid fuels include wood (see wood fuel), charcoal, peat, coal, Hexamine fuel tablets, and pellets made from wood (see wood pellets), corn, wheat, rye and other grains. Solid-fuel rocket technology also uses solid fuel (see solid propellants). Solid fuels have been used by humanity for many years to create fire. Coal was the fuel source which enabled the industrial revolution, from firing furnaces, to running steam engines. Wood was also extensively used to run steam locomotives. Both peat and coal are still used in electricity generation today. The use of some solid fuels (e.g. coal) is restricted or prohibited in some urban areas, due to unsafe levels of toxic emissions. The use of other solid fuels such as wood is decreasing as heating technology and the availability of good quality fuel improves. In some areas, smokeless coal is often the only solid fuel used. In Ireland, peat briquettes are used as smokeless fuel. They are also used to start a coal fire.

4.2.2 Liquid fuels

Main article: Liquid fuel
Liquid fuels are combustible or energy-generating

A gasoline station.

molecules that can be harnessed to create mechanical energy, usually producing kinetic energy; they also must take the shape of their container. It is the fumes of liquid fuels that are flammable instead of the fluid.

Most liquid fuels in widespread use are derived from the fossilized remains of dead plants and animals by exposure to heat and pressure in the Earth's crust. However, there are several types, such as hydrogen fuel (for automotive uses), ethanol, jet fuel and biodiesel which are all categorized as a liquid fuel. Emulsified fuels of oil-in-water such as orimulsion have been developed a way to make heavy oil fractions usable as liquid fuels. Many liquid fuels play a primary role in transportation and the economy.

Some common properties of liquid fuels are that they are easy to transport, and can be handled with relative ease. Also they are relatively easy to use for all engineering applications, and home use. Fuels like kerosene are rationed in some countries, for example available in government subsidized shops in India for home use.

Conventional diesel is similar to gasoline in that it is a mixture of aliphatic hydrocarbons extracted from petroleum. Kerosene is used in kerosene lamps and as a fuel for cooking, heating, and small engines. Natural gas, composed chiefly of methane, can be compressed to a liquid and used as a substitute for other traditional liquid fuels. LP gas is a mixture of propane and butane, both of which are easily compressible gases under standard atmospheric conditions. It offers many of the advantages of compressed natural gas (CNG), but is denser than air, does not burn as cleanly, and is much more easily compressed. Commonly used for cooking and space heating, LP gas and compressed propane are seeing increased use in motorized vehicles; propane is the third most commonly used motor fuel globally.

4.2.3 Gaseous fuels

Main article: Fuel gas

Fuel gas is any one of a number of fuels that under ordi-

A 20-pound (9.1 kg) propane cylinder.

nary conditions are gaseous. Many fuel gases are composed of hydrocarbons (such as methane or propane), hydrogen, carbon monoxide, or mixtures thereof. Such gases are sources of potential heat energy or light energy that can be readily transmitted and distributed through pipes from the point of origin directly to the place of consumption. Fuel gas is contrasted with liquid fuels and from solid fuels, though some fuel gases are liquefied for storage or transport. While their gaseous nature can be advantageous, avoiding the difficulty of transporting solid fuel and the dangers of spillage inherent in liquid fuels, it can also be dangerous. It is possible for a fuel gas to be undetected and collect in certain areas, leading to the risk of a gas explosion. For this reason, odorizers are added to most fuel gases so that they may be detected by a distinct smell. The most common type of fuel gas in current use is natural gas.

4.2.4 Biofuels

Main article: Biofuel

Biofuel can be broadly defined as solid, liquid, or gas fuel consisting of, or derived from biomass. Biomass can also be used directly for heating or power—known as *biomass fuel*. Biofuel can be produced from any carbon source that can be replenished rapidly e.g. plants. Many different plants and plant-derived materials are used for biofuel manufacture.

Perhaps the earliest fuel employed by humans is wood. Evidence shows controlled fire was used up to 1.5 million years ago at Swartkrans, South Africa. It is unknown which hominid species first used fire, as both *Australopithecus* and an early species of *Homo* were present at the sites.[6] As a fuel, wood has remained in use up until the present day, although it has been superseded for many purposes by other sources. Wood has an energy density of 10–20 MJ/kg.[7]

Recently biofuels have been developed for use in automotive transport (for example Bioethanol and Biodiesel), but there is widespread public debate about how carbon efficient these fuels are.

4.2.5 Fossil fuels

Main article: Fossil fuel

Fossil fuels are hydrocarbons, primarily coal and petroleum

Extraction of petroleum

(liquid petroleum or natural gas), formed from the fossilized remains of ancient plants and animals[8] by exposure to high heat and pressure in the absence of oxygen in the Earth's crust over hundreds of millions of years.[9] Commonly, the term fossil fuel also includes hydrocarbon-containing natural resources that are not derived entirely from biological sources, such as tar sands. These latter sources are properly known as *mineral fuels*.

Fossil fuels contain high percentages of carbon and include coal, petroleum, and natural gas.*[10] They range from volatile materials with low carbon:hydrogen ratios like methane, to liquid petroleum to nonvolatile materials composed of almost pure carbon, like anthracite coal. Methane can be found in hydrocarbon fields, alone, associated with oil, or in the form of methane clathrates. Fossil fuels formed from the fossilized remains of dead plants*[8] by exposure to heat and pressure in the Earth's crust over millions of years.*[11] This biogenic theory was first introduced by German scholar Georg Agricola in 1556 and later by Mikhail Lomonosov in the 18th century.

It was estimated by the Energy Information Administration that in 2007 primary sources of energy consisted of petroleum 36.0%, coal 27.4%, natural gas 23.0%, amounting to an 86.4% share for fossil fuels in primary energy consumption in the world.*[12] Non-fossil sources in 2006 included hydroelectric 6.3%, nuclear 8.5%, and others (geothermal, solar, tidal, wind, wood, waste) amounting to 0.9%.*[13] World energy consumption was growing about 2.3% per year.

Fossil fuels are non-renewable resources because they take millions of years to form, and reserves are being depleted much faster than new ones are being made. So we must conserve these fuels and use them judiciously. The production and use of fossil fuels raise environmental concerns. A global movement toward the generation of renewable energy is therefore under way to help meet increased energy needs. The burning of fossil fuels produces around 21.3 billion tonnes (21.3 gigatonnes) of carbon dioxide (CO_2) per year, but it is estimated that natural processes can only absorb about half of that amount, so there is a net increase of 10.65 billion tonnes of atmospheric carbon dioxide per year (one tonne of atmospheric carbon is equivalent to 44/12 or 3.7 tonnes of carbon dioxide).*[14] Carbon dioxide is one of the greenhouse gases that enhances radiative forcing and contributes to global warming, causing the average surface temperature of the Earth to rise in response, which the vast majority of climate scientists agree will cause major adverse effects. Fuels are a source of energy.

4.3 Nuclear

Main article: Nuclear fuel

Nuclear fuel is any material that is consumed to derive nuclear energy. Technically speaking, All matter can be a nuclear fuel because any element under the right conditions will release nuclear energy, but the materials commonly referred to as nuclear fuels are those that will produce energy without being placed under extreme duress. Nuclear fuel is a material that can be 'burned' by nuclear fission or fusion to derive nuclear energy. *Nuclear fuel* can refer to the fuel itself, or to physical objects (for example bundles composed

CANDU fuel bundles Two CANDU (*"CANada Deuterium Uranium"*) fuel bundles, each about 50 cm long, 10 cm in diameter. Photo courtesy of Atomic Energy of Canada Ltd.

of **fuel rods**) composed of the fuel material, mixed with structural, neutron moderating, or neutron reflecting materials.

Most nuclear fuels contain heavy fissile elements that are capable of nuclear fission. When these fuels are struck by neutrons, they are in turn capable of emitting neutrons when they break apart. This makes possible a self-sustaining chain reaction that releases energy with a controlled rate in a nuclear reactor or with a very rapid uncontrolled rate in a nuclear weapon.

The most common fissile nuclear fuels are uranium-235 (^{235}U) and plutonium-239 (^{239}Pu). The actions of mining, refining, purifying, using, and ultimately disposing of nuclear fuel together make up the nuclear fuel cycle. Not all types of nuclear fuels create power from nuclear fission. Plutonium-238 and some other elements are used to produce small amounts of nuclear power by radioactive decay in radioisotope thermoelectric generators and other types of atomic batteries. Also, light nuclides such as tritium (^3H) can be used as fuel for nuclear fusion. Nuclear fuel has the highest energy density of all practical fuel sources.

4.3.1 Fission

The most common type of nuclear fuel used by humans is heavy fissile elements that can be made to undergo nuclear fission chain reactions in a nuclear fission reactor; *nuclear fuel* can refer to the material or to physical objects (for example fuel bundles composed of fuel rods) composed of the fuel material, perhaps mixed with structural, neutron moderating, or neutron reflecting materials. The most common fissile nuclear fuels are ^{235}U and ^{239}Pu, and the actions of mining, refining, purifying, using, and ultimately disposing of these elements together make up the nuclear fuel cycle, which is important for its relevance to nuclear power generation and nuclear weapons.

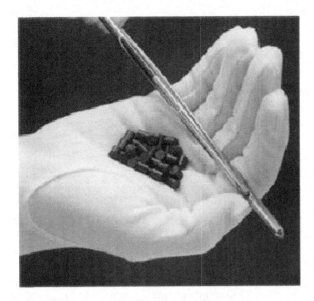

Nuclear fuel pellets are used to release nuclear energy.

4.3.2 Fusion

Fuels that produce energy by the process of nuclear fusion are currently not utilized by humans but are the main source of fuel for stars. Fusion fuels tend to be light elements such as hydrogen which will combine easily. Energy is required to start fusion by raising temperature so high all materials would turn into plasma, and allow nuclei to collide and stick together with each other before repelling due to electric charge. This process is called fusion and it can give out energy.

In stars that undergo nuclear fusion, fuel consists of atomic nuclei that can release energy by the absorption of a proton or neutron. In most stars the fuel is provided by hydrogen, which can combine to form helium through the proton-proton chain reaction or by the CNO cycle. When the hydrogen fuel is exhausted, nuclear fusion can continue with progressively heavier elements, although the net energy released is lower because of the smaller difference in nuclear binding energy. Once iron-56 or nickel-56 nuclei are produced, no further energy can be obtained by nuclear fusion as these have the highest nuclear binding energies. The elements then on use up energy instead of giving off energy when fused. Therefore, fusion stops and the star dies. In attempts by humans, fusion is only carried out with hydrogen (isotope of 2 and 3) to form helium-4 as this reaction gives out the most net energy. Electric confinement (ITER), inertial confinement(heating by laser) and heating by strong electric currents are the popular methods used. .*[15]

Fuel imports in 2005

4.4 World trade

World Bank reported that the USA was the top fuel importer in 2005 followed by the EU and Japan.

4.5 See also

- Alcohol fuel
- Alternative fuels
- Ammonia
- Battery (electricity)
- Bitumen-based fuel
- Biofuels
- Compressed natural gas
- Cryogenic fuel
- Emulsified fuel
- Fuel card
- Fuel cell
- Fuel management systems
- Fuel oil
- Fuel poverty
- Filling station
- Hydrogen economy
- Hydrogen fuel
- Liquid fuels
- List of energy topics
- Marine fuel management
- Propellant

- Recycled fuel
- Solid fuel
- World energy resources and consumption

4.6 Footnotes

[1] Leakey, Richard (1994). *Origin of Humankind*. Basic Books. ISBN 0-465-03135-8.

[2] Hall, Loretta (2007). "Charcoal Briquette". How Products Are Made. Retrieved 2007-10-01.

[3] One or more of the preceding sentences incorporates text from a publication now in the public domain: Chisholm, Hugh, ed. (1911). "Fuel". *Encyclopædia Britannica* (11th ed.). Cambridge University Press.

[4] "History of Coal Use". World Coal Institute. Retrieved 2006-08-10.

[5] Schmidt-Rohr, K (2015). "Why Combustions Are Always Exothermic, Yielding About 418 kJ per Mole of O_2". *J. Chem. Educ.* **92** (12): 2094–2099. doi:10.1021/acs.jchemed.5b00333.

[6] Rincon, Paul (22 March 2004). "Bones hint at first use of fire". BBC News. Retrieved 2007-09-11.

[7] Elert, Glenn (2007). "Chemical Potential Energy". The Physics Hypertextbook. Retrieved 2007-09-11.

[8] Dr. Irene Novaczek. "Canada's Fossil Fuel Dependency". Elements. Retrieved 2007-01-18.

[9] "Fossil fuel". EPA. Archived from the original on 12 March 2007. Retrieved 2007-01-18.

[10] "Fossil fuel".

[11] "Fossil fuel". EPA. Archived from the original on 12 March 2007. Retrieved 2007-01-18.

[12] "U.S. EIA International Energy Statistics". Retrieved 2010-01-12.

[13] "International Energy Annual 2006". Retrieved 2009-02-08.

[14] "US Department of Energy on greenhouse gases". Retrieved 2007-09-09.

[15] Fewell, M. P. (1995). "The atomic nuclide with the highest mean binding energy". *American Journal of Physics*. **63** (7): 653–658. Bibcode:1995AmJPh..63..653F. doi:10.1119/1.17828.

4.7 References

- Ratcliff, Brian; et al. (2000). *Chemistry 1*. Cambridge University press. ISBN 0-521-78778-5.

4.8 Further reading

- Directive 1999/94/EC of the European Parliament and of the council of 13 December 1999, relating to the availability of consumer information on fuel economy and CO2 emissions in respect of the marketing of new passenger cars PDF (140 KB).
- Council Directive 80/1268/EEC Fuel consumption of motor vehicles.

Chapter 5

Oxidizing agent

The international pictogram for oxidising chemicals.

Dangerous goods label for oxidising agents

In chemistry, an **oxidizing agent** (oxidant, oxidizer) is a substance that has the ability to oxidize other substances (cause them to lose electrons). Common oxidizing agents are oxygen, hydrogen peroxide and the halogens.

In one sense, an oxidizing agent is a chemical reaction that removes an electron from another atom. It is one component in an oxidation–reduction (redox) reaction. In the second sense, an oxidizing agent is a chemical species that transfers electronegative atoms, usually oxygen, to a substrate. Combustion, many explosives, and organic redox reactions involve atom-transfer reactions.

$Fe(C_5H_5)^+_2$, which accepts an electron to form $Fe(C_5H_5)_2$.[1]

Extensive tabulations of ranking the electron accepting properties of various reagents (redox potentials) are available, see Standard electrode potential (data page).

5.1 Electron acceptors

Electron acceptors participate in electron-transfer reactions. In this context, the oxidizing agent is called an **electron acceptor** and the reducing agent is called an electron donor. A classic oxidizing agent is the ferrocenium ion

5.1.1 Mechanism

Of great interest to chemists are the details of the electron transfer event, which can be described as inner sphere or outer sphere.

5.3. DANGEROUS MATERIALS DEFINITION

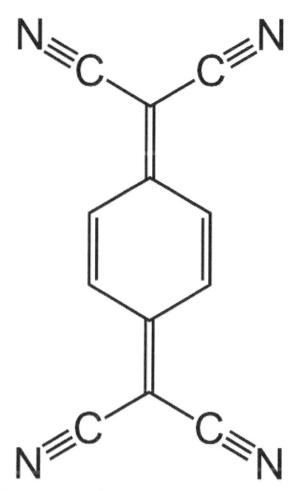

Tetracyanoquinodimethane is an organic electron-acceptor.

5.2 Atom-transfer reagents

In more common usage, an oxidising agent transfers oxygen atoms to a substrate. In this context, the oxidising agent can be called an oxygenation reagent or oxygen-atom transfer (OAT) agent.*[2] Examples include MnO_4^- (permanganate), CrO_4^{2-} (chromate), OsO_4 (osmium tetroxide), and especially ClO_4^- (perchlorate). Notice that these species are all oxides.

In some cases, these oxides can also serve as electron acceptors, as illustrated by the conversion of MnO_4^- to MnO_4^{2-}, manganate.

5.2.1 Common oxidizing agents (O-atom transfer agents)

- Oxygen (O_2)
- Ozone (O_3)
- Hydrogen peroxide (H_2O_2) and other inorganic peroxides, Fenton's reagent
- Fluorine (F_2), chlorine (Cl_2), and other halogens
- Nitric acid (HNO_3) and nitrate compounds
- Sulfuric acid (H_2SO_4)
- Peroxydisulfuric acid ($H_2S_2O_8$)
- Peroxymonosulfuric acid (H_2SO_5)
- Chlorite, chlorate, perchlorate, and other analogous halogen compounds
- Hypochlorite and other hypohalite compounds, including household bleach (NaClO)
- Hexavalent chromium compounds such as chromic and dichromic acids and chromium trioxide, pyridinium chlorochromate (PCC), and chromate/dichromate compounds
- Permanganate compounds such as potassium permanganate
- Sodium perborate
- Nitrous oxide (N_2O)
- Potassium nitrate (KNO_3), the oxidizer in black powder
- Sodium bismuthate

5.3 Dangerous materials definition

The dangerous materials definition of an **oxidizing agent** is a substance that can cause or contribute to the combustion of other material.*[3] By this definition some materials that are classified as oxidising agents by analytical chemists are not classified as oxidising agents in a dangerous materials sense. An example is potassium dichromate, which does not pass the dangerous goods test of an oxidising agent.

The U.S. Department of Transportation defines oxidizing agents specifically. There are two definitions for oxidizing agents governed under DOT regulations. These two are Class 5; Division 5.1 and Class 5; Division 5.2. Division 5.1 "means a material that may, generally by yielding oxygen, cause or enhance the combustion of other materials." Division 5.1 of the DOT code applies to solid oxidizers "if, when tested in accordance with the UN Manual of Tests and Criteria (IBR, see § 171.7 of this subchapter), its mean burning time is less than or equal to the burning time of a

3:7 potassium bromate/cellulose mixture." 5.1 of the DOT code applies to liquid oxidizers "if, when tested in accordance with the UN Manual of Tests and Criteria, it spontaneously ignites or its mean time for a pressure rise from 690 kPa to 2070 kPa gauge is less than the time of a 1:1 nitric acid (65 percent)/cellulose mixture." *[4]

5.4 Common oxidizing agents and their products

5.5 See also

- Combustion
- Dye
- Electrosynthesis
- Organic oxidation
- Organic redox reaction

5.6 References

[1] N. G. Connelly, W. E. Geiger (1996). "Chemical Redox Agents for Organometallic Chemistry". *Chemical Reviews*. **96** (2): 877–910. doi:10.1021/cr940053x. PMID 11848774.

[2] Smith, Michael B.; March, Jerry (2007), *Advanced Organic Chemistry: Reactions, Mechanisms, and Structure* (6th ed.), New York: Wiley-Interscience, ISBN 0-471-72091-7

[3] Australian Dangerous Goods Code, 6th Edition

[4] 49 CFR 172.127 General Requirements for Shipments and Packagings; Subpart D

Chapter 6

Explosive booster

An **explosive booster** is a sensitive explosive charge that acts as a bridge between a (relatively weak) conventional detonator and a low-sensitivity (but typically high-energy) explosive such as TNT. By itself, the initiating detonator would not deliver sufficient energy to set off the low-sensitivity charge. However, it detonates the primary charge (the booster), which then delivers an explosive shockwave that is sufficient to detonate the secondary, main, high-energy charge.

Unlike C4 plastic explosive, not all explosives can be detonated simply by inserting a detonator and firing it.

An initiator such as a shock tube, cannon fuse, or even a conventional detonator does not deliver sufficient shock to detonate charges comprising TNT, Composition B, ANFO and many other high explosives. Therefore, some form of "booster" is required to amplify the energy released by the detonator so that the main charge will detonate.

Tetryl was once a very popular chemical for booster charges, particularly during World War II, but has been largely superseded by other compositions, e.g. a small cylinder or pellet of phlegmatized RDX or PETN (slightly larger than the actual detonator) into which the detonator itself is inserted.

Note: booby traps and improvised explosive devices frequently use plastic explosive as the booster charge, for example, some C4 or Semtex stuffed into the empty fuze pocket of a 120mm mortar shell. This is because any standard detonator will initiate plastic explosive as is.

When encountered in connection with artillery shells or air dropped bombs, a booster charge is sometimes referred to as the "gaine". See detonators.

At a purely technical level, a sufficiently large detonator would initiate high explosives without the need for a booster charge. However, there are very good reasons why this method is never used. Firstly, there is a major safety issue, i.e. detonators are (like all primary explosives) much more sensitive to shock, heat, and friction than an explosive booster. Therefore, minimising the amount of primary explosive that users must store or carry greatly reduces the likelihood of serious accidents. An additional economic reason for using explosive booster charges is that chemical compounds used in detonators (e.g. lead styphnate) are comparatively expensive to produce and encapsulate when compared to the manufacturing costs of explosive boosters.

A common form for boosters is to cast the explosive material into a cylindrical shell made of cardboard or plastic; these are accordingly known as **cast boosters**.

6.1 Gallery

- Cross-sectional view of an M4 mine showing the detonator and adjacent booster charge surrounded by the main explosive charge of TNT

- Cross-sectional view of a BLU-43 Dragontooth cluster munition showing detonator and adjacent booster charge

- Cut-away view of an M14 antipersonnel landmine. No booster is required because the main explosive filling is tetryl, which is sufficiently sensitive to be initiated by the detonator alone

- Cut-away view of an RPG-2 rocket grenade showing booster charge

- A group of 105mm artillery shells with plastic explosive stuffed into their fuze pockets to act as booster charges. Each of the 5 shells has been linked together with red detcord to make them detonate simultaneously. To turn this assembly into a booby trap, the final step would be to connect an M142 firing device to the detcord and hide everything under some form of cover e.g. newspapers or a bed-sheet.

Chapter 7

Explosive train

A **triggering sequence**, also called an **explosive train**, is a sequence of events that culminates in the detonation of explosives. For safety reasons, most widely used high explosives are difficult to detonate. A primary explosive of higher sensitivity is used to trigger a uniform and predictable detonation of the main body of the explosive. Although the primary explosive itself is generally a more sensitive and expensive compound, it is only used in small quantities and in relatively safely packaged forms. By design there are low explosives and high explosives made such that the low explosives are highly sensitive (i.e. their 'Figure of Insensitivity' is low) and high explosives are comparatively insensitive. This not only affords inherent safety to the usage of explosives during handling and transport, but also necessitates an explosive triggering sequence or explosive train. The explosive triggering sequence or the explosive train essentially consists of an 'initiator', an 'intermediary' and the 'high explosive'.

For example, a match will not cause plastic explosive to explode, but it will light a fuse which will detonate a primary explosive that will shock a secondary high explosive and cause it to detonate. In this way, even very insensitive explosives may be used; the primary detonates a "booster" charge that then detonates the main charge. Triggering sequences are used in the mining industry for the detonation of ANFO and other cheap, bulk, and insensitive explosives that can not be fired by only a blasting cap or similar item.

7.1 Low explosive train

An example of a low-explosive train is a rifle cartridge, which consists of

1. a primer consisting of a small amount of primary high explosive which initiates the explosive train

2. an igniter which is initiated by the primer and creates a flame that ignites the propellant

3. a propellant consisting of a secondary low explosive that emits a large amount of gas as it deflagrates.

7.2 High explosive train

High-explosives trains can be either two-step (e.g., detonator and dynamite) or three-step (e.g., detonator, booster of primary explosive, and main charge of secondary explosive).

7.2.1 Primary components

A high explosive train includes three primary high explosive components which are used to initiate explosives:

1. Fuse or fuze
2. Primer
3. Detonator

Detonators are often made from tetryl and fulminates.

7.2.2 Secondary components

In an explosive train there are two secondary high explosive components:

1. Boosters
2. Bursting charges, also known as main charges

Examples of bursting charges are

- TNT
- Composition B
- RDX
- PETN

7.2.3 Tertiary components

In some cases, the main charge is so insensitive that using typical primary materials becomes impractical due to large amount required. Thus, an explosive booster is used to deliver sufficient shockwave to the main charge.

The most significant tertiary material in widespread use is ANFO.

7.3 References

Chapter 8

Detonation velocity

Explosive velocity, also known as **detonation velocity** or **velocity of detonation** (VoD), is the velocity at which the shock wave front travels through a detonated explosive. The data listed for a specific substance is usually a rough prediction based upon gas behavior theory (see Chapman-Jouguet condition), as in practice it is difficult to measure. Explosive velocities are always faster than the local speed of sound in the material.

If the explosive is confined before detonation, such as in an artillery shell, the force produced is focused on a much smaller area, and the pressure is massively intensified. This results in explosive velocity that is higher than if the explosive had been detonated in open air. Unconfined velocities are often approximately 70 to 80 percent of confined velocities.*[1]

Explosive velocity is increased with smaller particle size (*i.e.* increased spatial density), increased charge diameter, and increased confinement (*i.e.* higher pressure).*[1]

Typical detonation velocities in gases range from 1800 m/s to 3000 m/s. Typical velocities in solid explosives often range beyond 4000 m/s to 10300 m/s.

VoD can be measured by using the Dautriche method. General - the time lag between the initiation of two ends of, a length of detonating fuse of known velocity of detonation, inserted radially into an explosive charge at a known distance (d) apart, causes the two detonation fronts travelling in opposite direction along the length of the detonating fuse to meet at a point (A L) away from the centre of the fuse. Knowing the distance (d), the velocity of the detonation (V_1) of the detonating fuse, the velocity of detonation (V) of the explosive is calculated and is expressed in km/s.

8.1 See also

- Table of explosive detonation velocities
- Brisance
- Detonation
- Explosion
- Deflagration
- Flame speed
- Gurney equations

8.2 References

[1] GlobalSecurity.org

Chapter 9

Sensitivity (explosives)

Sensitivity of explosives is the degree to which an explosive can be initiated by impact, heat, or friction.[1]

Sensitivity, along with stability and brisance are three of the most significant properties of explosives that affect their use and application. All explosive compounds have a certain amount of energy required to initiate. If an explosive is too sensitive, it may go off accidentally. A safer explosive is less sensitive and will not explode if accidentally dropped or mishandled. However, such explosives are more difficult to initiate intentionally.

9.1 Explosive train

Less sensitive explosives can be initiated by smaller quantities of more sensitive explosives, called primers or detonators, such as blasting caps. The use of increasingly less sensitive explosive materials to create an escalating chain reaction is known as an explosive train, initiation sequence, or firing train.

9.2 Classifications

High explosives are conventionally subdivided into two explosives classes, differentiated by sensitivity:

- **Primary explosives** are extremely sensitive to mechanical shock, friction, and heat, to which they will respond by burning rapidly or detonating.

- **Secondary explosives**, also called **base explosives**, are relatively insensitive to shock, friction, and heat.

9.3 References

[1] *NAVSEA OP 5, Volume 1*. U.S. Navy.

Chapter 10

Use forms of explosives

Explosive materials are produced in numerous physical forms for their use in mining, engineering, or military applications. The different physical forms and fabrication methods are grouped together in several **useful forms of explosives**.

Explosives are sometimes used in their pure forms, but most common applications transform or modify them.

These useful forms are commonly categorized as:[1]

- Pressings
- Castings
- Polymer bonded
- Putties (a.k.a. plastic explosives)
- Rubberized
- Extrudable
- Binary
- Blasting agents
- Slurries and gels
- Dynamites

10.1 Pressings

10.2 Castings

Castings, or castable explosives, are explosive materials or mixtures in which at least one component can be safely melted at a temperature which is safe to handle the other components, and which are normally produced by casting or pouring the molten mixture or material into a form or use container.

In modern usage, **Trinitrotoluene** or **TNT** is the basic meltable explosive used in essentially all castable explosives.

Other ingredients found in modern castable explosives include:[1]

- Active, energetic or explosive ingredients:
    - Aluminum powder
    - Ammonium nitrate
    - Ammonium picrate
    - Barium nitrate
    - EDNA
    - HMX
    - Lead nitrate
    - PETN
    - Sodium picrate
    - RDX
    - Tetryl
- Inert ingredients
    - Boric acid
    - Calcium chloride
    - Wax
    - Silica, often in the form of silica fume (Cab-o-sil for example)

Common castable explosives include:

- Amatol
- Baratol
- Boracitol
- Composition B

- Cyclotol
- Octol
- Pentolite
- Plumbatol
- Tritonal
- Torpex
- IMX-101

10.3 Polymer bonded

Polymer-bonded explosives, also known as Plastic-bonded explosives or simply **PBX**, are a relatively solid and inflexible explosive form containing a powdered explosive material and a polymer (plastic) binder. These are usually carefully mixed, often with a very thin coating of the polymer onto the powder grains of the explosive material, and then hot pressed to form dense solid blocks of PBX material.

There are numerous PBX explosives, mostly based on RDX, HMX, or TATB explosive materials. An extensive but by no means complete list of PBX materials is in the main Polymer-bonded explosive article. The major naming systems for PBX use:

- LX-# (Lawrence Livermore National Laboratory developed PBXes)
- PBX #### (Los Alamos National Laboratory developed PBXes)
- PBXN-# (United States Navy developed PBXes)

LX numbers range from 1 to 17. PBX system numbers start around 9000 and use numerous scattered numbers between there and 9700.

Some commonly known PBXes are:

- LX-17
- PBX 9502
- PBX 9404
- LX-11
- LX-14

PBXes are notable for their use in modern Nuclear weapons. Modern US and British nuclear warheads nearly all use insensitive PBX types using only TATB explosive, to increase safety in case of accidents.

10.4 Putties, aka Plastic explosives

Technically known as **putties**, but more commonly **Plastic explosives**, these mixtures are a thick, flexible, moldable solid material that can be shaped and will retain that shape after forming, much like clay. Putties normally contain mostly RDX explosive, but may include some PETN (Semtex, for example).

Some common putties are:

- C4
- (Now-obsolete) Composition C
- Semtex
- PE-4

10.5 Rubberized

Rubberized explosives are flat sheets of solid but flexible material, a mixture of a powdered explosive (commonly RDX or PETN) and a synthetic or natural rubber compound. Rubberized sheet explosives are commonly used for explosive welding and for various other industrial and military applications. Rubberized explosives can be cut to specific shape, bent around solid surfaces, glued or taped in place, or simply laid on relatively flat surfaces.

Some common rubberized explosives include:[1]

- **Detasheet** - a discontinued DuPont product
    - **Deta Flex** - a DuPont military version of Detasheet
    - **LX-02-1** - a DuPont Deta Flex variant used by the US Department of Energy nuclear weapons programs
- **Primasheet** - current Ensign-Bickford product line
    - **Primasheet 1000** - Primasheet 1000 using PETN
    - **Primasheet 2000** - Primasheet 2000 using RDX

10.6 Extrudable

Extrudable explosives are an extremely viscous liquid, similar in properties to silicone based caulking materials used in construction. It is used in similar ways - stored in a container, then extruded out a nozzle into thin cracks, holes, or along surfaces.

Some extrudable explosives can then be hardened using a heat curing process. Others will remain a viscous fluid permanently.

Common extrudable explosives include:

- Setting extrudables
    - LX-13
    - XTX-8003
    - XTX-8004
- Non-setting extrudables
    - Demex-400

10.7 Binary

Binary explosives are **cap-sensitive** (detonatable with a standard #8 blasting cap) two-part explosives mixtures, shipped separately and combined at the use site.

Many of these mixtures are based on Ammonium nitrate as an oxidizer plus a volatile fuel, but unlike ANFO (ammonium nitrate fuel oil explosive) these binaries can be detonated by blasting caps. ANFO requires high explosive boosters to detonate it.

Most binary explosives are a slurry after mixing, but some form a fluid with solid components dissolved into liquid ones.

Some common binary explosives include:

- Kinestik
- Kinepouch
- Kinepak
- Boulder-Busters
- Marine Pac
- ASTRO-PAK

The historical but now uncommon Astrolite explosive is also a binary explosive.

This category is somewhat unusual in that a single explosives researcher, Gerald Hurst, was responsible for inventing and developing most of the explosive mixtures now in use."[2]

10.8 Blasting agents

Blasting agents are explosive materials or mixtures which are not detonatable by standard #8 blasting caps.

The best known blasting agent is ANFO explosive, a mixture containing primarily ammonium nitrate with a small quantity (typically around 6%) of fuel oil, most commonly diesel fuel. Other fuels and additives are used as well.

While ANFO is often made on-site using fertilizer grade ammonium nitrate, blasting agents can also be purchased in prepackaged form, usually in metal or cardboard cylinders. Some brand names of packaged blasting agents include:

- Nitramon
- Nitramite
- Pellite
- Carbomite
- Vibronite
- Dynatex
- Hydratol
- Anoil

10.9 Slurries and gels

10.10 Dynamites

It is usually sold in the form of a stick roughly eight inches (20 cm) long and one inch (2.5 cm) in diameter but other sizes also exist.

Dynamite is considered a "high explosive", which means it detonates rather than deflagrates.

The chief uses of dynamite used to be in construction, mining and demolition.

However, newer explosives and techniques have replaced dynamite in many applications.

Dynamite is still used, mainly as bottom charge or in underwater blasting.

10.11 References

[1] Cooper, Paul W. (1996). "Chapter 4: Use forms of explosives". *Explosives Engineering*. Wiley-VCH. pp. 51–66. ISBN 0-471-18636-8.

10.11. REFERENCES

[2] Astrolite usenet posts archived at Yarchive, accessed 2008-12-28

Chapter 11

Combustibility

German test apparatus for determining combustibility at Technische Universität Braunschweig.

Combustibility is a measure of how easily a substance will set on fire, through fire or combustion. This is an important property to consider when a substance is used for construction or is being stored. It is also important in processes that produce combustible substances as a by-product. Special precautions are usually required for substances that are easily combustible. These measures may include installation of fire sprinklers or storage remote from possible sources of ignition.

Substances with low combustibility may be selected for construction where the fire risk needs to be reduced. Like apartment buildings, houses, offices and so on. If combustible resources are used there is greater chance of fire accidents and deaths. Fire resistant substances are preferred for building materials and furnishings.

11.1 Code Definitions

For an Authority Having Jurisdiction, combustibility is defined by the local code. In the National Building Code of Canada, it is defined as follows:

- *Combustible: A material which fails to meet acceptance criteria of CAN/ULC-S114, Standard Method of Test for Determination of Noncombustibility in Building Materials.*

This leads to the definition of **noncombustible**:

- *Non-combustible: means that a material meets the acceptance criteria of CAN4-S114, "Standard Method of Test for Determination of Non-Combustibility in Building Materials".*

BS 476-4:1970 defines a test for combusibility in which 3 specimens of a material are heated in a furnace. Non-combustibile materials are defined as those for which none of the 3 specimens either:

- cause the temperature reading from either of two thermocouples to rise by 50 degrees Celsius or more above the initial furnace temperature, or

- is observed to flame continuously for 10 seconds or more inside the furnace.

Otherwise, the material shall be deemed combustible.

11.2 Fire testing

Various countries have tests for determining noncombustibility of materials. Most involve the heating of a specified quantity of the test specimen for a set duration. Usually, the material cannot support combustion and must not undergo a certain loss of mass. As a rule of thumb, concrete, steel, ceramics, in other words inorganic substances pass these tests, which permits them to be mentioned in building codes as being suitable and sometimes even mandated for use in certain applications. In Canada, for instance, firewalls must be made of concrete.

11.3 Relevance in construction

In building construction, buildings are typically divided into combustible and noncombustible ones. The code provisions and safety measures that must be taken into account in the design and construction of a building depend to a significant extent upon whether the structure is made from noncombustible elements, such as concrete, brick and structural steel, or a combustible element such as wood. Combustible structures have more stringent limits on maximum building height and area.

11.4 Combustible dust

Main article: Dust explosion

A number of industrial processes produce combustible dust as a by-product. The most common being wood dust. Combustible dust has been defined as: *a solid material composed of distinct particles or pieces, regardless of size, shape, or chemical composition, which presents a fire or deflagration hazard when suspended in air or some other oxidizing medium over a range of concentrations.*[1] In addition to wood, combustible dusts include metals, especially magnesium, titanium and aluminum, as well as other carbon-based dusts.[1] There are at least a 140 known substances that produce combustible dust.[2]:38[3] While the particles in a combustible dusts may be of any size, normally they have a diameter of less than 420 μm.[1][note 1] As of 2012, the United States Occupational Safety and Health Administration has yet to adopt a comprehensive set of rules on combustible dust.[4]

When suspended in air (or any oxidizing environment), the fine particles of combustible dust present a potential for explosions. Accumulated dust, even when not suspended in air, remains a fire hazard. The National Fire Protection Association (U.S.) specifically addresses the prevention of fires and dust explosions in agricultural and food products facilities in NFPA Code section 61,[5] and other industries in NFPA Code sections 651–664.[note 2] Collectors designed to reduce airborne dust account for more than 40 percent of all dust explosions.[6] Other important processes are grinding and pulverizing, transporting powders, filing silos and containers (which produces powder), and the mixing and blending of powders.[7]

Investigation of 200 dust explosions and fires, between 1980 to 2005, indicated *approximately 100 fatalities and 600 injuries.*[2]:105–106 In January 2003, a polyethylene powder explosion and fire at the West Pharmaceutical Services plant in Kinston, North Carolina resulted in the deaths of six workers and injuries to 38 others.[2]:104 In February 2008 an explosion of sugar dust rocked the Imperial Sugar Company's plant at Port Wentworth, Georgia,[8] resulting in thirteen deaths.[9]

11.5 Related matters

The flammability article describes further the subcategorisations of combustible matters. Here, further fire tests are involved in quantifying the degree of flammability or combustibility.

11.5.1 The chemistry underlying the fire testing and resulting code classifications

The degree of flammability or combustibility depends largely upon the chemical composition of the subject material, as well as the ratio of mass versus surface area. As an example, paper is made from wood. A piece of paper catches on fire quite easily, whereas a heavy oak desk is much harder to ignite, although the wood fibre is the same in each substance, be it a piece of paper or a wooden board. Also, Antoine Lavoisier's law of conservation of mass, states that matter can be neither created nor destroyed, only altered. Therefore, the combustion or burning of a substance causes a chemical change, but does not decrease the mass of the original matter. The mass of the remains (ash, water, carbon dioxide, and other gases) is the same as it was prior to the burning of the matter. Whatever is not left behind in ashes and remains, literally went up in smoke, but it all went somewhere and the atoms of which the substance consisted before the fire still exist after the fire, even though they may be present in other phases and molecules.

11.6 References

[1] United States Occupational Safety and Health Administration (2009) "Hazard Communication Guidance for Combustible Dusts", OSHA 3371-08, Occupational Safety and Health Administration, U.S. Department of Labor

[2] United States Chemical Safety and Hazard Investigation Board (17 November 2006), *Investigation Report No. 2006-H-1, Combustible Dust Hazard Study* (PDF), Washington, D.C.: U.S. Chemical Safety and Hazard Investigation Board, OCLC 246682805

[3] National Materials Advisory Board, Panel on Classification of Combustible Dusts of the Committee on Evaluation of Industrial Hazards (1980) *Classification of combustible dusts in accordance with the national electrical code* Publication NMAB 353-3, National Research Council (U.S.), Washington, D.C., OCLC 8391202

[4] Smith, Sandy (7 February 2012) "Only OSHA Has Not Adopted Chemical Safety Board Recommendations Stemming from Imperial Sugar Explosion" *EHS Today*

[5] "NFPA 61 Standard for the Prevention of Fires and Dust Explosions in Agricultural and Food Processing Facilities"

[6] Zalosh, Robert *et al.* (April 2005) "Dust Explosion Scenarios and Case Histories in the CCPS Guidelines for Safe Handling of Powders and Bulk Solids" *39th AIChE Loss Prevention Symposium Session on Dust Explosions* Atlanta, Georgia

[7] O'Brien, Michael (2008) "Controlling Static Hazards is Key to Preventing Combustible Cloud Explosions" Newton Gale, Inc.

[8] *The chief executive, John C. Sheptor, said the probable cause of the explosion was sugar dust building up in storage areas, which could have been ignited by static electricity or a spark.* Dewan, Shaila (9 February 2008). "Lives and a Georgia Community's Anchor Are Lost". *The New York Times*. Retrieved 7 May 2012.

[9] Chapman, Dan (13 April 2008). "Sugar refinery near Savannah determined to rebuild". *The Atlanta Journal-Constitution*. Archived from the original on June 29, 2011. Retrieved 7 May 2012.

11.7 Notes

[1] I.e. they can pass through a U.S. No. 40 standard sieve.

[2] E.g. NFPA 651 (aluminium), NFPA 652 (magnesium), NFPA 655 (sulphur)

11.8 See also

- Flammability
- Fire
- Fire protection
- Fire test
- Underwriters Laboratories
- Technische Universität Braunschweig
- Explosive material

11.9 External links

- CAN4-S114 CAN/ULC-S114 Abstract
- iBMB/TU Braunschweig Governmental Lab for Testing Building Materials
- BAM Abstract and Picture of Noncombustibility Test in Progress
- ASTM E136 Standard Test Method for Behavior of Materials in a Vertical Tube Furnace at 750°C abstract
- "Combustible Dust: Agricultural Related Fires and Explosions Increasing, but Preventable" Division of Occupational Safety and Health, N.C. Department of Labor
- Combustible Dust: A Major Hot Work Hazard" Division of Occupational Safety and Health, N.C. Department of Labor

Chapter 12

Flammability

DIN4102 Flammability Class B1 Vertical Shaft Furnace at Technische Universität Braunschweig, Germany.

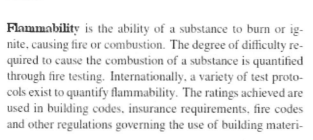

Sample Holder for DIN4102 Flammability Class B1 Vertical Shaft Furnace

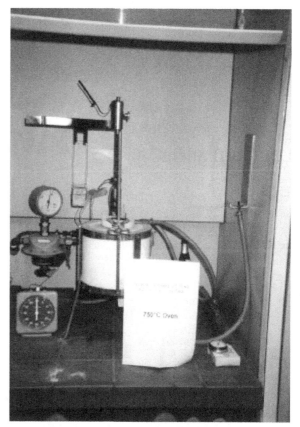

750 °C Furnace to test A1 and A2 Class Combustibility per DIN4102 Part 1 at TU Braunschweig

Flammability is the ability of a substance to burn or ignite, causing fire or combustion. The degree of difficulty required to cause the combustion of a substance is quantified through fire testing. Internationally, a variety of test protocols exist to quantify flammability. The ratings achieved are used in building codes, insurance requirements, fire codes and other regulations governing the use of building materials as well as the storage and handling of highly flammable substances inside and outside of structures and in surface and air transportation. For instance, changing an occupancy by altering the flammability of the contents requires the owner of a building to apply for a building permit to make sure that the overall fire protection design basis of the facility can take the change into account.

CHAPTER 12. FLAMMABILITY

The international pictogram for flammable chemicals.

12.1 Definitions

Historically, *flammable*, *inflammable* and *combustible* meant *capable of burning*.*[1] The word "inflammable" came through French from the Latin *inflammāre* = "to set fire to," where the Latin preposition "in-"*[2] means "in" as in "indoctrinate", rather than "not" as in "invisible" and "ineligible".

The word "inflammable" may be erroneously thought to mean "non-flammable".*[3] The erroneous usage of the word "inflammable" is a significant safety hazard. Therefore, since the 1950s, efforts to put forward the use of "flammable" in place of "inflammable" were accepted by linguists, and it is now the accepted standard in American English and British English.*[4]*[5] Antonyms of "flammable/inflammable" include: *non-flammable*, *non-inflammable*, *incombustible*, *non-combustible*, *ininflammable*, *not flammable*, and *fireproof*.

Flammable is used for materials which ignite more easily than other materials thus are more dangerous and more highly regulated. Less easily ignited or which burn less vigorously are *combustible*. For example, in the United States flammable liquids by definition have a flash point below 100 °F (38 °C) where combustible liquids have a flash point above 100 °F (38 °C). "Flammable solids are solids that are readily combustible, or may cause or contribute to fire through friction. Readily combustible solids are powdered, granular, or pasty substances which are dangerous if they can be easily ignited by brief contact with an ignition source, such as a burning match, and if the flame spreads rapidly."
[6] The technical definitions vary between countries so the United Nations created the Globally Harmonized System of Classification and Labelling of Chemicals which defines the flash point temperature of flammable liquids to be between 0 and 140 °F (60 °C) and combustible liquids between 140 °F (60 °C) and 200 °F (93 °C).[6]

12.2 Testing

A fire test can be conducted to determine the degree of flammability. Test standards used to make this determination but are not limited to the following:

- Underwriters Laboratories UL 94 Flammability Testing

- International Electrotechnical Commission IEC 60707, 60695-11-10 and 60695-11-20

- International Organization for Standardization ISO 9772 and 9773.

- National Fire Protection Association NFPA 287 Standard Test Methods for Measurement of Flammability of Materials in Cleanrooms Using a Fire Propagation Apparatus (FPA)

- NFPA 701: Standard Methods of Fire Tests for Flame Propagation of Textiles and Films

- NFPA 850: Recommended Practice for Fire Protection for Electric Generating Plants and High Voltage Direct Current Converter Stations

12.3 Categorization of building materials

- DIN4102 A1 noncombustible rockwool

- DIN4102 A2 gypsum fireproofing plaster leavened with polystyrene beads

- DIN 4102 B1 (difficult to ignite/often self-extinguishing) Silicone caulking used as a component in firestopping piping penetration

- DIN 4102 B2: Timber, normal combustibility

- DIN 4102 B3: Polyurethane foam (easy to ignite = lots of hydrocarbon bonds usually)

Materials can be tested for the degree of flammability and combustibility in accordance with the German DIN 4102. DIN 4102, as well as its British cousin BS 476 include for testing of passive fire protection systems, as well as some of its constituent materials.

The following are the categories in order of degree of combustibility as well as flammability:

A more recent industrial standard is the European EN 13501-1 - Fire classification of construction products and building elements - which roughly replaces A2 with A2/B, B1 with C, B2 with D/E and B3 with F.

B3 or F rated materials may not be used in building unless combined with another material which reduces the flammability of those materials.

12.4 Important characteristics

12.4.1 Flash point

A material's flash point is a metric of how easy it is to ignite the vapor of the material as it evaporates into the atmosphere. A lower flash point indicates higher flammability. Materials with flash points below 100 °F (38 °C) are regulated in the United States by OSHA as potential workplace hazards.

12.4.2 Vapor pressure

- The vapor pressure of a liquid, which varies with its temperature, is a measure of how much the vapor of the liquid tends to concentrate in the surrounding atmosphere as the liquid evaporates. Vapor pressure is a major determinant of the flash point, with higher vapor pressures leading to lower flash points and higher flammability.

12.5 Furniture flammability

Flammability of furniture is of concern as cigarettes and candle accidents can trigger domestic fires. In 1975, California began implementing Technical Bulletin 117 (TB 117), which required that materials such as polyurethane foam used to fill furniture be able to withstand a small open flame, equivalent to a candle, for at least 12 seconds.*[7] In polyurethane foam, furniture manufacturers typically meet TB 117 with additive halogenated organic flame retardants. Although no other U.S. states had similar standards, because California has such a large market manufacturers meet TB 117 in products that they distribute across the United States. The proliferation of flame retardants, and especially halogenated organic flame retardants, in furniture across the United States is strongly linked to TB 117. When it became apparent that the risk-benefit ratio of this approach was unfavorable and industry had used falsified documentation (i.e. see David Heimbach) for the use of flame retardants, California modified TB 117 to require that fabric covering upholstered furniture meet a smolder test replacing the open flame test.*[8] Gov. Jerry Brown signed the modified TB117-2013 which became effective in 2014.*[9]

12.6 Examples of flammable substances

Flammable substances include, but are not limited to:

- Gasoline - Petrol / a complicated mixture of hydrocarbons that includes isomers of octane, C_8H_{18}
- Ethanol / CH_3CH_2OH
- Rubber
- Isopropyl alcohol / $CH_3CH(OH)CH_3$
- Methanol / CH_3OH
- Wood
- Acetone / CH_3COCH_3
- Paper
- Nitromethane / CH_3NO_2

12.7 Examples of nonflammable liquids

- Water
- Carbon tetrachloride

12.8 Classification of flammability

The US Government uses the Hazardous Materials Identification System (HMIS) standard for flammability ratings, as do many US regulatory agencies, and also the US National Fire Protection Association (NFPA).

The ratings are as follows:

12.9 Codes

12.9.1 Flammability

For existing buildings, fire codes focus on maintaining the occupancies as originally intended. In other words, if a portion of a building were designed as an apartment, one could not suddenly load it with flammable liquids and turn it into a gas storage facility, because the fire load and smoke development in that one apartment would be so immense as to overtax the active fire protection as well as the passive fire protection means for the building. The handling and use of flammable substances inside a building is subject to the local fire code, which is ordinarily enforced by the local fire prevention officer.

12.10 See also

- Fire test
- Fire protection
- Active fire protection
- Passive fire protection
- Flammable liquids
- Flammable limit

12.11 References

[1] inflammable, a. (n.) 1. combustible a. and n. 1. *Oxford English Dictionary*. 2nd ed. 2009. CD-rom.

[2] "flammable". *The American Heritage® Dictionary of the English Language*. 5th ed. Houghton Mifflin Harcourt Publishing Company. 2014. accessed 3/11/2015

[3] Sherk, Bill. "fireproof", *500 Years of New Words*. Toronto: Dundurn, 2004. 96. Print.

[4] Garner, Bryan A., *Garner's Modern American Usage*. 3rd ed. New York: Oxford UP, 2009. 357. Print.

[5] "INFLAMMABLE". *Common Errors in English Usage*. Washington State University. Retrieved 30 June 2012.

[6] *The Guide to The Globally Harmonized System of Classification and Labelling of Chemicals (GHS)*. Occupational Safety & Health Administration, U.S. Department of Labor.

[7] California Department of Consumer Affairs, Bureau of Home Furnishings (2000). Technical Bulletin 117: Requirements, test procedure and apparatus for testing the flame retardance of resilient filling (PDF) (Report). pp. 1–8.

[8] "Notice of Proposed New Flammability Standards for Upholstered Furniture/Articles Exempt from Flammability Standards". Department of Consumer Affairs, Bureau of Electronic and Appliance Repair, Home Furnishings and Thermal Insulation.

[9] "Calif. law change sparks debate over use of flame retardants in furniture". PBS Newshour. January 1, 2014. Retrieved November 1, 2014.

12.12 External links

- Videos showing flammability of cables based on jacket rating
- Fire Performance of Ageing Cable Compounds, NFPA Treatise by Dr. Perry Marteny
- Fire Testing Laboratory

Chapter 13

Deflagration

A log in a fireplace.

Deflagration (Lat: *de* + *flagrare*, "to burn down") is a term describing subsonic combustion propagating through heat transfer; hot burning material heats the next layer of cold material and ignites it. Most "fire" found in daily life, from flames to explosions, is deflagration. Deflagration is different from detonation, which propagates supersonically through shock waves. This means that when a substance deflagrates, it burns extremely quickly instead of detonating. Black powder is an example of a substance that deflagrates; when it is ignited, black powder burns extremely quickly (so fast in fact that the burn is sometimes mistaken for a detonation).

13.1 Applications

In engineering applications, deflagrations are easier to control than detonations. Consequently, they are better suited when the goal is to move an object (a bullet in a gun, or a piston in an internal combustion engine) with the force of the expanding gas. Typical examples of deflagrations are the combustion of a gas-air mixture in a gas stove or a fuel-air mixture in an internal combustion engine, and the rapid burning of gunpowder in a firearm or of pyrotechnic mixtures in fireworks. Deflagration systems and products can also be used in mining, demolition and stone quarrying via gas pressure blasting as a beneficial alternative to high explosives.

13.2 Oil/wax fire and water

Adding water to a burning hydrocarbon such as oil or wax produces a deflagration. The water boils rapidly and ejects the burning material as a fine spray of droplets. A deflagration then occurs as the fine mist of oil ignites and burns extremely rapidly. These are particularly common in chip pan fires, which are responsible for one in five household fires in Britain.*[1]

13.3 Flame physics

The underlying flame physics can be understood with the help of an idealized model consisting of a uniform one-dimensional tube of unburnt and burned gaseous fuel, separated by a thin transitional region of width δ in which the burning occurs. The burning region is commonly referred to as the flame or flame front. In equilibrium, thermal diffusion across the flame front is balanced by the heat supplied by burning.

There are two characteristic timescales which are important here. The first is the thermal diffusion timescale τ_d, which is approximately equal to

$$\tau_d \simeq \delta^2/\kappa$$

where κ is the thermal diffusivity. The second is the burning timescale τ_b that strongly decreases with temperature, typically as

$$\tau_b \propto \exp[\Delta U/(k_B T_f)]$$

where ΔU is the activation barrier for the burning reaction and T_f is the temperature developed as the result of burning; the value of this so-called "flame temperature" can be determined from the laws of thermodynamics.

For a stationary moving deflagration front, these two timescales must be equal: the heat generated by burning is equal to the heat carried away by heat transfer. This makes it possible to calculate the characteristic width δ of the flame front:

$$\tau_b = \tau_d$$

thus

$$\delta \simeq \sqrt{\kappa \tau_b}$$

Now, the thermal flame front propagates at a characteristic speed S_l, which is simply equal to the flame width divided by the burn time:

$$S_l \simeq \delta / \tau_b \simeq \sqrt{\kappa / \tau_b}$$

This simplified model neglects the change of temperature and thus the burning rate across the deflagration front. This model also neglects the possible influence of turbulence. As a result, this derivation gives only the laminar flame speed -- hence the designation S_l.

13.4 Damaging events

Damage to buildings, equipment and people can result from a large-scale, short-duration deflagration. The potential damage is primarily a function of the total amount of fuel burned in the event (total energy available), the maximum flame velocity that is achieved, and the manner in which the expansion of the combustion gases is contained.

In free-air deflagrations, there is a continuous variation in deflagration effects relative to the maximum flame velocity. When flame velocities are low, the effect of a deflagration is to release heat. Some authors use the term flash fire to describe these low-speed deflagrations. At flame velocities near the speed of sound, the energy released is in the form of pressure and the results resemble a detonation. Between these extremes, both heat and pressure are released.

When a low-speed deflagration occurs within a closed vessel or structure, pressure effects can produce damage due to expansion of gases as a secondary effect. The heat released by the deflagration causes the combustion gases and excess air to expand thermally. The net result is that the volume of the vessel or structure must expand to accommodate the hot combustion gases, or the vessel must be strong enough to withstand the additional internal pressure, or it fails, allowing the gases to escape. The risks of deflagration inside waste storage drums is a growing concern in storage facilities.

13.5 See also

- Pressure piling

13.6 References

[1] UK Fire Service advice on chip pan fires

Chapter 14

Detonation

For other uses, see Detonation (disambiguation).

Detonation (from Latin *detonare*, meaning "to thunder down") is a type of combustion involving a supersonic exothermic front accelerating through a medium that eventually drives a shock front propagating directly in front of it. Detonations occur in both conventional solid and liquid explosives,[1] as well as in reactive gases. The velocity of detonation in solid and liquid explosives is much higher than that in gaseous ones, which allows the wave system to be observed with greater detail (higher resolution).

Detonation of a 500-ton TNT explosive charge during Operation Sailor Hat. The initial shock wave is visible on the water surface, and a shock condensation cloud is visible overhead.

A very wide variety of fuels may occur as gases, droplet fogs, or dust suspensions. Oxidants include halogens, ozone, hydrogen peroxide and oxides of nitrogen. Gaseous detonations are often associated with a mixture of fuel and oxidant in a composition somewhat below conventional flammability ratios. They happen most often in confined systems, but they sometimes occur in large vapor clouds. Other materials, such as acetylene, ozone, and hydrogen peroxide are detonable in the absence of oxygen; a more complete list is given by both Stull[2] and Bretherick.[3]

Processes involved in the transition between deflagration and detonation are covered thoroughly for gases by Nettleton.[4]

14.1 Theories

The simplest theory to predict the behaviour of detonations in gases is known as Chapman-Jouguet (CJ) theory, developed around the turn of the 20th century. This theory, described by a relatively simple set of algebraic equations, models the detonation as a propagating shock wave accompanied by exothermic heat release. Such a theory confines the chemistry and diffusive transport processes to an infinitely thin zone.

A more complex theory was advanced during World War II independently by Zel'dovich, von Neumann, and W. Doering.[5][6][7] This theory, now known as ZND theory, admits finite-rate chemical reactions and thus describes a detonation as an infinitely thin shock wave followed by a zone of exothermic chemical reaction. With a reference frame of a stationary shock, the following flow is subsonic, so that an acoustic reaction zone follows immediately behind the lead front, the Chapman-Jouguet condition.[8][9] There is also some evidence that the reaction zone is semi-metallic in some explosives.[10]

Both theories describe one-dimensional and steady wave fronts. However, in the 1960s, experiments revealed that gas-phase detonations were most often characterized by unsteady, three-dimensional structures, which can only in an averaged sense be predicted by one-dimensional steady theories. Indeed, such waves are quenched as their structure is destroyed.[11][12] The Wood-Kirkwood detonation theory can correct for some of these limitations.[13]

Experimental studies have revealed some of the conditions needed for the propagation of such fronts. In confinement, the range of composition of mixes of fuel and oxidant and self-decomposing substances with inerts are slightly below the flammability limits and for spherically expanding fronts well below them."[14] The influence of increasing the concentration of diluent on expanding individual detonation cells has been elegantly demonstrated."[15] Similarly their size grows as the initial pressure falls."[16] Since cell widths must be matched with minimum dimension of containment, any wave overdriven by the initiator will be quenched.

Mathematical modeling has steadily advanced to predicting the complex flow fields behind shocks inducing reactions."[17]"[18] To date, none has adequately described how structure is formed and sustained behind unconfined waves.

14.2 Applications

When used in explosive devices, the main cause of damage from a detonation is the supersonic blast front (a powerful shock wave) in the surrounding area. This is a significant distinction from deflagrations where the exothermic wave is subsonic and maximum pressures are at most one quarter as great. Therefore, detonation is most often used for explosives and the acceleration of projectiles. However, detonation waves may also be used for less destructive purposes, including deposition of coatings to a surface"[19] or cleaning of equipment (e.g. slag removal"[20]) and even explosively welding together metals that would otherwise fail to fuse. Pulse detonation engines use the detonation wave for aerospace propulsion."[21] The first flight of an aircraft powered by a pulse detonation engine took place at the Mojave Air & Space Port on January 31, 2008."[22]

14.3 In engines and firearms

Unintentional detonation when deflagration is desired is a problem in some devices. In internal combustion engines it is called engine knocking or pinging or pinking, and it causes a loss of power and excessive heating of certain components. In firearms, it may cause catastrophic and potentially lethal failure.

14.4 Etymology

Classical Latin *detonare* means "to stop thundering", as in weather. The modern meaning developed later.

14.5 See also

- Carbon detonation
- Detonator
- Detonation of an explosive charge
- Detonation diamond
- Detonation flame arrester
- Sympathetic detonation
- Nuclear testing
- Predetonation
- Chapman-Jouguet condition
- Engine knocking
- Deflagration
- Relative effectiveness factor

14.6 References

[1] Fickett; Davis (1979). *Detonation*. Univ. California Press. ISBN 978-0-486-41456-0.

[2] Stull (1977). *Fundamentals of fire and explosion*. Monograph Series. **10**. A.I.Chem.E. p. 73.

[3] Bretherick (1979). *Handbook of Reactive Chemical Hazards*. London: Butterworths. ISBN 978-0-12-372563-9.

[4] Nettleton (1987). *Gaseous Detonations: Their Nature, Effects and Control*. London: Butterworths. ISBN 978-0-412-27040-6.

[5] Zel'dovich; Kompaneets (1960). *Theory of Detonation*. New York: Academic Press. ASIN B000WB4XGE.

[6] von Neumann. Progress report on the theory of detonation waves, OSRD Report No. 549 (Report).

[7] Doring, W. (1943). "Über den Detonationsvorgang in Gasen". *Annalen der Physik*. **43** (6–7): 421. Bibcode:1943AnP...435..421D. doi:10.1002/andp.19434350605.

[8] Chapman, David Leonard (January 1899). "On the rate of explosion in gases". *Philosophical Magazine*. Series 5. London: Taylor & Francis. **47** (284): 90–104. doi:10.1080/14786449908621243. ISSN 1941-5982. LCCN sn86025845.

[9] Jouguet, Jacques Charles Emile (1905). "Sur la propagation des réactions chimiques dans les gaz" [On the propagation of chemical reactions in gases] (PDF). *Journal des Mathématiques Pures et Appliquées*. 6. **1**: 347–425. Continued in Continued in Jouguet, Jacques Charles Emile (1906). "Sur la propagation des réactions chimiques dans les gaz" [On the propagation of chemical reactions in gases] (PDF). *Journal des Mathématiques Pures et Appliquées*. 6. **2**: 5–85.

[10] Reed, Evan J.; Riad Manaa, M.; Fried, Laurence E.; Glaesemann, Kurt R.; Joannopoulos, J. D. (2007). "A transient semimetallic layer in detonating nitromethane". *Nature Physics*. **4** (1): 72–76. Bibcode:2008NatPh...4...72R. doi:10.1038/nphys806.

[11] Edwards, D.H.; Thomas, G.O. & Nettleton, M.A. (1979). "The Diffraction of a Planar Detonation Wave at an Abrupt Area Change". *Journal of Fluid Mechanica*. **95** (1): 79–96. Bibcode:1979JFM....95...79E. doi:10.1017/S002211207900135X.

[12] D. H. Edwards; G. O. Thomas; M. A. Nettleton (1981). A. K. Oppenheim; N. Manson; R.I. Soloukhin; J.R. Bowen, eds. "Diffraction of a Planar Detonation in Various Fuel-Oxygen Mixtures at an Area Change". *Progress in Astronautics & Aeronautics*. **75**: 341. doi:10.2514/5.9781600865497.0341.0357. ISBN 978-0-915928-46-0.

[13] Glaesemann, Kurt R.; Fried, Laurence E. (2007). "Improved wood–kirkwood detonation chemical kinetics". *Theoretical Chemistry Accounts*. **120** (1–3): 37–43. doi:10.1007/s00214-007-0303-9.

[14] Nettleton, M. A. (1980). "Detonation and flammability limits of gases in confined and unconfined situations". *Fire prevention science and technology*. Fire Prevention Society (UK) (23): 29. ISSN 0305-7844.

[15] Munday, G.; Ubbelohde, A.R. & Wood, I.F. (1968). "Fluctuating Detonation in Gases". *Proceedings of the Royal Society A*. **306** (1485): 171–178. Bibcode:1968RSPSA.306..171M. doi:10.1098/rspa.1968.0143.

[16] Barthel, H. O. (1974). "Predicted Spacings in Hydrogen-Oxygen-Argon Detonations". *Physics of Fluids*. **17** (8): 1547–1553. Bibcode:1974PhFl...17.1547B. doi:10.1063/1.1694932.

[17] Oran; Boris (1987). *Numerical Simulation of Reactive Flows*. Elsevier Publishers.

[18] Sharpe, G.J.; Quirk, J.J. (2008). "Nonlinear cellular dynamics of the idealized detonation model: Regular cells". *Combustion Theory and Modelling*. **12** (1): 1–21. Bibcode:2007CTM....12....1S. doi:10.1080/13647830701335749.

[19] Nikolaev, Yu.A.; Vasil'ev, A.A.; Ul'yanitskii & B.Yu. (2003). "Gas Detonation and its Application in Engineering and Technologies (Review)". *Combustion, Explosion, and Shock Waves*. **39** (4): 382–410. doi:10.1023/A:1024726619703.

[20] Huque, Z.; Ali, M.R. & Kommalapati, R. (2009). "Application of pulse detonation technology for boiler slag removal". *Fuel Processing Technology*. **90** (4): 558–569. doi:10.1016/j.fuproc.2009.01.004.

[21] Kailasanath, K. (2000). "Review of Propulsion Applications of Detonation Waves". *AIAA Journal*. **39** (9): 1698–1708. Bibcode:2000AIAAJ..38.1698K. doi:10.2514/2.1156.

[22] Norris, G. (2008). "Pulse Power: Pulse Detonation Engine-powered Flight Demonstration Marks Milestone in Mojave". *Aviation Week & Space Technology*. **168** (7): 60.

14.7 External links

- Youtube video demonstrating physics of a blast wave
- GALCIT Explosion Dynamics Laboratory Detonation Database

Chapter 15

Brisance

Brisance /brɪˈzɑːns/ is the shattering capability of a high explosive, determined mainly by its detonation pressure. The term can be traced from the French verb "briser" (to break or shatter) ultimately derived from the Celtic word "brissim" (to break).*[1] Brisance is of practical importance for determining the effectiveness of an explosion in fragmenting shells, bomb casings, grenades, structures, and the like. The sand crush test and Trauzl lead block test are commonly used to determine the relative brisance in comparison to TNT (which is considered a standard reference for many purposes).

Fragmentation occurs by the action of the transmitted shock wave, the strength of which depends on the detonation pressure of the explosive. Generally, the higher this pressure, the finer the fragments generated. High detonation pressure correlates with high detonation velocity, the speed at which the detonation wave propagates through the explosive, but not necessarily with the explosive's total energy (or work capacity), some of which may be released after passage of the detonation wave. A more brisant explosive, therefore, projects smaller fragments but not necessarily at a higher velocity than a less brisant one.

One of the most brisant of the conventional explosives is cyclotrimethylene trinitramine (also known as RDX or Hexogen).*[2] RDX is the explosive agent in the plastic explosive commonly known as C-4, constituting 91% RDX by mass.*[3]

15.1 See also

- Relative effectiveness factor
- Table of explosive detonation velocities

15.2 References

[1] "Brisance". *Dictionary.com Unabridged*. Random House, Inc. Retrieved 31 March 2014.

[2] *TM 9-1300-214*. US Army. Archived August 16, 2010, at the Wayback Machine.

[3] "Explosives – Compounds". *Global Security*.

- A. Bailey & S.G. Murray, *Explosives, Propellants & Pyrotechnics*, Brassey's (UK) Ltd., London, 1989.

Chapter 16

Pressure

This article is about pressure in the physical sciences. For other uses, see Pressure (disambiguation).

Pressure (symbol: p or P) is the force applied perpendic-

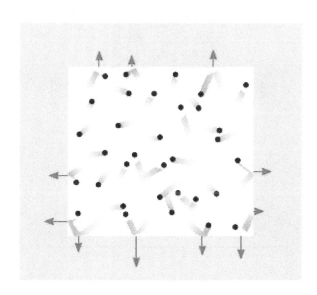

Pressure as exerted by particle collisions inside a closed container.

ular to the surface of an object per unit area over which that force is distributed. Gauge pressure (also spelled *gage* pressure)*[lower-alpha 1] is the pressure relative to the ambient pressure.

Various units are used to express pressure. Some of these derive from a unit of force divided by a unit of area; the SI unit of pressure, the pascal (Pa), for example, is one newton per square metre; similarly, the pound-force per square inch (psi) is the traditional unit of pressure in the imperial and US customary systems. Pressure may also be expressed in terms of standard atmospheric pressure; the atmosphere (atm) is equal to this pressure and the torr is defined as $1/760$ of this. Manometric units such as the centimetre of water, millimetre of mercury, and inch of mercury are used to express pressures in terms of the height of column of a particular fluid in a manometer.

16.1 Definition

Pressure is the amount of force acting per unit area. The symbol for it is p or P.*[1] The IUPAC recommendation for pressure is a lower-case p.*[2] However, upper-case P is widely used. The usage of P vs p depends on the field in which one is working, on the nearby presence of other symbols for quantities such as power and momentum, and on writing style.

16.1.1 Formula

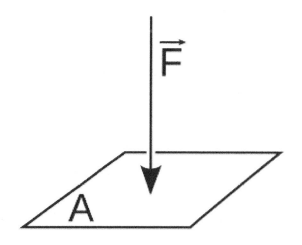

Mathematically:

$$p = \frac{F}{A}$$

where:

p is the pressure,

F is the normal force,

A is the area of the surface on contact.

Pressure is a scalar quantity. It relates the vector surface element (a vector normal to the surface) with the normal force acting on it. The pressure is the scalar proportionality constant that relates the two normal vectors:

$$d\mathbf{F}_n = -p\,d\mathbf{A} = -p\,\mathbf{n}\,dA$$

The minus sign comes from the fact that the force is considered towards the surface element, while the normal vector points outward. The equation has meaning in that, for any surface S in contact with the fluid, the total force exerted by the fluid on that surface is the surface integral over S of the right-hand side of the above equation.

It is incorrect (although rather usual) to say "the pressure is directed in such or such direction". The pressure, as a scalar, has no direction. The force given by the previous relationship to the quantity has a direction, but the pressure does not. If we change the orientation of the surface element, the direction of the normal force changes accordingly, but the pressure remains the same.

Pressure is transmitted to solid boundaries or across arbitrary sections of fluid *normal to* these boundaries or sections at every point. It is a fundamental parameter in thermodynamics, and it is conjugate to volume.

16.1.2 Units

The SI unit for pressure is the pascal (Pa), equal to one newton per square metre (N/m^2 or kg·m^{-1}·s^{-2}). This name for the unit was added in 1971;[3] before that, pressure in SI was expressed simply in newtons per square metre.

Other units of pressure, such as pounds per square inch and bar, are also in common use. The CGS unit of pressure is the barye (Ba), equal to 1 dyn·cm^{-2} or 0.1 Pa. Pressure is sometimes expressed in grams-force or kilograms-force per square centimetre (g/cm^2 or kg/cm^2) and the like without properly identifying the force units. But using the names kilogram, gram, kilogram-force, or gram-force (or their symbols) as units of force is expressly forbidden in SI. The technical atmosphere (symbol: at) is 1 kgf/cm^2 (98.0665 kPa or 14.223 psi).

Since a system under pressure has potential to perform work on its surroundings, pressure is a measure of potential energy stored per unit volume. It is therefore related to energy density and may be expressed in units such as joules per cubic metre (J/m^3, which is equal to Pa). Mathematically:

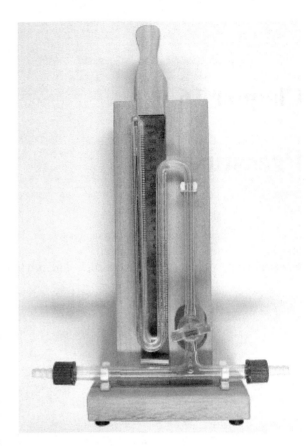

Mercury column

$$p = \frac{F \times distance}{A \times distance} = \frac{Work}{Volume} = \frac{Energy(J)}{Volume(m^3)}$$

Some meteorologists prefer the hectopascal (hPa) for atmospheric air pressure, which is equivalent to the older unit millibar (mbar). Similar pressures are given in kilopascals (kPa) in most other fields, where the hecto- prefix is rarely used. The inch of mercury is still used in the United States. Oceanographers usually measure underwater pressure in decibars (dbar) because pressure in the ocean increases by approximately one decibar per metre depth.

The standard atmosphere (atm) is an established constant. It is approximately equal to typical air pressure at earth mean sea level and is defined as 101325 Pa.

Because pressure is commonly measured by its ability to displace a column of liquid in a manometer, pressures are often expressed as a depth of a particular fluid (e.g., centimetres of water, millimetres of mercury or inches of mercury). The most common choices are mercury (Hg) and water; water is nontoxic and readily available, while mercury's high density allows a shorter column (and so a smaller manometer) to be used to measure a given pressure. The pressure exerted by a column of liquid of height h and den-

16.1. DEFINITION

sity ϱ is given by the hydrostatic pressure equation $p = \varrho gh$, where g is the gravitational acceleration. Fluid density and local gravity can vary from one reading to another depending on local factors, so the height of a fluid column does not define pressure precisely. When millimetres of mercury or inches of mercury are quoted today, these units are not based on a physical column of mercury; rather, they have been given precise definitions that can be expressed in terms of SI units. One millimetre of mercury is approximately equal to one torr. The water-based units still depend on the density of water, a measured, rather than defined, quantity. These *manometric units* are still encountered in many fields. Blood pressure is measured in millimetres of mercury in most of the world, and lung pressures in centimetres of water are still common.

Underwater divers use the metre sea water (msw or MSW) and foot sea water (fsw or FSW) units of pressure, and these are the standard units for pressure gauges used to measure pressure exposure in diving chambers and personal decompression computers. A msw is defined as 0.1 bar, and is not the same as a linear metre of depth, and 33.066 fsw = 1 atm.*[4] Note that the pressure conversion from msw to fsw is different from the length conversion: 10 msw = 32.6336 fsw, while 10 m = 32.8083 ft

Gauge pressure is often given in units with 'g' appended, e.g. 'kPag', 'barg' or 'psig', and units for measurements of absolute pressure are sometimes given a suffix of 'a', to avoid confusion, for example 'kPaa', 'psia'. However, the US National Institute of Standards and Technology recommends that, to avoid confusion, any modifiers be instead applied to the quantity being measured rather than the unit of measure*[5] For example, "p_g = 100 psi" rather than "p = 100 psig".

Differential pressure is expressed in units with 'd' appended; this type of measurement is useful when considering sealing performance or whether a valve will open or close.

Presently or formerly popular pressure units include the following:

- atmosphere (atm)
- manometric units:
  - centimetre, inch, millimetre (torr) and micrometre (mTorr, micron) of mercury
  - Height of equivalent column of water, including millimetre (mm H 2O), centimetre (cm H 2O), metre, inch, and foot of water
- imperial and customary units:
  - kip, short ton-force, long ton-force, pound-force, ounce-force, and poundal per square inch
  - short ton-force and long ton-force per square inch
  - fsw (feet sea water) used in underwater diving, particularly in connection with diving pressure exposure and decompression
- non-SI metric units:
  - bar, decibar, millibar
    - msw (metres sea water), used in underwater diving, particularly in connection with diving pressure exposure and decompression
  - kilogram-force, or kilopond, per square centimetre (technical atmosphere)
  - gram-force and tonne-force (metric ton-force) per square centimetre
  - barye (dyne per square centimetre)
  - kilogram-force and tonne-force per square metre
  - sthene per square metre (pieze)

16.1.3 Examples

As an example of varying pressures, a finger can be pressed against a wall without making any lasting impression; however, the same finger pushing a thumbtack can easily damage the wall. Although the force applied to the surface is the same, the thumbtack applies more pressure because the point concentrates that force into a smaller area. Pressure is transmitted to solid boundaries or across arbitrary sections of fluid *normal to* these boundaries or sections at every point. Unlike stress, pressure is defined as a scalar quantity. The negative gradient of pressure is called the force density.

Another example is of a common knife. If we try to cut a fruit with the flat side it obviously will not cut. But if we take the thin side, it will cut smoothly. The reason is that the flat side has a greater surface area (less pressure) and so it does not cut the fruit. When we take the thin side, the surface area is reduced and so it cuts the fruit easily and quickly. This is one example of a practical application of pressure.

For gases, pressure is sometimes measured not as an *absolute pressure*, but relative to atmospheric pressure; such measurements are called *gauge pressure*. An example of this is the air pressure in an automobile tire, which might be said to be "220 kPa (32 psi)", but is actually 220 kPa (32 psi) above atmospheric pressure. Since atmospheric pressure at sea level is about 100 kPa (14.7 psi), the absolute pressure in the tire is therefore about 320 kPa (46.7 psi). In technical work, this is written "a gauge pressure of 220 kPa (32 psi)". Where space is limited, such as on pressure gauges, name plates, graph labels, and table headings, the

16.1.4 Scalar nature

In a static gas, the gas as a whole does not appear to move. The individual molecules of the gas, however, are in constant random motion. Because we are dealing with an extremely large number of molecules and because the motion of the individual molecules is random in every direction, we do not detect any motion. If we enclose the gas within a container, we detect a pressure in the gas from the molecules colliding with the walls of our container. We can put the walls of our container anywhere inside the gas, and the force per unit area (the pressure) is the same. We can shrink the size of our "container" down to a very small point (becoming less true as we approach the atomic scale), and the pressure will still have a single value at that point. Therefore, pressure is a scalar quantity, not a vector quantity. It has magnitude but no direction sense associated with it. Pressure acts in all directions at a point inside a gas. At the surface of a gas, the pressure force acts perpendicular (at right angle) to the surface.

A closely related quantity is the stress tensor σ, which relates the vector force $\vec{F}$ to the vector area $\vec{A}$ via the linear relation $\vec{F} = \sigma \vec{A}$.

This tensor may be expressed as the sum of the viscous stress tensor minus the hydrostatic pressure. The negative of the stress tensor is sometimes called the pressure tensor, but in the following, the term "pressure" will refer only to the scalar pressure.

According to the theory of general relativity, pressure increases the strength of a gravitational field (see stress–energy tensor) and so adds to the mass-energy cause of gravity. This effect is unnoticeable at everyday pressures but is significant in neutron stars, although it has not been experimentally tested.[7]

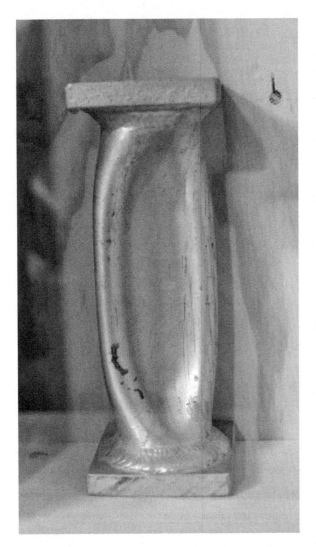

The effects of an external pressure of 700 bar on an aluminum cylinder with 5 mm wall thickness

use of a modifier in parentheses, such as "kPa (gauge)" or "kPa (absolute)", is permitted. In non-SI technical work, a gauge pressure of 32 psi is sometimes written as "32 psig" and an absolute pressure as "32 psia", though the other methods explained above that avoid attaching characters to the unit of pressure are preferred.[6]

Gauge pressure is the relevant measure of pressure wherever one is interested in the stress on storage vessels and the plumbing components of fluidics systems. However, whenever equation-of-state properties, such as densities or changes in densities, must be calculated, pressures must be expressed in terms of their absolute values. For instance, if the atmospheric pressure is 100 kPa, a gas (such as helium) at 200 kPa (gauge) (300 kPa [absolute]) is 50% denser than the same gas at 100 kPa (gauge) (200 kPa [absolute]). Focusing on gauge values, one might erroneously conclude the first sample had twice the density of the second one.

16.2 Types

16.2.1 Fluid pressure

Fluid pressure is the pressure at some point within a fluid, such as water or air (for more information specifically about liquid pressure, see section below).

Fluid pressure occurs in one of two situations:

1. an open condition, called "open channel flow", e.g. the ocean, a swimming pool, or the atmosphere.

2. a closed condition, called "closed conduit", e.g. a water line or gas line.

Pressure in open conditions usually can be approximated as

the pressure in "static" or non-moving conditions (even in the ocean where there are waves and currents), because the motions create only negligible changes in the pressure. Such conditions conform with principles of fluid statics. The pressure at any given point of a non-moving (static) fluid is called the **hydrostatic pressure**.

Closed bodies of fluid are either "static", when the fluid is not moving, or "dynamic", when the fluid can move as in either a pipe or by compressing an air gap in a closed container. The pressure in closed conditions conforms with the principles of fluid dynamics.

The concepts of fluid pressure are predominantly attributed to the discoveries of Blaise Pascal and Daniel Bernoulli. Bernoulli's equation can be used in almost any situation to determine the pressure at any point in a fluid. The equation makes some assumptions about the fluid, such as the fluid being ideal*[8] and incompressible.*[8] An ideal fluid is a fluid in which there is no friction, it is inviscid *[8] (zero viscosity).*[8] The equation for all points of a system filled with a constant-density fluid is

$$\frac{p}{\gamma} + \frac{v^2}{2g} + z = \text{const} \ ^*[9]$$

where:

- p = pressure of the fluid
- $\gamma = \varrho g$ = density·acceleration of gravity = specific weight of the fluid.*[8]
- v = velocity of the fluid
- g = acceleration of gravity
- z = elevation
- $\frac{p}{\gamma}$ = pressure head
- $\frac{v^2}{2g}$ = velocity head

Applications

- Hydraulic brakes
- Artesian well
- Blood pressure
- Hydraulic head
- Plant cell turgidity
- Pythagorean cup

16.2.2 Explosion or deflagration pressures

Explosion or deflagration pressures are the result of the ignition of explosive gases, mists, dust/air suspensions, in unconfined and confined spaces.

16.2.3 Negative pressures

Low pressure chamber in Bundesleistungszentrum Kienbaum, Germany

While **pressures** are, in general, positive, there are several situations in which negative pressures may be encountered:

- When dealing in relative (gauge) pressures. For instance, an absolute pressure of 80 kPa may be described as a gauge pressure of −21 kPa (i.e., 21 kPa below an atmospheric pressure of 101 kPa).

- When attractive intermolecular forces (e.g., van der Waals forces or hydrogen bonds) between the particles of a fluid exceed repulsive forces due to thermal motion. These forces explain ascent of sap in tall plants. An apparent negative pressure must act on water molecules at the top of any tree taller than 10 m, which is the pressure head of water that balances the atmospheric pressure. Intermolecular forces maintain cohesion of columns of sap that run continuously in xylem from the roots to the top leaves.*[10]

- The Casimir effect can create a small attractive force due to interactions with vacuum energy; this force is sometimes termed "vacuum pressure" (not to be confused with the negative *gauge pressure* of a vacuum).

- For non-isotropic stresses in rigid bodies, depending on how the orientation of a surface is chosen, the same distribution of forces may have a component of positive pressure along one surface normal, with a component of negative pressure acting along another surface normal.
  - The stresses in an electromagnetic field are generally non-isotropic, with the pressure normal to one surface element (the normal stress) being negative, and positive for surface elements perpendicular to this.

- In the cosmological constant.

16.2.4 Stagnation pressure

Stagnation pressure is the pressure a fluid exerts when it is forced to stop moving. Consequently, although a fluid moving at higher speed will have a lower static pressure, it may have a higher stagnation pressure when forced to a standstill. Static pressure and stagnation pressure are related by:

$$p_0 = \frac{1}{2}\rho v^2 + p$$

where

p_0 is the stagnation pressure
v is the flow velocity
p is the static pressure.

The pressure of a moving fluid can be measured using a Pitot tube, or one of its variations such as a Kiel probe or Cobra probe, connected to a manometer. Depending on where the inlet holes are located on the probe, it can measure static pressures or stagnation pressures.

16.2.5 Surface pressure and surface tension

There is a two-dimensional analog of pressure – the lateral force per unit length applied on a line perpendicular to the force.

Surface pressure is denoted by π and shares many similar properties with three-dimensional pressure. Properties of surface chemicals can be investigated by measuring pressure/area isotherms, as the two-dimensional analog of Boyle's law, $\pi A = k$, at constant temperature.

$$\pi = \frac{F}{l}$$

Surface tension is another example of surface pressure, but with a reversed sign, because "tension" is the opposite to "pressure".

16.2.6 Pressure of an ideal gas

Main article: Ideal gas law

In an ideal gas, molecules have no volume and do not interact. According to the ideal gas law, pressure varies linearly with temperature and quantity, and inversely with volume.

$$p = \frac{nRT}{V}$$

where:

p is the absolute pressure of the gas
n is the amount of substance
T is the absolute temperature
V is the volume
R is the ideal gas constant.

Real gases exhibit a more complex dependence on the variables of state.[11]

16.2.7 Vapor pressure

Main article: Vapor pressure

Vapor pressure is the pressure of a vapor in thermodynamic equilibrium with its condensed phases in a closed system. All liquids and solids have a tendency to evaporate into a gaseous form, and all gases have a tendency to condense back to their liquid or solid form.

The atmospheric pressure boiling point of a liquid (also known as the normal boiling point) is the temperature at which the vapor pressure equals the ambient atmospheric pressure. With any incremental increase in that temperature, the vapor pressure becomes sufficient to overcome atmospheric pressure and lift the liquid to form vapor bubbles inside the bulk of the substance. Bubble formation deeper in the liquid requires a higher pressure, and therefore higher temperature, because the fluid pressure increases above the atmospheric pressure as the depth increases.

The vapor pressure that a single component in a mixture contributes to the total pressure in the system is called partial vapor pressure.

16.2.8 Liquid pressure

See also: Fluid statics § Pressure in fluids at rest

When a person swims under the water, water pressure is felt acting on the person's eardrums. The deeper that person swims, the greater the pressure. The pressure felt is due to the weight of the water above the person. As someone swims deeper, there is more water above the person and therefore greater pressure. The pressure a liquid exerts depends on its depth.

Liquid pressure also depends on the density of the liquid. If someone was submerged in a liquid more dense than water, the pressure would be correspondingly greater. The pressure due to a liquid in liquid columns of constant density or

16.2. TYPES

at a depth within a substance is represented by the following formula:

$$p = \rho g h$$

where:

- p is liquid pressure
- g is gravity at the surface of overlaying material
- ρ is density of liquid
- h is height of liquid column or depth within a substance

Another way of saying this same formula is the following:

$$p = \text{density weight} \times \text{depth}$$

The pressure a liquid exerts against the sides and bottom of a container depends on the density and the depth of the liquid. If atmospheric pressure is neglected, liquid pressure against the bottom is twice as great at twice the depth; at three times the depth, the liquid pressure is threefold; etc. Or, if the liquid is two or three times as dense, the liquid pressure is correspondingly two or three times as great for any given depth. Liquids are practically incompressible – that is, their volume can hardly be changed by pressure (water volume decreases by only 50 millionths of its original volume for each atmospheric increase in pressure). Thus, except for small changes produced by temperature, the density of a particular liquid is practically the same at all depths.

Atmospheric pressure pressing on the surface of a liquid must be taken into account when trying to discover the *total* pressure acting on a liquid. The total pressure of a liquid, then, is $\rho g h$ plus the pressure of the atmosphere. When this distinction is important, the term *total pressure* is used. Otherwise, discussions of liquid pressure refer to pressure without regard to the normally ever-present atmospheric pressure.

It is important to recognize that the pressure does not depend on the *amount* of liquid present. Volume is not the important factor – depth is. The average water pressure acting against a dam depends on the average depth of the water and not on the volume of water held back. For example, a wide but shallow lake with a depth of 3 m (10 ft) exerts only half the average pressure that a small 6 m (20 ft) deep pond does (note that the *total force* applied to the longer dam will be greater, due to the greater total surface area for the pressure to act upon, but for a given 5-foot section of each dam, the 10 ft deep water will apply half the force of 20 ft deep water). A person will feel the same pressure whether his/her head is dunked a metre beneath the surface of the water in a small pool or to the same depth in the middle of a large lake. If four vases contain different amounts of water but are all filled to equal depths, then a fish with its head dunked a few centimetres under the surface will be acted on by water pressure that is the same in any of the vases. If the fish swims a few centimetres deeper, the pressure on the fish will increase with depth and be the same no matter which vase the fish is in. If the fish swims to the bottom, the pressure will be greater, but it makes no difference what vase it is in. All vases are filled to equal depths, so the water pressure is the same at the bottom of each vase, regardless of its shape or volume. If water pressure at the bottom of a vase were greater than water pressure at the bottom of a neighboring vase, the greater pressure would force water sideways and then up the narrower vase to a higher level until the pressures at the bottom were equalized. Pressure is depth dependent, not volume dependent, so there is a reason that water seeks its own level.

Restating this as energy equation, the energy per unit volume in an ideal, incompressible liquid is constant throughout its vessel. At the surface, gravitational potential energy is large but liquid pressure energy is low. At the bottom of the vessel, all the gravitational potential energy is converted to pressure energy. The sum of pressure energy and gravitational potential energy per unit volume is constant throughout the volume of the fluid and the two energy components change linearly with the depth.[12] Mathematically, it is described by Bernoulli's equation where velocity head is zero and comparisons per unit volume in the vessel are:

$$\frac{p}{\gamma} + z = \text{const}$$

Terms have the same meaning as in section Fluid pressure.

16.2.9 Direction of liquid pressure

An experimentally determined fact about liquid pressure is that it is exerted equally in all directions.[13] If someone is submerged in water, no matter which way that person tilts his/her head, the person will feel the same amount of water pressure on his/her ears. Because a liquid can flow, this pressure isn't only downward. Pressure is seen acting sideways when water spurts sideways from a leak in the side of an upright can. Pressure also acts upward, as demonstrated when someone tries to push a beach ball beneath the surface of the water. The bottom of a boat is pushed upward by water pressure (buoyancy).

When a liquid presses against a surface, there is a net force that is perpendicular to the surface. Although pressure doesn't have a specific direction, force does. A submerged triangular block has water forced against each point from many directions, but components of the force that are not perpendicular to the surface cancel each other out, leaving only a net perpendicular point.*[13] This is why water spurting from a hole in a bucket initially exits the bucket in a direction at right angles to the surface of the bucket in which the hole is located. Then it curves downward due to gravity. If there are three holes in a bucket (top, bottom, and middle), then the force vectors perpendicular to the inner container surface will increase with increasing depth – that is, a greater pressure at the bottom makes it so that the bottom hole will shoot water out the farthest. The force exerted by a fluid on a smooth surface is always at right angles to the surface. The speed of liquid out of the hole is $\sqrt{2gh}$, where h is the depth below the free surface.*[13] Interestingly, this is the same speed the water (or anything else) would have if freely falling the same vertical distance h.

16.2.10 Kinematic pressure

$P = p/\rho_0$

is the kinematic pressure, where p is the pressure and ρ_0 constant mass density. The SI unit of P is m^2/s^2. Kinematic pressure is used in the same manner as kinematic viscosity ν in order to compute Navier–Stokes equation without explicitly showing the density ρ_0.

Navier–Stokes equation with kinematic quantities
$$\frac{\partial u}{\partial t} + (u\nabla)u = -\nabla P + \nu\nabla^2 u$$

16.3 See also

- Atmospheric pressure
- Blood pressure
- Boyle's Law
- Combined gas law
- Conversion of units
- Critical point (thermodynamics)
- Dynamic pressure
- Hydraulics
- Internal pressure
- Kinetic theory
- Microphone
- Orders of magnitude (pressure)
- Partial pressure
- Pressure measurement
- Pressure sensor
- Sound pressure
- Spouting can
- Timeline of temperature and pressure measurement technology
- Units conversion by factor-label
- Vacuum
- Vacuum pump
- Vertical pressure variation

16.4 Notes

[1] The preferred spelling varies by country and even by industry. Further, both spellings are often used *within* a particular industry or country. Industries in British English-speaking countries typically use the "gauge" spelling.

16.5 References

[1] Giancoli, Douglas G. (2004). *Physics: principles with applications*. Upper Saddle River, N.J.: Pearson Education. ISBN 0-13-060620-0.

[2] McNaught, A. D.; Wilkinson, A.; Nic, M.; Jirat, J.; Kosata, B.; Jenkins, A. (2014). *IUPAC. Compendium of Chemical Terminology, 2nd ed. (the "Gold Book"*). 2.3.3. Oxford: Blackwell Scientific Publications. doi:10.1351/goldbook.P04819. ISBN 0-9678550-9-8.

[3] "14th Conference of the International Bureau of Weights and Measures". Bipm.fr. Retrieved 2012-03-27.

[4] US Navy (2006). *US Navy Diving Manual, 6th revision*. United States: US Naval Sea Systems Command. pp. 2–32. Retrieved 2008-06-15.

[5] "Rules and Style Conventions for Expressing Values of Quantities". NIST. Retrieved 2009-07-07.

[6] NIST, *Rules and Style Conventions for Expressing Values of Quantities*, Sect. 7.4.

[7] "Einstein's gravity under pressure". Springerlink.com. Retrieved 2012-03-27.

[8] Finnemore, John, E. and Joseph B. Franzini (2002). *Fluid Mechanics: With Engineering Applications*. New York: McGraw Hill, Inc. pp. 14–29. ISBN 978-0-07-243202-2.

[9] NCEES (2011). *Fundamentals of Engineering: Supplied Reference Handbook*. Clemson, South Carolina: NCEES. p. 64. ISBN 978-1-932613-59-9.

[10] Karen Wright (March 2003). "The Physics of Negative Pressure". Discover. Retrieved 31 January 2015.

[11] P. Atkins, J. de Paula *Elements of Physical Chemistry*, 4th Ed, W.H. Freeman, 2006. ISBN 0-7167-7329-5.

[12] Streeter, V.L., *Fluid Mechanics*, Example 3.5, McGraw–Hill Inc. (1966), New York.

[13] Hewitt 251 (2006)

16.6 External links

- *Introduction to Fluid Statics and Dynamics* on Project PHYSNET
- Pressure being a scalar quantity

Chapter 17

Blasting cap

Class B blasting caps

A **blasting cap** is a small sensitive primary explosive device generally used to detonate a larger, more powerful and less sensitive secondary explosive such as TNT, dynamite, or plastic explosive.

Blasting caps come in a variety of types, including non-electric caps, electric caps, and fuse caps. They are used in commercial mining, excavation, and demolition. Electric types are set off by a short burst of current conducted from a blasting machine by a long wire to the cap to ensure safety. Traditional fuse caps have a fuse which is ignited by a flame source, such as a match or a lighter.

17.1 Description

The need for blasting caps came from the development of safer explosives. Different explosives require different amounts of energy (their activation energy) to detonate. Most commercial explosives are formulated with a high activation energy, so they are stable and safe to handle and will not explode if accidentally dropped, mishandled, or exposed to fire. These are called secondary explosives. However they are correspondingly difficult to detonate intentionally, and require a small initiating explosion.

A blasting cap contains an easy-to-ignite primary explosive that provides the initial activation energy to start the detonation in the main charge. Explosives commonly used in blasting caps include mercury fulminate, lead azide, lead styphnate and tetryl and DDNP. The blasting cap is stored separately and not inserted into the main explosive charge until just before use, keeping the main charge safe.

Blasting caps are hazardous for untrained personnel to handle and they are sometimes not recognized as explosives due to their appearance, leading to injuries.

17.2 Types

17.2.1 Pyrotechnic fuse blasting cap

The oldest and simplest type of cap, fuse caps are a metal cylinder, closed at one end. From the open end inwards, there is first an empty space into which a pyrotechnic fuse is inserted and crimped, then a pyrotechnic ignition mix, a primary explosive, and then the main detonating explosive charge.

The primary hazard of pyrotechnic blasting caps is that for proper usage, the fuse must be inserted and then crimped into place by crushing the base of the cap around the fuse. If the tool used to crimp the cap is used too close to the explosives, the primary explosive compound can detonate during crimping. A common hazardous practice is crimping caps with one's teeth; an accidental detonation can cause serious injury to the mouth.

Fuse type blasting caps are still in active use today. They are the safest type to use around certain types of electromagnetic interference, and they have a built in time delay as the fuse burns down.

17.2. TYPES

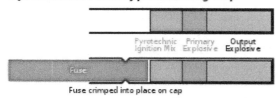

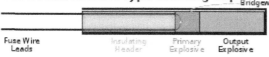

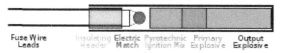

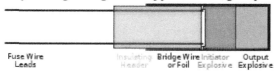

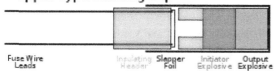

17.2.2 Solid pack electric blasting cap

Solid pack electric blasting caps use a thin bridgewire in direct contact (hence solid pack) with a primary explosive, which is heated by electric current and causes the detonation of the primary explosive. That primary explosive then detonates a larger charge of secondary explosive.

Some solid pack fuses incorporate a small pyrotechnic delay element, up to a few hundred milliseconds, before the cap fires.

17.2.3 Match or fusehead electric blasting cap

Match type blasting caps use an electric match (insulating sheet with electrodes on both sides, a thin bridgewire soldered across the sides, all dipped in ignition and output mixes) to initiate the primary explosive, rather than direct contact between the bridgewire and the primary explosive. The match can be manufactured separately from the rest of the cap and only assembled at the end of the process.

Match type caps are now the most common type found worldwide.

17.2.4 Exploding bridgewire detonator or blasting cap

Main article: Exploding-bridgewire detonator

This type of detonator was invented in the 1940s as part of the Manhattan project to develop nuclear weapons. The design goal was to produce a detonator which acted very rapidly and predictably. Both Match and Solid Pack type electric caps take a few milliseconds to fire, as the bridgewire heats up and heats the explosive to the point of detonation. Explosive bridgewire or **EBW** detonators use a higher voltage electric charge and a very thin bridgewire, .04 inch long, .0016 diameter, (1 mm long, 0.04 mm diameter). Instead of heating up the explosive, the EBW detonator wire is heated so quickly by the high firing current that the wire actually vaporizes and explodes due to electric resistance heating. That electrical driven explosion then fires the detonator's initiator explosive (usually PETN).

Some similar detonators use a thin metal foil instead of a wire, but operate in the same manner as true bridgewire detonators.

In addition to firing very quickly when properly activated, EBW detonators are safe from stray static electricity and other electric current. Enough current and the bridgewire may melt, but it is small enough that it cannot detonate the initiator explosive unless the full, high voltage high current charge passes through the bridgewire. EBW detonators are used in many civilian applications where radio signals, static electricity, or other electrical hazards might cause accidents with conventional electric detonators.

17.2.5 Slapper detonator or blasting cap

Main article: Slapper detonator

Slapper detonators are an improvement on EBW detonators. Slappers, instead of directly using the exploding foil to detonate the initiator explosive, use the electrical vaporization of the foil to drive a small circle of insulating material such as PET film or kapton down a circular hole in an additional disc of insulating material. At the far end of that hole is a pellet of conventional initiator explosive.

The conversion efficiency of energy from electricity into kinetic energy of the flying disk or slapper can be 20-40%.

Since the slapper impacts a wide area, 40 thousandths or (roughly one mm across) of the explosive, rather than a thin line or point as in an exploding foil or bridgewire detonator, the detonation is more regular and requires less energy. Reliable detonation requires raising a minimum volume of explosive to temperatures and pressures at which detonation starts. If energy is deposited at a single point, it can radiate away in the explosive in all directions in rarefaction or expansion waves, and only a small volume is efficiently heated or compressed. The flier disc loses impact energy at its sides to rarefaction waves, but a conical volume of explosive is efficiently shock compressed.

Slapper detonators are used in nuclear weapons. These components require large quantities of energy to initiate, making them extremely unlikely to accidentally discharge.

17.2.6 Laser ordnance initiators

The use of a laser to initiate a carbon-doped explosive via a fiber optic. These initiators are highly reliable, and unintentional initiation is very difficult as without the correct laser initiation system, or a completely independent initiation system, these components are not capable of being controlled remotely.

17.3 History

The first blasting cap or detonator was demonstrated in 1746 when a Dr. Watson of the Royal Society showed that the electric spark of a friction machine could ignite black powder, by way of igniting a flammable substance mixed in with the black powder.

In 1750, Benjamin Franklin in Philadelphia made a commercial blasting cap consisting of a paper tube full of black powder, with wires leading in both sides and wadding sealing up the ends. The two wires came close but did not touch, so a large electric spark discharge between the two wires would fire the cap.

In 1822 a hot wire detonator was produced by Dr Robert Hare, although attempts along similar lines had earlier been attempted by the Italians Volta and Cavallo.*[1] Using one strand separated out of a multistrand wire as the hot bridgewire, this blasting cap ignited a pyrotechnic mixture (believed to be potassium chlorate/arsenic/sulphur) and then a charge of tamped black powder.

In 1863 Alfred Nobel introduced the first pyrotechnic fuse blasting cap, using mercury fulminate to detonate nitroglycerin.

In 1868, H. Julius Smith introduced a cap that combined a spark gap ignitor and mercury fulminate, the first electric cap able to detonate dynamite.

In 1875, Perry "Pell" Gardiner and Smith independently developed and marketed caps which combined the hot wire detonator with mercury fulminate explosive. These were the first generally modern type blasting caps. Modern caps use different explosives and separate primary and secondary explosive charges, but are generally very similar to the Gardiner and Smith caps.

Electric match caps were developed in the early 1900s in Germany, and spread to the US in the 1950s when ICI International purchased Atlas Powder Co. These match caps have become the predominant world standard cap type.

17.4 See also

- Blasting machine

17.5 References

[1] http://www.standingwellback.com/home/2012/11/18/inventing-detonators.html

- Cooper, Paul W., *Explosives Engineering*, New York: Wiley-VCH, 1996. ISBN 0-471-18636-8

17.6 External links

- 1956 safety film "Blasting Cap - Danger!" from Prelinger Archives
- Modelling and Simulation of Burst Phenomenon in Electrically Exploded Foils

Chapter 18

Percussion cap

For a description of the primers that replaced percussion caps in breechloaded cartridges, see Centerfire ammunition.

The **percussion cap**, introduced circa 1820, was the cru-

Single-shot caplock pistol used to assassinate Abraham Lincoln. This type of small handgun is known as a Derringer.

cial invention that enabled muzzleloading firearms to fire reliably in any weather.*[1] This gave rise to the caplock or percussionlock system.

Before this development, firearms used flintlock ignition systems that produced flint-on-steel sparks to ignite a pan of priming powder and thereby fire the gun's main powder charge (the flintlock mechanism replaced older ignition systems such as the matchlock and wheellock). Flintlocks were prone to misfire in wet weather, and many flintlock firearms were later converted to the more reliable percussion system.

The percussion cap is a small cylinder of copper or brass with one closed end. Inside the closed end is a small amount of a shock-sensitive explosive material such as fulminate of mercury. The percussion cap is placed over a hollow metal "nipple" at the rear end of the gun barrel. Pulling the trigger releases a hammer that strikes the percussion cap and ignites the explosive primer. The flame travels through the hollow nipple to ignite the main powder charge. Percussion caps were, and still are, made in small sizes for pistols and larger sizes for rifles and muskets.*[1]

While the metal percussion cap was the most popular and widely used type of primer, their small size made them difficult to handle under the stress of combat or while riding a horse. Accordingly, several manufacturers developed alternative, "auto-priming" systems. The "Maynard tape primer", for example, used a roll of paper "caps" much like today's toy cap gun. The Maynard tape primer was fitted to some firearms used in the mid-nineteenth century and a few saw brief use in the American Civil War. Other disc or pellet-type primers held a supply of tiny fulminate detonator discs in a small magazine. Cocking the hammer automatically advanced a disc into position. However, these automatic feed systems were difficult to make with the manufacturing systems in the early and mid-nineteenth century and generated more problems than they solved. They were quickly shelved in favor of a single percussion cap that, while awkward to handle in some conditions, could be carried in sufficient quantities to make up for occasionally dropping one while a jammed tape primer system reduced the rifle to an awkward club.*[1]

The first practical solution for the problem of handling percussion caps in battle was the Prussian 1841 (Dreyse needle gun), which used a long needle to penetrate a paper cartridge filled with black powder and strike the percussion cap that was fastened to the base of the bullet. While it had a number of problems, it was widely used by the Prussians and other German states in the mid-nineteenth century and was a major factor in the 1866 Austro-Prussian War.

In the 1850s, the percussion cap was first integrated into a metallic cartridge, which contained the bullet, powder charge and primer. By the late 1860s, breech-loading metallic cartridges had made the percussion cap system obsolete. Today, reproduction percussion firearms are popular for recreational shooters and percussion caps are still available (though some modern muzzleloaders use shotshell primers instead of caps). Most percussion caps now use non-corrosive compounds such as lead styphnate.*[1]

18.1 History

Inverted percussion pistol, 9.5 mm; made by gunsmith Correvon, Morges, 1854. On display at Morges military museum.

The percussion cap replaced the flint, the steel "frizzen", and the powder pan of the flint-lock mechanism. It was only generally applied to the British military musket (the Brown Bess) in 1842, a quarter of a century after the invention of percussion powder and after an elaborate government test at Woolwich in 1834. The first percussion firearm produced for the US military was the percussion carbine version (c.1833) of the M1819 Hall rifle.

The discovery of fulminates was made by Edward Charles Howard (1774–1816) in 1800.[2][3] The invention that made the percussion cap possible using the recently discovered fulminates was patented by the Rev. Alexander John Forsyth of Belhelvie, Aberdeenshire, Scotland in 1807.[1]

This early system coined "Percussion Lock" operated in a near identical fashion to flintlock firearms and utilized fulminating primer made of fulminate of mercury, chlorate of potash, sulphur, and charcoal, which was ignited by concussion.[4][5] It was an invention born of necessity: Rev. Forsyth had noticed that sitting birds would startle when smoke puffed from the powder pan of his flintlock shotgun, giving them sufficient warning to escape the shot. His invention of a fulminate-primed firing mechanism deprived the birds of their early warning system, both by avoiding the initial puff of smoke from the flintlock powder pan, as well as shortening the interval between the trigger pull and the shot leaving the muzzle.

Fulminate-primed guns were also less likely to misfire than flintlock guns. However, it was not until after Forsyth's patents expired that the conventional percussion cap system was developed. The percussion cap helped lead to the self-contained cartridge, where the bullet is held in by the casing, the casing is filled with gunpowder, and a primer is at the end.

Joshua Shaw, an English-born American, is sometimes credited with the development of the first metallic percussion cap in 1814, but his claim remains clouded with controversy as he did not patent the idea until 1822. Furthermore, according to Lewis Winant, the US government's decision to award Shaw $25,000 as compensation for his invention was actually a mistake. Congress believed Shaw's patent was the earliest and awarded him a large sum of money based on this belief. However, a patent for the percussion cap was filed by François Prélat in 1818, four years before Shaw's.[6] Shaw's percussion caps used a mixture of fulminate of mercury, chlorate of potash, and ground glass contained in a small metallic cup. Other possible claimants include François Prélat, Joseph Manton, Col. Peter Hawker, and most likely of all, Joseph Egg (nephew of Durs Egg).

This invention was gradually improved, and came to be used, first in a steel cap, and then in a copper cap, by various gunmakers and private individuals before coming into general military use nearly thirty years later.

The alteration of the military flintlock to the percussion musket was easily accomplished by replacing the powder pan and steel "frizzen" with a nipple, and by replacing the cock or hammer that held the flint by a smaller hammer formed with a hollow made to fit around the nipple when released by the trigger. On the nipple was placed the copper cap containing the detonating composition, now made of three parts of chlorate of potash, two of fulminate of mercury and one of powdered glass. The hollow in the hammer contained the fragments of the cap if it fragmented, reducing the risk of injury to the firer's eyes.

The detonating cap, thus invented and adopted, brought about the invention of the modern cartridge case, and rendered possible the general adoption of the breech-loading principle for all varieties of rifles, shotguns and pistols.

Caps are used in cartridges, grenades, rocket-propelled grenades, and rescue flares. Percussion caps are also used in land mine fuzes, boobytrap firing devices and anti-handling devices.

18.1.1 Firing devices and fuze mechanisms

As a rule, most purpose-made military booby-trap firing devices contain some form of spring-loaded firing pin designed to strike a percussion cap connected to a detonator at one end. The detonator is inserted into an explosive charge —e.g., C4 or a block of TNT. Triggering the booby-trap (e.g., by pulling on a trip-wire) releases the cocked firing pin that flips forward to strike the percussion cap, firing both it and the attached detonator. The resulting shock-wave from the detonator sets off the main explosive charge.

- USSR booby trap firing device – pull fuze: normally connected to a tripwire. Percussion cap is clearly labelled
- Alternative design of USSR booby trap firing device – pull fuze: normally connected to tripwire. Percussion cap is clearly labelled
- USSR boobytrap firing device – pressure fuze: victim steps on loose floorboard with fuze concealed underneath
- Pencil detonator – a British time fuze used in covert operations during World War II
- Cross-sectional view of a Japanese Type 99 grenade showing percussion primer
- Cross-sectional view of the fuze fitted to a German S-mine. Percussion cap is clearly labelled
- Percussion cap nipples, the ignition flame travels though the hole.
- Percussion caps

18.2 See also

- Cap gun
- Caplock mechanism
- Internal ballistics
- Tubes and primers for ammunition

18.3 References

[1] Fadala, Sam (17 November 2006). *The Complete Blackpowder Handbook*. Iola, Wisconsin: Gun Digest Books. pp. 159–161. ISBN 0-89689-390-1.

[2] Howard, Edward (1800) "On a New Fulminating Mercury," *Philosophical Transactions of the Royal Society of London* **90** (1): 204–238.

[3] Edward Charles Howard at National Portrait Gallery

[4] Percussion lock

[5] Samuel Parkes, *The chemical catechism : with notes, illustrations, and experiments*, New York : Collins and Co., 1818, page 494 (page 494 online, see "LVI. A New Kind of Gunpowder.")

[6] "Early Percussion Firearms". Spring Books. 2015-10-25.

- Winant, L. (1956). *Early percussion firearms*. Bonanza Books

Chapter 19

Shock wave

"Shockwave" redirects here. For other uses, see Shockwave (disambiguation).
"Bombshock" redirects here. For the Transformers character, see Micromasters.

In physics, a **shock wave** (also spelled **shockwave**), or

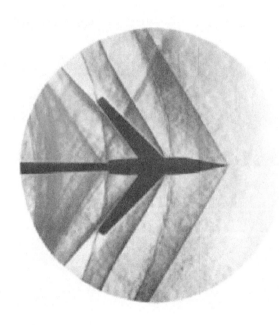

Schlieren photograph of an attached shock on a sharp-nosed supersonic body.

shock, is a type of propagating disturbance. When a wave moves faster than the local speed of sound in a fluid it is a shock wave. Like an ordinary wave, a shock wave carries energy, and can propagate through a medium; however it is characterized by an abrupt, nearly discontinuous change in pressure, temperature and density of the medium.*[1] In supersonic flows, expansion is achieved through an expansion fan also known as a Prandtl-Meyer expansion fan.

Unlike solitons (another kind of nonlinear wave), the energy of a shock wave dissipates relatively quickly with distance. Also, the accompanying expansion wave approaches and eventually merges with the shock wave, partially can-

celling it out. Thus the sonic boom associated with the passage of a supersonic aircraft is the sound wave resulting from the degradation and merging of the shock wave and the expansion wave produced by the aircraft.

When a shock wave passes through matter, energy is preserved but entropy increases. This change in the matter's properties manifests itself as a decrease in the energy which can be extracted as work, and as a drag force on supersonic objects; shock waves are strongly irreversible processes.

19.1 Terminology

Shock waves can be:

- Normal: at 90° (perpendicular) to the shock medium's flow direction.

- Oblique: at an angle to the direction of flow.

- Bow: Occurs upstream of the front (bow) of a blunt object when the upstream flow velocity exceeds Mach 1.

Some other terms

- Shock Front: an alternative name for the shock wave itself

- Contact Front: in a shock wave caused by a driver gas (for example the "impact" of a high explosive on the surrounding air), the boundary between the driver (explosive products) and the driven (air) gases. The Contact Front trails the Shock Front.

19.2 In supersonic flows

The abruptness of change in the features of the medium, that characterize shock waves, can be viewed as a phase

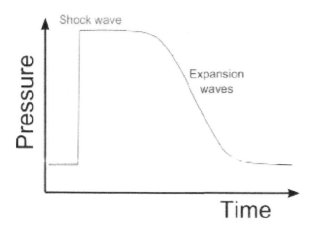

Pressure-time diagram at an external observation point for the case of a supersonic object propagating past the observer. The leading edge of the object causes a shock (left, in red) and the trailing edge of the object causes an expansion (right, in blue).

transition: the pressure-time diagram of a supersonic object propagating shows how the transition induced by a shock wave is analogous to a *dynamic phase transition*.

When an object (or disturbance) moves faster than the information about it can propagate into the surrounding fluid, fluid near the disturbance cannot react or "get out of the way" before the disturbance arrives. In a shock wave the properties of the fluid (density, pressure, temperature, flow velocity, Mach number) change almost instantaneously. Measurements of the thickness of shock waves in air have resulted in values around 200 nm (about $10^{*}-5$ in),[2] which is on the same order of magnitude as the mean free gas molecule path. In reference to the continuum, this implies the shock wave can be treated as either a line or a plane if the flow field is two-dimensional or three-dimensional, respectively.

Shock waves form when the speed of a fluid changes by more than the speed of sound.[3] At the region where this occurs, sound waves travelling against the flow reach a point where they cannot travel any further upstream and the pressure progressively builds in that region; a high pressure shock wave rapidly forms.

Shock waves are not conventional sound waves; a shock wave takes the form of a very sharp change in the gas properties. Shock waves in air are heard as a loud "crack" or "snap" noise. Over longer distances, a shock wave can change from a nonlinear wave into a linear wave, degenerating into a conventional sound wave as it heats the air and loses energy. The sound wave is heard as the familiar "thud" or "thump" of a sonic boom, commonly created by the supersonic flight of aircraft.

The shock wave is one of several different ways in which a gas in a supersonic flow can be compressed. Some other methods are isentropic compressions, including Prandtl-Meyer compressions. The method of compression of a gas results in different temperatures and densities for a given pressure ratio which can be analytically calculated for a non-reacting gas. A shock wave compression results in a loss of total pressure, meaning that it is a less efficient method of compressing gases for some purposes, for instance in the intake of a scramjet. The appearance of pressure-drag on supersonic aircraft is mostly due to the effect of shock compression on the flow.

19.3 Normal shocks

In elementary fluid mechanics utilizing ideal gases, a shock wave is treated as a discontinuity where entropy increases over a nearly infinitesimal region. Since no fluid flow is discontinuous, a control volume is established around the shock wave, with the control surfaces that bound this volume parallel to the shock wave (with one surface on the pre-shock side of the fluid medium and one on the post-shock side). The two surfaces are separated by a very small depth such that the shock itself is entirely contained between them. At such control surfaces, momentum, mass flux and energy are constant; within combustion, detonations can be modelled as heat introduction across a shock wave. It is assumed the system is adiabatic (no heat exits or enters the system) and no work is being done. The Rankine–Hugoniot conditions arise from these considerations.

Taking into account the established assumptions, in a system where the downstream properties are becoming subsonic: the upstream and downstream flow properties of the fluid are considered isentropic. Since the total amount of energy within the system is constant, the stagnation enthalpy remains constant over both regions. Though, entropy is increasing; this must be accounted for by a drop in stagnation pressure of the downstream fluid.

19.4 Other shocks

19.4.1 Oblique shocks

When analyzing shock waves in a flow field, which are still attached to the body, the shock wave which is deviating at some arbitrary angle from the flow direction is termed oblique shock. These shocks require a component vector analysis of the flow; doing so allows for the treatment of the flow in an orthogonal direction to the oblique shock as a normal shock.

19.4.2 Bow shocks

When an oblique shock is likely to form at an angle which can not remain on the surface, a nonlinear phenomenon arises where the shock wave will form a continuous pattern around the body. These are termed bow shocks. In these cases, the 1d flow model is not valid and a complex analysis is needed to predict the pressure forces which are exerted on the surface.

19.5 Shock waves due to nonlinear steepening

Shock waves can form due to steepening of ordinary waves. The best-known example of this phenomenon is ocean waves that form breakers on the shore. In shallow water, the speed of surface waves is dependent on the depth of the water. An incoming ocean wave has a slightly higher wave speed near the crest of each wave than near the troughs between waves, because the wave height is not infinitesimal compared to the depth of the water. The crests overtake the troughs until the leading edge of the wave forms a vertical face and spills over to form a turbulent shock (a breaker) that dissipates the wave's energy as sound and heat.

Similar phenomena affect strong sound waves in gas or plasma, due to the dependence of the sound speed on temperature and pressure. Strong waves heat the medium near each pressure front, due to adiabatic compression of the air itself, so that high pressure fronts outrun the corresponding pressure troughs. While shock formation by this process does not normally happen to sound waves in Earth's atmosphere, it is thought to be one mechanism by which the solar chromosphere and corona are heated, via waves that propagate up from the solar interior.

19.6 Analogies

A shock wave may be described as the furthest point upstream of a moving object which "knows" about the approach of the object. In this description, the shock wave position is defined as the boundary between the zone having no information about the shock-driving event and the zone aware of the shock-driving event, analogous with the light cone described in the theory of special relativity.

To produce a shock wave, an object in a given medium (such as air or water) must travel faster than the local speed of sound. In the case of an aircraft travelling at high subsonic speed, regions of air around the aircraft may be travelling at exactly the speed of sound, so that the sound waves leaving the aircraft pile up on one another, similar to a traffic jam on a motorway. When a shock wave forms, the local air pressure increases and then spreads out sideways. Because of this amplification effect, a shock wave can be very intense, more like an explosion when heard at a distance (not coincidentally, since explosions create shock waves).

Analogous phenomena are known outside fluid mechanics. For example, particles accelerated beyond the speed of light in a refractive medium (where the speed of light is less than that in a vacuum, such as water) create visible shock effects, a phenomenon known as Cherenkov radiation.

19.7 Phenomena types

Below are a number of examples of shock waves, broadly grouped with similar shock phenomena:

19.7.1 Moving shock

- Usually consists of a shock wave propagating into a stationary medium

- In this case, the gas ahead of the shock is stationary (in the laboratory frame) and the gas behind the shock can be supersonic in the laboratory frame. The shock propagates with a wavefront which is normal (at right angles) to the direction of flow. The speed of the shock is a function of the original pressure ratio between the two bodies of gas.

- Moving shocks are usually generated by the interaction of two bodies of gas at different pressure, with a shock wave propagating into the lower pressure gas and an expansion wave propagating into the higher pressure gas.

- Examples: Balloon bursting, Shock tube, shock wave from explosion.

19.7.2 Detonation wave

Main article: Detonation

- A detonation wave is essentially a shock supported by a trailing exothermic reaction. It involves a wave travelling through a highly combustible or chemically unstable medium, such as an oxygen-methane mixture or a high explosive. The chemical reaction of the medium occurs following the shock wave, and the chemical energy of the reaction drives the wave forward.

19.7. PHENOMENA TYPES

Shock wave propagating into a stationary medium, ahead of the fireball of an explosion. The shock is made visible by the shadow effect (Trinity explosion.)

- A detonation wave follows slightly different rules from an ordinary shock since it is driven by the chemical reaction occurring behind the shock wavefront. In the simplest theory for detonations, an unsupported, self-propagating detonation wave proceeds at the Chapman-Jouguet flow velocity. A detonation will also cause a shock of type 1, above to propagate into the surrounding air due to the overpressure induced by the explosion.

- When a shock wave is created by high explosives such as TNT (which has a detonation velocity of 6,900 m/s), it will always travel at high, supersonic velocity from its point of origin.

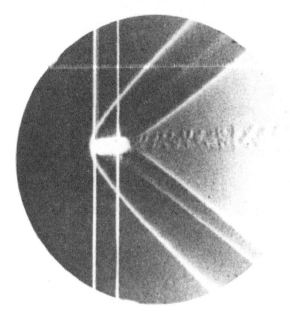

Schlieren photograph of the detached shock on a bullet in supersonic flight, published by Ernst Mach and Peter Salcher in 1887.

19.7.3 Bow shock (detached shock)

Main article: Bow shock (aerodynamics)

- These shocks are curved and form a small distance in front of the body. Directly in front of the body, they stand at 90 degrees to the oncoming flow and then curve around the body. Detached shocks allow the same type of analytic calculations as for the attached shock, for the flow near the shock. They are a topic of continuing interest, because the rules governing the shock's distance ahead of the blunt body are complicated and are a function of the body's shape. Additionally, the shock standoff distance varies drastically with the temperature for a non-ideal gas, causing large differences in the heat transfer to the thermal protection system of the vehicle. See the extended discussion on this topic at Atmospheric reentry. These follow the "strong-shock" solutions of the analytic equations, meaning that for some oblique shocks very close to the deflection angle limit, the downstream Mach number is subsonic. See also bow shock or oblique shock

- Such a shock occurs when the maximum deflection angle is exceeded. A detached shock is commonly seen

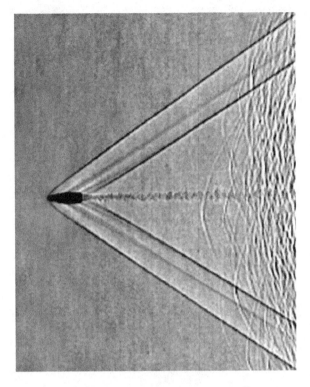

Shadowgram of shock waves from a supersonic bullet fired from a rifle. The shadowgraph optical technique reveals that the bullet is moving at about a Mach number of 1.9. Left- and right-running bow waves and tail waves stream back from the bullet and its turbulent wake is also visible. Patterns at the far right are from unburned gunpowder particles ejected by the rifle.

on blunt bodies, but may also be seen on sharp bodies at low Mach numbers.

- Examples: Space return vehicles (Apollo, Space shuttle), bullets, the boundary (Bow shock) of a magnetosphere. The name "bow shock" comes from the example of a bow wave, the detached shock formed at the bow (front) of a ship or boat moving through water, whose slow surface wave speed is easily exceeded (see ocean surface wave).

19.7.4 Attached shock

- These shocks appear as *attached* to the tip of sharp bodies moving at supersonic speeds.

- Examples: Supersonic wedges and cones with small apex angles.

- The attached shock wave is a classic structure in aerodynamics because, for a perfect gas and inviscid flow field, an analytic solution is available, such that the pressure ratio, temperature ratio, angle of the wedge and the downstream Mach number can all be calculated knowing the upstream Mach number and the shock angle. Smaller shock angles are associated with higher upstream Mach numbers, and the special case where the shock wave is at 90° to the oncoming flow (Normal shock), is associated with a Mach number of one. These follow the "weak-shock" solutions of the analytic equations.

19.7.5 In rapid granular flows

Shock waves can also occur in rapid flows of dense granular materials down inclined channels or slopes. Strong shocks in rapid dense granular flows can be studied theoretically and analyzed to compare with experimental data. Consider a configuration in which the rapidly moving material down the chute impinges on an obstruction wall erected perpendicular at the end of a long and steep channel. Impact leads to a sudden change in the flow regime from a fast moving supercritical thin layer to a stagnant thick heap. This flow configuration is particularly interesting because it is analogous to some hydraulic and aerodynamic situations associated with flow regime changes from supercritical to subcritical flows.

19.7.6 In astrophysics

Main article: Shock waves in astrophysics

Astrophysical environments feature many different types of shock waves. Some common examples are supernovae shock waves or blast waves travelling through the interstellar medium, the bow shock caused by the Earth's magnetic field colliding with the solar wind and shock waves caused by galaxies colliding with each other. Another interesting type of shock in astrophysics is the quasi-steady reverse shock or termination shock that terminates the ultra relativistic wind from young pulsars.

Meteor entering events

The Tunguska event and the 2013 Russian meteor event are the best documented evidence of the shock wave produced by a massive meteoroid.

When the 2013 meteor entered into the Earth's atmosphere with an energy release equivalent to 100 or more kilotons of TNT, dozens of times more powerful than the atomic bomb dropped on Hiroshima, the meteor's shock wave produced damages as in a supersonic jet's flyby (directly underneath the meteor's path) and as a detonation wave, with the circular shock wave centred at the meteor explosion, causing

19.8 Technological applications

Damage caused by a meteor's shock wave.

multiple instances of broken glass in the city of Chelyabinsk and neighbouring areas (pictured).

19.8 Technological applications

In the examples below, the shock wave is controlled, produced by (ex. airfoil) or in the interior of a technological device, like a turbine.

19.8.1 Recompression shock

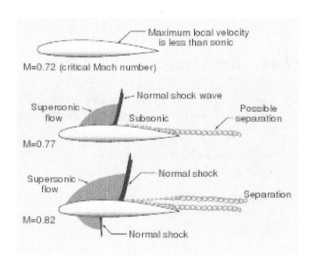

Recompression shock on a transonic flow airfoil, at and above critical Mach number.

- These shocks appear when the flow over a transonic body is decelerated to subsonic speeds.
- Examples: Transonic wings, turbines

- Where the flow over the suction side of a transonic wing is accelerated to a supersonic speed, the resulting re-compression can be by either Prandtl-Meyer compression or by the formation of a normal shock. This shock is of particular interest to makers of transonic devices because it can cause separation of the boundary layer at the point where it touches the transonic profile. This can then lead to full separation and stall on the profile, higher drag, or shock buffet, a condition where the separation and the shock interact in a resonance condition, causing resonating loads on the underlying structure.

19.8.2 Pipe flow

- This shock appears when supersonic flow in a pipe is decelerated.

- Examples:

  - In Supersonic Propulsion -- ramjet, scramjet, unstart.
  - In Flow Control -- needle valve, choked venturi.

- In this case the gas ahead of the shock is supersonic (in the laboratory frame), and the gas behind the shock system is either supersonic (*oblique shocks*) or subsonic (a *normal shock*) (Although for some oblique shocks very close to the deflection angle limit, the downstream Mach number is subsonic.) The shock is the result of the deceleration of the gas by a converging duct, or by the growth of the boundary layer on the wall of a parallel duct.

19.8.3 Combustion engines

The wave disk engine (also named "Radial Internal Combustion Wave Rotor") is a kind of pistonless rotary engine that utilizes *shock waves* to transfer energy between a high-energy fluid to a low-energy fluid, thereby increasing both temperature and pressure of the low-energy fluid.

19.8.4 Memristors

In memristors, under externally-applied electric field, shock waves can be launched across the transition-metal oxides, creating fast and non-volatile resistivity changes.*[4]

19.9 Shock capturing and detection

Advanced techniques are needed to capture shock waves and to detect shock waves in both numerical computations and experimental observations.*[5]*[6]*[7]*[8]*[9]*[10]*[11]

Computational fluid dynamics is commonly used to obtain the flow field with shock waves. Though shock waves are sharp discontinuities, in numerical solutions of fluid flow with discontinuities (shock wave, contact discontinuity or slip line), the shock wave can be smoothed out by low-order numerical method (due to numerical dissipation) or there are spurious oscillations near shock surface by high-order numerical method (due to Gibbs phenomena).

There exist some other discontinuities in fluid flow than the shock wave. The slip surface (3D) or slip line (2D) is a plane across which the tangent velocity is discontinuous, while pressure and normal velocity are continuous. Across the contact discontinuity, the pressure and velocity are continuous and the density is discontinuous. A strong expansion wave or shear layer may also contain high gradient regions which appear to be a discontinuity. Some common features of these flow structures and shock waves and the insufficient aspects of numerical and experimental tools lead to two important problems in practices: (1) some shock waves can not be detected or their positions are detected wrong, (2) some flow structures which are not shock waves are wrongly detected to be shock waves.

In fact, correct capturing and detection of shock waves are important since shock waves have the following influences: (1) causing loss of total pressure, which may be a concern related to scramjet engine performance, (2)providing lift for wave-rider configuration, as the oblique shock wave at lower surface of the vehicle can produce high pressure to generate lift, (3)leading to wave drag of high-speed vehicle which is harmful to vehicle performance, (4)inducing severe pressure load and heat flux, e.g. the Type IV shock–shock interference could yield a 17 times heating increase at vehicle surface, (5)interacting with other structures, such as boundary layers, to produce new flow structures such as flow separation, transition, etc.

19.10 See also

- Atmospheric focusing
- Atmospheric reentry
- Čerenkov radiation
- Explosion
- Hydraulic jump
- Joule–Thomson effect*[12]
- Kerner's breakdown minimization principle
- Mach wave
- Magnetopause
- Moreton wave
- Normal shock tables
- Oblique shock
- Prandtl–Meyer expansion fan
- Shocks and Discontinuities (MHD)
- Shock (mechanics)
- Sonic boom
- Three-phase traffic theory
- Traffic congestion: Reconstruction with Kerner's three-phase theory
- Supercritical airfoil
- Undercompressive shock wave
- Unstart
- Shock diamond
- Kelvin wake pattern

19.11 References

[1] Anderson, John D. Jr. (January 2001) [1984], *Fundamentals of Aerodynamics* (3rd ed.), McGraw-Hill Science/Engineering/Math, ISBN 0-07-237335-0

[2] [Introduction To Fluid Mechanics Fourth Edition, Robert W. Fox, Alan T. McDonald ISBN 0-471-54852-9]

[3] Settles, Gary S. (2006), *High-speed Imaging of Shock Wave, Explosions and Gunshots*, **94** (1), American Scientist, pp. 22–31

[4] Tang, Shao; Tesler, Federico; Marlasca, Fernando Gomez; Levy, Pablo; Dobrosavljević, V.; Rozenberg, Marcelo (2016-03-15). "Shock Waves and Commutation Speed of Memristors". *Physical Review X*. **6** (1). Bibcode:2016PhRvX...6a1028T. doi:10.1103/physrevx.6.011028.

[5] Wu ZN,Xu YZ,etc (2013), *Review of shock wave detection method in CFD post-processing*, **26** (3), Chinese Journal of Aeronautics, pp. 501–513

[6] Solem, J. C.; Veeser, L. (1977). "Exploratory laser-driven shock wave studies" (PDF). *Los Alamos Scientific Laboratory Report LA-6997*.

[7] Veeser, L. R.; Solem, J. C. (1978). "Studies of Laser-driven shock waves in aluminum". *Physical Review Letters*. **40** (21): 1391. Bibcode:1978PhRvL..40.1391V. doi:10.1103/PhysRevLett.40.1391.

[8] Solem, J. C.; Veeser, L. R. (1978). "Laser-driven shock wave studies". *Proceedings of Symposium on the Behavior of Dense Media Under High Dynamic Pressure. (Editions due Commissriat a l'Energie Atomique, Centre d'Etudes Nucleaires de Saclay, Paris)* (Los Alamos Scientific Laboratory Report LA-UR-78-1039): 463–476.

[9] Veeser, L.; Solem, J. C.; Lieber, A. (1979). "Impedance-match experiments using laser-driven shock waves". *Applied Physics Letters*. **35**: 761. Bibcode:1979ApPhL..35..761V. doi:10.1063/1.90961.

[10] Solem, J. C.; Veeser, L.; Lieber, A. (1979). "Impedance-match experiments using laser-driven shock waves". *Proceedings of 7th International AIRAPT Conference, High Pressure Science and Technology, Le Creusot, France, July 30-August 3, 1979. (Pergamon Press, Oxford, England)*: 971.

[11] Veeser, L.; Lieber, A.; Solem, J. C. (1979). "Planar streak camera laser-driven shockwave studies". *Proceedings of International Conference on Lasers '79, Orlando, FL, 17 December 17, 1979.* LA-UR-79-3509; CONF-791220-3. (Los Alamos Scientific Lab., NM): 45.

[12] Hoover, Wm G., Carol G. Hoover, and Karl P. Travis. "Shock-Wave Compression and Joule-Thomson Expansion." Physical review letters 112.14 (2014): 144504.

19.12 External links

- NASA Glenn Research Center information on:
  - Oblique Shocks
  - Multiple Crossed Shocks
  - Expansion Fans
- Selkirk college: Aviation intranet: High speed (supersonic) flight
  - Energy loss in a shock wave, normal and oblique shock waves
  - Formation of a normal shock wave
- Fundamentals of compressible flow, 2007
- KB Commercial finite-element educational software to simulate shocks and detonations.
- NASA 2015 Schlieren image shock wave T-38C

19.13 Further reading

- Krehl, Peter O. K. (2011). "Shock wave physics and detonation physics —a stimulus for the emergence of numerous new branches in science and engineering". *European Physical Journal H*. **36**: 85. Bibcode:2011EPJH...36...85K. doi:10.1140/epjh/e2011-10037-x.

Chapter 20

Binary explosive

A **binary explosive** or **two-component explosive** is an explosive consisting of two components, neither of which is explosive by itself, which have to be mixed in order to become explosive. Examples of common binary explosives include Oxyliquit (liquid oxygen/combustible powder), ANFO (ammonium nitrate/fuel oil), Kinestik (ammonium nitrate/nitromethane), Tannerite (ammonium nitrate/aluminum), and FIXOR (nitroethane/physical sensitizer).

Binary explosives are often used in commercial applications because of their greater handling safety.

20.1 See also

- Binary (chemical weapon)
- Category:Binary explosives

20.2 External links

- [wrc.navair-rdte.navy.mil/warfighter_enc/weapons/ordnance/types.htm] Types of Explosives
- FIXOR, a commercial binary explosive sold for mine clearance
- Binary/Two Component Explosives, from a presentation by the N. C. Dept. of Transportation

Chapter 21

Improvised explosive device

Ammunition rigged for an IED discovered by Iraqi police in Baghdad in November 2005

This Cougar in Al Anbar, Iraq, was hit by a directed charge IED approximately 300–500 lbs in size.

An **improvised explosive device** (**IED**) is a bomb constructed and deployed in ways other than in conventional military action. It may be constructed of conventional military explosives, such as an artillery round, attached to a detonating mechanism. IEDs are commonly used as **roadside bombs**.

IEDs are generally seen in heavy terrorist actions or in unconventional warfare by guerrillas or commando forces in a theater of operations. In the second Iraq War, IEDs were used extensively against US-led invasion forces and by the end of 2007 they had become responsible for approximately 63% of coalition deaths in Iraq.[1] They are also used in Afghanistan by insurgent groups, and have caused over 66% of coalition casualties in the 2001–present Afghanistan War.[2]

IEDs were also used extensively by cadres of the rebel Tamil Tiger (LTTE) organization against military targets in Sri Lanka.[3][4]

21.1 Background

A portable X-ray generator and a portable flat panel detector are used to inspect a suspicious carrying case.

The term comes from the British Army in the 1970s, after the Provisional Irish Republican Army (IRA) used bombs made from agricultural fertilizer and Semtex smuggled from Libya to make highly effective boobytrap devices or remote-controlled bombs.

An IED is a bomb fabricated in an improvised manner incorporating destructive, lethal, noxious, pyrotechnic, or incendiary chemicals and designed to destroy or incapacitate personnel or vehicles. In some cases, IEDs are used to distract, disrupt, or delay an opposing force, facilitating another type of attack."[5] IEDs may incorporate military or commercially sourced explosives, and often combine both types, or they may otherwise be made with homemade explosives (HME).

An IED has five components: a switch (activator), an initiator (fuse), container (body), charge (explosive), and a power source (battery). An IED designed for use against armoured targets such as personnel carriers or tanks will be designed for armour penetration, by using a shaped charge that creates an explosively formed penetrator. IEDs are extremely diverse in design and may contain many types of initiators, detonators, penetrators, and explosive loads.

Antipersonnel IEDs typically also contain fragmentation-generating objects such as nails, ball bearings or even small rocks to cause wounds at greater distances than blast pressure alone could. IEDs are triggered by various methods, including remote control, infrared or magnetic triggers, pressure-sensitive bars or trip wires (victim-operated). In some cases, multiple IEDs are wired together in a daisy chain to attack a convoy of vehicles spread out along a roadway.

IEDs made by inexperienced designers or with substandard materials may fail to detonate, and in some cases, they actually detonate on either the maker or the emplacer of the device. Some groups, however, have been known to produce sophisticated devices constructed with components scavenged from conventional munitions and standard consumer electronics components, such as mobile phones, washing machine timers, pagers, or garage door openers. The sophistication of an IED depends on the training of the designer and the tools and materials available.

IEDs may use artillery shells or conventional high-explosive charges as their explosive load as well as homemade explosives. However, the threat exists that toxic chemical, biological, or radioactive (dirty bomb) material may be added to a device, thereby creating other life-threatening effects beyond the shrapnel, concussive blasts and fire normally associated with bombs. Chlorine liquid has been added to IEDs in Iraq, producing clouds of chlorine gas.

A **vehicle-borne IED**, or **VBIED**, is a military term for a car bomb or truck bomb but can be any type of transportation such as a bicycle, motorcycle, donkey, etc. They are typically employed by insurgents, and can carry a relatively large payload. They can also be detonated from a remote location. VBIEDs can create additional shrapnel through the destruction of the vehicle itself and use vehicle fuel as an incendiary weapon. The act of a person's being in this vehicle and detonating it is known as an SVBIED suicide.

Of increasing popularity among insurgent forces in Iraq is the house-borne IED, or HBIED from the common military practice of clearing houses; insurgents rig an entire house to detonate and collapse shortly after a clearing squad has entered.

21.2 Historical use

The fougasse was improvised for centuries, eventually inspiring factory-made land mines. Ernst Jünger mentions in his war memoir the systematic use of IEDs and booby traps to cover the retreat of German troops at the Somme region during the First World War. Another early example of coordinated large-scale use of IEDs was the Belarusian Rail War launched by Belarusian guerrillas against the Germans during World War II."[6]"[7] Both command-detonated and delayed-fuse IEDs were used to derail thousands of German trains during 1943–1944."[8]

21.2.1 Afghanistan

U.S. Marines with Explosive Ordnance Disposal (EOD) destroy an Improvised Explosive Device (IED) cache in southern Afghanistan in June 2010.

Starting six months before the invasion of Afghanistan by the USSR on 27 December 1979, the Afghan Mujahideen were supplied with large quantities of military supplies. Among those supplies were many types of anti-tank mines. The insurgents often removed the explosives from several foreign anti-tank mines, and combined the explosives in tin cooking-oil cans for a more powerful blast. By combining the explosives from several mines and placing them in tin cans, the insurgents made them more powerful, but sometimes also easier to detect by Soviet sappers using mine detectors. After an IED was detonated, the insurgents often used direct-fire weapons such as machine guns and rocket-propelled grenades to continue the attack.

21.2. HISTORICAL USE

Afghan insurgents operating far from the border with Pakistan did not have a ready supply of foreign anti-tank mines. They preferred to make IEDs from Soviet unexploded ordnance. The devices were rarely triggered by pressure fuses. They were almost always remotely detonated. Since the 2001 invasion of Afghanistan, the Taliban and its supporters have used IEDs against NATO and Afghan military and civilian vehicles. This has become the most common method of attack against NATO forces, with IED attacks increasing consistently year on year.

According to a report by the Homeland Security Market Research in the USA, the number of IEDs used in Afghanistan had increased by 400 percent since 2007 and the number of troops killed by them by 400 percent, and those wounded by 700 percent. It has been reported that IEDs are the number one cause of death among NATO troops in Afghanistan.[9]

A brigade commander said that sniffer dogs are the most reliable way of detecting IEDs.[10] However, statistical evidence gathered by the US Army Maneuver Support Center at Fort Leonard Wood, MO shows that the dogs are not the most effective means of detecting IEDs. The U.S. Army's 10th Mountain Division was the first unit to introduce explosive detection dogs[11] in southern Afghanistan. In less than two years the dogs discovered 15 tons of illegal munitions, IED's, and weapons.[12]

In July 2012 it was reported that "sticky bombs", magnetically adhesive IED's that were prevalent in the Iraq War, showed up in Afghanistan.[13][14]

21.2.2 India

IEDs are increasingly being used by Maoists in India.[15]

On 13 July 2011, three IEDs were used by the Insurgency in Jammu and Kashmir to carry out a coordinated attack on the city of Mumbai, killing 19 people and injuring 130 more.[16][17]

On 21 February 2013, two IEDs were used to carry out bombings in the Indian city of Hyderabad. The bombs exploded in Dilsukhnagar, a crowded shopping area of the city, within 150 metres of each other.[18]

On 17 April 2013, Two kilos of explosives used in Bangalore bomb blast at Malleshwaram area, leaving 16 injured and no fatalities. Intelligence sources have said the bomb was an Improvised Explosive Device or IED.[19]

On 21 May 2014, Indinthakarai village supporters of the Kudankulam Nuclear Power Plant were targeted by opponents using over half a dozen crude "country-made bombs". It was further reported that there had been at least four similar bombings in Tamil Nadu during the preceding year.[20]

On 28 December 2014, a minor explosion took place near the Coconut Grove restaurant at Church Street in Bangalore on Sunday around 8:30 pm. One woman was killed and another injured in the blast.[21]

During the 2016 Pathankot attack, several casualties came from IEDs.[22]

21.2.3 Iraq

A Stryker lies on its side following a buried IED blast in Iraq. (2007)

Controlled explosion of IED, US Army in Iraq

In the 2003–2011 Iraq War, IEDs have been used extensively against Coalition forces and by the end of 2007 they have been responsible for at least 64% of Coalition deaths in Iraq.[1]

Beginning in July 2003, the Iraqi insurgency used IEDs to target invading coalition vehicles. According to the Washington Post, 64% of U.S deaths in Iraq occurred due to IEDs.[23] A French study[24] showed that in Iraq, from March 2003 to November 2006, on a global 3,070 deaths in the US-led invading coalition soldiers, 1,257 were caused by IEDs, i.e. 41%. That is to say more than in the "normal fights" (1027 dead, 34%). Insurgents now use the bombs to target not only invading coalition vehicles but Iraqi police as well.

Common locations for placing these bombs on the ground include animal carcasses, soft drink cans, and boxes. Typically they explode underneath or to the side of the vehicle to cause the maximum amount of damage; however, as vehicle armor was improved on military vehicles, insurgents began placing IEDs in elevated positions such as on road signs, utility poles, or trees, in order to hit less protected areas.

IEDs in Iraq may be made with artillery or mortar shells or with varying amounts of bulk or homemade explosives. Early during the Iraq war, the bulk explosives were often obtained from stored munitions bunkers to include stripping landmines of their explosives.

Despite the increased armor, IEDs have been killing military personnel and civilians with greater frequency. May 2007 was the deadliest month for IED attacks thus far, with a reported 89 of the 129 invading coalition casualties coming from an IED attack.*[1] According to the Pentagon, 250,000 tons (out of 650,000 tons total) of Iraqi heavy ordnance were looted, providing a large supply of ammunition for the insurgents.

In October 2005, the UK government charged that Iran was supplying insurgents with the technological know-how to make shaped charge IEDs.*[25] Both Iranian and Iraqi government officials denied the allegations.*[26]*[27]

21.2.4 United Kingdom/Republic of Ireland

Oil-drum roadside IED removed from culvert in 1984

Throughout The Troubles, the Provisional IRA made extensive use of IEDs in their 1969–97 campaign. They used barrack buster mortars and remote controlled IEDs. Members of the IRA developed and counter-developed devices and tactics. IRA bombs became highly sophisticated, fea-

Wheelbarrow counter-IED robot on streets of Northern Ireland in 1978

turing anti-handling devices such as a mercury tilt switch or microswitches. These devices would detonate the bomb if it was moved in any way. Typically, the safety-arming device used was a clockwork Memopark timer, which armed the bomb up to 60 minutes after it was placed*[28] by completing an electrical circuit supplying power to the anti-handling device. Depending on the particular design (e.g., boobytrapped briefcase or car bomb) an independent electrical circuit supplied power to a conventional timer set for the intended time delay, e.g. 40 minutes. However, some electronic delays developed by IRA technicians could be set to accurately detonate a bomb weeks after it was hidden, which is what happened in the Brighton hotel bomb attack of 1984. Initially, bombs were detonated either by timer or by simple command wire. Later, bombs could be detonated by radio control. Initially, simple servos from radio-controlled aircraft were used to close the electrical circuit and supply power to the detonator. After the British developed jammers, IRA technicians introduced devices that required a sequence of pulsed radio codes to arm and detonate them. These were harder to jam.

Roadside bombs were extensively used by the IRA. Typically, a roadside bomb was placed in a drain or culvert along a rural road and detonated by remote control when British security forces vehicles were passing. As a result of the use of these bombs, the British military stopped transport by road in areas such as South Armagh, and used helicopter transport instead to avoid the danger.

Most IEDs used commercial or homemade explosives, although the use of Semtex-H smuggled in from Libya in the 1980s was also common from the mid-1980s onward. Bomb Disposal teams from 321 EOD manned by Ammunition Technicians were deployed in those areas to deal with the IED threat. The IRA also used secondary devices to catch British reinforcements sent in after an initial blast as occurred in the Warrenpoint Ambush. Between 1970 and 2005, the IRA detonated 19,000 improvised explosive devices (IEDs) in the Northern Ireland and Britain, an average of one every 17 hours for three and a half decades, arguably making it "the biggest terrorist bombing campaign in history".*[29]

In the early 1970s, at the height of the IRA campaign, the British Army unit tasked with rendering safe IEDs, 321 EOD, sustained significant casualties while engaged in bomb disposal operations. This mortality rate was far higher than other high risk occupations such as deep sea diving, and a careful review was made of how men were selected for EOD operations. The review recommended bringing in psychometric testing of soldiers to ensure those chosen had the correct mental preparation for high risk bomb disposal duties.

The IRA came up with ever more sophisticated designs and deployments of IEDs. Booby Trap or Victim Operated IEDs (VOIEDs), became commonplace. The IRA engaged in an ongoing battle to gain the upper hand in electronic warfare with remote controlled devices. The rapid changes in development led 321 EOD to employ specialists from DERA (now Dstl, an agency of the MOD), the Royal Signals, and Military Intelligence. This approach by the British army to fighting the IRA in Northern Ireland led to the development and use of most of the modern weapons, equipment and techniques now used by EOD Operators throughout the rest of the world today.

The bomb disposal operations were led by Ammunition Technicians and Ammunition Technical Officers from 321 EOD, and were trained at the Felix Centre at the Army School of Ammunition.

21.2.5 Lebanon

The Lebanese National Resistance Front, the Popular Front for the Liberation of Palestine, other resistance groups in Lebanon, and later Hezbollah, made extensive use of IEDs to resist Israeli forces after Israel's invasion of Lebanon in 1982. Israel withdrew from Beirut, Northern Lebanon, and Mount Lebanon in 1985, whilst maintaining its occupation of Southern Lebanon. Hezbollah frequently used IEDs to attack Israeli military forces in this area up until the Israeli withdrawal, and the liberation of Lebanon in May 2000.

One such bomb killed Israeli Brigadier General Erez Gerstein*[30] on February 28, 1999, the highest-ranking Israeli to die in Lebanon since Yekutiel Adam's death in 1982.

Also in the 2006 War in Lebanon, a Merkava Mark II tank was hit by a pre-positioned Hezbollah IED, killing all 4 IDF servicemen on board,*[31] the first of two IEDs to damage a Merkava tank.

21.2.6 Libya

Homemade IEDs are used extensively during the post-civil war violence in Libya, mostly in the city of Benghazi against police stations, cars or foreign embassies.*[32]*[33]*[34]

21.2.7 Nepal

IEDs were also widely used in the 10-years long civil war of the Maoists in Nepal, ranging from those bought from illicit groups in India and China, to self-made devices. Typically used devices were pressure cooker bombs, socket bombs, pipe bombs, bucket bombs, etc. The devices were used more for the act of terrorizing the urban population rather than for fatal causes, placed in front of governmental offices, street corners or road sides. Mainly, the home-made IEDs were responsible for destruction of majority of structures targeted by the Maoists and assisted greatly in spreading terror among the public.

21.2.8 Russia

IEDs have also been popular in Chechnya, where Russian forces were engaged in fighting with rebel elements. While no concrete statistics are available on this matter, bombs have accounted for many Russian deaths in both the First Chechen War (1994–1996) and the Second (1999–2008).

21.2.9 Syria

During the Syrian Civil War, militant insurgents were using IEDs to attack buses, trucks and tanks.*[35]*[36] Additionally, the Syrian Air Force has used barrel bombs to attack cities and other largely civilian targets. Such barrel bombs consist of barrels filled with high explosives, oil, and shrapnel, and are dropped from helicopters.*[37]*[38]

21.2.10 United States

In the 1995 Oklahoma City bombing, Timothy McVeigh and Terry Nichols built an IED with ammonium nitrate fertilizer, nitromethane, and stolen commercial explosives in a rental truck, with sandbags used to concentrate the explosive force in the desired direction. McVeigh detonated it next to the Alfred P. Murrah Federal Building, killing 168 people, 19 of whom were children.

In January 2011, a shaped pipe bomb was discovered and defused at a Martin Luther King Jr. memorial march in

Spokane, Washington. The FBI said that the bomb was specifically designed to cause maximum harm as the explosive device was, according to the *Los Angeles Times*, packed with fishing weights covered in rat poison, and may have been racially motivated. No one was injured during the event.

On April 15, 2013, as the annual Boston Marathon race was concluding, two bombs were detonated seconds apart close to the finish line. Initial FBI response indicated suspicion of IED pressure cooker bombs.

On September 17–19, 2016, several explosions occurred in Manhattan and New Jersey. The sources of the explosions were all found to be IEDs of various types, such as pressure cooker bombs and pipe bombs.

21.2.11 Vietnam

IEDs were used during the Vietnam War by the Viet Cong against land- and river-borne vehicles as well as personnel.*[39] They were commonly constructed using materials from unexploded American ordnance.*[40] Thirty-three percent of U.S. casualties in Vietnam and twenty-eight percent of deaths were officially attributed to mines; these figures include losses caused by both IEDs and commercially manufactured mines.*[41]

The *Grenade in a Can* was a simple and effective booby trap. A hand grenade with the safety pin removed and safety lever compressed was placed into a container such as a tin can, with a length of string or tripwire attached to the grenade. The can was fixed in place and the string was stretched across a path or doorway opening and firmly tied down. In alternative fashion, the string could be attached to the moving portion of a door or gate. When the grenade was pulled out of the can by a person or vehicle placing tension on the string, the spring-loaded safety lever would release and the grenade would explode.

The *rubber band grenade* was another booby trap. To make this device, a Viet Cong guerrilla would wrap a strong rubber band around the spring-loaded safety lever of a hand grenade and remove the pin. The grenade was then hidden in a hut. American and South Vietnamese soldiers would burn huts regularly to prevent them from being inhabited again, or to expose foxholes and tunnel entrances, which were frequently concealed within these structures. When a hut with the booby trap was torched, the rubber band on the grenade would melt, releasing the safety lever and blowing up the hut. This would often wound the soldiers with burning bamboo and metal fragments. This booby trap was also used to destroy vehicles when the modified grenade was placed in the fuel tank. The rubber band would be eaten away by the chemical action of the fuel, releasing the safety lever and detonating the grenade.

Another variant was the *Mason jar grenade*. The safety pin of hand grenades would be pulled and the grenades would be placed in glass Ball Mason jars, which would hold back the safety lever. The safety lever would release upon the shattering of the jar and the grenade would detonate. This particular variant was popular with helicopter warfare, and were used as improvised anti-personnel cluster bombs during air raids. They were easy to dump out of the flight door over a target, and the thick Ball Mason glass was resistant to premature shattering. They could also be partially filled with gasoline or jellied gasoline, Napalm, to add to their destructive nature.

21.3 Types

21.3.1 By warhead

The *Dictionary of Military and Associated Terms* (JCS Pub 1-02) includes two definitions for improvised devices: improvised explosive devices (IED) and improvised nuclear device (IND).*[42] These definitions address the *Nuclear* and *Explosive* in *CBRNe*. That leaves chemical, biological and radiological undefined. Four definitions have been created to build on the structure of the JCS definition. Terms have been created to standardize the language of first responders and members of the military and to correlate the operational picture.*[43]

Explosive

A device placed or fabricated in an improvised manner incorporating destructive, lethal, noxious, pyrotechnic, or incendiary chemicals and designed to destroy, incapacitate, harass, or distract. It may incorporate military stores, but is normally devised from non-military components.*[5]

Chemical

A device incorporating the toxic attributes of chemical materials designed to result in the dispersal of these toxic chemical materials for the purpose of creating a primary patho-physiological toxic effect (morbidity and mortality), or secondary psychological effect (causing fear and behavior modification) on a larger population. Such devices may be fabricated in a completely improvised manner or may be an improvised modification to an existing weapon.

Biological

A device incorporating biological materials designed to result in the dispersal of vector borne biological material for the purpose of creating a primary patho-physiological toxic effect (morbidity and mortality), or secondary psychological effect (causing fear and behavior modification) on a larger population. Such devices are fabricated in a completely improvised manner.

Radiological

A speculative device incorporating radioactive materials designed to result in the dispersal of radioactive material for the purpose of area denial and economic damage, and/or for the purpose of creating a primary patho-physiological toxic effect (morbidity and mortality), or secondary psychological effect (causing fear and behavior modification) on a larger population. Such devices may be fabricated in a completely improvised manner or may be an improvised modification to an existing nuclear weapon. Also called a Radiological Dispersion Device (RDD) or "dirty bomb".

Incendiary

A device making use of exothermic chemical reactions designed to result in the rapid spread of fire for the purpose of creating a primary patho-physiological effect (morbidity and mortality), or secondary psychological effect (causing fear and behavior modification) on a larger population or it may be used with the intent of gaining a tactical advantage. Such devices may be fabricated in a completely improvised manner or may be an improvised modification to an existing weapon. A common type of this is the Molotov cocktail.

Explosively formed penetrator/projectiles (EFPs)

IEDs have been deployed in the form of explosively formed projectiles (EFP), a special type of shaped charge that is effective at long standoffs from the target (50 meters or more), however they are not accurate at long distances. This is because of how they are produced. The large "slug" projected from the explosion has no stabilization because it has no tail fins and it does not spin like a bullet from a rifle. Without this stabilization the trajectory can not be accurately determined beyond 50 meters. An EFP is essentially a cylindrical shaped charge with a machined concave metal disc (often copper) in front, pointed inward. The force of the shaped charge turns the disc into a high velocity slug, capable of penetrating the armor of most vehicles in Iraq.

Improvised explosive device in Iraq. The concave copper shape on top defines an explosively formed penetrator/projectile

Directionally focused charges

Directionally focused charges (also known as directionally focused fragmentary charges) are very similar to EFPs, with the main difference being that the top plate is usually flat and not concave. It also is not made with machined copper but much cheaper cast or cut metal. The contents of the canister are usually nuts, bolts, ball bearings and other similar shrapnel products and explosive.

21.3.2 By delivery mechanism

Car

Main article: Car bomb

A vehicle may be laden with explosives, set to explode by remote control or by a passenger/driver, commonly known as a car bomb or vehicle-borne IED (VBIED, pronounced *vee-bid*). On occasion the driver of the car bomb may have been coerced into delivery of the vehicle under duress, a situation known as a proxy bomb. Distinguishing features are low-riding vehicles with excessive weight, vehicles with only one passenger, and ones where the interior of the vehicles look as if they have been stripped down and built back up. Car bombs can carry thousands of pounds of explosives and may be augmented with shrapnel to increase fragmen-

Artillery shells and gasoline cans discovered in the back of a pickup truck in Iraq

tation. The U.S. State Department has published a guide on car bomb awareness.[44]

Boat

Boats laden with explosives can be used against ships and areas connected to water. An early example of this type was the Japanese Shinyo suicide boats during World War II. The boats were laden with explosives and attempted to ram Allied ships, sometimes successfully, having sunk or severely damaged several American ships by war's end. Suicide bombers used a boat-borne IED to attack the USS Cole. US and UK troops have also been killed by boat-borne IEDs in Iraq.[24][45]

Animal

Main article: Animal-borne bomb attacks

Monkeys and war pigs were used as incendiaries around 1000 AD. More famously the "anti-tank dog" and "bat bomb" were developed during World War II. In recent times, a two-year-old child and seven other people were killed by explosives strapped to a horse in the town of Chita in Colombia[46] The carcasses of certain animals were also used to conceal explosive devices by the Iraqi insurgency.[47]

Collar

IEDs strapped to the necks of farmers have been used on at least three occasions by guerrillas in Colombia, as a way of extortion.[48][49] American pizza delivery man Brian Douglas Wells was killed in 2003 by an explosive fastened to his neck, purportedly under duress from the maker of the bomb.[50] In 2011 a schoolgirl in Sydney, Australia had a suspected collar bomb attached to her by an attacker in her home. The device was removed by police after a ten-hour operation and proved to be a hoax.[51]

Suicide

Suicide bombing usually refers to an individual wearing explosives and detonating them in order to kill others including themselves, a technique pioneered by LTTE (Tamil Tigers).[52] The bomber will conceal explosives on and around their person, commonly using a vest (or possibly a prosthetic[53]) and will use a timer or some other trigger to detonate the explosives. The logic behind such attacks is the belief that an IED delivered by a human has a greater chance of achieving success than any other method of attack. In addition, there is the psychological impact of fighters prepared to deliberately sacrifice themselves for their cause.[54]

Surgically implanted Main article: Surgically implanted explosive device

In May 2012 American counter-terrorism officials leaked their acquisition of documents describing the preparation and use of surgically implanted improvised explosive devices.[55][56][57] The devices were designed to evade detection. The devices were described as containing no metal, so they could not be detected by X-rays.

Security officials referred to bombs being surgically implanted into suicide bombers' "love handles".[55]

According to *The Daily Mirror* UK security officials at MI-6 asserted that female bombers could travel undetected carrying the explosive chemicals in otherwise standard breast implants.[58][59] The bomber would blow up the implanted explosives by injecting a chemical trigger.[57]

Rocket

Main article: Lob bomb

In 2008, rocket-propelled IEDs, dubbed *Improvised Rocket Assisted Munitions, Improvised Rocket Assisted Mortars* and *(IRAM)* by the military, came to be employed in numbers against U.S. forces in Iraq. They have been described as propane tanks packed with explosives and powered by 107 mm rockets.[60] They are similar to some Provisional IRA barrack buster mortars. New types of IRAMs including Volcano IRAM, are used during Syrian Civil War.[61]

Improvised Mortar Improvised mortar has been used by many insurgent groups including during civil war in Syria and Boko Haram insurgency.*[62] IRA used improvised mortars called barrack busters.

Improvised Artillery

Improvised artillery including *hell cannons* is used by rebel forces during Syrian Civil War.

21.3.3 By trigger mechanism

Wire

Command-wire improvised, explosive devices (CWIED) use an electrical firing cable that affords the user complete control over the device right up until the moment of initiation.*[54]

Radio

The trigger for a radio-controlled improvised explosive device (RCIED) is controlled by radio link. The device is constructed so that the receiver is connected to an electrical firing circuit and the transmitter operated by the perpetrator at a distance. A signal from the transmitter causes the receiver to trigger a firing pulse that operates the switch. Usually the switch fires an initiator; however, the output may also be used to remotely arm an explosive circuit. Often the transmitter and receiver operate on a matched coding system that prevents the RCIED from being initiated by spurious radio frequency signals.*[54] An RCIED can be triggered from any number of different mechanisms including car alarms, wireless door bells, cell phones, pagers and encrypted GMRS radios.*[54]

Cell phone

A radio-controlled IED (RCIED) incorporating a cell phone that is modified and connected to an electrical firing circuit. Cell phones operate in the UHF band in line of sight with base transceiver station (BTS) antennae sites. In the common scenario, receipt of a paging signal by phone is sufficient to initiate the IED firing circuit.*[54]

Victim-operated

Victim-operated improvised explosive devices (VOIED), also known as booby traps, are designed to function upon contact with a victim. VOIED switches are often well hidden from the victim or disguised as innocuous everyday objects. They are operated by means of movement. Switching methods include tripwire, pressure mats, spring-loaded release, push, pull or tilt. Common forms of VOIED include the under-vehicle IED (UVIED), improvised landmines, and mail bombs.*[54]

Infrared

The British accused Iran and Hezbollah of teaching Iraqi fighters to use infrared light beams to trigger IEDs. As the occupation forces became more sophisticated in interrupting radio signals around their convoys, the insurgents adapted their triggering methods.*[63] In some cases, when a more advanced method was disrupted, the insurgents regressed to using uninterruptible means, such as hard wires from the IED to detonator; however, this method is much harder to effectively conceal. It later emerged however, that these "advanced" IEDs were actually old IRA technology. The infrared beam method was perfected by the IRA in the early '90s after it acquired the technology from a botched undercover British Army operation. Many of the IEDs being used against the invading coalition forces in Iraq were originally developed by the British Army who unintentionally passed the information on to the IRA.*[64] The IRA taught their techniques to the Palestine Liberation Organisation and the knowledge spread to Iraq.*[65]

21.4 Counterefforts

A U.S. Marine in Iraq shown with a robot used for disposal of buried devices

Main article: Counter-IED efforts

Israeli IDF Caterpillar D9 armored bulldozer, which is used by the IDF Combat Engineering Corps for clearing heavy belly charges and booby-trapped buildings.

Counter-IED efforts are done primarily by military, law enforcement, diplomatic, financial, and intelligence communities and involve a comprehensive approach to countering the threat networks that employ IEDs, not just efforts to defeat the devices themselves.

21.4.1 Detection and disarmament

Because the components of these devices are being used in a manner not intended by their manufacturer, and because the method of producing the explosion is limited only by the science and imagination of the perpetrator, it is not possible to follow a step-by-step guide to detect and disarm a device that an individual has only recently developed. As such, explosive ordnance disposal (IEDD) operators must be able to fall back on their extensive knowledge of the first principles of explosives and ammunition, to try and deduce what the perpetrator has done, and only then to render it safe and dispose of or exploit the device. Beyond this, as the stakes increase and IEDs are emplaced not only to achieve the direct effect, but to deliberately target IEDD operators and cordon personnel, the IEDD operator needs to have a deep understanding of tactics to ensure he is neither setting up any of his team or the cordon troops for an attack, nor walking into one himself. The presence of chemical, biological, radiological, or nuclear (CBRN) material in an IED requires additional precautions. As with other missions, the EOD operator provides the area commander with an assessment of the situation and of support needed to complete the mission.

Military and law enforcement personnel from around the world have developed a number of render-safe procedures (RSPs) to deal with IEDs. RSPs may be developed as a result of direct experience with devices or by applied research designed to counter the threat. The supposed effectiveness of IED jamming systems, including vehicle- and personally-mounted systems, has caused IED technology to essentially regress to command-wire detonation methods.*[66] These are physical connections between the detonator and explosive device and cannot be jammed. However, these types of IEDs are more difficult to emplace quickly, and are more readily detected.

Military forces and law enforcement from India, Canada, United Kingdom, Israel, Spain, and the United States are at the forefront of counter-IED efforts, as all have direct experience in dealing with IEDs used against them in conflict or terrorist attacks. From the research and development side, programs such as the new Canadian Unmanned Systems Challenge will bring student groups together to invent an unmanned device to both locate IEDs and pinpoint the insurgents.*[67]

21.5 See also

- List of notable 3D printed weapons and parts
- Acetone peroxide
- Blast fishing
- Dragon Runner
- Improvised firearm
- JIEDDO
- Metalith

Types of device

- Barrel bomb
- Blast bomb
- Car bomb
- Fougasse
- Land mine
- Letter bomb
- Molotov cocktail
- Nail bomb
- Pipe bomb
- Pressure cooker bomb

- Radiological weapon
- Satchel charge
- Sidolówka Grenade
- Time bomb (explosive)

21.6 References

[1] iCasualties: OIF - Deaths by IED Archived January 13, 2009, at the Wayback Machine.

[2] "home.mytelus.com". home.mytelus.com. Retrieved 2012-05-11.

[3] "Suicide Terrorism: A Global Threat". Pbs.org. Retrieved 2009-10-18.

[4] "13 killed in blasts, arson in Sri Lanka". Chennai, India: Hindu.com. 2006-04-13. Retrieved 2009-10-18.

[5] *NATO Glossary of Terms and Definitions (AAP-6)* (PDF). North Atlantic Treaty Organization. 2010. p. 2-1-2.

[6] State Archival Service. "Historical background". *World War Two*. Republic of Belarus, Ministry of Justice, Department of Archives and Records Management. Retrieved 4 Dec 2008.

[7] "Belarus during the Great Patriotic War". *History*. belarus.by. Retrieved 4 Dec 2008.

[8] Stockfish, David; Yariv Eldar; Daniella HarPaz Mechnikov (1970). *Dokszyc-Parafianow Memorial Book — Belarus (Sefer Dokshitz-Parafianov)*. Tel Aviv: Association of Former Residents of Dokszyce-Parafianow in Israel. p. 274.

[9] "Combating the No. 1 killer of troops in Afghanistan". Afghanistan.blogs.cnn.com. 2010-05-06. Retrieved 2012-05-11.

[10] Johnson, Andrew (2010-01-10). "Taliban make 'undetectable' bombs out of wood". Independent.co.uk. Retrieved 2012-05-11.

[11] http://www.patriotdog.com/bomb-dog-services.html

[12] government contract GSO7F-5391P

[13] "Sticky bombs, like those used in Iraq, now appearing in Afghanistan".

[14] "Sticky bombs showing up in Afghanistan".

[15] Sethi, Aman (2010-04-04). "Troop fatality figures show changing Maoist strategy". Chennai, India: The Hindu.

[16] "Three blasts in Mumbai, 18 dead, over 130 injured". NDTV. Retrieved 17 July 2011.

[17] "Blasts: ATS claims good leads, suicide bomber ruled out". DD News. Retrieved 17 July 2011.

[18] http://www.dnaindia.com/india/report_hyderabad-blasts-indian-mujahideen-suspected-ammon 1803037

[19] NDTV, NDTV (April 17, 2013). "Bangalore blast: Two kilos of explosives used, say police; CCTV footage offers clues". *NDTV*. Retrieved April 17, 2013.

[20] Sudipto Mondal. "Explosions at village near Kudankulam plant: Reports". *Hindustan Times*. Retrieved 11 December 2014.

[21] "Minor explosion at Church Street in Bengaluru". *Deccan Herald*. Retrieved 29 December 2014.

[22] "Pathankot operation continues; 2 terrorists still holed up - Rediff.com India News".

[23] "More Attacks, Mounting Casualties". *The Washington Post*. September 30, 2007. Retrieved 2009-10-18.

[24] Jean-Pierre Steinhoffer : " Irak : les pertes de la Coalition par EEI ", in *le Casoar* January 2007.

[25] "Middle East | Iran 'behind attacks on British'". BBC News. 2005-10-05. Retrieved 2009-10-18.

[26] "Middle East | Blair warns Iran over Iraq bombs". BBC News. 2005-10-06. Retrieved 2009-10-18.

[27] "British Official Warns Iran Not to Meddle in Iraq". Nyjtimes.com. 2004-06-08. Retrieved 2009-10-18.

[28] Parry, Gareth; Pallister, David. *Timer clue to Brighton bombing*, The Guardian; 10 May 10, 1986

[29] "IRA TECHNOLOGY".

[30] Eiran, Ehud (May 2007). *The Essence of Longing: General Erez Gerstein and the War in Lebanon* (in Hebrew). Miskal — Yedioth Ahronoth Books and Chemed Books.

[31] Arkin, William M. (Aug 2007). "Divine Victory for Whom? Airpower in the 2006 Israel-Hezbollah War" (PDF). *Strategic Studies Quarterly*. Maxwell Air Force Base, Alabama: United States Air ForceAir Education and Training Command Air University. Winter 2007: 9. Retrieved 3 Dec 2008.

[32] IED Attack in Benghazi Embassy of the United States, Tripoli-Libya, 6 June 2012

[33] UK experts help Libya with IED detection Libya Herald, 1 October 2012

[34] IED explodes in front of Benghazi police station, injures 3 Tavernkeepers.com, 5 November 2012

[35] Syrian security forces set off Damascus bombs blamed on al-Qaida – defectors Guardian, 18 May 2012

[36] "Like Afghan Counterparts, Syrian Rebels Now Using IEDs". 25 July 2012.

[37] BBC, 5 February 2014

[38] BBC, 20 December 2013

[39] "Mine Warfare in South Vietnam". History.navy.mil. Retrieved 2009-10-18.

[40] "American Experience | Vietnam Online | Transcript | PBS". pbs.org. Retrieved 2009-10-18.

[41] "In Its Own Words". Hrw.org. Retrieved 2009-10-18.

[42] "JP 1-02 Department of Defense Dictionary of Military and Associated Terms" (PDF). Retrieved 2009-10-18.

[43] "CBRNe World pages" (PDF). Archived from the original (PDF) on March 25, 2009. Retrieved 2009-10-18.

[44] "When broken down vehicles go boom! - WikiLeaks".

[45] "UK | Iraq boat attack personnel named". BBC News. 2006-11-14. Retrieved 2009-10-18.

[46] "Americas | 'Horse bomb' hits Colombia town". BBC News. 2003-09-11. Retrieved 2009-10-18.

[47] Improvised Explosive Devices (IEDs) -Iraq GlobalSecurity.org

[48] "Americas | Experts defuse necklace bomb". BBC News. 2003-07-01. Retrieved 2009-10-18.

[49] "AMERICAS | 'Necklace' bomb halts Colombia talks". BBC News. 2000-05-16. Retrieved 2009-10-18.

[50] Caniglia, John (July 11, 2007). ""Brian Wells"Erie bombing 'victim' was in on bank robbery". *Plain Dealer*.

[51] "'Bomb' device attached to Mosman schoolgirl was a 'very, very elaborate hoax'". smh.com.au. 2011-08-04. Retrieved 4 August 2011.

[52] "IISS Armed Conflict Database". Acd.iiss.org. Retrieved 2009-10-18.

[53] "DHS Warns Of Pregnant Prosthetic Belly Bombings".

[54] Hunter, Major Chris (2008). *Eight Lives Down*. London: Corgi Books. ISBN 978-0-552-15571-7.

[55] Daniel Klaidman, Christopher Dickey (2012-05-14). "Ibrahim al-Asiri: The Body Bomb Menace". Daily Beast. Retrieved 2012-05-14. Newsweek has learned that U.S. intelligence officials circulated a secret report that laid out in vivid detail how doctors working for al-Asiri had developed the surgical technique. An American government source familiar with the report described it as 15 to 20 pages, single spaced, and replete with schematics and pictures. "It was almost like something you'd see in Scientific American," the source said. mirror

[56] David Pescovitz (2012-05-14). "You da bomb! (surgically-implanted explosives)". Boing boing. Retrieved 2012-05-14. According to Newsweek, US intelligence officials report that al Qaeda's explosives expert Ibrahim al-Asiri and medical doctors have been designing bombs to be surgically implanted into the bodies of suicide bombers. The idea is that the technique would somehow foil airport scanners. Gives a whole new meaning to the phrase, "You da bomb!" mirror

[57] Anissa Haddadi (2012-05-14). "Al-Qaida's 'Body Bombs' increase Fears of Global Attacks by Master Bomb-Maker Ibrahim Hassan Tali al-Asiri". International Business Times. Retrieved 2012-05-14. Experts and intelligence sources say the terrorists could use the powerful explosive pentaerythritol tetranitrate, known as PETN and insert it in the bodies of would-be suicide bombers. According to reports they would then be able to detonate the implanted explosives via injections. The bombs would not be detectable to airport body scanner, increasing risks of attacks similar to the 2011 September attack on the Twin Towers in New York and on the Pentagon. mirror

[58] "Breast bombers: Doctors trained to plant explosives inside chest of female suicide bombers". The Daily Mirror. 2012-05-14. Retrieved 2012-05-14. MI6 chiefs believe doctors have been trained to plant explosives inside the breasts of female suicide bombers. mirror

[59] Lines, Andy (2013-08-16). "Breast implants suicide bomb threat: Heathrow on high alert over "credible" intelligence". The Daily Mirror. Retrieved 2013-08-21. Security has been beefed up after intelligence al-Qaeda is plotting attacks on airlines flying out of London.

[60] Londoño, Ernesto (July 10, 2008). "U.S. Troops in Iraq Face A Powerful New Weapon: Use of Rocket-Propelled Bombs Spreads". Washington Post. p. A01.

[61] "A new type of Volcano rocket spotted in Idlib".

[62] https://www.youtube.com/watch?v=_wEEovjWZZk

[63] "Bomb Making Skills Spread Globally", *National Defense* magazine, June 2007 Archived August 14, 2007, at the Wayback Machine.

[64] Harkin, Greg; Elliott, Francis; Whitaker, Raymond (2005-10-16). "Revealed: IRA bombs killed eight British soldiers in Iraq, "This Britain". UK —Independent.co.uk". London: News.independent.co.uk. Retrieved 2009-10-18.

[65] Independent.ie (2010-04-09). "independent.ie". independent.ie. Retrieved 2012-05-11.

[66] John Pike. "Warlock Green / Warlock Red / AN/VLQ −9 or −10 SHORTSTOP Countermeasure". Globalsecurity.org. Retrieved 2009-10-18.

[67] "Messenger, Scott (2009-03-01). "The Unmanned Mission". Retrieved on 2009-03-26". Unlimitedmagazine.com. Retrieved 2009-10-18.

21.7 External links

- IED News at DefenceTalk

21.7. EXTERNAL LINKS

- Discussion of US and Taliban IED Strategies, Gareth Porter, The Real News Network
- CFR-TV Episode 7 – video of a blue VBIED detonated from a distance
- Transcript of PBS *Frontline* episode *Private Warriors*
- IED Definition Structure Applied to the CBRN Threats (p9-11)
- Strategy for Countering IEDs - Chris Hunter
- Clearing Bombs in Afghanistan - slideshow by *Life magazine*
- JKnIFE The Joint IED Defeat Organization (JIEDDO) Knowledge and Information Fusion Exchange (JKnIFE) *CAC Required

Chapter 22

Insensitive munition

Insensitive munitions are munitions that are designed to withstand stimuli representative of severe but credible accidents. The current range of stimuli are shock, (from bullets, fragments and shaped charge jets), heat (from fires or an adjacent thermal events) and adjacent detonating munitions. A munition can have its vulnerability reduced by a number of means used on their own or in combination such as a reduced vulnerability energetic material, design features, additions or changes to packaging etc.*[1] The munition must still retain its terminal effect and performance within acceptable parameters.

22.1 Description

Insensitive munitions (IM) will only burn (rather than explode) when subjected to fast or slow heating, bullets, shrapnel, shaped charges or the detonation of another nearby munition. The term refers to warheads, bombs, rocket motors, although different countries' armed forces may have their own definitions.

Due to "accidents, and the subsequent loss of human life, cost of repairing and replacing material, and the toll taken on operational readiness and capability, Insensitive Munitions (IM) improvements are mandated by law in the U.S." *[2]

Three approaches are taken when designing insensitive munitions: Firstly, the high energy device can be protected and transported with an external protection of some kind. Some munition shipping containers are designed to provide some protection and thermal insulation. Secondly, the chemistry of the high energy fill is chosen to provide a higher degree of stability, for example by using plastic bonded explosives. Lastly, the casings of high energy devices can be designed in such a way as to allow venting or some other form of pressure relief in a fire.

Beyond the three approaches above, other threats need addressing when designing IM, e.g., slow and fast cook-off, sympathetic detonation, bullet and fragment impact, and shaped charge jet impact. Extensive testing requirements for potential IM candidates to address these threats are extremely costly. Modeling programs are being designed to simulate the threat of bullet and fragment impact in an effort to reduce testing costs. One of the most promising methods that engineers and scientists within the U.S. Department of Defense (DoD) are employing to help to enhance IM performance is by using advanced multiphysics modeling programs.*[2] Also, another effort is underway developing 2-D numerical code that will simulate the threat of slow and fast cook-off.*[3]

22.2 Insensitive high explosives

Insensitive munitions are almost always filled with fire resistant, shock resistant **insensitive high explosives** (**IHE**) such as triaminotrinitrobenzene (TATB) or various insensitive explosive mixtures, or plastic/polymer-bonded explosives, which are similar to reactive materials. TATB particularly will not detonate if impacted by typical fragments or burned in a fire.

A new IHE called Insensitive Munitions Explosive (IMX-101), has been qualified and approved by the U.S. Army to replace trinitrotoluene (TNT). IMX-101 is said to have the "same lethality as traditional TNT, but is far less likely to explode if dropped, shot at or hit by a roadside bomb during transport" .*[4] This IHE has been tested and proven to be a safer alternative within large-caliber projectiles currently utilized by the Army and Marine Corps.

Other insensitive high explosives, are nitroguanidine, 1,1-diamino-2,2-dinitroethylene aka FOX-7, [[4,10-dinitro-2,6,8,12-tetraoxa-4,10-diazatetracyclo[5.5.0.05,9.03,11]-dodecane]] known as TEX.*[5]

IHEs often combine amino groups and nitro groups in the same molecule.

22.2.1 Origin

Following the 1966 Palomares B-52 crash and the 1968 Thule Air Base B-52 crash, concerns were raised by accident investigators about the high explosive used in the nuclear devices, which had detonated on impact. Efforts were started to find an explosive that was stable enough to withstand the forces involved in an aircraft accident.[6] The Lawrence Livermore National Laboratory developed the "Susan Test" —a standard test designed to simulate an aircraft accident by squeezing and nipping explosive material between metal surfaces of a test projectile. Following experiments with this device, the Los Alamos National Laboratory developed a new safer type of explosive, called insensitive high explosive (IHE), for use in U.S. nuclear weapons.[7]

IHE explosives can withstand impacts up to 1,500 feet per second (460 m/s), as opposed to conventional HE, which will detonate at only 100 feet per second (30 m/s).[8]

22.2.2 Use in nuclear weapons

Insensitive high explosives have been available to the United States military for use in its nuclear weapons since 1979—by 1991, 25% of the country's nuclear stockpile was using IHE.[9] Most modern American nuclear weapons, and at least those of the United Kingdom, are manufactured using insensitive munition designs. These are almost exclusively TATB plastic bonded explosive (LX-17-0 and PBX-9502). Conventional high explosives are still used in missiles and nuclear artillery shells where weight and volume is a factor (IHE by weight contains only two-thirds the energy of HE, so more is needed to achieve the same effect).[9]

22.3 See also

- Hexanitrostilbene
- Dunnite

22.4 References

[1] shrapnel

[2] DeFisher, S.; Pfau, D; Dyka, C. (2010). "Insensitive Munitions Modeling Improvement Efforts" (PDF).

[3] Aydemir, E.; Ulas, A. (2011). "A numerical study on the thermal initiation of a confined explosive in 2-D geometry". *Journal of Hazardous Materials*. **186** (1): 396–400. doi:10.1016/j.jhazmat.2010.11.015.

[4] Picatinny Public Affairs (2010) Army approves safer explosive to replace TNT. Retrieved from http://www.army.mil/-news/2010/08/11/43553-army-approves-safer-explosive-to-replace-tnt/

[5] E.-C. Koch, TEX - 4,10-Dinitro-2,6,8,12-tetraoxa-4,10-diazatetracyclo[5.5.0.05,9.03,11]-dodecane, *Propellants Explos. Pyrotech.* **2015**,40

[6] Jonas A. Zukas; William P. Walters (2002). *Explosive Effects and Applications*. Springer. pp. 305–307. ISBN 0-387-95558-5.

[7] Nathan E. Busch (2004). *No end in sight*. University Press of Kentucky. pp. 50–51. ISBN 0-8131-2323-2.

[8] Sidney David Drell (2007). *Nuclear weapons, scientists, and the post-Cold War challenge*. World Scientific. pp. 147–150. ISBN 981-256-896-4.

[9] "How Safe is Safe?". *Bulletin of Atomic Scientists*. April 1991. pp. 34–40.

22.5 External links

- History of Insensitive Munition by Ray Beauregard
- Global Security
- Shrapnel

Chapter 23

Chemical explosive

The vast majority of explosives are **chemical explosives**. Explosives usually have less potential energy than fuels, but their high rate of energy release produces a great blast pressure. TNT has a detonation velocity of 6,940 m/s compared to 1,680 m/s for the detonation of a pentane-air mixture, and the 0.34-m/s stoichiometric flame speed of gasoline combustion in air.

The properties of the explosive indicate the class into which it falls. In some cases explosives can be made to fall into either class by the conditions under which they are initiated. In sufficiently large quantities, almost all low explosives can undergo a Deflagration to Detonation Transition (DDT). For convenience, low and high explosives may be differentiated by the shipping and storage classes.

23.1 Chemical explosive reaction

A chemical explosive is a compound or mixture which, upon the application of heat or shock, decomposes or rearranges with extreme rapidity, yielding much gas and heat. Many substances not ordinarily classed as explosives may do one, or even two, of these things. For example, at high temperatures (> 2000 °C) a mixture of nitrogen and oxygen can be made to react rapidly and yield the gaseous product nitric oxide; yet the mixture is not an explosive since it does not evolve heat, but rather absorbs heat.

$$N_2 + O_2 \rightarrow 2\,NO - 43{,}200 \text{ calories (or 180 kJ)}$$
per mole of N_2

For a chemical to be an explosive, it must exhibit all of the following:

- Rapid expansion (i.e., rapid production of gases or rapid heating of surroundings)
- Evolution of heat
- Rapidity of reaction
- Initiation of reaction
- Blast Theory

23.2 Sensitiser

A sensitiser is a powdered or fine particulate material that is sometimes used to create voids that aid in the initiation or propagation of the detonation wave. It may be as high-tech as glass beads or as simple as seeds.

23.3 Measurement of chemical explosive reaction

The development of new and improved types of ammunition requires a continuous program of research and development. Adoption of an explosive for a particular use is based upon both proving ground and service tests. Before these tests, however, preliminary estimates of the characteristics of the explosive are made. The principles of thermochemistry are applied for this process.

Thermochemistry is concerned with the changes in internal energy, principally as heat, in chemical reactions. An explosion consists of a series of reactions, highly exothermic, involving decomposition of the ingredients and recombination to form the products of explosion. Energy changes in explosive reactions are calculated either from known chemical laws or by analysis of the products.

For most common reactions, tables based on previous investigations permit rapid calculation of energy changes. Products of an explosive remaining in a closed calorimetric bomb (a constant-volume explosion) after cooling the bomb back to room temperature and pressure are rarely those present at the instant of maximum temperature and pressure. Since only the final products may be analyzed conveniently, indirect or theoretical methods are often used to determine the maximum temperature and pressure values.

Some of the important characteristics of an explosive that can be determined by such theoretical computations are:

- Oxygen balance
- Heat of explosion or reaction
- Volume of products of explosion
- Potential of the explosive

23.4 Balancing chemical explosion equations

In order to assist in balancing chemical equations, an order of priorities is presented in table 1. Explosives containing C, H, O, and N and/or a metal will form the products of reaction in the priority sequence shown. Some observation you might want to make as you balance an equation:

- The progression is from top to bottom; you may skip steps that are not applicable, but you never back up.
- At each separate step there are never more than two compositions and two products.
- At the conclusion of the balancing, elemental nitrogen, oxygen, and hydrogen are always found in diatomic form.

Example, TNT:

$C_6H_2(NO_2)_3CH_3: \rightarrow : 7C + 5H + 3N + 6O$

Using the order of priorities in table 1, priority 4 gives the first reaction products:

$7C + 6O \rightarrow 6CO$ with one mol of carbon remaining

Next, since all the oxygen has been combined with the carbon to form CO, priority 7 results in:

$3N \rightarrow 1.5N_2$

Finally, priority 9 results in: $5H \rightarrow 2.5H_2$

The balanced equation, showing the products of reaction resulting from the detonation of TNT is:

$C_6H_2(NO_2)_3CH_3 \rightarrow 6CO + 2.5H_2 + 1.5N_2 + C$

Notice that partial moles are permitted in these calculations. The number of moles of gas formed is 10. The product carbon is a solid.

23.5 Example of thermochemical calculations

The PETN reaction will be examined as an example of thermo-chemical calculations.

PETN: $C(CH_2ONO_2)_4$

Molecular weight = 316.15 g/mol

Heat of formation = 119.4 kcal/mol

(1) Balance the chemical reaction equation. Using table 1, priority 4 gives the first reaction products:

$5C + 12O \rightarrow 5CO + 7O$

Next, the hydrogen combines with remaining oxygen:

$8H + 7O \rightarrow 4H_2O + 3O$

Then the remaining oxygen will combine with the CO to form CO and CO_2.

$5CO + 3O \rightarrow 2CO + 3CO_2$

Finally the remaining nitrogen forms in its natural state (N_2).

$4N \rightarrow 2N_2$

The balanced reaction equation is:

$C(CH_2ONO_2)_4 \rightarrow 2CO + 4H_2O + 3CO_2 + 2N_2$

(2) Determine the number of molar volumes of gas per mole. Since the molar volume of one gas is equal to the molar volume of any other gas, and since all the products of the PETN reaction are gaseous, the resulting number of molar volumes of gas (N_m) is:

$N_m = 2 + 4 + 3 + 2 = 11\ V_{molar}/mol$

(3) Determine the potential (capacity for doing work). If the total heat liberated by an explosive under constant volume conditions (Q_m) is converted to the equivalent work units, the result is the potential of that explosive.

The heat liberated at constant volume (Q_{mv}) is equivalent to the heat liberated at constant pressure (Q_{mp}) plus that heat converted to work in expanding the surrounding medium. Hence, $Q_{mv} = Q_{mp}$ + work (converted).

a. $Q_{mp} = Q_{fi}$ (products) $- Q_{fk}$ (reactants)

where: Q_f = heat of formation (see table 1)

For the PETN reaction:

$Q_{mp} = 2(26.343) + 4(57.81) + 3(94.39) - (119.4) = 447.87$ kcal/mol

(If the compound produced a metallic oxide, that heat of formation would be included in Q_{mp}.)

b. Work $= 0.572 N_m = 0.572(11) = 6.292$ kcal/mol

As previously stated, Q_{mv} converted to equivalent work units is taken as the potential of the explosive.

c. Potential $J = Q_{mv}$ $(4.185 \times 10^6$ kg)(MW) $= 454.16$ (4.185×10^6) $316.15 = 6.01 \times 10^6$ J kg

This product may then be used to find the relative strength (RS) of PETN, which is

d. RS = Pot (PETN) = 6.01×10^6 = 2.21 Pot (TNT) 2.72×10^6

23.6 References

Chapter 24

Nuclear explosive

See also: Nuclear Weapon

A **nuclear explosive** is an explosive device that derives its energy from nuclear reactions. Almost all nuclear explosive devices that have been designed and produced are nuclear weapons intended for warfare.

Other, non-warfare, applications for nuclear explosives have occasionally been proposed. For example, nuclear pulse propulsion is a form of spacecraft propulsion that would use nuclear explosives to provide impulse to a spacecraft. A similar application is the proposal to use nuclear explosives for asteroid deflection. From 1958 to 1965 the United States government ran a project to design a nuclear explosive powered nuclear pulse rocket called Project Orion. Never built, this vessel would use repeated nuclear explosions to propel itself and was considered surprisingly practical. It is thought to be a feasible design for interstellar travel.

The 1962 Sedan nuclear test formed a crater 100 m (330 ft) deep with a diameter of about 390 m (1,300 ft), as a means of investigating the possibilities of using peaceful nuclear explosions for large-scale earth moving.

Nuclear explosives were once considered for use in large-scale excavation. A nuclear explosion could be used to create a harbor, or a mountain pass, or possibly large underground cavities for use as storage space. It was thought that detonating a nuclear explosive in oil-rich rock could make it possible to extract more from the deposit, e.g. note the Canadian Project Oilsand. From 1958 to 1973 the U. S government exploded 28 nuclear test-shots in a project called the Operation Plowshare. The purpose of the operation was to use peaceful nuclear explosions for moving and lifting enormous amounts of earth and rock during construction projects such as building reservoirs. The Soviet Union conducted a much more vigorous program of 122 nuclear tests, some with multiple devices, between 1965 and 1989 under the auspices of Program No. 7-Nuclear Explosions for the National Economy.

As controlled nuclear fusion has proven difficult to use as an energy source, an alternate proposal for producing fusion power has been to detonate nuclear fusion explosives inside very large underground chambers and then using the heat produced, which would be absorbed by a molten salt coolant which would also absorb neutrons. The 1970s PACER (fusion) project investigated fusion detonation as a power source.

Failure to meet objectives, along with the realization of the dangers of nuclear fallout and other residual radioactivity, and with the enactment of various agreements such as the Partial Test Ban Treaty and the Outer Space Treaty, has led to the termination of most of these programs.

24.1 External links

- Nuclear Weapons Frequently Asked Questions

Chapter 25

Nuclear weapon

"A-bomb" redirects here. For other uses, see A-bomb (disambiguation).

The mushroom cloud of the atomic bombing of the Japanese city of Nagasaki on August 9, 1945 rose some 11 miles (18 km) above the bomb's hypocenter.

A **nuclear weapon** is an explosive device that derives its destructive force from nuclear reactions, either fission (fission bomb) or a combination of fission and fusion (thermonuclear weapon). Both reactions release vast quantities of energy from relatively small amounts of matter. The first test of a fission ("atomic") bomb released the same amount of energy as approximately 20,000 tons of TNT (84 TJ). The first thermonuclear ("hydrogen") bomb test released the same amount of energy as approximately 10 million tons of TNT (42 PJ).

A thermonuclear weapon weighing little more than 2,400 pounds (1,100 kg) can produce an explosive force comparable to the detonation of more than 1.2 million tons of TNT (5.0 PJ).*[1] A nuclear device no larger than traditional bombs can devastate an entire city by blast, fire, and radiation. Nuclear weapons are considered weapons of mass destruction, and their use and control have been a major focus of international relations policy since their debut.

Nuclear weapons have been used twice in nuclear warfare, both times by the United States against Japan near the end of World War II. On August 6, 1945, the U.S. Army Air Forces detonated a uranium gun-type fission bomb nicknamed "Little Boy" over the Japanese city of Hiroshima; three days later, on August 9, the U.S. Army Air Forces detonated a plutonium implosion-type fission bomb codenamed "Fat Man" over the Japanese city of Nagasaki. The bombings resulted in the deaths of approximately 200,000 civilians and military personnel from acute injuries sustained from the explosions.*[2] The ethics of the bombings and their role in Japan's surrender remain the subject of scholarly and popular debate.

Since the atomic bombings of Hiroshima and Nagasaki, nuclear weapons have been detonated on over two thousand occasions for the purposes of testing and demonstration. Only a few nations possess such weapons or are suspected of seeking them. The only countries known to have detonated nuclear weapons—and acknowledge possessing them—are (chronologically by date of first test) the United States, the Soviet Union (succeeded as a nuclear power by Russia), the United Kingdom, France, the People's Republic of China, India, Pakistan, and North Korea. Israel is also believed to possess nuclear weapons, though in a policy of deliberate ambiguity, it does not acknowledge having them. Germany, Italy, Turkey, Belgium and the Netherlands are nuclear weapons sharing states.*[3]*[4]*[5]

The nuclear non-proliferation treaty aimed to reduce the spread of nuclear weapons, but its effectiveness has been questioned, and political tensions remained high in the 1970s and 1980s. As of 2016, 16,000 nuclear weapons are stored at sites in 14 countries and many are ready for immediate use. Modernisation of weapons continues to occur.*[6]

25.1 Types

Main article: Nuclear weapon design

There are two basic types of nuclear weapons: those that

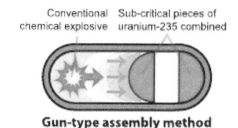

Gun-type assembly method

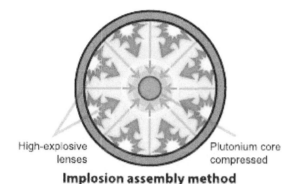

Implosion assembly method

The two basic fission weapon designs

derive the majority of their energy from nuclear fission reactions alone, and those that use fission reactions to begin nuclear fusion reactions that produce a large amount of the total energy output.

25.1.1 Fission weapons

All existing nuclear weapons derive some of their explosive energy from nuclear fission reactions. Weapons whose explosive output is exclusively from fission reactions are commonly referred to as **atomic bombs** or **atom bombs** (abbreviated as **A-bombs**). This has long been noted as something of a misnomer, as their energy comes from the nucleus of the atom, just as it does with fusion weapons.

In fission weapons, a mass of fissile material (enriched uranium or plutonium) is assembled into a supercritical mass —the amount of material needed to start an exponentially growing nuclear chain reaction—either by shooting one piece of sub-critical material into another (the "gun" method) or by compressing using explosive lenses a sub-critical sphere of material using chemical explosives to many times its original density (the "implosion" method). The latter approach is considered more sophisticated than the former and only the latter approach can be used if the fissile material is plutonium.

A major challenge in all nuclear weapon designs is to ensure that a significant fraction of the fuel is consumed before the weapon destroys itself. The amount of energy released by fission bombs can range from the equivalent of just under a ton to upwards of 500,000 tons (500 kilotons) of TNT (4.2 to 2.1×10^8 GJ).*[7]

All fission reactions necessarily generate fission products, the radioactive remains of the atomic nuclei split by the fission reactions. Many fission products are either highly radioactive (but short-lived) or moderately radioactive (but long-lived), and as such are a serious form of radioactive contamination if not fully contained. Fission products are the principal radioactive component of nuclear fallout.

The most commonly used fissile materials for nuclear weapons applications have been uranium-235 and plutonium-239. Less commonly used has been uranium-233. Neptunium-237 and some isotopes of americium may be usable for nuclear explosives as well, but it is not clear that this has ever been implemented, and even their plausible use in nuclear weapons is a matter of scientific dispute.*[8]

25.1.2 Fusion weapons

Main article: Thermonuclear weapon

The other basic type of nuclear weapon produces a large proportion of its energy in nuclear fusion reactions. Such fusion weapons are generally referred to as **thermonuclear weapons** or more colloquially as **hydrogen bombs** (abbreviated as **H-bombs**), as they rely on fusion reactions between isotopes of hydrogen (deuterium and tritium). All such weapons derive a significant portion, and sometimes a majority, of their energy from fission. This is because a fission reaction is required as a "trigger" for the fusion reactions, and the fusion reactions can themselves trigger additional fission reactions.*[9]

Only six countries—United States, Russia, United Kingdom, People's Republic of China, France and India—have conducted thermonuclear weapon tests. (Whether India has detonated a "true", multi-staged thermonuclear weapon is controversial.)*[10] North Korea claims to have tested a fusion weapon as of January 2016, though this claim is disputed.*[11] Thermonuclear weapons are considered much more difficult to successfully design and execute than prim-

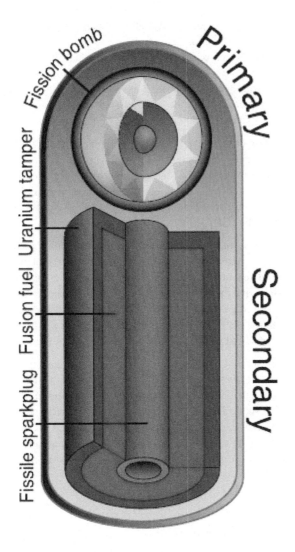

The basics of the Teller–Ulam design for a hydrogen bomb: a fission bomb uses radiation to compress and heat a separate section of fusion fuel.

known as a "stage", with the fission bomb as the "primary" and the fusion capsule as the "secondary". In large, megaton-range hydrogen bombs, about half of the yield comes from the final fissioning of depleted uranium.*[7]

Virtually all thermonuclear weapons deployed today use the "two-stage" design described above, but it is possible to add additional fusion stages—each stage igniting a larger amount of fusion fuel in the next stage. This technique can be used to construct thermonuclear weapons of arbitrarily large yield, in contrast to fission bombs, which are limited in their explosive force. The largest nuclear weapon ever detonated, the Tsar Bomba of the USSR, which released an energy equivalent of over 50 megatons of TNT (210 PJ), was a three-stage weapon. Most thermonuclear weapons are considerably smaller than this, due to practical constraints from missile warhead space and weight requirements.*[12]

Edward Teller, often referred to as the "father of the hydrogen bomb"

itive fission weapons. Almost all of the nuclear weapons deployed today use the thermonuclear design because it is more efficient.

Thermonuclear bombs work by using the energy of a fission bomb to compress and heat fusion fuel. In the Teller-Ulam design, which accounts for all multi-megaton yield hydrogen bombs, this is accomplished by placing a fission bomb and fusion fuel (tritium, deuterium, or lithium deuteride) in proximity within a special, radiation-reflecting container. When the fission bomb is detonated, gamma rays and X-rays emitted first compress the fusion fuel, then heat it to thermonuclear temperatures. The ensuing fusion reaction creates enormous numbers of high-speed neutrons, which can then induce fission in materials not normally prone to it, such as depleted uranium. Each of these components is

Fusion reactions do not create fission products, and thus contribute far less to the creation of nuclear fallout than fission reactions, but because all thermonuclear weapons contain at least one fission stage, and many high-yield thermonuclear devices have a final fission stage, thermonuclear weapons can generate at least as much nuclear fallout as fission-only weapons.

25.1.3 Other types

Main articles: boosted fission weapon, neutron bomb, and radiological bomb

There are other types of nuclear weapons as well. For example, a boosted fission weapon is a fission bomb that increases its explosive yield through a small amount of fusion reactions, but it is not a fusion bomb. In the boosted bomb, the neutrons produced by the fusion reactions serve primarily to increase the efficiency of the fission bomb. There are two types of boosted fission bomb: internally boosted, in which a deuterium-tritium mixture is injected into the bomb core, and externally boosted, in which concentric shells of lithium-deuteride and depleted uranium are layered on the outside of the fission bomb core.

Some weapons are designed for special purposes; a neutron bomb is a thermonuclear weapon that yields a relatively small explosion but a relatively large amount of neutron radiation; such a device could theoretically be used to cause massive casualties while leaving infrastructure mostly intact and creating a minimal amount of fallout. The detonation of any nuclear weapon is accompanied by a blast of neutron radiation. Surrounding a nuclear weapon with suitable materials (such as cobalt or gold) creates a weapon known as a salted bomb. This device can produce exceptionally large quantities of long-lived radioactive contamination. It has been conjectured that such a device could serve as a "doomsday weapon" because such a large quantity of radioactivities with half-lives of decades, lifted into the stratosphere where wind currents would distribute it around the globe, would make all life on the planet extinct.

In connection with the Strategic Defense Initiative, research into the Nuclear pumped laser was conducted under the Dod program Project Excalibur but this did not result in a working weapon. The concept involves the tapping of the energy of an exploding nuclear bomb to power a single-shot laser which is directed at a distant target.

During the Starfish Prime high-altitude nuclear test in 1962, an unexpected effect was produced which is called a Nuclear electromagnetic pulse. This is an intense flash of electromagnetic energy produced by a rain of high energy electrons which in turn are produced by a nuclear bomb's gamma rays. This flash of energy can permanently destroy or disrupt electronic equipment if insufficiently shielded. It has been proposed to use this effect to disable an enemy's military and civilian infrastructure as an adjunct to other nuclear or conventional military operations against that enemy. Because the effect is produced by very high altitude nuclear detonations, it can produce damage to electronics over a very wide, even continental, geographical area.

Research has been done into the possibility of pure fusion bombs: nuclear weapons that consist of fusion reactions without requiring a fission bomb to initiate them. Such a device might provide a simpler path to thermonuclear weapons than one that required development of fission weapons first, and pure fusion weapons would create significantly less nuclear fallout than other thermonuclear weapons, because they would not disperse fission products. In 1998, the United States Department of Energy divulged that the United States had " made a substantial investment" in the past to develop pure fusion weapons, but that, "The U.S. does not have and is not developing a pure fusion weapon", and that, "No credible design for a pure fusion weapon resulted from the DOE investment".*[13]

Antimatter, which consists of particles resembling ordinary matter particles in most of their properties but having opposite electric charge, has been considered as a trigger mechanism for nuclear weapons.*[14] A major obstacle is the difficulty of producing antimatter in large enough quantities, and there is no evidence that it is feasible beyond the military domain.*[15] However, the U.S. Air Force funded studies of the physics of antimatter in the Cold War, and began considering its possible use in weapons, not just as a trigger, but as the explosive itself.*[16] A fourth generation nuclear weapon design is related to, and relies upon, the same principle as Antimatter-catalyzed nuclear pulse propulsion.*[17]

Most variation in nuclear weapon design is for the purpose of achieving different yields for different situations, and in manipulating design elements to attempt to minimize weapon size.*[7]

25.2 Weapons delivery

See also: Nuclear weapons delivery, nuclear triad, Strategic bomber, Intercontinental ballistic missile, and Submarine-launched ballistic missile

Nuclear weapons delivery—the technology and systems used to bring a nuclear weapon to its target—is an important aspect of nuclear weapons relating both to nuclear weapon design and nuclear strategy. Additionally, development and maintenance of delivery options is among the most resource-intensive aspects of a nuclear weapons program: according to one estimate, deployment costs accounted for 57% of the total financial resources spent by the United States in relation to nuclear weapons since 1940.*[18]

Historically the first method of delivery, and the method used in the two nuclear weapons used in warfare, was as a gravity bomb, dropped from bomber aircraft. This is usually the first method that countries developed, as it does not place many restrictions on the size of the weapon and *weapon miniaturization* requires considerable weapons de-

The first nuclear weapons were gravity bombs, such as this "Fat Man" weapon dropped on Nagasaki, Japan. They were very large and could only be delivered by heavy bomber aircraft

A demilitarized and commercial launch of the Russian Strategic Rocket Forces R-36 ICBM; also known by the NATO reporting name: SS-18 Satan. Upon its first fielding in the late 1960s, the SS-18 remains the single highest throw weight missile delivery system ever built.

sign knowledge. It does, however, limit attack range, response time to an impending attack, and the number of weapons that a country can field at the same time.

With the advent of miniaturization, nuclear bombs can be delivered by both strategic bombers and tactical fighter-bombers, allowing an air force to use its current fleet with little or no modification. This method may still be considered the primary means of nuclear weapons delivery; the majority of U.S. nuclear warheads, for example, are free-fall gravity bombs, namely the B61.*[7]

Montage of an inert test of a United States Trident SLBM (submarine launched ballistic missile), from submerged to the terminal, or re-entry phase, of the multiple independently targetable reentry vehicles

More preferable from a strategic point of view is a nuclear weapon mounted onto a missile, which can use a ballistic trajectory to deliver the warhead over the horizon. Although even short-range missiles allow for a faster and less vulnerable attack, the development of long-range intercontinental ballistic missiles (ICBMs) and submarine-launched ballistic missiles (SLBMs) has given some nations the ability to plausibly deliver missiles anywhere on the globe with a high likelihood of success.

More advanced systems, such as multiple independently targetable reentry vehicles (MIRVs), can launch multiple warheads at different targets from one missile, reducing the chance of a successful missile defense. Today, missiles are most common among systems designed for delivery of nuclear weapons. Making a warhead small enough to fit onto a missile, though, can be difficult.*[7]

Tactical weapons have involved the most variety of delivery types, including not only gravity bombs and missiles but also artillery shells, land mines, and nuclear depth charges and torpedoes for anti-submarine warfare. An atomic mortar was also tested at one time by the United States. Small, two-man portable tactical weapons (somewhat misleadingly referred to as suitcase bombs), such as the Special Atomic Demolition Munition, have been developed, although the difficulty of combining sufficient yield with portability limits their military utility.*[7]

25.3 Nuclear strategy

Main articles: Nuclear strategy and Deterrence theory
See also: Nuclear peace, Essentials of Post–Cold War Deterrence, Single Integrated Operational Plan, nuclear warfare, and On Thermonuclear War

Nuclear warfare strategy is a set of policies that deal with preventing or fighting a nuclear war. The policy of trying to prevent an attack by a nuclear weapon from another country by threatening nuclear retaliation is known as the strategy of nuclear deterrence. The goal in deterrence is to always maintain a second strike capability (the ability of a country to respond to a nuclear attack with one of its own) and potentially to strive for first strike status (the ability to completely destroy an enemy's nuclear forces before they could retaliate). During the Cold War, policy and military theorists in nuclear-enabled countries worked out models of what sorts of policies could prevent one from ever being attacked by a nuclear weapon, and developed weapon game theory models that create the greatest and most stable deterrence conditions.

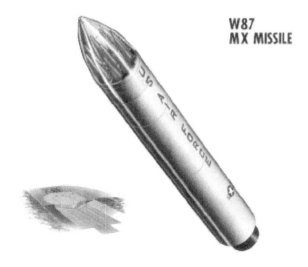

The now decommissioned United States' Peacekeeper missile was an ICBM developed to entirely replace the minuteman missile in the late 1980s. Each missile, like the heavier lift Russian SS-18 Satan, could contain up to ten nuclear warheads (shown in red), each of which could be aimed at a different target. A factor in the development of MIRVs was to make complete missile defense very difficult for an enemy country.

Different forms of nuclear weapons delivery (see above) allow for different types of nuclear strategies. The goals of any strategy are generally to make it difficult for an enemy to launch a pre-emptive strike against the weapon system and difficult to defend against the delivery of the weapon during a potential conflict. Sometimes this has meant keeping the weapon locations hidden, such as deploying them on submarines or land mobile transporter erector launchers whose locations are very hard for an enemy to track, and other times, this means protecting them by burying them in hardened missile silo bunkers.

Other components of nuclear strategies have included using missile defense (to destroy the missiles before they land) or implementation of civil defense measures (using early-warning systems to evacuate citizens to safe areas before an attack).

Note that weapons designed to threaten large populations, or to generally deter attacks are known as *strategic weapons*. Weapons designed for use on a battlefield in military situations are called *tactical weapons*.

There are critics of the very idea of nuclear strategy for waging nuclear war who have suggested that a nuclear war between two nuclear powers would result in mutual annihilation. From this point of view, the significance of nuclear weapons is purely to deter war because any nuclear war would immediately escalate out of mutual distrust and fear, resulting in mutually assured destruction. This threat of national, if not global, destruction has been a strong motivation for anti-nuclear weapons activism.

Critics from the peace movement and within the military establishment have questioned the usefulness of such weapons in the current military climate. According to an advisory opinion issued by the International Court of Justice in 1996, the use of (or threat of use of) such weapons would generally be contrary to the rules of international law applicable in armed conflict, but the court did not reach an opinion as to whether or not the threat or use would be lawful in specific extreme circumstances such as if the survival of the state were at stake.

Another deterrence position in nuclear strategy is that nuclear proliferation can be desirable. This view argues that, unlike conventional weapons, nuclear weapons successfully deter all-out war between states, and they succeeded in doing this during the Cold War between the U.S. and the Soviet Union.*[19] In the late 1950s and early 1960s, Gen. Pierre Marie Gallois of France, an adviser to Charles DeGaulle, argued in books like *The Balance of Terror: Strategy for the Nuclear Age* (1961) that mere possession of a nuclear arsenal, what the French called the *force de frappe*, was enough to ensure deterrence, and thus concluded that the spread of nuclear weapons could increase international stability. Some very prominent neo-realist scholars, such as the late Kenneth Waltz, formerly a Political Science at UC Berkeley and Adjunct Senior Research Scholar at Columbia University, and John Mearsheimer of University of Chicago, have also argued along the lines of Gallois. Specifically, these scholars have advocated some forms of nuclear proliferation, arguing that it would decrease the likelihood of total war, especially in troubled regions of the world where there exists a unipolar nuclear weapon state. Aside from the public opinion that opposes proliferation in any form, there are two schools of thought on the matter: those, like Mearsheimer, who favor selective proliferation,*[20] and those of Kenneth Waltz, who was somewhat more non-interventionist.*[21]*[22]

The threat of potentially suicidal terrorists possessing nuclear weapons (a form of nuclear terrorism) complicates the decision process. The prospect of mutually assured destruction may not deter an enemy who expects to die in the confrontation. Further, if the initial act is from a stateless terrorist instead of a sovereign nation, there is no fixed nation or fixed military targets to retaliate against. It has been argued by the New York Times, especially after the September 11, 2001 attacks, that this complication is the sign of the next age of nuclear strategy, distinct from the relative stability of the Cold War.*[23] In 1996, the United States adopted a policy of allowing the targeting of its nuclear weapons at terrorists armed with weapons of mass destruction.*[24]

Robert Gallucci, president of the John D. and Catherine T. MacArthur Foundation, argues that although traditional deterrence is not an effective approach toward terrorist groups bent on causing a nuclear catastrophe, Gallucci believes that "the United States should instead consider a policy of expanded deterrence, which focuses not solely on the would-be nuclear terrorists but on those states that may deliberately transfer or inadvertently lead nuclear weapons and materials to them. By threatening retaliation against those states, the United States may be able to deter that which it cannot physically prevent." .*[25]

Graham Allison makes a similar case, arguing that the key to expanded deterrence is coming up with ways of tracing nuclear material to the country that forged the fissile material. "After a nuclear bomb detonates, nuclear forensics cops would collect debris samples and send them to a laboratory for radiological analysis. By identifying unique attributes of the fissile material, including its impurities and contaminants, one could trace the path back to its origin." *[26] The process is analogous to identifying a criminal by fingerprints. "The goal would be twofold: first, to deter leaders of nuclear states from selling weapons to terrorists by holding them accountable for any use of their own weapons; second, to give leader every incentive to tightly secure their nuclear weapons and materials." *[26]

25.4 Governance, control, and law

Main articles: Nuclear Non-Proliferation Treaty, Strategic Arms Limitation Talks, Intermediate-Range Nuclear Forces Treaty, START I, Strategic Offensive Reductions Treaty, Comprehensive Nuclear-Test-Ban Treaty, and New START

Because of the immense military power they can confer,

The International Atomic Energy Agency was created in 1957 to encourage peaceful development of nuclear technology while providing international safeguards against nuclear proliferation.

the political control of nuclear weapons has been a key issue for as long as they have existed; in most countries the use of nuclear force can only be authorized by the head of government or head of state.*[27] Controls and regulations governing nuclear weapons are man-made, and so are imperfect. Therefore, there is an inherent danger of "accidents, mistakes, false alarms, blackmail, theft, and sabotage" .*[28]

In the late 1940s, lack of mutual trust was preventing the United States and the Soviet Union from making ground towards international arms control agreements. The Russell–Einstein Manifesto was issued in London on July 9, 1955 by Bertrand Russell in the midst of the Cold War. It highlighted the dangers posed by nuclear weapons and called for world leaders to seek peaceful resolutions to international conflict. The signatories included eleven pre-eminent intellectuals and scientists, including Albert Einstein, who signed it just days before his death on April 18, 1955. A few days after the release, philanthropist Cyrus S. Eaton offered to sponsor a conference—called for in the manifesto—in Pugwash, Nova Scotia, Eaton's birthplace. This conference was to be the first of the Pugwash Conferences on Science and World Affairs, held in July 1957.

By the 1960s steps were being taken to limit both the proliferation of nuclear weapons to other countries and the environmental effects of nuclear testing. The Partial Test Ban Treaty (1963) restricted all nuclear testing to underground nuclear testing, to prevent contamination from nuclear fallout, whereas the Nuclear Non-Proliferation Treaty (1968) attempted to place restrictions on the types of activities signatories could participate in, with the goal of allowing the transference of non-military nuclear technology to member countries without fear of proliferation.

In 1957, the International Atomic Energy Agency (IAEA) was established under the mandate of the United Nations to encourage development of peaceful applications for nuclear technology, provide international safeguards against its misuse, and facilitate the application of safety measures in its use. In 1996, many nations signed the Comprehensive Test Ban Treaty,*[29] which prohibits all testing of nuclear weapons. A testing ban imposes a significant hindrance to nuclear arms development by any complying country.*[30] The Treaty requires the ratification by 44 specific states before it can go into force; as of 2012, the ratification of eight of these states is still required.*[29]

Additional treaties and agreements have governed nuclear weapons stockpiles between the countries with the two largest stockpiles, the United States and the Soviet Union, and later between the United States and Russia. These include treaties such as SALT II (never ratified), START I (expired), INF, START II (never ratified), SORT, and New START, as well as non-binding agreements such as SALT I and the Presidential Nuclear Initiatives*[31] of 1991. Even when they did not enter into force, these agreements helped limit and later reduce the numbers and types of nuclear weapons between the United States and the Soviet Union/Russia.

Nuclear weapons have also been opposed by agreements between countries. Many nations have been declared Nuclear-Weapon-Free Zones, areas where nuclear weapons production and deployment are prohibited, through the use of treaties. The Treaty of Tlatelolco (1967) prohibited any production or deployment of nuclear weapons in Latin America and the Caribbean, and the Treaty of Pelindaba (1964) prohibits nuclear weapons in many African countries. As recently as 2006 a Central Asian Nuclear Weapon Free Zone was established amongst the former Soviet republics of Central Asia prohibiting nuclear weapons.

In the middle of 1996, the International Court of Justice, the highest court of the United Nations, issued an Advisory Opinion concerned with the "Legality of the Threat or Use of Nuclear Weapons". The court ruled that the use or threat of use of nuclear weapons would violate various articles of international law, including the Geneva Conventions, the Hague Conventions, the UN Charter, and the Universal Declaration of Human Rights. In view of the unique, destructive characteristics of nuclear weapons, the International Committee of the Red Cross calls on States to ensure that these weapons are never used, irrespective of whether they consider them lawful or not.*[32]

Additionally, there have been other, specific actions meant to discourage countries from developing nuclear arms. In the wake of the tests by India and Pakistan in 1998, economic sanctions were (temporarily) levied against both countries, though neither were signatories with the Nuclear Non-Proliferation Treaty. One of the stated *casus belli* for the initiation of the 2003 Iraq War was an accusation by the United States that Iraq was actively pursuing nuclear arms (though this was soon discovered not to be the case as the program had been discontinued). In 1981, Israel had bombed a nuclear reactor being constructed in Osirak, Iraq, in what it called an attempt to halt Iraq's previous nuclear arms ambitions; in 2007, Israel bombed another reactor being constructed in Syria.

In 2013, Mark Diesendorf says that governments of France, India, North Korea, Pakistan, UK, and South Africa have used nuclear power and/or research reactors to assist nuclear weapons development or to contribute to their supplies of nuclear explosives from military reactors.*[33]

25.4.1 Disarmament

Main article: Nuclear disarmament
See also: Nuclear Tipping Point
For statistics on possession and deployment, see List of states with nuclear weapons.

Nuclear disarmament refers to both the act of reduc-

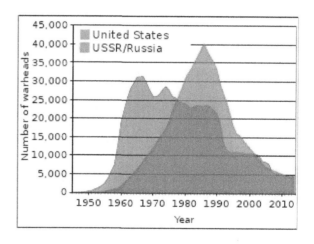

The USSR and United States nuclear weapon stockpiles throughout the Cold War until 2015, with a precipitous drop in total numbers following the end of the Cold War in 1991.

ing or eliminating nuclear weapons and to the end state of a nuclear-free world, in which nuclear weapons are completely eliminated.

Beginning with the 1963 Partial Test Ban Treaty and continuing through the 1996 Comprehensive Test Ban Treaty, there have been many treaties to limit or reduce nuclear weapons testing and stockpiles. The 1968 Nuclear Non-Proliferation Treaty has as one of its explicit conditions that all signatories must "pursue negotiations in good faith" towards the long-term goal of "complete disarmament". The nuclear weapon states have largely treated that aspect of the agreement as "decorative" and without force.*[34]

Only one country —South Africa —has ever fully renounced nuclear weapons they had independently developed. The former Soviet republics of Belarus, Kazakhstan, and Ukraine returned Soviet nuclear arms stationed in their countries to Russia after the collapse of the USSR.

Proponents of nuclear disarmament say that it would lessen the probability of nuclear war occurring, especially accidentally. Critics of nuclear disarmament say that it would undermine the present nuclear peace and deterrence and would lead to increased global instability. Various American elder statesmen,*[35] who were in office during the Cold War period, have been advocating the elimination of nuclear weapons. These officials include Henry Kissinger, George Shultz, Sam Nunn, and William Perry. In January 2010, Lawrence M. Krauss stated that "no issue carries more importance to the long-term health and security of humanity than the effort to reduce, and perhaps one day, rid the world of nuclear weapons".*[36]

Ukrainian workers use equipment provided by the U.S. Defense Threat Reduction Agency to dismantle a Soviet-era missile silo. After the end of the Cold War, Ukraine and the other non-Russian, post-Soviet republics relinquished Soviet nuclear stockpiles to Russia.

In the years after the end of the Cold War, there have been numerous campaigns to urge the abolition of nuclear weapons, such as that organized by the Global Zero movement, and the goal of a "world without nuclear weapons" was advocated by United States President Barack Obama in an April 2009 speech in Prague.*[37] A CNN poll from April 2010 indicated that the American public was nearly evenly split on the issue.*[38]

Some analysts have argued that nuclear weapons have made the world relatively safer, with peace through deterrence and through the stability–instability paradox, including in south Asia.*[39]*[40] Kenneth Waltz has argued that nuclear weapons have helped keep an uneasy peace, and further nuclear weapon proliferation might even help avoid the large scale conventional wars that were so common prior to their invention at the end of World War II.*[22] But former Secretary Henry Kissinger says there is a new danger, which cannot be addressed by deterrence: "The classical notion of deterrence was that there was some consequences before which aggressors and evildoers would recoil. In a world of suicide bombers, that calculation doesn't operate in any comparable way".*[41] George Shultz has said, "If you think of the people who are doing suicide attacks, and people like that get a nuclear weapon, they are almost by definition not deterrable".*[42]

25.4.2 United Nations

Main article: United Nations Office for Disarmament Affairs

The UN Office for Disarmament Affairs (UNODA) is a department of the United Nations Secretariat established in January 1998 as part of the United Nations Secretary-General Kofi Annan's plan to reform the UN as presented in his report to the General Assembly in July 1997.*[43]

Its goal is to promote nuclear disarmament and non-proliferation and the strengthening of the disarmament regimes in respect to other weapons of mass destruction, chemical and biological weapons. It also promotes disarmament efforts in the area of conventional weapons, especially land mines and small arms, which are often the weapons of choice in contemporary conflicts.

25.5 Controversy

See also: Nuclear weapons debate and History of the anti-nuclear movement

25.5.1 Ethics

Even before the first nuclear weapons had been developed, scientists involved with the Manhattan Project were divided over the use of the weapon. The role of the two atomic bombings of the country in Japan's surrender and the U.S.'s ethical justification for them has been the subject of scholarly and popular debate for decades. The question of whether nations should have nuclear weapons, or test them, has been continually and nearly universally controversial.*[44]

25.5.2 Notable nuclear weapons accidents

Main article: Nuclear and radiation accidents

- February 13, 1950: a Convair B-36B crashed in northern British Columbia after jettisoning a Mark IV atomic bomb. This was the first such nuclear weapon loss in history.

- May 22, 1957: a 42,000-pound Mark-17 hydrogen bomb accidentally fell from a bomber near Albuquerque, New Mexico. The detonation of the device's conventional explosives destroyed it on impact and formed a crater 25-feet in diameter on land owned by the University of New Mexico. According to a researcher at the Natural Resources Defense Council, it was one of the most powerful bombs made to date.*[45]

- June 7, 1960: the 1960 Fort Dix IM-99 accident destroyed a Boeing CIM-10 Bomarc nuclear missile and shelter and contaminated the BOMARC Missile Accident Site in New Jersey.

- January 24, 1961: the 1961 Goldsboro B-52 crash occurred near Goldsboro, North Carolina. A B-52 Stratofortress carrying two Mark 39 nuclear bombs broke up in mid-air, dropping its nuclear payload in the process.*[46]*[47]

- 1965 Philippine Sea A-4 crash, where a Skyhawk attack aircraft with a nuclear weapon fell into the sea.*[48] The pilot, the aircraft, and the B43 nuclear bomb were never recovered.*[49] It was not until 1989 that the Pentagon revealed the loss of the one-megaton bomb.*[50]

- January 17, 1966: the 1966 Palomares B-52 crash occurred when a B-52G bomber of the USAF collided with a KC-135 tanker during mid-air refuelling off the coast of Spain. The KC-135 was completely destroyed when its fuel load ignited, killing all four crew members. The B-52G broke apart, killing three of the seven crew members aboard.*[51] Of the four Mk28 type hydrogen bombs the B-52G carried,*[52] three were found on land near Almería, Spain. The non-nuclear explosives in two of the weapons detonated upon impact with the ground, resulting in the contamination of a 2-square-kilometer (490-acre) (0.78 square mile) area by radioactive plutonium. The fourth, which fell into the Mediterranean Sea, was recovered intact after a 2½-month-long search.*[53]

- January 21, 1968: the 1968 Thule Air Base B-52 crash involved a United States Air Force (USAF) B-52 bomber. The aircraft was carrying four hydrogen bombs when a cabin fire forced the crew to abandon the aircraft. Six crew members ejected safely, but one who did not have an ejection seat was killed while trying to bail out. The bomber crashed onto sea ice in Greenland, causing the nuclear payload to rupture and disperse, which resulted in widespread radioactive contamination.

- September 18–19, 1980: the Damascus Accident, occurred in Damascus, Arkansas, where a Titan missile equipped with a nuclear warhead exploded. The accident was caused by a maintenance man who dropped a socket from a socket wrench down an 80-foot shaft, puncturing a fuel tank on the rocket. Leaking fuel resulted in a hypergolic fuel explosion, jettisoning the W-53 warhead beyond the launch site.*[54]*[55]*[56]

25.5.3 Nuclear testing and fallout

Main article: Nuclear fallout
See also: Downwinders

Over 500 atmospheric nuclear weapons tests were con-

Over 2,000 nuclear tests have been conducted in over a dozen different sites around the world. Red Russia/Soviet Union, blue France, light blue United States, violet Britain, black Israel, orange China, yellow India, brown Pakistan, green North Korea and light green (territories exposed to nuclear bombs)

ducted at various sites around the world from 1945 to 1980. Radioactive fallout from nuclear weapons testing was first drawn to public attention in 1954 when the Castle Bravo hydrogen bomb test at the Pacific Proving Grounds contaminated the crew and catch of the Japanese fishing boat *Lucky Dragon*.*[57] One of the fishermen died in Japan seven months later, and the fear of contaminated tuna led to a temporary boycotting of the popular staple in Japan. The incident caused widespread concern around the world, especially regarding the effects of nuclear fallout and atmospheric nuclear testing, and "provided a decisive impetus for the emergence of the anti-nuclear weapons movement in many countries" .*[57]

As public awareness and concern mounted over the possible health hazards associated with exposure to the nuclear fallout, various studies were done to assess the extent of

This view of downtown Las Vegas shows a mushroom cloud in the background. Scenes such as this were typical during the 1950s. From 1951 to 1962 the government conducted 100 atmospheric tests at the nearby Nevada Test Site.

the hazard. A Centers for Disease Control and Prevention/National Cancer Institute study claims that fallout from atmospheric nuclear tests would lead to perhaps 11,000 excess deaths amongst people alive during atmospheric testing in the United States from all forms of cancer, including leukemia, from 1951 to well into the 21st century.*[58]*[59] As of March 2009, the U.S. is the only nation that compensates nuclear test victims. Since the Radiation Exposure Compensation Act of 1990, more than $1.38 billion in compensation has been approved. The money is going to people who took part in the tests, notably at the Nevada Test Site, and to others exposed to the radiation.*[60]*[61]

In addition, leakage of byproducts of nuclear weapon production into groundwater has been an ongoing issue, particularly at the Hanford site.*[62]

25.6 Effects of nuclear explosions on human health

Main article: Effects of nuclear explosions on human health

Some scientists estimate that if there were a nuclear war resulting in 100 Hiroshima-size nuclear explosions on cities, it could cause significant loss of life in the tens of millions from long term climatic effects alone. The climatology hypothesis is that *if* each city firestorms, a great deal of soot could be thrown up into the atmosphere which could blanket the earth, cutting out sunlight for years on end, causing the disruption of food chains, in what is termed a Nuclear Winter.*[63]*[64]

The medical effects of the atomic bomb on Hiroshima upon humans can be put into the four categories below, with the effects of larger thermonuclear weapons producing blast and thermal effects so large that there would be a negligible number of survivors close enough to the center of the blast who would experience prompt/acute radiation effects, which were observed after the 16 kiloton yield Hiroshima bomb, due to its relatively low yield:*[65]*[66]

- Initial stage—the first 1–9 weeks, in which are the greatest number of deaths, with 90% due to thermal injury and/or blast effects and 10% due to super-lethal radiation exposure.

- Intermediate stage—from 10–12 weeks. The deaths in this period are from ionizing radiation in the median lethal range - LD50

- Late period—lasting from 13–20 weeks. This period has some improvement in survivors' condition.

- Delayed period—from 20+ weeks. Characterized by numerous complications, mostly related to healing of thermal and mechanical injuries, and if the individual was exposed to a few hundred to a thousand Millisieverts of radiation, it is coupled with infertility, sub-fertility and blood disorders. Furthermore, ionizing radiation above a dose of around 50-100 Millisievert exposure has been shown to statistically begin increasing one's chance of dying of cancer sometime in their lifetime over the normal unexposed rate of ~25%, in the long term, a heightened rate of cancer, proportional to the dose received, would begin to be observed after ~5+ years, with lesser problems such as eye cataracts and other more minor effects in other organs and tissue also being observed over the long term.

Fallout exposure - Depending on if further afield individuals Shelter in place or evacuate perpendicular to the direction of the wind, and therefore avoid contact with the fallout plume, and stay there for the days and weeks after the nuclear explosion, their exposure to fallout, and therefore their total dose, will vary. With those who do shelter in place, and or evacuate, experiencing a total dose that would be negligible in comparison to someone who just went about their life as normal.*[67]*[68]

Staying indoors until after the most hazardous fallout isotope, I-131 decays away to 0.1% of its initial quantity after ten half lives - which is represented by 80 days in I-131s case, would make the difference between likely contracting Thyroid cancer or escaping completely from this substance depending on the actions of the individual.*[69]

25.6.1 Public opposition

See also: History of the anti-nuclear movement and International Day against Nuclear Tests

Peace movements emerged in Japan and in 1954 they con-

Women Strike for Peace during the Cuban Missile Crisis

Demonstration against nuclear testing in Lyon, France, in the 1980s.

verged to form a unified "Japanese Council Against Atomic and Hydrogen Bombs". Japanese opposition to nuclear weapons tests in the Pacific Ocean was widespread, and "an estimated 35 million signatures were collected on petitions calling for bans on nuclear weapons" .*[70]

In the United Kingdom, the first Aldermaston March organised by the Campaign for Nuclear Disarmament(CND) took place at Easter 1958, when, according to the CND, several thousand people marched for four days from Trafalgar Square, London, to the Atomic Weapons Research Establishment close to Aldermaston in Berkshire, England, to demonstrate their opposition to nuclear weapons.*[71]*[72] The Aldermaston marches continued into the late 1960s when tens of thousands of people took part in the four-day marches.*[70]

In 1959, a letter in the *Bulletin of Atomic Scientists* was the start of a successful campaign to stop the Atomic Energy Commission dumping radioactive waste in the sea 19 kilometres from Boston.*[73] In 1962, Linus Pauling won the Nobel Peace Prize for his work to stop the atmospheric testing of nuclear weapons, and the "Ban the Bomb" movement spread.*[44]

In 1963, many countries ratified the Partial Test Ban Treaty prohibiting atmospheric nuclear testing. Radioactive fallout became less of an issue and the anti-nuclear weapons movement went into decline for some years.*[57]*[74] A resurgence of interest occurred amid European and American fears of nuclear war in the 1980s.*[75]

25.7 Costs and technology spin-offs

See also: Global Positioning System, Nuclear weapons delivery, History of computers, ENIAC, and Swords to ploughshares

According to an audit by the Brookings Institution, between 1940 and 1996, the U.S. spent $8.78 trillion in present-day terms*[76] on nuclear weapons programs. 57 percent of which was spent on building nuclear weapons delivery systems. 6.3 percent of the total, $551 billion in present-day terms, was spent on environmental remediation and nuclear waste management, for example cleaning up the Hanford site, and 7 percent of the total, $617 billion was spent on making nuclear weapons themselves.*[77]

25.8 Non-weapons uses

Main article: Peaceful nuclear explosion

Peaceful nuclear explosions are nuclear explosions conducted for non-military purposes, such as activities related to economic development including the creation of canals. During the 1960s and 70s, both the United States and the Soviet Union conducted a number of PNEs. Six of the explosions by the Soviet Union are considered to have been of an applied nature, not just tests.

Subsequently the United States and the Soviet Union halted their programs. Definitions and limits are covered in the

Peaceful Nuclear Explosions Treaty of 1976.*[78]*[79] The Comprehensive Nuclear-Test-Ban Treaty of 1996 prohibits all nuclear explosions, regardless of whether they are for peaceful purposes or not.

25.9 See also

- *The Atomic Age* – Wikipedia book

25.9.1 History

- History of nuclear weapons
    - Atomic spies
    - German nuclear energy project
    - Japanese atomic program
    - Soviet atomic bomb project
    - Nuclear testing at Bikini Atoll
- Timeline of nuclear weapons development
- Los Alamos National Laboratory
- Lawrence Livermore National Laboratory
- Lists of nuclear disasters and radioactive incidents
- Nuclear and radiation accidents, including nuclear weapons accidents
    - Nevada Test Site
    - Project Gnome
- Military strategy
    - Civil Defense
    - Fractional Orbital Bombardment System
    - Mutual Assured Destruction
- Weapon of mass destruction
    - Nuclear strategy

25.9.2 More technical details

- Effects of nuclear explosions
- Intercontinental ballistic missile
- Nuclear blackout
- Neutron bomb
- Nuclear bombs and health
- Nuclear weapon yield

25.9.3 Popular culture

- Nuclear weapons in popular culture
- *The Butter Battle Book*

25.9.4 Proliferation and politics

- Agency for the Prohibition of Nuclear Weapons in Latin America and the Caribbean
- Comprehensive Test Ban Treaty
- International Court of Justice advisory opinion on legality of nuclear weapons
- List of states with nuclear weapons
- List of nuclear weapons
- Nth Country Experiment
- Nuclear close calls
- Nuclear Non-Proliferation Treaty
- Nuclear weapons and the United Kingdom
- The Letters of last resort (United Kingdom)
- Nuclear weapons and Russia
- Nuclear weapons and the United States
- Strategic Arms Limitation Talks
- Three Non-Nuclear Principles, of Japan

25.10 Notes and references

[1] Specifically the 1970 to 1980 designed and deployed US B83 nuclear bomb, with a yield of up to 1.2 megatons.

[2] "Frequently Asked Questions #1". Radiation Effects Research Foundation. Retrieved September 18, 2007. total number of deaths is not known precisely ... acute (within two to four months) deaths ... Hiroshima ... 90,000 − 166,000 ... Nagasaki ... 60,000 − 80,000

[3] "Federation of American Scientists: Status of World Nuclear Forces". Fas.org. Retrieved December 29, 2012.

[4] "Nuclear Weapons – Israel". Fas.org. January 8, 2007. Retrieved December 15, 2010.

[5] See also Mordechai Vanunu

[6] Ian Lowe, "Three minutes to midnight", *Australasian Science*, March 2016, p. 49.

[7] The best overall printed sources on nuclear weapons design are: Hansen, Chuck. *U.S. Nuclear Weapons: The Secret History*. San Antonio, TX: Aerofax, 1988; and the more-updated Hansen, Chuck, "Swords of Armageddon: U.S. Nuclear Weapons Development since 1945" (CD-ROM & download available). PDF. 2,600 pages. Sunnyvale, California. Chuklea Publications, 1995, 2007. ISBN 978-0-9791915-0-3 (2nd Ed.)

[8] David Albright and Kimberly Kramer (August 22, 2005), "Neptunium 237 and Americium: World Inventories and Proliferation Concerns" (PDF). Institute for Science and International Security. Retrieved October 13, 2011.

[9] Carey Sublette, Nuclear Weapons Frequently Asked Questions: 4.5.2 "Dirty" and "Clean" Weapons, accessed May 10, 2011.

[10] On India's alleged hydrogen bomb test, see Carey Sublette, What Are the Real Yields of India's Test?.

[11] McKirdy, Euan. "North Korea announces it conducted nuclear test". *CNN*. Retrieved 7 January 2016.

[12] Sublette, Carey. "The Nuclear Weapon Archive". Retrieved March 7, 2007.

[13] U.S. Department of Energy, Restricted Data Declassification Decisions, 1946 to the Present (RDD-8) (January 1, 2002), accessed November 20, 2011.

[14] "Page discussing the possibility of using antimatter as a trigger for a thermonuclear explosion". Cui.unige.ch. Retrieved May 30, 2013.

[15] Andre Gsponer; Jean-Pierre Hurni (1970). "Paper discussing the number of antiprotons required to ignite a thermonuclear weapon". *In G. Velarde and E. Minguez, eds., Proceedings of the International Conference on Emerging Nuclear Energy Systems, Madrid, June /July , (World Scientific, Singapore, 1987)* 166–169. Arxiv.org. 4 (30): arXiv:physics/0507114. arXiv:physics/0507114. Bibcode:2005physics...7114G.

[16] Keay Davidson; Chronicle Science Writer (October 4, 2004). "Air Force pursuing antimatter weapons: Program was touted publicly, then came official gag order". Sfgate.com. Retrieved May 30, 2013.

[17] "Fourth Generation Nuclear Weapons". Retrieved October 24, 2014.

[18] Stephen I. Schwartz, ed., *Atomic Audit: The Costs and Consequences of U.S. Nuclear Weapons Since 1940*. Washington, D.C.: Brookings Institution Press, 1998. See also Estimated Minimum Incurred Costs of U.S. Nuclear Weapons Programs, 1940–1996, an excerpt from the book. Archived November 21, 2008, at the Wayback Machine.

[19] Creveld, Martin Van (2000). "Technology and War II: Postmodern War?". In Charles Townshend. *The Oxford History of Modern War*. New York, USA: Oxford University Press. p. 349. ISBN 0-19-285373-2.

[20] Mearsheimer, John (2006). "Conversations in International Relations: Interview with John J. Mearsheimer (Part I)" (PDF). *International Relations*. **20** (1): 105–123. doi:10.1177/0047117806060939.See page 116

[21] Kenneth Waltz, "More May Be Better," in Scott Sagan and Kenneth Waltz, eds., *The Spread of Nuclear Weapons* (New York: Norton, 1995).

[22] Kenneth Waltz, "The Spread of Nuclear Weapons: More May Better, *Adelphi Papers*, no. 171 (London, International Institute for Strategic Studies, 1981).

[23] See, for example: Feldman, Noah. "Islam, Terror and the Second Nuclear Age," *New York Times Magazine* (October 29, 2006).

[24] Daniel Plesch & Stephen Young, "Senseless policy", *Bulletin of the Atomic Scientists*, November/December 1998, page 4. Fetched from URL on April 18, 2011.

[25] Gallucci, Robert (September 2006). "Averting Nuclear Catastrophe: Contemplating Extreme Responses to U.S. Vulnerability". *Annals of the American Academy of Political and Social Science*. **607**: 51–58. doi:10.1177/0002716206290457. Retrieved January 28, 2013.

[26] Allison, Graham (March 13, 2009). "How to Keep the Bomb From Terrorists". *Newsweek*. Retrieved January 28, 2013.

[27] In the United States, the President and the Secretary of Defense, acting as the National Command Authority, must *jointly* authorize the use of nuclear weapons.

[28] Eric Schlosser, Today's nuclear dillemma, *Bulletin of the Atomic Scientists*, November/December 2015, vol. 71 no. 6, 11-17.

[29] Preparatory Commission for the Comprehensive Nuclear-Test-Ban Treaty Organization (2010). "Status of Signature and Ratification". Accessed May 27, 2010. Of the "Annex 2" states whose ratification of the CTBT is required before it enters into force, China, Egypt, Iran, Israel, and the United States have signed but not ratified the Treaty. India, North Korea, and Pakistan have not signed the Treaty.

[30] Richelson, Jeffrey. *Spying on the bomb: American nuclear intelligence from Nazi Germany to Iran and North Korea*. New York: Norton, 2006.

[31] The Presidential Nuclear Initiatives (PNIs) on Tactical Nuclear Weapons At a Glance, Fact Sheet, Arms Control Association.

[32] Nuclear weapons and international humanitarian law International Committee of the Red Cross

[33] Mark Diesendorf (2013). "Book review: Contesting the future of nuclear power" (PDF). *Energy Policy*.

[34] Gusterson, Hugh, "Finding Article VI" *Bulletin of the Atomic Scientists* (January 8, 2007).

[35] Jim Hoagland (October 6, 2011). "Nuclear energy after Fukushima". *Washington Post*.

[36] Lawrence M. Krauss. The Doomsday Clock Still Ticks, *Scientific American*, January 2010, p. 26.

[37] Graham, Nick (April 5, 2009). "Obama Prague Speech On Nuclear Weapons". Huffingtonpost.com. Retrieved May 30, 2013.

[38] "CNN Poll: Public divided on eliminating all nuclear weapons". Politicalticker.blogs.cnn.com. April 12, 2010. Retrieved May 30, 2013.

[39] Krepon, Michael. "The Stability-Instability Paradox, Misperception, and Escalation Control in South Asia" (PDF). *Stimson*. Retrieved November 20, 2015.

[40] "Michael Krepon • The Stability-Instability Paradox". Retrieved October 24, 2014.

[41] Ben Goddard (January 27, 2010). "Cold Warriors say no nukes". *The Hill*.

[42] Hugh Gusterson (March 30, 2012). "The new abolitionists". *Bulletin of the Atomic Scientists*.

[43] ODS Team. "Renewing the United Nations: A Program for Reform (A/51/950)" (PDF). Daccess-dds-ny.un.org. Retrieved May 30, 2013.

[44] Jerry Brown and Rinaldo Brutoco (1997). *Profiles in Power: The Anti-nuclear Movement and the Dawn of the Solar Age*, Twayne Publishers, pp. 191–192.

[45] "Accident Revealed After 29 Years: H-Bomb Fell Near Albuquerque in 1957". Los Angeles Times. Associated Press. August 27, 1986. Retrieved 31 August 2014.

[46] Barry Schneider (May 1975). "Big Bangs from Little Bombs". *Bulletin of Atomic Scientists*. p. 28. Retrieved July 13, 2009.

[47] James C. Oskins; Michael H. Maggelet (2008). *Broken Arrow — The Declassified History of U.S. Nuclear Weapons Accidents*. lulu.com. ISBN 1-4357-0361-8. Retrieved December 29, 2008.

[48] "Ticonderoga Cruise Reports" (Navy.mil weblist of Aug 2003 compilation from cruise reports). Retrieved April 20, 2012. The National Archives hold[s] deck logs for aircraft carriers for the Vietnam Conflict.

[49] Broken Arrows at www.atomicarchive.com. Accessed August 24, 2007.

[50] "U.S. Confirms '65 Loss of H-Bomb Near Japanese Islands". *The Washington Post*. Reuters. May 9, 1989. p. A–27.

[51] Hayes, Ron (January 17, 2007). "H-bomb incident crippled pilot's career". Palm Beach Post. Archived from the original on June 16, 2011. Retrieved May 24, 2006.

[52] Maydew, Randall C. (1997). *America's Lost H-Bomb: Palomares, Spain, 1966*. Sunflower University Press. ISBN 978-0-89745-214-4.

[53] Long, Tony (January 17, 2008). "Jan. 17, 1966: H-Bombs Rain Down on a Spanish Fishing Village". WIRED. Retrieved February 16, 2008.

[54] Schlosser, Eric (2013). *Command and Control: Nuclear Weapons, the Damascus Accident, and the Illusion of Safety*. Penguin Press. ISBN 978-1-59420-227-8.

[55] Christ, Mark K. "Titan II Missile Explosion". *The Encyclopedia of Arkansas History & Culture*. Arkansas Historic Preservation Program. Retrieved 31 August 2014.

[56] Stumpf, David K. (2000). Christ, Mark K.; Slater, Cathryn H., eds. *"We Can Neither Confirm Nor Deny" Sentinels of History: Reflections on Arkansas Properties on the National Register of Historic Places*. Fayetteville, Arkansas: University of Arkansas Press.

[57] Rudig, Wolfgang (1990). "Anti-nuclear Movements: A World Survey of Opposition to Nuclear Energy". Longman. pp. 54–55.

[58] "Report on the Health Consequences to the American Population from Nuclear Weapons Tests Conducted by the United States and Other Nations". CDC. Retrieved December 7, 2013.

[59] Committee to Review the CDC-NCI Feasibility Study of the Health Consequences Nuclear Weapons Tests, National Research Council. "Exposure of the American Population to Radioactive Fallout from Nuclear Weapons Tests". Retrieved October 24, 2014.

[60] ABC News. "What governments offer to victims of nuclear tests". *ABC News*. Retrieved October 24, 2014.

[61] Radiation Exposure Compensation System: Claims to Date Summary of Claims Received by 06/11/2009

[62] Coghlan, Andy. "US nuclear dump is leaking toxic waste". *New Scientist*. Retrieved 12 March 2016.

[63] Philip Yam. Nuclear Exchange, *Scientific American*, June 2010, p. 24.

[64] Alan Robock and Owen Brian Toon. Local Nuclear War, Global Suffering, *Scientific American*, January 2010, p. 74-81.

[65] "Remm.nlm.gov".

[66] "Nuclear Warfare" (PDF). Nd.edu. p. 3.

[67] 7 hour rule: At 7 hours after detonation the fission product activity will have decreased to about 1/10 (10%) of its amount at 1 hour. At about 2 days (49 hours-7X7) the activity will have decreased to 1% of the 1-hour value. Falloutradiation.com

[68] "Nuclear Warfare" (PDF). p. 22.

[69] Oak Ridge Reservation (USDOE), EPA Facility ID: TN1890090003; Site and Radiological Assessment Branch, Division of Health Assessment and Consultation, Agency for Toxic Substances and Disease Registry. "PUBLIC HEALTH ASSESSMENT Iodine-131 Releases" (PDF). atsdr.cdc.gov. U.S. Center for Disease Control. Retrieved 21 May 2016.

[70] Jim Falk (1982). *Global Fission: The Battle Over Nuclear Power.* Oxford University Press. pp. 96–97

[71] "A brief history of CND". Cnduk.org. Retrieved May 30, 2013.

[72] "Early defections in march to Aldermaston". London: Guardian Unlimited. April 5, 1958.

[73] Jim Falk (1982). *Global Fission: The Battle Over Nuclear Power*, Oxford University Press, p. 93.

[74] Jim Falk (1982). *Global Fission: The Battle Over Nuclear Power*, Oxford University Press, p. 98.

[75] Spencer Weart, *Nuclear Fear: A History of Images* (Cambridge, Mass.: Harvard University Press, 1988), chapters 16 and 19.

[76] Federal Reserve Bank of Minneapolis Community Development Project. "Consumer Price Index (estimate) 1800–". Federal Reserve Bank of Minneapolis. Retrieved November 10, 2015.

[77] "Estimated Minimum Incurred Costs of U.S. Nuclear Weapons Programs, 1940–1996". *Brookings Institution*. Archived from the original on March 5, 2004. Retrieved November 20, 2015.

[78] "Announcement of Treaty on Underground Nuclear Explosions Peaceful Purposes (PNE Treaty)" (PDF). Gerald R. Ford Museum and Library. May 28, 1976.

[79] Peters, Gerhard; Woolley, John T. "Gerald R. Ford: "Message to the Senate Transmitting United States-Soviet Treaty and Protocol on the Limitation of Underground Nuclear Explosions," July 29, 1976". *The American Presidency Project*. University of California - Santa Barbara.

25.11 Bibliography

See also: List of books about nuclear issues

- Bethe, Hans Albrecht. *The Road from Los Alamos.* New York: Simon and Schuster, 1991. ISBN 0-671-74012-1
- DeVolpi, Alexander, Minkov, Vladimir E., Simonenko, Vadim A., and Stanford, George S. *Nuclear Shadowboxing: Contemporary Threats from Cold War Weaponry.* Fidlar Doubleday, 2004 (Two volumes, both accessible on Google Book Search) (Content of both volumes is now available in the 2009 trilogy by Alexander DeVolpi: *Nuclear Insights: The Cold War Legacy*)
- Glasstone, Samuel and Dolan, Philip J. *The Effects of Nuclear Weapons (third edition).* Washington, D.C.: U.S. Government Printing Office, 1977. Available online (PDF).
- *NATO Handbook on the Medical Aspects of NBC Defensive Operations (Part I – Nuclear).* Departments of the Army, Navy, and Air Force: Washington, D.C., 1996
- Hansen, Chuck. *U.S. Nuclear Weapons: The Secret History.* Arlington, TX: Aerofax, 1988
- Hansen, Chuck. "Swords of Armageddon: U.S. nuclear weapons development since 1945" (CD-ROM & download available). PDF. 2,600 pages. Sunnyvale, California, Chucklea Publications, 1995, 2007. ISBN 978-0-9791915-0-3 (2nd Ed.)
- Holloway, David. *Stalin and the Bomb.* New Haven: Yale University Press, 1994. ISBN 0-300-06056-4
- The Manhattan Engineer District, "The Atomic Bombings of Hiroshima and Nagasaki" (1946)
- (French) Jean-Hugues Oppel, *Réveillez le président*, Éditions Payot et rivages, 2007 (ISBN 978-2-7436-1630-4). The book is a fiction about the nuclear weapons of France; the book also contains about ten chapters on true historical incidents involving nuclear weapons and strategy.
- Smyth, Henry DeWolf. *Atomic Energy for Military Purposes.* Princeton, NJ: Princeton University Press, 1945. (Smyth Report – the first declassified report by the US government on nuclear weapons)
- *The Effects of Nuclear War*. Office of Technology Assessment, May 1979.
- Rhodes, Richard. *Dark Sun: The Making of the Hydrogen Bomb.* New York: Simon and Schuster, 1995. ISBN 0-684-82414-0
- Rhodes, Richard. *The Making of the Atomic Bomb.* New York: Simon and Schuster, 1986 ISBN 0-684-81378-5
- Schultz, George P. and Goodby, James E. *The War that Must Never be Fought*, Hoover Press, 2015, ISBN 978-0-8179-1845-3.

- Weart, Spencer R. *Nuclear Fear: A History of Images.* Cambridge, MA: Harvard University Press, 1988. ISBN 0-674-62836-5

- Weart, Spencer R. *The Rise of Nuclear Fear.* Cambridge, MA: Harvard University Press, 2012. ISBN 0-674-05233-1

25.12 External links

- Nuclear Weapon Archive from Carey Sublette is a reliable source of information and has links to other sources and an informative FAQ.

- The Federation of American Scientists provide solid information on weapons of mass destruction, including nuclear weapons and their effects

- Alsos Digital Library for Nuclear Issues — contains many resources related to nuclear weapons, including a historical and technical overview and searchable bibliography of web and print resources.

- Video archive of US, Soviet, UK, Chinese and French Nuclear Weapon Testing at sonicbomb.com

- The National Museum of Nuclear Science & History (United States)—located in Albuquerque, New Mexico; a Smithsonian Affiliate Museum

- Nuclear Emergency and Radiation Resources

- The Manhattan Project: Making the Atomic Bomb at AtomicArchive.com

- Los Alamos National Laboratory: History (U.S. nuclear history)

- *Race for the Superbomb*, PBS website on the history of the H-bomb

- Recordings of recollections of the victims of Hiroshima and Nagasaki

- The Woodrow Wilson Center's Nuclear Proliferation International History Project or NPIHP is a global network of individuals and institutions engaged in the study of international nuclear history through archival documents, oral history interviews and other empirical sources.

- NUKEMAP3D - a 3D nuclear weapons effects simulator powerd by Google Maps.

Chapter 26

Chemical energy

Not to be confused with chemical potential.

In chemistry, **chemical energy** is the potential of a chemical substance to undergo a transformation through a chemical reaction to transform other chemical substances. Examples include batteries, food, gasoline, and more. Breaking or making of chemical bonds involves energy, which may be either absorbed or evolved from a chemical system.

Energy that can be released (or absorbed) because of a reaction between a set of chemical substances is equal to the difference between the energy content of the products and the reactants, if the initial and final temperatures are the same. This change in energy can be estimated from the bond energies of the various chemical bonds in the reactants and products. It can also be calculated from $\Delta U^\circ_{f\,\text{reactants}}$, the internal energy of formation of the reactant molecules, and $\Delta U^\circ_{f\,\text{products}}$ the internal energy of formation of the product molecules. The internal energy change of a chemical process is equal to the heat exchanged if it is measured under conditions of constant volume and equal initial and final temperature, as in a closed container such as a bomb calorimeter. However, under conditions of constant pressure, as in reactions in vessels open to the atmosphere, the measured heat change is not always equal to the internal energy change, because pressure-volume work also releases or absorbs energy. (The heat change at constant pressure is called the enthalpy change; in this case the enthalpy of reaction, if initial and final temperatures are equal).

Another useful term is the heat of combustion, which is the energy mostly of the weak double bonds of molecular oxygen[1] released due to a combustion reaction and often applied in the study of fuels. Food is similar to hydrocarbon and carbohydrate fuels, and when it is oxidized to carbon dioxide and water, the energy released is analogous to the heat of combustion (though not assessed in the same way as a hydrocarbon fuel — see food energy).

Chemical potential energy is a form of potential energy related to the structural arrangement of atoms or molecules. This arrangement may be the result of chemical bonds within a molecule or otherwise. Chemical energy of a chemical substance can be transformed to other forms of energy by a chemical reaction. As an example, when a fuel is burned the chemical energy of molecular oxygen is converted to heat,[1] and the same is the case with digestion of food metabolized in a biological organism. Green plants transform solar energy to chemical energy (mostly of oxygen) through the process known as photosynthesis, and electrical energy can be converted to chemical energy and vice versa through electrochemical reactions.

The similar term chemical potential is used to indicate the potential of a substance to undergo a change of configuration, be it in the form of a chemical reaction, spatial transport, particle exchange with a reservoir, etc. It is *not* a form of potential energy itself, but is more closely related to free energy. The confusion in terminology arises from the fact that in other areas of physics not dominated by entropy, all potential energy is available to do useful work and drives the system to spontaneously undergo changes of configuration, and thus there is no distinction between "free" and "non-free" potential energy (hence the one word "potential"). However, in systems of large entropy such as chemical systems, the total amount of energy present (and conserved by the first law of thermodynamics) of which this Chemical Potential Energy is a part, is separated from the amount of that energy — Thermodynamic Free Energy (which Chemical potential is derived from) — which (appears to) drive the system forward spontaneously as its entropy increases (in accordance with the *second* law).

26.1 References

[1] Schmidt-Rohr, K (2015). "Why Combustions Are Always Exothermic, Yielding About 418 kJ per Mole of O_2". *J. Chem. Educ.* **92**: 2094–2099. doi:10.1021/acs.jchemed.5b00333.

Chapter 27

Explosives engineering

Explosives engineering is the field of science and engineering which is related to examining the behavior and usage of explosive materials.[1]

27.1 Topics

Some of the topics that explosives engineers study, research, and work on include:

- Development and characterization of new explosive materials in various forms
- Analysis of the physical process of detonation
- Explosive generated shock waves and their effects on materials
- Safety testing of explosives
- Analysis and engineering of rock blasting for mining
- Design and analysis of shaped charges and reactive armor
- Design and analysis of military explosives such as shells, aerial bombs, missile warheads, etc.

27.2 Organizations

- International Society of Explosives Engineers (ISEE)
- New Mexico Institute of Mining and Technology (New Mexico Tech)
- Missouri University of science and Technology [2]

27.3 See also

- Explosives
- Chapman–Jouguet condition
- Chemistry
- Civil engineer
- Chemical engineer
- Gurney equations
- Material science
- Physics
- Rock Blasting

27.4 References

[1] Cooper, Paul W. (1996). *Explosives Engineering*. Wiley-VCH. ISBN 0-471-18636-8.

[2] http://explosives.mst.edu/

27.5 External links

- http://www.isee.org/

Chapter 28

Explosives safety

Explosives safety originated as a formal program in the United States in the aftermath of World War I when several ammunition storage areas were destroyed in a series of mishaps. The most serious occurred at Picatinny Arsenal Ammunition Storage Depot, New Jersey, in July, 1926 when an electrical storm led to fires that caused explosions and widespread destruction. The severe property damage and 19 fatalities led Congress to empower a board of Army and Naval officers to investigate the Picatinny Arsenal disaster and determine if similar conditions existed at other ammunition depots. The board reported in its findings that this mishap could recur, prompting Congress to establish a permanent board of colonels to develop explosives safety standards and ensure compliance beginning in 1928. This organization evolved into the Department of Defense Explosives Safety Board (DDESB) and is chartered in Title 10 of the US Code. Today, the DDESB authors DOD Manual 6055.9, Ammunition and Explosives Safety Standards. It also evaluates scientific data which may adjust those standards, reviews and approves all explosives site plans for new construction, and conducts worldwide visits to locations containing US title munitions.

28.1 US Air Force

The United States Air Force counterpart to the DDESB is the Air Force Safety Center (AFSEC/SEW). Similarly safety functions are found at major command headquarters, intermediate command headquarters and at unit level as the weapons safety office. Quantity-Distance (QD) has evolved into the foundation of DOD 6055.9-STD, Ammunition and Explosives Safety Standards. The current Air Force regulation governing explosives safety is Air Force Manual (AFMAN) 91-201. AFMAN 91-201 was written using DODI 6055.9 as a parent regulation, and in most cases will follow the limitations set forth in the DODI (excluding mission specific requirements). The Air Force deviates from DODI 6055.9 using AFMAN 91-201 as their primary source document to allow for deviation from many of the requirements of the DODI as long as the risks of doing so are accepted at the appropriate level.

28.2 US Army

The United States Army counterpart to the DDESB is the U.S. Army Technical Center for Explosives Safety (USATCES). The USATCES is located with the Defense Ammunition Center on McAlester Army Ammunition Plant, near McAlester, Oklahoma. USATCES is responsible for providing ammunition and explosives (A&E) safety worldwide by acting as the field office of the Department of Army Safety responsible for A&E safety. The USATCES also acts as the Army agency having safety oversight of clean-up of Former Used Defense Sites (FUDS)[1][2] and Former Toxic Chemical Agent Sites where munitions from all branches of service disposed of A&E by burial or dumping up until the end of the Vietnam War. The USATCES acts as the Army's safety watchdog for disposal of chemical ammunition at the Army's Chemical Disposal Facilities. As part of Army's Ordinance Corps under TRADOC Specially trained Civilian Explosives Safety Personnel [Quality Assurance Specialist (Ammunition Surveillance) (QASAS)[3]] and Safety Specialist that have received specialized training in A&E Safety) from the USATCES are deployed worldwide, wherever the U.S. Army has A&E. Their mission is to provide A&E safety to the soldier, the public, and the environment making sure the Army's A&E is not only stored safely but ready, reliable, and lethal when the U.S. military needs it.

28.3 Net Explosives Weight (NEW)

The net explosives weight (NEW) (or TNT Equivalence) is based on explosives compounds that are equal to one pound of trinitrotoluene (TNT). A compound may weigh two pounds but have the blast effects of only one pound of TNT it is then said to have a NEW of one pound. If the compound weights one pound but has the blast effects of two pounds of TNT the NEW is considered as two pounds NEW. NEW is used to calculate QD by means of a formula of the type $D (ft) = K \cdot W^{1/3}$, where "D" is the distance in feet, "K" is a factor (also called K-factor) that is dependent upon the risk assumed or permitted, and "W" is the NEW in pounds. When metric units are used, the symbol "Q" denotes Net Explosive Quantity (NEQ) in kilograms. In the formula $D (m) = Km \cdot Q^{1/4}$, the distance "D" is expressed in meters. Thus, the units of the K-factor ("K" in the English system) are $ft/lb^{1/3}$ and ("Km" in the metric system) $m/kg^{1/3}$. The value of "K" in English units is approximately 2.52 times "Km." For example, if $D (m) = 6 \cdot Q^{1/3}$, then $D (ft) = 15.12 \cdot W^{1/3}$. Distance requirements determined by the formula with English units are sometimes expressed by the value of "K," using the terminology K9, K11, K18, to mean K = 9, K = 11, and K = 18.

28.4 Blast Wave Phenomena

A Blast Wave Phenomenon is an incident involving the violent release of energy created by detonation of an explosive device. The sudden and intense pressure disturbance is termed the "blast wave." The blast wave is characterized by an almost instantaneous rise from ambient pressure to a peak incident pressure (Pi). This pressure increase or "shock front," travels radially outward from the detonation point, with a diminishing velocity that is always in excess of the speed of sound in that medium. Gas molecules making up the front move at lower velocities. This velocity, which is called the "particle velocity," is associated with the "dynamic pressure," or the pressure formed by the winds produced by the shock front. As the shock front expands into increasingly larger volumes of the medium, the incident pressure decreases and, generally, the duration of the pressure-pulse increase. If the shock wave strikes a rigid surface (e.g., a building) at an angle to the direction of the wave's propagation, a reflected pressure is instantly developed on the surface and this pressure rises to a value that exceeds the incident pressure. This reflected pressure is a function of the incident wave's pressure and the angle formed between the rigid surface and the plane of the shock front.

28.5 Fragments

An important consideration in the analysis of the hazards associated with an explosion is the effect of any fragments produced. Fragmentation most commonly occur in high explosives events, fragmentation may occur in any incident involving ammunition and explosives (A&E). Depending on their origin, fragments are referred to as "primary" or "secondary" fragments.

Primary fragments result from the shattering of a container (e.g., shell casings, kettles, hoppers, and other containers used in the manufacture of explosives and rocket engine housings) in direct contact with the explosive. These fragments usually are small, initially travel at thousands of feet per second, and may be lethal at long distances from an explosion.

Secondary fragments are debris from structures and other items in close proximity to the explosion. These fragments, which are somewhat larger in size than primary fragments and initially travel at hundreds of feet per second, do not normally travel as far as primary fragments.

28.6 Thermal Hazards

Generally, thermal hazards from explosives events are of less concern than blast and fragment hazards. With the release of energy from an explosion is heat. The amount of heat varies with the energetic compound (explosive). All explosives compound molecules are potentially unstable held together with weak bonds in their outer shell. When this weak bond is broken heat and energy is violently released. It normally takes longer for the thermal blast to incur. Injury from thermal effects follows the blast and fragmentation effects which happen almost instantaneously. This does not imply that there is a time lapse between blast and fragmentation effects of explosives; in fact it happens so fast that humans cannot notice the delay without specialized equipment. The time available to react to a thermal event does increases survivability by rapid equipment designed to react in a fragment of a second. The primary effect of the thermal effect from an explosive detonation on structures, material, and ammunition and explosives (A&E) is their partial or total destruction by fire. The primary concern for explosives safety with a fire involving A&E is that it may transition to a more severe reaction, causing detonations of additional or more hazardous explosives devises and placing more people or property at a greater degree of risk of damage, destruction, injury, or death.

28.7 Susan Test

"Susan Test" redirects here. For the *Johnny Test* character, see List of Johnny Test characters § Susan and Mary Test.

Following the 1966 Palomares B-52 crash and the 1968 Thule Air Base B-52 crash, accident investigators concluded that the conventional explosives used at the time in nuclear weapons were not stable enough to withstand the forces involved in an aircraft accident. The finding triggered research by scientists in the United States into safer conventional explosives that could be used in nuclear weapons.*[4] The Lawrence Livermore National Laboratory developed the "Susan Test"—a standard test that uses a special projectile whose design simulates an aircraft accident by squeezing and nipping explosive material between metal surfaces. The test projectile is fired under controlled conditions at a hard surface to measure the reactions and thresholds of different explosives to an impact.

28.8 Explosives Safety Specialist

This is a highly trained and skilled civilian professional usually a QASAS or a Safety Specialist that has been trained to evaluate risk and hazards involved with conventional, guided missiles and toxic chemical ammunition operations. Department of Defense Standards requires that only trained and certified personnel are permitted to participate in operations involving ammunition, explosives, and/or explosive components, guided missiles, and toxic chemicals. They are responsible for providing protection from the effects of ammunition and explosives by evaluation of a set of standards developed by the Department of Defense and reinforced by additional regulations by the branch of military service responsible for the explosives item. They develop safety programs to minimize losses due to injuries and property damage. They try to eliminate unsafe practices and conditions on sites where ammunition and explosives (A&E) are used or stored. Military explosives safety specialist are deployed along with U.S. Military forces to maintain safe storage and use of A&E. They are responsible to recommend to military command ways to store A&E that reduce the risk of injury or death to service men and women in case of an accidental detonation or if the A&E supply is hit by enemy attack.

Much of the work of military explosives safety specialist is identical to their civilian counterparts. They have offices where they analyze data and write reports to upper commands on the storage of A&E. Much of their time is spent reviewing or preparing explosives safety site plans. An explosives site plan (ESS) is the composite risk management (CRM) process associated with explosives/toxic chemical activities to ensure the minimum risk to personnel, equipment, and assets, while meeting mission requirements. The damage or injury potential of explosions is determined by the separation distance between potential explosion sites (PES) and exposed sites (ES); the ability of the PES to suppress blast overpressure, primary and secondary fragments; and the ability of the ES to resist explosion effects. Planning for the proper location and construction of A&E facilities and surrounding facilities exposed to A&E facilities is a key element of the explosives/toxic chemical site planning process. This management process also ensures that risks above those normally accepted for A&E activities are identified and approved at the proper level of command.

Explosives Safety Specialist must often travel to different storage sites to verify that the military installation is meeting the service explosives safety regulations.

Explosives Safety Specialist often works with other safety professionals. They are required to know OSHA, EPA, NFPA and other consensus standards when looking at safety and if these regulations are stricter than their service regulation they must apply these standards and regulations. They must also know Alcohol, Tobacco, and Firearms (ATF) regulations dealing with A&E and apply those standards if it is required. They must be able to convince people the need for following prescribes explosives safety standards/regulations. They must also work with ammunition cleanup sites insuring that safety laws and regulations as well as industry standards are followed. They should be good at solving problems.

The military is not the only industry to use explosives safety specialist but are by far the largest employer. Mining and construction also use explosives safety specialist to evaluate hazard and risk from explosives and blasting operations. Ammunition and explosives manufactures also use these professionals. Outside the military explosives safety specialist must apply and be knowledgeable of ATF, OSHA, EPA, NFPA, as well as state and local regulations dealing with safety of A&E.

28.9 See also

- Explosion protection
- Explosion vent
- Explosive material
- Explosives shipping classification system

28.10 References

[1] 1 azdeq.gov retrieved 2011-11-23

[2] 2 U.S. Army Corps of Engineers (USACE). retrieved 2011-11-23

[3] apd.army.mil retrieved 2011-11-23

[4] Jonas A. Zukas, William P. Walters (2002). *Explosive Effects and Applications*. Springer. pp. 305–307. ISBN 0-387-95558-5.

- [1][Picatinny: History. (n.d.). Retrieved February 7, 2015, from http://www.pica.army.mil/PicatinnyPublic/about/history.asp]

28.11 External links

- Explosives Safety Support
- ddesb.pentagon
- retrieved 2011-11-23 nasa.gov

Chapter 29
Examples of Military Weapons Explosions

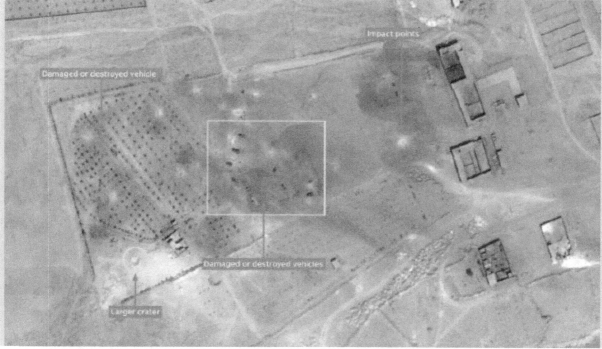

29.3. REFERENCES

Hypothetical nuclear 'mine' attack

Approx size of crater of Hawthorne Ridge mine

Rough guess of 8kt nuclear mine 100m deep

Types of Missiles

1. Conventional guided missiles
- Air-to-air missile
- Air-to-surface missile
- Anti-ballistic missile
- Anti-tank guided missile
- Surface-to-air missile
- Surface-to-surface missile

2. Cruise missiles

3. Ballistic missiles
- Short Range Ballistic Missile
  - Range < 1000 Km
- Medium Range Ballistic Missile
  - Range 1000 – 3000 Km
- Intermediate Range Ballistic Missile
  - Range 3000 – 5500 Km
- Intercontinental Ballistic Missile
  - Range > 5500 Km

Chapter 30

Strength (explosive)

In explosive materials, **strength** is the parameter determining the ability of the explosive to move the surrounding material. It is related to the total gas yield of the reaction, and the amount of heat produced. *Cf.* brisance.

The strength, or *potential*, of an explosive is the total work that can be performed by the gas resulting from its explosion, when expanded adiabatically from its original volume, until its pressure is reduced to atmospheric pressure and its temperature to 15°C. The potential is therefore the total quantity of heat given off at constant volume when expressed in equivalent work units and is a measure of the strength of the explosive.

Explosive strength is measured by, for example, the Trauzl lead block test.

An explosion may occur under two general conditions: the first, unconfined, as in the open air where the pressure (atmospheric) is constant; the second, confined, as in a closed chamber where the volume is constant. The same amount of heat energy is liberated in each case, but in the unconfined explosion, a certain amount is used as work energy in pushing back the surrounding air, and therefore is lost as heat. In a confined explosion, where the explosive volume is small (such as occurs in the powder chamber of a firearm), practically all the heat of explosion is conserved as useful energy. If the quantity of heat liberated at constant volume under adiabatic conditions is calculated and converted from heat units to equivalent work units, the potential or capacity for work results.

Therefore, if

Q_{mp} represents the total quantity of heat given off by a mole of explosive of 15°C and constant pressure (atmospheric);

Q_{mv} represents the total heat given off by a mole of explosive at 15°C and constant volume; and

W represents the work energy expended in pushing back the surrounding air in an unconfined explosion and thus is not available as net theoretical heat;

Then, because of the conversion of energy to work in the constant pressure case,

$$Q_{mv} = Q_{mp} + W$$

from which the value of Q_{mv} may be determined. Subsequently, the potential of a mole of an explosive may be calculated. Using this value, the potential for any other weight of explosive may be determined by simple proportion.

Using the principle of the initial and final state, and heat of formation table (resulting from experimental data), the heat released at constant pressure may be readily calculated.

$$Q_{mp} = \sum_{1}^{m} v_i Q_{fi} - \sum_{1}^{n} v_k Q_{fk}$$

where:

Q_{fi} = heat of formation of product i at constant pressure

Q_{fk} = heat of formation of reactant k at constant pressure

v = number of moles of each product/reactants (m is the number of products and n the number of reactants)

The work energy expended by the gaseous products of detonation is expressed by:

$$W = P\,dv$$

With pressure constant and negligible initial volume, this expression reduces to:

$$W = P \cdot V_2$$

Since heats of formation are calculated for standard atmospheric pressure (101 325 Pa, where 1 Pa = 1 N/m^2) and 15°C, V_2 is the volume occupied by the product gases under these conditions. At this point

W/mol = (101 325 N/m^2)(23.63 l/mol)(1 m^3/1000 l) = 2394 N·m/mol = 2394 J/mol

and by applying the appropriate conversion factors, work can be converted to units of kilocalories.

W/mol = 0.572 kcal/mol

Once the chemical reaction has been balanced, one can calculate the volume of gas produced and the work of expansion. With this completed, the calculations necessary to determine potential may be accomplished.

For TNT:

$C_6H_2(NO_2)_3CH_3 \rightarrow 6CO + 2.5H_2 + 1.5N_2 + C$

for 10 mol

Then:

Q_{mp} = 6(26.43) − 16.5 = 142.08 kcal/mol

Note: Elements in their natural state (H_2, O_2, N_2, C, etc.) are used as the basis for heat of formation tables and are assigned a value of zero. See table 12-2.

Q_{mv} = 142.08 + 0.572(10) = 147.8 kcal/mol

As previously stated, Q_{mv} converted to equivalent work units is the potential of the explosive. (MW = Molecular Weight of Explosive)

Potential = Q_{mv} kcal/mol × 4185 J/kcal × 10^3 g/kg × 1 mol/(mol·g)

Potential = Q_{mv} (4.185 × 10^6) J/(mol·kg)

For TNT,

Potential = 147.8 (4.185 × 10^6)/227.1 = 2.72 × 10^6 J/kg

Rather than tabulate such large numbers, in the field of explosives, TNT is taken as the standard explosive, and others are assigned strengths relative to that of TNT. The potential of TNT has been calculated above to be 2.72 × 10^6 J/kg. Relative strength (RS) may be expressed as

R.S. = Potential of Explosive/(2.72 × 10^6)

Chapter 31

Gurney equations

The **Gurney equations** are a set of mathematical formulas used in explosives engineering to relate how fast an explosive will accelerate a surrounding layer of metal or other material when the explosive detonates. This determines how fast fragments are released by military explosives, how quickly shaped charge explosives accelerate their liners inwards, and in other calculations such as explosive welding where explosives force two metal sheets together and bond them.[1]

The equations were first developed in the 1940s by Ronald Gurney[2] and have been expanded on and added to significantly since that time.

31.1 Underlying physics

When an explosive surrounded by a metallic or other solid shell detonates, the outer shell is accelerated both by the initial detonation shock wave and by the expansion of the detonation gas products contained by the outer shell. Gurney modeled how energy was distributed between the metal shell and the detonation gases, and developed formulas that accurately describe the acceleration results.

Gurney made a simplifying assumption that there is a linear velocity gradient in the explosive detonation product gases. This works well for most configurations, but see the section Anomalous predictions below.

31.1.1 Definitions and units

The Gurney equations relate the following quantities:

C - The mass of the explosive charge

M - The mass of the accelerated shell or sheet of material (usually metal). The shell or sheet is often referred to as the *flyer*, or *flyer plate*.

V or V_m - Velocity of accelerated flyer after explosive detonation.

N - The mass of a tamper shell or sheet on the other side of the explosive charge, if present.

$\sqrt{2E}$ - The Gurney constant for a given explosive. This is expressed in units of velocity (millimeters per microsecond, for example) and compares the relative flyer velocity produced by different explosive materials.

For imploding systems, where a hollow explosive charge accelerates an inner mass towards the center, the calculations additionally take into account:

R_o - Outside radius of the explosive charge.

R_i - Inside radius of the explosive charge.

31.1.2 Gurney constant and detonation velocity

As a simple approximate equation, the physical value of $\sqrt{2E}$ is usually very close to 1/3 of the detonation velocity of the explosive material for standard explosives.[1] For a typical set of military explosives, the value of $\frac{D}{\sqrt{2E}}$ ranges from between 2.79 and 3.15.

Note that $\frac{mm}{\mu s}$ is dimensionally equal to kilometers per second, a more familiar unit for many applications.

31.1.3 Fragmenting versus nonfragmenting outer shells

The Gurney equations give a result that assumes the flyer plate remains intact throughout its acceleration. For some configurations, this is true; explosive welding, for example, uses a thin sheet of explosive to evenly accelerate flat plates of metal and collide them, and the plates remain solid throughout. However, for many configurations where materials are accelerated outwards, the expanding shell fractures due to stretching. When it fractures, it usually breaks into many small fragments due to the combined effects of ongoing expansion of the shell and stress relief waves moving into the material from fracture points.*[1]

For brittle metal shells, the fragment velocities are typically about 80% of the value predicted by the Gurney formulas.

31.1.4 Effective charge volume for small diameter charges

The basic Gurney equations for flat sheets assume that the sheet of material is large diameter.

Small explosive charges, where the explosives diameter is not significantly larger than its thickness, have reduced effectiveness as gas and energy are lost to the sides.*[1]

This loss is empirically modeled as reducing the effective explosive charge mass C to an effective value C_{eff} which is the volume of explosives contained within a 60° cone with its base on the explosives/flyer boundary.

Putting a cylindrical tamper around the explosive charge reduces that side loss effectively, as analyzed by Benham.

31.1.5 Anomalous predictions

In 1996, Hirsch described a performance region, for relatively small ratios of $\frac{M}{C}$ in which the Gurney equations misrepresent the actual physical behavior. *[3]

The range of values for which the basic Gurney equations generated anomalous values is described by (for flat asymmetrical and open-faced sandwich configurations):

$\frac{M}{C}\left[\left(4\frac{N}{C}\right)+1\right] < \frac{1}{2}$

For an open-faced sandwich configuration (see below), this corresponds to values of $\frac{M}{C}$ of 0.5 or less. For a sandwich with tamper mass equal to explosive charge mass ($\frac{N}{C} \geq 1.0$) a flyer plate mass of 0.1 or less of the charge mass will be anomalous.

This error is due to the configuration exceeding one of the underlying simplifying assumptions used in the Gurney equations, that there is a linear velocity gradient in the explosive product gases. For values of $\frac{M}{C}$ outside the anomalous region, this is a good assumption. Hirsch demonstrated that as the total energy partition between the flyer plate and gases exceeds unity, the assumption breaks down, and the Gurney equations become less accurate as a result.

Complicating factors in the anomalous region include detailed gas behavior of the explosive products, including the reaction products' heat capacity ratio, γ.

Modern explosives engineering utilizes computational analysis methods which avoid this problem.

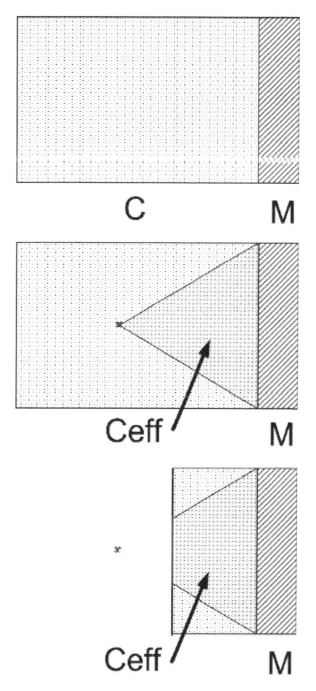

Effective charge mass for thin charges - a 60° cone

31.2 Equations

31.2.1 Cylindrical charge

For the simplest case, a long hollow cylinder of metal is filled completely with explosives. The cylinder's walls are accelerated outwards as described by:*[1]

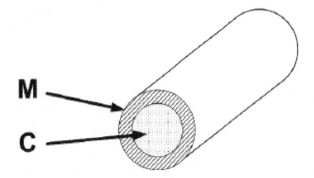

Cylindrical charge of mass C and flyer shell of mass M

$$\frac{V}{\sqrt{2E}} = \left(\frac{M}{C} + \frac{1}{2}\right)^{-1/2}$$

This configuration is a first-order approximation for most military explosive devices, including artillery shells, bombs, and most missile warheads. These use mostly cylindrical explosive charges.

31.2.2 Spherical charge

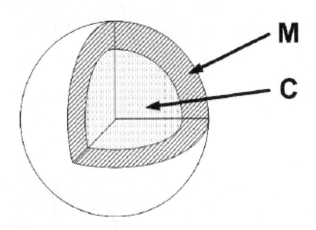

Center-initiated spherical charge - spherical explosive charge of mass C and spherical flyer shell of mass M

A spherical charge, initiated at its center, will accelerate a surrounding flyer shell as described by:[*][1]

$$\frac{V}{\sqrt{2E}} = \left(\frac{M}{C} + \frac{3}{5}\right)^{-1/2}$$

This model approximates the behavior of military grenades, and some cluster bomb submunitions.

31.2.3 Symmetrical sandwich

A flat layer of explosive with two identical heavy flat flyer plates on each side will accelerate the plates as described by:[*][1]

$$\frac{V}{\sqrt{2E}} = \left(2\frac{M}{C} + \frac{1}{3}\right)^{-1/2}$$

Symmetrical sandwich - flat explosives layer of mass C and two flyer plates of mass M each

Symmetrical sandwiches are used in some Reactive armor applications, on heavily armored vehicles such as main battle tanks. The inward-firing flyer will impact the vehicle main armor, causing damage if the armor is not thick enough, so these can only be used on heavier armored vehicles. Lighter vehicles use open-face sandwich reactive armor (see below). However, the dual moving plate method of operation of a symmetrical sandwich offers the best armor protection.

31.2.4 Asymmetrical sandwich

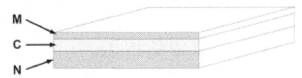

Asymmetrical sandwich - flat explosives layer of mass C, flyer plates of different masses M and N

A flat layer of explosive with two flat flyer plates of different masses will accelerate the plates as described by:[*][1][*][4][*][5]

Let: $A = \frac{1+2\frac{M}{C}}{1+2\frac{N}{C}}$

$$\frac{V_M}{\sqrt{2E}} = \left(\frac{1+A^3}{3(1+A)} + A^2\frac{N}{C} + \frac{M}{C}\right)^{-1/2}$$

31.2.5 Infinitely tamped sandwich

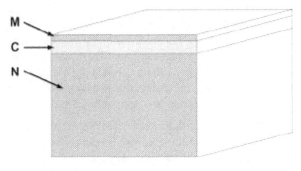

Infinitely tamped sandwich - flat explosives layer of mass C, flyer plate of mass M, and infinitely heavy backing tamper

31.2. EQUATIONS

When a flat layer of explosive is placed on a practically infinitely thick supporting surface, and topped with a flyer plate of material, the flyer plate will be accelerated as described by:[1]

$$\frac{V_M}{\sqrt{2E}} = \left(\frac{M}{C} + \frac{1}{3}\right)^{-1/2}$$

31.2.6 Open-faced sandwich

Open-faced sandwich (no tamping) - flat explosives layer of mass C and single flyer plate of mass M

A single flat sheet of explosives with a flyer plate on one side, known as an "open-faced sandwich", is described by:[1]

Since:

$$N = 0$$

then:

$$A = 1 + 2\left(\frac{M}{C}\right)$$

which gives:

$$\frac{V}{\sqrt{2E}} = \left[\frac{1+(1+2\frac{M}{C})^3}{6(1+\frac{M}{C})} + \frac{M}{C}\right]^{-1/2}$$

Open-faced sandwich configurations are used in Explosion welding and some other metalforming operations.

It is also a configuration commonly used in reactive armour on lightly armored vehicles, with the open face down towards the vehicle's main armor plate. This minimizes the reactive armor units damage to the vehicle structure during firing.

31.2.7 Imploding cylinder

A hollow cylinder of explosive, initiated evenly around its surface, with an outer tamper and inner hollow shell which is then accelerated inwards ("imploded") rather than outwards is described by the following equations.[6]

Unlike other forms of the Gurney equation, implosion forms (cylindrical and spherical) must take into account the shape of the control volume of the detonating shell of explosives and the distribution of momentum and energy within the detonation product gases. For cylindrical implosions, the geometry involved is simplified to include the inner and outer radii of the explosive charge, R_i and R_o.

$$\beta = \frac{R_o}{R_i}$$

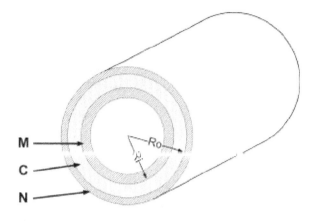

Uniformly initiated cylindrical charge imploding an inner mass - cylinder shell explosive charge of mass C, outer tamper layer of mass N, and inner imploding cylindrical flyer shell of mass M, with inner explosive charge radius R_i and outer charge radius of R_o.

$$a = 1$$

$$A = \frac{V_o}{V_i} = \frac{\left(\frac{M}{C} + a\left(\frac{M}{C}\right)(\beta-1) + \frac{\beta+2}{3(\beta+1)}\right)}{\left(\frac{N}{C} + \frac{2\beta+1}{3(\beta+1)}\right)}$$

$$\frac{V_m}{\sqrt{2E}} = \left[A\left\{\frac{\left(\frac{M}{C} + \frac{\beta+1}{6(\beta+1)}\right)}{A} + A\left(\frac{N}{C} + \frac{3\beta+1}{6(\beta+1)}\right) - 1/3\right\}\right]^{-1/2}$$

While the imploding cylinder equations are fundamentally similar to the general equation for asymmetrical sandwiches, the geometry involved (volume and area within the explosive's hollow shell, and expanding shell of detonation product gases pushing inwards and out) is more complicated, as the equations demonstrate.

The constant a was experimentally and analytically determined to be 1.0.

31.2.8 Imploding spherical

A special case is a hollow sphere of explosives, initiated evenly around its surface, with an outer tamper and inner hollow shell which is then accelerated inwards ("imploded") rather than outwards, is described by:[6]

$$\beta = \frac{R_o}{R_i}$$

$$a = 1$$

$$A = \frac{V_o}{V_i} = \frac{\left[\frac{M}{C} + (a\frac{M}{C})(\beta^2 - 1) + \frac{\beta^2+2\beta+3}{4(\beta^2+\beta+1)}\right]}{\left(\frac{N}{C} + \frac{3\beta^2+2\beta+1}{4(\beta^2+\beta+1)}\right)}$$

$$\frac{V_m}{\sqrt{2E}} = \left[A\left\{\frac{\left(\frac{M}{C} + \frac{\beta^2+3\beta+6}{10(\beta^2+\beta+1)}\right)}{A} + A\left(\frac{N}{C} + \frac{6\beta^2+3\beta+1}{10(\beta^2+\beta+1)}\right) - \frac{3\beta^2+4\beta+3}{10(\beta^2+\beta+1)}\right\}\right]^{-1/2}$$

The spherical Gurney equation has applications in early nuclear weapons design.

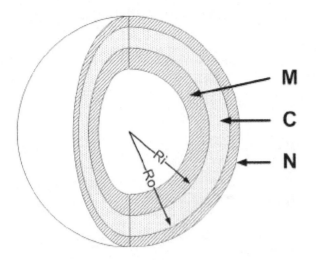

Uniformly initiated spherical charge imploding an inner mass - spherical shell explosive charge of mass C, outer tamper layer of mass N, and inner imploding spherical flyer shell of mass M

31.3 Applications

- Nuclear weapon

31.4 See also

- Explosives engineering
- Explosive velocity
- Table of explosive detonation velocities

31.5 References

[1] Cooper, Paul W. (1996). "Acceleration, Formation, and Flight of Fragments". *Explosives Engineering*. Wiley-VCH. pp. 385–394. ISBN 0-471-18636-8.

[2] Gurney, R. W. (1943). "The Initial Velocities of Fragments from Bombs, Shells, and Grenades, BRL-405". Ballistic Research Laboratory, Aberdeen, Maryland.

[3] Hirsch, E. (1995). "On the Inconsistency of the Asymmetric-Sandwich Gurney Formula When Used to Model Thin Plate Propulsion". *Propellants, Explosives, Pyrotechnics*. **20** (4): 178–181. doi:10.1002/prep.19950200404.

[4] Jones, G. E.; Kennedy, J. E.; Bertholf, L. D. (1980). "Ballistics calculations of R. W. Gurney". *Am. J. Phys.* **48** (4): 264–269. doi:10.1119/1.12135.

[5] Kennedy, J. E. (March 1979). *Explosive Output for Driving Metal*. Behavior and Utilization of Explosives Symposium (12th). ASME/UNM.

[6] Hirsch, E. (1986). "Simplified and Extended Gurney Formulas for Imploding Cylinders and Spheres". *Propellants, Explosives, Pyrotechnics*. **11** (1): 6–9. doi:10.1002/prep.19860110103.

Chapter 32

Nitroglycerin

Nitroglycerin (NG), also known as **nitroglycerine**, **trinitroglycerin (TNG)**, **trinitroglycerine**, **nitro**, **glyceryl trinitrate (GTN)**, or **1,2,3-trinitroxypropane**, is a heavy, colorless, oily, explosive liquid most commonly produced by nitrating glycerol with white fuming nitric acid under conditions appropriate to the formation of the nitric acid ester. Chemically, the substance is an organic nitrate compound rather than a nitro compound, yet the traditional name is often retained. Invented in 1847, nitroglycerin has been used as an active ingredient in the manufacture of explosives, mostly dynamite, and as such it is employed in the construction, demolition, and mining industries. Since the 1880s, it has been used by the military as an active ingredient, and a gelatinizer for nitrocellulose, in some solid propellants, such as cordite and ballistite.

Nitroglycerin is also a major component in double-based smokeless gunpowders used by reloaders. Combined with nitrocellulose, there are hundreds of powder combinations used by rifle, pistol, and shotgun reloaders.

For over 130 years, nitroglycerin has been used medically as a potent vasodilator (dilation of the vascular system) to treat heart conditions, such as angina pectoris and chronic heart failure. Though it was previously known that these beneficial effects are due to nitroglycerin being converted to nitric oxide, a potent venodilator, it was not until 2002 that the enzyme for this conversion was discovered to be mitochondrial aldehyde dehydrogenase.*[3] Nitroglycerin is available in sublingual tablets, sprays, and patches.*[4] Other potential suggested uses include adjunct therapy in prostate cancer.*[5]

32.1 History

Nitroglycerin was the first practical explosive produced that was stronger than black powder. It was first synthesized by the Italian chemist Ascanio Sobrero in 1847, working under Théophile-Jules Pelouze at the University of Turin. Sobrero initially called his discovery *pyroglycerine* and warned vigorously against its use as an explosive.

Nitroglycerin was later adopted as a commercially useful explosive by Alfred Nobel, who experimented with safer ways to handle the dangerous compound after his younger brother, Emil Oskar Nobel, and several factory workers were killed in an explosion at the Nobels' armaments factory in 1864 in Heleneborg, Sweden.*[6]

One year later, Nobel founded Alfred Nobel & Company in Germany and built an isolated factory in the Krümmel hills of Geesthacht near Hamburg. This business exported a liquid combination of nitroglycerin and gunpowder called "Blasting Oil", but this was extremely unstable and difficult to handle, as evidenced in numerous catastrophes. The buildings of the Krümmel factory were destroyed twice.*[7]

In April 1866, three crates of nitroglycerin were shipped to California for the Central Pacific Railroad, which planned to experiment with it as a blasting explosive to expedite the construction of the 1,659-foot (506 m)-long Summit Tunnel through the Sierra Nevada Mountains. One of the crates exploded, destroying a Wells Fargo company office in San Francisco and killing 15 people. This led to a complete ban on the transportation of liquid nitroglycerin in California. The on-site manufacture of nitroglycerin was thus required for the remaining hard-rock drilling and blasting required for the completion of the First Transcontinental Railroad in North America.*[8]

Liquid nitroglycerin was widely banned elsewhere as well, and these legal restrictions led to Alfred Nobel and his company's developing dynamite in 1867. This was made by mixing nitroglycerin with diatomaceous earth ("*kieselgur*" in German) found in the Krümmel hills. Similar mixtures, such as "dualine" (1867), "lithofracteur" (1869), and "gelignite" (1875), were formed by mixing nitroglycerin with other inert absorbents, and many combinations were tried by other companies in attempts to get around Nobel's tightly held patents for dynamite.

Dynamite mixtures containing nitrocellulose, which increases the viscosity of the mix, are commonly known as "gelatins".

Following the discovery that amyl nitrite helped alleviate chest pain, Dr. William Murrell experimented with the use of nitroglycerin to alleviate angina pectoris and to reduce the blood pressure. He began treating his patients with small diluted doses of nitroglycerin in 1878, and this treatment was soon adopted into widespread use after Murrell published his results in the journal *The Lancet* in 1879.[9] A few months before his death in 1896, Alfred Nobel was prescribed nitroglycerine for this heart condition, writing to a friend: "Isn't it the irony of fate that I have been prescribed nitro-glycerin, to be taken internally! They call it Trinitrin, so as not to scare the chemist and the public." [10] The medical establishment also used the name "glyceryl trinitrate" for the same reason.

32.1.1 Wartime production rates

Large quantities of nitroglycerin were manufactured during World War I and World War II for use as military propellants and in military engineering work. During World War I, HM Factory, Gretna, the largest propellant factory in Britain, produced about 800 tonne of cordite RDB per week. This amount took at least 336 tons of nitroglycerin per week (assuming no losses in production). The Royal Navy had its own factory at the Royal Navy Cordite Factory, Holton Heath in Dorset, England. A large cordite factory was also built in Canada during World War I. The Canadian Explosives Limited cordite factory at Nobel, Ontario, was designed to produce 1,500,000 lb (680 t) of cordite per month, requiring about 286 tonnes of nitroglycerin per month.

32.2 Instability and desensitization

In its pure form, nitroglycerin is a contact explosive, with physical shock causing it to explode, and it degrades over time to even more unstable forms. This makes nitroglycerin highly dangerous to transport or use. In its undiluted form, it is one of the world's most powerful explosives, comparable to the more recently developed RDX and PETN.

Early in its history, it was discovered that liquid nitroglycerin can be "desensitized" by cooling it to about 5 to 10 °C (40 to 50 °F). At this temperature nitroglycerin freezes, contracting upon solidification. Thawing it out can be extremely sensitizing, especially if impurities are present or the warming is too rapid.[11] It is possible to chemically "desensitize" nitroglycerin to a point where it can be considered approximately as "safe" as modern high explosives, such as by the addition of approximately 10% to 30% ethanol, acetone,[12] or dinitrotoluene. (The percentage varies with the desensitizing agent used.) Desensitization requires extra effort to reconstitute the "pure" product. Failing this, it must be assumed that desensitized nitroglycerin is substantially more difficult to detonate, possibly rendering it useless as an explosive for practical application.

A serious problem in the use of nitroglycerin results from its high freezing point 13 °C (55 °F). Solid nitroglycerin is much less sensitive to shock than the liquid, a feature that is common in explosives. In the past, nitroglycerin was often shipped in the frozen state, but this resulted in a high number of accidents during the thawing process just before its use. This disadvantage is overcome by using mixtures of nitroglycerin with other polynitrates. For example, a mixture of nitroglycerin and ethylene glycol dinitrate freezes at −29 °C (−20 °F).[13]

32.3 Detonation

Nitroglycerin and any diluents can certainly deflagrate, i.e., burn. The explosive power of nitroglycerin derives from detonation: energy from the initial decomposition causes a strong pressure wave that detonates the surrounding fuel. This is a self-sustained shock wave that propagates through the explosive medium at 30 times the speed of sound as a near-instantaneous pressure-induced decomposition of the fuel into a white-hot gas. Detonation of nitroglycerin generates gases that would occupy more than 1,200 times the original volume at ordinary room temperature and pressure. The heat liberated raises the temperature to about 5,000 °C (9,000 °F).[14] This is entirely different from deflagration, which depends solely upon available fuel regardless of pressure or shock. The decomposition results in much higher ratio of energy to gas moles released compared to other explosives, making it one of the hottest detonating high explosives.

32.4 Manufacturing

Nitroglycerin can be produced by acid catalyzed nitration of glycerol (glycerine).

Nitroglycerine synthesis: [15] [16] [17]

The industrial manufacturing process often reacts glycerol with a nearly 1:1 mixture of concentrated sulfuric acid and concentrated nitric acid. This can be produced by mixing white fuming nitric acid—a quite expensive pure nitric acid in which the oxides of nitrogen have been removed, as opposed to red fuming nitric acid, which contains nitrogen oxides—and concentrated sulfuric acid. More often, this mixture is attained by the cheaper method of mixing fuming sulfuric acid, also known as oleum—sulfuric acid containing excess sulfur trioxide—and azeotropic nitric acid (consisting of about 70 percent nitric acid, with the rest being water).

The sulfuric acid produces protonated nitric acid species, which are attacked by glycerol's nucleophilic oxygen atoms. The nitro group is thus added as an ester $C-O-NO_2$ and water is produced. This is different from an electrophilic aromatic substitution reaction in which nitronium ions are the electrophile.

The addition of glycerol results in an exothermic reaction (i.e., heat is produced), as usual for mixed-acid nitrations. If the mixture becomes too hot, it results in a runaway reaction, a state of accelerated nitration accompanied by the destructive oxidation of organic materials by the hot nitric acid and the release of poisonous nitrogen dioxide gas at high risk of an explosion. Thus, the glycerin mixture is added slowly to the reaction vessel containing the mixed acid (not acid to glycerin). The nitrator is cooled with cold water or some other coolant mixture and maintained throughout the glycerin addition at about 22 °C (72 °F), much below which the esterification occurs too slowly to be useful. The nitrator vessel, often constructed of iron or lead and generally stirred with compressed air, has an emergency trap door at its base, which hangs over a large pool of very cold water and into which the whole reaction mixture (called the charge) can be dumped to prevent an explosion, a process referred to as drowning. If the temperature of the charge exceeds about 30 °C (86 °F) (actual value varying by country) or brown fumes are seen in the nitrator's vent, then it is immediately drowned.

32.5 Use as an explosive and a propellant

Main articles: Dynamite, Ballistite, Cordite, smokeless powder, and Gelignite

The main use of nitroglycerin, by tonnage, is in explosives such as dynamite and in propellants.

Nitroglycerin is an oily liquid that may explode when subjected to heat, shock or flame.

Alfred Nobel developed the use of nitroglycerin as a blasting explosive by mixing nitroglycerin with inert absorbents, particularly "*kieselguhr*," or diatomaceous earth. He named this explosive dynamite and patented it

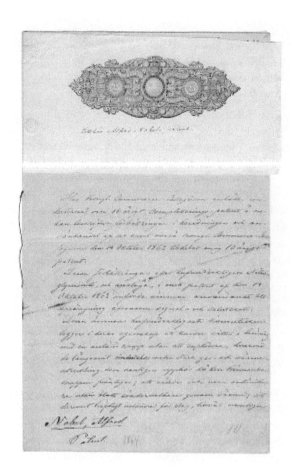

Alfred Nobel's patent application from 1864

in 1867.[18] It was supplied ready for use in the form of sticks, individually wrapped in greased waterproof paper. Dynamite and similar explosives were widely adopted for civil engineering tasks, such as in drilling highway and railroad tunnels, for mining, for clearing farmland of stumps, in quarrying, and in demolition work. Likewise, military engineers have used dynamite for construction and demolition work.

Nitroglycerin was also used as an ingredient in military propellants for use in firearms.

Nitroglycerin has been used in conjunction with hydraulic fracturing, a process used to recover oil and gas from shale formations. The technique involves displacing and detonating nitroglycerin in natural or hydraulically induced fracture systems, or displacing and detonating nitroglycerin in hydraulically induced fractures followed by wellbore shots using pelletized TNT.[19]

Nitroglycerin has an advantage over some other high explosives, that on detonation it produces practically no visible smoke. Therefore, it is useful as an ingredient in the formulation of various kinds of "smokeless powder".[20]

Its sensitivity has limited the usefulness of nitroglycerin as a military explosive, and less sensitive explosives such as TNT, RDX, and HMX have largely replaced it in munitions. It remains important in military engineering, and combat engineers still use dynamite.

Alfred Nobel then developed ballistite, by combining nitroglycerin and guncotton. He patented it in 1887. Ballistite was adopted by a number of European governments, as a military propellant. Italy was the first to adopt it. The British Government and the Commonwealth governments adopted cordite instead, which had been developed by Sir Frederick Abel and Sir James Dewar of the United Kingdom in 1889. The original Cordite Mk I consisted of 58% nitroglycerin, 37% guncotton, and 5.0% petroleum jelly. Ballistite and cordite were both manufactured in the forms of *cords*.

Smokeless powders were originally developed using nitrocellulose as the sole explosive ingredient. Therefore, they were known as *single-base* propellants. A range of smokeless powders that contain both nitrocellulose and nitroglycerin, known as *double-base* propellants, were also developed. Smokeless powders were originally supplied only for military use, but they were also soon developed for civilian use and were quickly adopted for sports. Some are known as sporting powders. *Triple-base* propellants contain nitrocellulose, nitroglycerin, and nitroguanidine, but are reserved mainly for extremely high-caliber ammunition rounds such as those used in tank cannons and naval artillery.

Blasting gelatin, also known as *gelignite*, was invented by Nobel in 1875, using nitroglycerin, wood pulp, and sodium or potassium nitrates. This was an early low-cost, flexible explosive.

32.6 Medical use

Main article: Medical use of nitroglycerin

Nitroglycerin belongs to a group of drugs called nitrates, which includes many other nitrates like isosorbide dinitrate (Isordil) and isosorbide mononitrate (Imdur, Ismo, Monoket).*[21] These agents all exert their effect by being converted to nitric oxide in the body by mitochondrial aldehyde dehydrogenase,*[3] and nitric oxide is a potent natural vasodilator.

In medicine, nitroglycerin is used as a medicine for angina pectoris, a painful symptom of ischemic heart disease caused by inadequate flow of blood and oxygen to the heart. Nitroglycerin corrects the imbalance between the flow of oxygen and blood to the heart.*[22] The principal action of nitroglycerin is venodilation (widening of the venous blood vessels). At low doses, nitroglycerin will dilate veins more than arteries, thereby reducing preload; this is thought to be its primary mechanism of action. But at higher doses, it also dilates arteries, thereby reducing afterload. It is also a potent antihypertensive agent. In cardiac treatment, the lowering of pressure in the arteries reduces the pressure against which the heart must pump, thereby decreasing afterload.*[21] Dilating the veins decreases cardiac preload and lowers the oxygen requirement of the heart whilst at the same time reducing ventricular transmural pressure thereby improving coronary blood flow. Improved myocardial oxygen demand vs oxygen delivery ratio leads to the following therapeutic effects during episodes of angina pectoris: subsiding of chest pain, decrease of blood pressure, increase of heart rate, and orthostatic hypotension. Patients experiencing angina when doing certain physical activities can often prevent symptoms by taking nitroglycerin 5 to 10 minutes before the activity.

Nitroglycerin is available in tablets, ointment, solution for intravenous use, transdermal patches, or sprays administered sublingually. Some forms of nitroglycerin last much longer in the body than others. It has been shown that continuous exposure to nitrates can cause the body to stop responding normally to this medicine. Experts recommend that the patches be removed at night, allowing the body a few hours to restore its responsiveness to nitrates. Shorter-acting preparations can be used several times a day with less risk of the body's getting used to this drug.*[23] Nitroglycerin was first used by William Murrell to treat angina attacks in 1878, with the discovery published that same year.*[9]*[24]

32.7 Industrial exposure

Infrequent exposure to high doses of nitroglycerin can cause severe headaches known as "NG head" or "bang head". These headaches can be severe enough to incapacitate some people; however, humans develop a tolerance to and dependence on nitroglycerin after long-term exposure. Withdrawal can (rarely) be fatal;*[25] withdrawal symptoms include chest pain and heart problems and if unacceptable may be treated with re-exposure to nitroglycerin or other suitable organic nitrates.*[26]

For workers in nitroglycerin (NTG) manufacturing facilities, the effects of withdrawal sometimes include "Sunday Heart Attacks" in those experiencing regular nitroglycerin exposure in the workplace, leading to the development of tolerance for the venodilating effects. Over the weekend, the workers lose the tolerance and, when they are re-exposed on Monday, the drastic vasodilation produces a fast heart rate, dizziness, and a headache, this is referred to as "Monday Disease." *[27]*[28]

People can be exposed to nitroglycerin in the workplace by breathing it in, skin absorption, swallowing it, or eye contact. The Occupational Safety and Health Administration (OSHA) has set the legal limit (permissible exposure limit) for nitroglycerin exposure in the workplace as 0.2 ppm (2 mg/m^3) skin exposure over an 8-hour workday. The National Institute for Occupational Safety and Health (NIOSH) has set a recommended exposure limit (REL) of 0.1 mg/m^2 skin exposure over an 8-hour workday. At levels of 75 mg/m^3, nitroglycerin is immediately dangerous to life and health.*[29]

32.8 See also

- Erythritol tetranitrate
- Ethylene glycol dinitrate
- Mannitol hexanitrate
- Methyl nitrate
- Tetranitratoxycarbon
- Xylitol pentanitrate
- RE factor

32.9 References

[1] https://www.osha.gov/SLTC/healthguidelines/nitroglycerin/recognition.html

[2] "NIOSH Pocket Guide to Chemical Hazards #0456". National Institute for Occupational Safety and Health (NIOSH).

[3] Chen, Z; Foster, MW; Zhang, J; Mao, L; Rockman, HA; Kawamoto, T; Kitagawa, K; Nakayama, KI; et al. (2005). "An essential role for mitochondrial aldehyde dehydrogenase in nitroglycerin bioactivation". *Proc. Natl. Acad. Sci. USA.* **102** (34): 12159–12164. Bibcode:2005PNAS..10212159C. doi:10.1073/pnas.0503723102. PMC 1189320☉. PMID 16103363.

[4] http://web.ebscohost.com/src/detail?vid=17&hid=7&sid=7e55c0c3-4b92-4b24-ac2d-b2091791a502%40sessionmgr14&bdata=JnNpdGU9c3JjLWxpdmU%3d#db=hxh&AN=9703191987

[5] Daily Mail: "How dynamite could help destroy prostate cancer" Retrieved 2010-02-23

[6] NobelPrize.org: Emil Nobel.

[7] NobelPrize.org: Krümmel.

[8] "Transcontinental Railroad – People & Events: Nitroglycerin". *American Experience*, PBS.

[9] Sneader, Walter. *Drug Discovery: A History*. John Wiley and Sons, 2005 ISBN 0-471-89980-1.

[10] History of TNG

[11] "Tales of Destruction-Thawing can be Hell".

[12] "Tales of Destruction – Is Nitroglicerine in This?"

[13] "nitroglycerin". *Britannica*. Retrieved 2005-03-23.

[14] Encyclopaedia Britannica.

[15] "Zusammensetzung der Zuckerasche". *Annalen der Chemie und Pharmacie*. **64** (3): 398–399. 1848. doi:10.1002/jlac.18480640364.

[16] "Ueber Nitroglycerin". *Annalen der Chemie und Pharmacie*. **92** (3): 305–306. 1854. doi:10.1002/jlac.18540920309.

[17] Di Carlo, F. J. (1975). "Nitroglycerin Revisited: Chemistry, Biochemistry, Interactions". *Drug Metabolism Reviews*. **4** (1): 1–38. doi:10.3109/03602537508993747. PMID 812687.

[18] Mary Bellis. "Alfred Nobel and the History of Dynamite". About.com Money.

[19] Miller, J. S.; Johansen, R. T. (1976). "Fracturing Oil Shale with Explosives for In Situ Recovery." (PDF). *Shale Oil, Tar Sand and Related Fuel Sources*. American Chemical Society: 151. Retrieved 27 March 2015.

[20] "Nitroglycerin".

[21] Omudhome Ogbru, PharmD. "nitroglycerin, Nitro-Bid: Drug Facts, Side Effects and Dosing". *MedicineNet*.

[22] Omudhome Ogbru, PharmD. "nitroglycerin, Nitro-Bid: Drug Facts, Side Effects and Dosing". *MedicineNet*.

[23] Nitroglycerin for angina, February 1997, Vol. 7.

[24] Smith, E; Hart, F. D. (1971). "William Murrell, physician and practical therapist". *British Medical Journal*. **3** (5775): 632–633. doi:10.1136/bmj.3.5775.632. PMC 1798737☉. PMID 4998847.

[25] Amdur, Mary O.; Doull, John. Casarett and Doull's Toxicology. 4th edition Pub: Elsevier 1991 ISBN 0071052399

[26] John B. Sullivan, Jr.; Gary R. Krieger (2001). *Clinical Environmental Health and Toxic Exposures: Latex*. Lippincott Williams & Wilkins. pp. 264–. ISBN 978-0-683-08027-8. Retrieved 23 April 2013.

[27] Marsh N, Marsh A (2000). "A short history of nitroglycerine and nitric oxide in pharmacology and physiology". *Clin. Exp. Pharmacol. Physiol.* **27** (4): 313–9. doi:10.1046/j.1440-1681.2000.03240.x. PMID 10779131. Retrieved 2015-10-16.

[28] Assembly of Life Sciences (U.S.). Advisory Center on Toxicology. *Toxicological Reports*. National Academies. pp. 115–. NAP:11288. Retrieved 23 April 2013.

[29] "CDC - NIOSH Pocket Guide to Chemical Hazards - Nitroglycerine" . *www.cdc.gov*. Retrieved 2015-11-21.

32.10 External links

- "Nitroglycerine! Terrible Explosion and Loss of Lives in San Francisco" . *Central Pacific Railroad Photographic History Museum*. Retrieved 2005-03-23. – 1866 Newspaper article

- WebBook page for C3H5N3O9

- CDC - NIOSH Pocket Guide to Chemical Hazards

- The Tallini Tales of Destruction Detailed and horrific stories of the historical use of nitroglycerin-filled torpedoes to restart petroleum wells.

- Dynamite and TNT at *The Periodic Table of Videos* (University of Nottingham)

Chapter 33

Acetone peroxide

Acetone peroxide is an organic peroxide and a primary high explosive. It is produced by the oxidation of acetone to yield a mixture of linear monomer and cyclic dimer, trimer, and tetramer forms. The trimer is known as **triacetone triperoxide (TATP)** or **tri-cyclic acetone peroxide (TCAP)**. Acetone peroxide takes the form of a white crystalline powder with a distinctive bleach-like odor and can explode if subjected to heat, friction, or shock. As a non-nitrogenous explosive, TATP has historically been more difficult to detect, and it has been implicated as the explosive used in terrorist attacks in Europe (2016 Brussels bombings) in 2016 and earlier.

33.1 History

Acetone peroxide (specifically, triacetone triperoxide) was discovered in 1895 by Richard Wolffenstein.[1] He was the first researcher to receive a patent for using the peroxide as an explosive compound.

In 1900 Bayer and Villiger described the first synthesis of the dimer and described use of acids for the synthesis of both peroxides.[2] Work on this methodology, and on the various products obtained, was further investigated in the mid-20th century by Milas and Golubović.[3]

33.2 Chemistry

The chemical name acetone peroxide is most commonly used to refer to the cyclic trimer *triacetone triperoxide* (TATP: synonyms, tri-cyclic acetone peroxide, TCAP: peroxyacetone), obtained by a reaction between hydrogen peroxide and acetone in an acid-catalyzed nucleophilic addition, although various further monomeric and dimeric forms are possible.

Specifically, two dimers, one cyclic ($C_6H_{12}O_4$) and one open chain ($C_6H_{14}O_4$), as well as an open chain monomer ($C_3H_8O_4$),[4] can also be formed; under a particular set

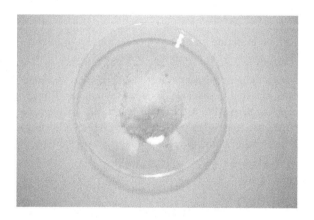

Synthesis of tri-cyclic acetone peroxide.

of conditions of reagent and acid catalyst concentration, the cyclic trimer is the primary product.[3] A tetrameric form has also been described, under different catalytic conditions.[5] Under neutral conditions, the reaction is reported to produce the monomeric organic peroxide.[3]

Tetrameric acetone peroxide

Organic peroxides in general are sensitive, dangerous explosives, and all forms of acetone peroxide are sensitive to initiation. TATP decomposes explosively; examination of the explosive decomposition of TATP predicts "formation of acetone and ozone as the main decomposition products and not the intuitively expected oxidation products."[6] Very little heat is created by the explosive decomposition of TATP; the foregoing computational analysis suggests that TATP decomposition as an entropic explosion.[6] However, this hypothesis has been challenged as not conforming to actual measurements.[7] The tetrameric form of acetone peroxide, prepared under neutral conditions using a tin catalyst (with a chelator or general inhibitor of radical chemistry present), is reported to be more chemically stable, although still a very dangerous primary explosive.*[5]

Some forms of acetone peroxide are prone to loss by sublimation and evaporation.

Several methods can be used for trace analysis of TATP,*[8] including gas chromatography/mass spectrometry (GC/MS)*[9]*[10]*[11]*[12]*[13] high performance liquid chromatography/mass spectrometry (HPLC/MS),*[14]*[15]*[16]*[17]*[18] and HPLC with post-column derivitization.*[19]

33.3 Industrial uses

Ketone peroxides, including acetone peroxide and methyl ethyl ketone peroxide, find application, alongside other compounds such as benzoyl peroxide, as initiators for polymerization reactions—e.g. silicone or polyester resins, in the making of fiberglass-reinforced composites. For these uses, the peroxides are typically in the form of a dilute solution in an organic solvent; methyl ethyl ketone is more common for this purpose, as it is stable in storage.

Acetone peroxides are common and unwanted by-products of oxidation reactions, such as those used in phenol syntheses.

Acetone peroxide and benzoyl peroxide are used as flour bleaching agents to bleach and "mature" flour.*[20]

Due to their explosive nature, their presence in chemical processes creates potential hazardous situations. Numerous methods are used to reduce their appearance as byproducts —for instance, shifting pH to more alkaline, adjusting reaction temperature, or adding inhibitors of their production.*[21]

33.4 Use in improvised explosive devices

See also: Improvised explosive device

TATP and the other explosive forms of acetone peroxide belong to the few high explosives that do not contain nitrogen,*[22] and so can pass undetected through explosive detection scanners designed to detect nitrogenous explosives.*[23] Because of its high susceptibility to accidental detonation (and resulting "workplace accidents" in bomb-making shops), TATP has been referred to as the "Mother of Satan."*[22] It is used by terrorists for its ability to evade detection aimed at nitrogenous explosives, and due to its low cost and the ease with which its precursors can be obtained.*[22] It has been described in popular media as easily prepared from readily available retail ingredients, such as hair bleach and nail polish remover.*[24]

As such, TATP has been used in bomb and suicide attacks and in improvised explosive devices, including the London bombings on 7 July 2005, where four suicide bombers killed 52 people and injured more than 700.*[25]*[26] It was one of the explosives used by the "shoe bomber" Richard Reid*[26] and was used by the suicide bombers in the November 2015 Paris attacks*[24] and 2016 Brussels bombings.*[27]

33.5 References

[1] • Wolffenstein R (1895). "Über die Einwirkung von Wasserstoffsuperoxyd auf Aceton und Mesityloxyd" [On the effect of hydrogen peroxide on acetone and mesityl oxide]. *Berichte der Deutschen Chemischen Gesellschaft* (in German). **28** (2): 2265–2269. doi:10.1002/cber.189502802208.; Wolfenstein R (1895) Deutsches Reich Patent 84,953; Matyáš R, Pachman J (2013). *Primary Explosives*. Berlin: Springer. p. 262. ISBN 978-3-642-28436-6.

[2] Baeyer A, Villiger V (1900). "Über die Einwirkung des Caro'schen Reagens auf Ketone" [On the effect of Caro's reagent on ketones]. *Berichte der deutschen chemischen Gesellschaft*. **33** (1): 858–864. doi:10.1002/cber.190003301153.; See also Baeyer A, Villiger V (1900). "Über die Nomenclatur der Superoxyde und die Superoxyde der Aldehyde" [On the nomenclature of peroxides and the peroxide of aldehyde]. *Berichte der deutschen chemischen Gesellschaft*. **33** (2): 2479–2487. doi:10.1002/cber.190003302185.

[3] Milas NA, Golubović A (1959). "Studies in Organic Peroxides. XXVI. Organic Peroxides Derived from Acetone and Hydrogen Peroxide". *Journal of the American Chemical Society*. **81** (24): 6461–6462. doi:10.1021/ja01533a033.

[4] This is not the DMDO monomer referred to in the Chembox, but rather the open chain, dihydro monomer described by Milas & Goluboviç, op. cit.

[5] Jiang H, Chu G, Gong H, Qiao Q (1999). "Tin Chloride Catalysed Oxidation of Acetone with Hydrogen Peroxide to Tetrameric Acetone Peroxide". *Journal of Chemical Research*. **28** (4): 288–289. doi:10.1039/a809955c.

[6] Dubnikova F, Kosloff R, Almog J, Zeiri Y, Boese R, Itzhaky H, Alt A, Keinan E (Feb 2005). "Decomposition of triacetone triperoxide is an entropic explosion" (PDF). *Journal of the American Chemical Society*. **127** (4): 1146–59. doi:10.1021/ja0464903. PMID 15669854.

[7] Sinditskii VP, Koltsov VI, Egorshev, VY, Patrikeev DI, Dorofeeva OV (2014). "Thermochemistry of cyclic acetone peroxides". *Thermochimica Acta*. **585**: 10–15. doi:10.1016/j.tca.2014.03.046.

[8] Schulte-Ladbeck R, Vogel M, Karst U (Oct 2006). "Recent methods for the determination of peroxide-based explosives". *Analytical and Bioanalytical Chemistry*. **386** (3): 559–65. doi:10.1007/s00216-006-0579-y. PMID 16862379.

[9] Muller D, Levy A, Shelef R, Abramovich-Bar S, Sonenfeld D, Tamiri T (Sep 2004). "Improved method for the detection of TATP after explosion". *Journal of Forensic Sciences*. **49** (5): 935–8. PMID 15461093.

[10] Stambouli A, El Bouri A, Bouayoun T, Bellimam MA (Dec 2004). "Headspace-GC/MS detection of TATP traces in post-explosion debris". *Forensic Science International*. 146 Suppl: S191–4. doi:10.1016/j.forsciint.2004.09.060. PMID 15639574.

[11] Oxley JC, Smith JL, Shinde K, Moran J (2005). "Determination of the Vapor Density of Triacetone Triperoxide (TATP) Using a Gas Chromatography Headspace Technique". *Propellants, Explosives, Pyrotechnics*. **30** (2): 127. doi:10.1002/prep.200400094.

[12] Sigman ME, Clark CD, Fidler R, Geiger CL, Clausen CA (2006). "Analysis of triacetone triperoxide by gas chromatography/mass spectrometry and gas chromatography/tandem mass spectrometry by electron and chemical ionization". *Rapid Communications in Mass Spectrometry*. **20** (19): 2851–7. doi:10.1002/rcm.2678. PMID 16941533.

[13] Romolo FS, Cassioli L, Grossi S, Cinelli G, Russo MV (Jan 2013). "Surface-sampling and analysis of TATP by swabbing and gas chromatography/mass spectrometry". *Forensic Science International*. **224** (1-3): 96–100. doi:10.1016/j.forsciint.2012.11.005. PMID 23219697.

[14] Widmer L, Watson S, Schlatter K, Crowson A (Dec 2002). "Development of an LC/MS method for the trace analysis of triacetone triperoxide (TATP)". *The Analyst*. **127** (12): 1627–32. doi:10.1039/B208350G. PMID 12537371.

[15] Xu X, van de Craats AM, Kok EM, de Bruyn PC (Nov 2004). "Trace analysis of peroxide explosives by high performance liquid chromatography-atmospheric pressure chemical ionization-tandem mass spectrometry (HPLC-APCI-MS/MS) for forensic applications". *Journal of Forensic Sciences*. **49** (6): 1230–6. PMID 15568694.

[16] Cotte-Rodríguez I, Hernandez-Soto H, Chen H, Cooks RG (Mar 2008). "In situ trace detection of peroxide explosives by desorption electrospray ionization and desorption atmospheric pressure chemical ionization". *Analytical Chemistry*. **80** (5): 1512–9. doi:10.1021/ac7020085. PMID 18247583.

[17] Sigman ME, Clark CD, Caiano T, Mullen R (2008). "Analysis of triacetone triperoxide (TATP) and TATP synthetic intermediates by electrospray ionization mass spectrometry". *Rapid Communications in Mass Spectrometry*. **22** (2): 84–90. doi:10.1002/rcm.3335. PMID 18058960.

[18] Sigman ME, Clark CD, Painter K, Milton C, Simatos E, Frisch JL, McCormick M, Bitter JL (Feb 2009). "Analysis of oligomeric peroxides in synthetic triacetone triperoxide samples by tandem mass spectrometry". *Rapid Communications in Mass Spectrometry*. **23** (3): 349–56. doi:10.1002/rcm.3879. PMID 19125413.

[19] Schulte-Ladbeck R, Kolla P, Karst U (Feb 2003). "Trace analysis of peroxide-based explosives". *Analytical Chemistry*. **75** (4): 731–5. doi:10.1021/ac020392n. PMID 12622359.

[20] Ferrari CG, Higashiuchi K, Podliska JA (1963). "Flour Maturing and Bleaching with Acyclic Acetone Peroxides" (PDF). *Cereal Chemistry*. **40**: 89–100.

[21] Costantini, Michel (1991-03-26) Destruction of acetone peroxide. United States Patent 5003109. Freepatentsonline.com. Retrieved on 2013-02-03.

[22] Glas K (2006-11-06). "TATP: Countering the Mother of Satan". The Future of Things. Retrieved 24 September 2009. The tremendous devastative force of TATP, together with the relative ease of making it, as well as the difficulty in detecting it, made TATP one of the weapons of choice for terrorists

[23] "Feds are all wet on airport security". Star-Ledger (Newark, New Jersey). 2006-08-24. Retrieved 11 September 2009. At the moment, Watts said, the screening devices are set to detect nitrogen-based explosives, a category that doesn't include TATP

[24] Callimachi R, Rubin AJ, Fourquet L (2016-03-19). "A View of ISIS's Evolution in New Details of Paris Attacks". *The New York Times*.

[25] Naughton P (2005-07-15). "TATP is suicide bombers' weapon of choice". *The Times (UK)*. Archived from the original on 10 February 2008.

[26] Vince G (15 July 2005). "Explosives linked to London bombings identified". *New Scientist*.

[27] ""La mère de Satan" ou TATP, l'explosif préféré de l'EI" ["Mother of Satan" or TATP, the preferred explosive of IE]. *LeVif.be Express* (in French).

33.6 External links

- ChemSub Online: Acetone peroxide – Triacetone triperoxide.

Chapter 34

Trinitrotoluene

"TNT" redirects here. For other uses, see TNT (disambiguation).

Trinitrotoluene (/ˌtraɪˌnaɪtroʊˈtɒljuːˌiːn, -ljəˌwiːn/;[4][5] **TNT**), or more specifically **2,4,6-trinitrotoluene**, is a chemical compound with the formula $C_6H_2(NO_2)_3CH_3$. This yellow-colored solid is sometimes used as a reagent in chemical synthesis, but it is best known as an explosive material with convenient handling properties. The explosive yield of TNT is considered to be the standard measure of bombs and other explosives. In chemistry, TNT is used to generate charge transfer salts.

While the two words are sometimes used interchangeably in common conversation, TNT is not the same as dynamite, a special formulation of nitroglycerin for use as an industrial explosive.

34.1 History

TNT was first prepared in 1863 by German chemist Julius Wilbrand[6] and originally used as a yellow dye. Its potential as an explosive was not appreciated for several years, mainly because it was so difficult to detonate and because it was less powerful than alternatives. Its explosive properties were first discovered by another German chemist, Carl Haeussermann, in 1891.[7] TNT can be safely poured when liquid into shell cases, and is so insensitive that in 1910, it was exempted from the UK's Explosives Act 1875 and was not considered an explosive for the purposes of manufacture and storage.[8]

The German armed forces adopted it as a filling for artillery shells in 1902. TNT-filled armour-piercing shells would explode after they had penetrated the armour of British capital ships, whereas the British lyddite-filled shells tended to explode upon striking armour, thus expending much of their energy outside the ship.[8] The British started replacing lyddite with TNT in 1907.

The United States Navy continued filling armor-piercing

Trinitrotoluene melting at 81 °C

shells with explosive D after some other nations had switched to TNT; but began filling naval mines, bombs, depth charges, and torpedo warheads with burster charges of crude *grade B* TNT with the color of brown sugar and requiring an explosive booster charge of granular crystallized *grade A* TNT for detonation. High-explosive shells were filled with *grade A* TNT, which became preferred for this other use as industrial chemical capacity became available for removing xylene and similar hydrocarbons from the toluene feedstock and other nitrotoluene isomer byproducts from the nitrating reactions.[9]

TNT is still widely used by the United States military, as well as construction companies around the world. The majority of TNT currently used by the US military is manufac-

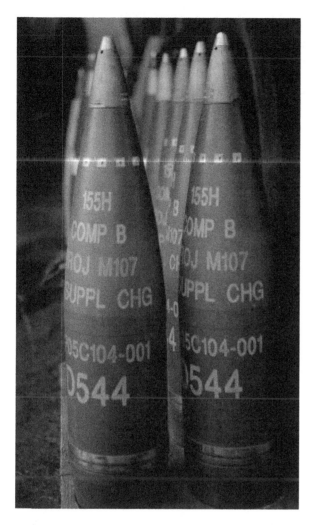

M107 artillery shells. All are labelled to indicate a filling of "Comp B" (mixture of TNT and RDX) and have fuzes fitted

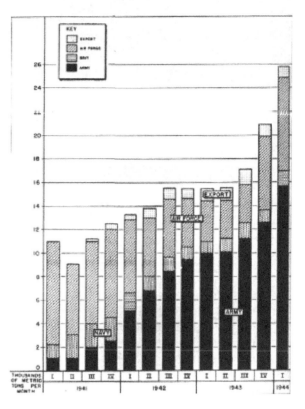

Analysis of TNT production by branch of the German army between 1941 and the first quarter of 1944 shown in thousands of tons per month

Detonation of the 500-ton TNT explosive charge as part of Operation Sailor Hat in 1965. The white blast-wave is visible on the water surface and a shock condensation cloud is visible overhead.

tured by Radford Army Ammunition Plant near Radford, Virginia.

34.2 Preparation

In industry, TNT is produced in a three-step process. First, toluene is nitrated with a mixture of sulfuric and nitric acid to produce mononitrotoluene (MNT). The MNT is separated and then renitrated to dinitrotoluene (DNT). In the final step, the DNT is nitrated to trinitrotoluene (TNT) using an anhydrous mixture of nitric acid and oleum. Nitric acid is consumed by the manufacturing process, but the diluted sulfuric acid can be reconcentrated and reused. After nitration, TNT is stabilized by a process called sulfitation, where the crude TNT is treated with aqueous sodium sulfite solution to remove less stable isomers of TNT and other undesired reaction products. The rinse water from sulphitation is known as red water and is a significant pollutant and waste product of TNT manufacture."[10]

World War I-era HE artillery shell for a 9.2 inch howitzer. The red band indicates it is filled and the green band (marked "Trotyl") indicates that the filling is TNT

Control of nitrogen oxides in feed nitric acid is very important because free nitrogen dioxide can result in oxidation of the methyl group of toluene. This reaction is highly exothermic and carries with it the risk of a runaway reaction leading to an explosion.

In the laboratory, 2,4,6-trinitrotoluene is produced by a two-step process. A nitrating mixture of concentrated nitric and sulfuric acids is used to nitrate toluene to a mixture of mono- and di-nitrotoluene isomers, with careful cooling to maintain temperature. The nitrated toluenes are then separated, washed with dilute sodium bicarbonate to remove oxides of nitrogen, and then carefully nitrated with a mixture of fuming nitric acid and sulfuric acid. Towards the end of the nitration, the mixture is heated on a steam bath. The trinitrotoluene is separated, washed with a dilute solution of sodium sulfite and then recrystallized from alcohol.

34.3 Applications

TNT is one of the most commonly used explosives for military, industrial, and mining applications. TNT has been used in conjunction with hydraulic fracturing, a process used to recover oil and gas from shale formations. The technique involves displacing and detonating nitroglycerin in hydraulically induced fractures followed by wellbore shots using pelletized TNT.*[11]

TNT is valued partly because of its insensitivity to shock and friction, with reduced risk of accidental detonation compared to more sensitive explosives such as nitroglycerin. TNT melts at 80 °C (176 °F), far below the temperature at which it will spontaneously detonate, allowing it to be poured or safely combined with other explosives. TNT nei-

ther absorbs nor dissolves in water, which allows it to be used effectively in wet environments. To detonate, TNT must be triggered by a pressure wave from a starter explosive, called an explosive booster.

Although blocks of TNT are available in various sizes (e.g. 250 g, 500 g, 1,000 g), it is more commonly encountered in synergistic explosive blends comprising a variable percentage of TNT plus other ingredients. Examples of explosive blends containing TNT include:

- Amatex: (ammonium nitrate and RDX) *[12]
- Amatol:(ammonium nitrate *[13])
- Ammonal: (ammonium nitrate and aluminium powder plus sometimes charcoal).
- Baratol: (barium nitrate and wax *[14])
- Composition B (RDX and paraffin wax *[15])
- Composition H6
- Cyclotol (RDX) *[16]
- Ednatol
- Hexanite *[17](hexanitrodiphenylamine*[18]*[19]).
- Minol
- Octol
- Pentolite
- Picratol
- Tetrytol
- Torpex
- Tritonal

34.4 Explosive character

Upon detonation, TNT decomposes as follows:

$$2\ C_7H_5N_3O_6 \rightarrow 3\ N_2 + 5\ H_2O + 7\ CO + 7\ C$$
$$2\ C_7H_5N_3O_6 \rightarrow 3\ N_2 + 5\ H_2 + 12\ CO + 2\ C$$

The reaction is exothermic but has a high activation energy in the gas phase (~62 kcal/mol). The condensed phases (solid or liquid) show markedly lower activation energies of roughly 35 kcal/mol due to unique bimolecular decomposition routes at elevated densities.*[20] Because of the production of carbon, TNT explosions have a sooty appearance. Because TNT has an excess of carbon, explosive mixtures with oxygen-rich compounds can yield more energy per kilogram than TNT alone. During the 20th century, amatol, a mixture of TNT with ammonium nitrate was a widely used military explosive.

TNT can be detonated with a high velocity initiator or by efficient concussion.*[21]

For many years, TNT used to be the reference point for the Figure of Insensitivity. TNT had a rating of exactly 100 on the "F of I" scale. The reference has since been changed to a more sensitive explosive called RDX, which has an F of I rating of 80.

34.5 Energy content

See also: TNT equivalent

The heat of detonation utilized by NIST is 4184 J/g

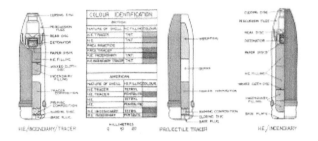

Cross-sectional view of Oerlikon 20 mm cannon shells (dating from circa 1945) showing color codes for TNT and pentolite fillings

(4.184 MJ/kg).*[22] The energy density of TNT is used as a reference-point for many other explosives, including nuclear weapons, the energy content of which is measured in equivalent kilotons (~4.184 terajoules) or megatons (~4.184 petajoules) of TNT. The heat of combustion is 14.5 megajoules per kilogram, which requires that some of the carbon in TNT react with atmospheric oxygen, which does not occur in the initial event.*[23]

For comparison, gunpowder contains 3 megajoules per kilogram, dynamite contains 7.5 megajoules per kilogram, and gasoline contains 47.2 megajoules per kilogram (though gasoline requires an oxidant, so an optimized gasoline and O_2 mixture contains 10.4 megajoules per kilogram).

34.6 Detection

Various methods can be used to detect TNT including optical and electrochemical sensors and explosive-sniffing dogs.

In 2013, researchers from the Indian Institutes of Technology using noble-metal quantum clusters could detect TNT at the sub-zeptomolar (10^*-18 mol/m^3) level.*[24]

34.7 Safety and toxicity

TNT is poisonous, and skin contact can cause skin irritation, causing the skin to turn a bright yellow-orange color. During the First World War, munition workers who handled the chemical found that their skin turned bright yellow, which resulted in their acquiring the nickname "canary girls" or simply "canaries."

People exposed to TNT over a prolonged period tend to experience anemia and abnormal liver functions. Blood and liver effects, spleen enlargement and other harmful effects on the immune system have also been found in animals that ingested or breathed trinitrotoluene. There is evidence that TNT adversely affects male fertility.*[25] TNT is listed as a possible human carcinogen, with carcinogenic effects demonstrated in animal experiments (rat), although effects upon humans so far amount to none [according to IRIS of March 15, 2000].*[26] Consumption of TNT produces red urine through the presence of breakdown products and not blood as sometimes believed.*[27]

Some military testing grounds are contaminated with TNT. Wastewater from munitions programs including contamination of surface and subsurface waters may be colored pink because of the presence of TNT. Such contamination, called "pink water", may be difficult and expensive to remedy.

TNT is prone to exudation of dinitrotoluenes and other isomers of trinitrotoluene. Even small quantities of such impurities can cause such effect. The effect shows especially in projectiles containing TNT and stored at higher temperatures, e.g. during summer. Exudation of impurities leads to formation of pores and cracks (which in turn cause increased shock sensitivity). Migration of the exudated liquid into the fuze screw thread can form *fire channels*, increasing the risk of accidental detonations; fuze malfunction can result from the liquids migrating into its mechanism.*[28] Calcium silicate is mixed with TNT to mitigate the tendency towards exudation.*[29]

34.8 Ecological impact

Because of its use in construction and demolition, TNT has become the most widely used explosive, and thus its toxicity is the most characterized and reported. Residual TNT from manufacture, storage, and use can pollute water, soil, atmosphere, and biosphere.

The concentration of TNT in contaminated soil can reach 50 g/kg of soil, where the highest concentrations can be found on or near the surface. In the last decade, the United States Environmental Protection Agency (USEPA) has declared TNT a pollutant whose removal is priority.*[30] The USEPA maintains that TNT levels in soil should not exceed 17.2 gram per kilogram of soil and 0.01 milligrams per liter of water.*[31]

34.8.1 Aqueous solubility

Dissolution is a measure of the rate that solid TNT in contact with water is dissolved. The relatively low aqueous solubility of TNT causes the dissolution of solid particles to be continuously released to the environment over extended periods of time.*[32] Studies have shown that the TNT dissolved slower in saline water than in freshwater. However, when salinity was altered, TNT dissolved at the same speed (Figure 2).*[33] Because TNT is moderately soluble in water, it can migrate through subsurface soil, and cause groundwater contamination.*[34]

34.8.2 Soil adsorption

Adsorption is a measure of the distribution between soluble and sediment adsorbed contaminants following attainment of equilibrium. TNT and its transformation products are known to adsorb to surface soils and sediments, where they undergo reactive transformation or remained stored.*[35] The movement or organic contaminants through soils is a function of their ability to associate with the mobile phase (water) and a stationary phase (soil). Materials that associate strongly with soils move slowly through soil. Materials that associate strongly with water move through water with rates approaching that of ground water movement.

The association constant for TNT with a soil is 2.7 to 11 liters per kilogram of soil.*[36] This means that TNT has a one- to tenfold tendency to adhere to soil particulates than not when introduced into the soil.*[32] Hydrogen bonding and ion exchange are two suggested mechanisms of adsorption between the nitro functional groups and soil colloids.

The number of functional groups on TNT influences the ability to adsorb into soil. Adsorption coefficient values have been shown to increase with an increase in the number of amino groups. Thus, adsorption of the TNT decomposition product 2,4-diamino-6-nitrotoluene (2,4-DANT) was greater than that for 4-amino-2,6-dinitrotoluene (4-ADNT), which was greater than that for TNT.*[32] Lower adsorption coefficients for 2,6-DNT compared to 2,4-DNT can be attributed to the steric hindrance of the NO_3 group in the ortho position.

Research has shown that in freshwater environments, with a high abundances of Ca^*2+, the adsorption of TNT and its transformation products to soils and sediments may be lower than observed in a saline environment, dominated by K^*+ and Na^*+. Therefore, when considering the adsorption of TNT, the type of soil or sediment and the ionic composition and strength of the ground water are important factors.*[37]

The association constants for TNT and its degradation products with clays have been determined. Clay minerals have a significant effect on the adsorption of energetic compounds. It should be noted that soil properties, such as organic carbon content and cation exchange capacity had significant impacts of the adsorption coefficients reported in the table below.

Additional studies have shown that the mobility of TNT degradation products is likely to be lower "than TNT in subsurface environments where specific adsorption to clay minerals dominates the sorption process." *[37] Thus, the mobility of TNT and its transformation products are dependent on the characteristics of the sorbent.*[37] The mobility of TNT in groundwater and soil has been extrapolated from "sorption and desorption isotherm models determined with humic acids, in aquifer sediments, and soils" .*[37] From these models, it is predicted that TNT has a low retention and transports readily in the environment.*[30]

Compared to other explosives, TNT has a higher association constant with soil, meaning it adheres more with soil than with water. Conversely, other explosives, such as RDX and HMX with low association constants (ranging from 0.06 to 7.3 L/kg and 0 to 1.6 L/kg respectively) can move more rapidly in water.*[32]

34.8.3 Chemical breakdown

TNT is a reactive molecule and is particularly prone to react with reduced components of sediments or photodegradation in the presence of sunlight. TNT is thermodynamically and kinetically capable of reacting with a wide number of components of many environmental systems. This includes wholly abiotic reactants, like photons, hydrogen sulfide, Fe^*2+, or microbial communities, both oxic and anoxic.

Soils with high clay contents or small particle sizes and high total organic carbon content have been shown to promote TNT transformation. Possible TNT transformations include reduction of one, two, or three nitro-moieties to amines and coupling of amino transformation products to form dimers. Formation of the two monoamino transformation products, 2-ADNT and 4-ADNT are energetically favored, and therefore are observed in contaminated soils and ground water. The diamino products are energetically less favorable, and even less likely are the triamino products.

The transformation of TNT is significantly enhanced under anaerobic conditions as well as under highly reducing conditions. TNT transformations in soils can occur both biologically and abiotically.*[37]

Photolysis is a major process that impacts the transformation of energetic compounds. The alteration of a molecule in photolysis occurs in the presence of direct absorption of light energy by the transfer of energy from a photosensitized compound. Phototransformation of TNT "results in the formation of nitrobenzenes, benzaldehydes, azodicarboxylic acids, and nitrophenols, as a result of the oxidation of methyl groups, reduction of nitro groups, and dimer formation." *[32]

Evidence of the photolysis of TNT has been seen due to the color change to pink of the wastewaters when exposed to sunlight. Photolysis was more rapid in river water than in distilled water. Ultimately, photolysis affects the fate of TNT primarily in the aquatic environment but could also affect the reaction when exposed to sunlight on the soil surface.*[37]

34.8.4 Biodegradation

The ligninolytic physiological phase and manganese peroxidase system of fungi can cause a very limited amount of mineralization of TNT in a liquid culture; though not in soil. An organism capable of the remediation of large amounts of TNT in soil has yet to be discovered.*[38] Both wild and transgenic plants can phytoremediate explosives from soil and water.*[39]

34.9 See also

- TNT equivalent
- RE factor
- List of explosives used during World War II
- Dynamite (Difference from TNT)
- IMX-101
- Table of explosive detonation velocities
- Phlegmatized
- Environmental fate of TNT

34.10 References

[1] 2,4,6-Trinitrotoluene. inchem.org

[2] "NIOSH Pocket Guide to Chemical Hazards #0641". National Institute for Occupational Safety and Health (NIOSH).

[3] "2,4,6-Trinitrotoluene". *Immediately Dangerous to Life and Health*. National Institute for Occupational Safety and Health (NIOSH).

[4] "Trinitrotoluene". *Merriam-Webster Dictionary*.

[5] "Trinitrotoluene". *Dictionary.com Unabridged*. Random House.

[6] Wilbrand, J. (1863). "Notiz über Trinitrotoluol". *Annalen der Chemie und Pharmacie*. **128** (2): 178–179. doi:10.1002/jlac.18631280206.

[7] https://books.google.co.uk/books?id=PmuqCHDC3pwC&pg=PA404

[8] Brown GI (1998). *The Big Bang: a History of Explosives*. Sutton Publishing. pp. 151–153. ISBN 0-7509-1878-0.

[9] Fairfield AP (1921). *Naval Ordnance*. Lord Baltimore Press. pp. 49–52.

[10] Urbanski T (1964). *Chemistry and Technology of Explosives*. **1**. Pergamon Press. pp. 389–91. ISBN 0-08-010238-7.

[11] Miller, J. S.; Johansen, R. T. (1976). "Fracturing Oil Shale with Explosives for In Situ Recovery." (PDF). *Shale Oil, Tar Sand and Related Fuel Sources*. American Chemical Society: 151. Retrieved 27 March 2015.

[12] Campbell J (1985). *Naval weapons of World War Two*. London: Conway Maritime Press. p. 100. ISBN 978-0-85177-329-2.

[13] *U.S. Explosive Ordnance, Bureau of Ordnance*. Washington, D.C.: U.S. Department of the Navy. 1947. p. 580.

[14] Explosives – Compounds

[15] Military Specification MIL-C-401

[16] Cooper PW (1996). *Explosives Engineering*. Wiley-VCH. ISBN 0-471-18636-8.

[17] DEPARTMENT OF THE TREASURY:Bureau of Alcohol, Tobacco and Firearms GlobalSecurity.org Retrieved 2011-12-02

[18] [secondary source] webpages:submarine torpedo explosive Retrieved 2011-12-02

[19] *scribd.com* website showing copy of a North American Intelligence document see:page 167 Retrieved 2011-12-02

[20] Furman et al. (2014), Decomposition of Condensed Phase Energetic Materials: Interplay between Uni- and Bimolecular Mechanisms, J. Am. Chem. Soc., 2014, 136 (11), pp 4192–4200. http://pubs.acs.org/doi/abs/10.1021/ja410020f

[21] *Merck Index*, 13th Edition, **9801**

[22] NIST Guide for the Use of the International System of Units (SI): Appendix B8—Factors for Units Listed Alphabetically

[23] Babrauskas, Vytenis (2003). *Ignition Handbook*. Issaquah, WA: Fire Science Publishers/Society of Fire Protection Engineers. p. 453. ISBN 0-9728111-3-3.

[24] Grad, Paul (April 2013). "Quantum clusters serve as ultrasensitive detectors". *Chemical Engineering*.

[25] Toxicological Profile for 2,4,6-Trinitrotoluene. atsdr.cdc.gov

[26] from U.S. Environmental Protection Agency's Integrated Risk Information System (IRIS) *within the* NLM Hazardous Substances Databank – Trinitrotoluene

[27] "2,4,6-Trinitrotoluene" (PDF). Agency for Toxic Substances and Disease Registry. Retrieved 2010-05-17.

[28] Akhavan J (2004). *The Chemistry of Explosives*. Royal Society of Chemistry. pp. 11–. ISBN 978-0-85404-640-9.

[29] "Explosive & Propellant Additives". islandgroup.com.

[30] Esteve-Núñez A, Caballero A, Ramos JL (2001). "Biological degradation of 2,4,6-trinitrotoluene". *Microbiol. Mol. Biol. Rev.* **65** (3): 335–52, table of contents. doi:10.1128/MMBR.65.3.335-352.2001. PMC 99030⊖. PMID 11527999.

[31] Ayoub K, van Hullebusch ED, Cassir M, Bermond A (2010). "Application of advanced oxidation processes for TNT removal: A review". *J. Hazard. Mater.* **178** (1-3): 10–28. doi:10.1016/j.jhazmat.2010.02.042. PMID 20347218.

[32] Pichte J (2012). "Distribution and Fate of Military Explosives and Propellants in Soil: A Review". *Applied and Environmental Soil Science*. **2012**: 1–33. doi:10.1155/2012/617236.

[33] Brannon JM, Price CB, Yost SL, Hayes C, Porter B (2005). "Comparison of environmental fate and transport process descriptors of explosives in saline and freshwater systems". *Mar. Pollut. Bull.* **50** (3): 247–51. doi:10.1016/j.marpolbul.2004.10.008. PMID 15757688.

[34] Halasz A, Groom C, Zhou E, Paquet L, Beaulieu C, Deschamps S, Corriveau A, Thiboutot S, Ampleman G, Dubois C, Hawari J (2002). "Detection of explosives and their degradation products in soil environments". *J Chromatogr A*. **963** (1-2): 411–8. PMID 12187997.

[35] Douglas TA, Johnson L, Walsh M, Collins C (2009). "A time series investigation of the stability of nitramine and nitroaromatic explosives in surface water samples at ambient temperature". *Chemosphere*. **76** (1): 1–8. doi:10.1016/j.chemosphere.2009.02.050. PMID 19329139.

[36] Haderlein SB, Weissmahr KW, Schwarzenbach RP (January 1996). "Specific Adsorption of Nitroaromatic Explosives and Pesticides to Clay Minerals". *Environmental Science & Technology*. **30** (2): 612–622. doi:10.1021/es9503701.

[37] Pennington JC, Brannon JM (February 2002). "Environmental fate of explosives". *Thermochimica Acta*. **384** (1-2): 163–172. doi:10.1016/S0040-6031(01)00801-2.

[38] Hawari J, Beaudet S, Halasz A, Thiboutot S, Ampleman G (2000). "Microbial degradation of explosives: biotransformation versus mineralization". *Appl. Microbiol. Biotechnol.* **54** (5): 605–18. doi:10.1007/s002530000445. PMID 11131384.

[39] Panz K, Miksch K (2012). "Phytoremediation of explosives (TNT, RDX, HMX) by wild-type and transgenic plants". *J. Environ. Manage.* **113**: 85–92. doi:10.1016/j.jenvman.2012.08.016. PMID 22996005.

34.11 External links

- Dynamite and TNT at *The Periodic Table of Videos* (University of Nottingham)

- free software website *sonicbomb.com* containing a video bank and additionally pages for discussion of nuclear device testing Video showing detonation [Published on 2005-12-20] : Operation Blowdown

- *youtube.com* video showing the shockwave and typical black smoke cloud from detonation of 160 kilograms of pure TNT

- *liveleak.com* video of demolition training using half pound blocks of pure TNT

- CDC – NIOSH Pocket Guide to Chemical Hazards

Chapter 35

Nitrocellulose

Nitrocellulose (also known as **cellulose nitrate**, **flash paper**, **flash cotton**, **guncotton**, and **flash string**) is a highly flammable compound formed by nitrating cellulose through exposure to nitric acid or another powerful nitrating agent. When used as a propellant or low-order explosive, it was originally known as **guncotton**.

Partially nitrated cellulose has found uses as a plastic film and in inks and wood coatings.*[2] In 1862 the first manmade plastic, nitrocellulose, (branded Parkesine) was created by Alexander Parkes from cellulose treated with nitric acid and a solvent. In 1868, American inventor John Wesley Hyatt developed a plastic material he named **Celluloid**, improving on Parkes' invention by plasticizing the nitrocellulose with camphor so that it could be processed into finished form and used as a photographic film. Celluloid was used by Kodak, and other suppliers, from the late 1880s as a film base in photography, X-ray films, and motion picture films, and was known as nitrate film. After numerous fires caused by unstable nitrate films, "safety film" (cellulose acetate film) started to be used from the 1930s in the case of X-ray stock and from 1948 for motion picture film.

35.1 Guncotton/Nitrocellulose

35.1.1 Discovery

Henri Braconnot discovered in 1832 that nitric acid, when combined with starch or wood fibers, would produce a lightweight combustible explosive material, which he named *xyloïdine*.*[3] A few years later in 1838, another French chemist, Théophile-Jules Pelouze (teacher of Ascanio Sobrero and Alfred Nobel), treated paper and cardboard in the same way.*[4] Jean-Baptiste Dumas obtained a similar material, which he called *nitramidine*.*[5] These substances were highly unstable and were not practical explosives.

However, around 1846 Christian Friedrich Schönbein, a German-Swiss chemist, discovered a more practical solution.*[6]

As he was working in the kitchen of his home in Basel, he spilled a bottle of concentrated nitric acid on the kitchen table. He reached for the nearest cloth, a cotton apron, and wiped it up. He hung the apron on the stove door to dry, and, as soon as it was dry, there was a flash as the apron ignited. His preparation method was the first to be widely imitated—one part of fine cotton wool to be immersed in 15 parts of an equal blend of sulfuric and nitric acids. After two minutes, the cotton was removed and washed in cold water to set the esterification level and remove all acid residue. It was then slowly dried at a temperature below 40 °C (about 100 °F). Schönbein collaborated with the Frankfurt professor Rudolf Christian Böttger, who had discovered the process independently in the same year. By coincidence, a third chemist, the Brunswick professor F. J. Otto had also produced guncotton in 1846 and was the first to publish the process, much to the disappointment of Schönbein and Böttger.*[7]

The process uses nitric acid to convert cellulose into cellulose nitrate and water:

$$3HNO_3 + C_6H_{10}O_5 \rightarrow C_6H_7(NO_2)_3O_5 + 3H_2O$$

The sulfuric acid is present as a catalyst to produce the nitronium ion, NO_2^+. The reaction is first order and proceeds by electrophilic substitution at the C-OH centers of the cellulose.*[8]

35.1.2 Industrial production

The power of guncotton made it suitable for blasting. As a projectile driver, it had around six times the gas generation of an equal volume of black powder and produced less smoke and less heating.

The patent rights for the manufacture of gun cotton were obtained by John Hall & Son in 1846, and industrial manufacture of the explosive began at a purpose-built factory at Faversham's Marsh Works in Kent, England a year later. However, the manufacturing process was not properly un-

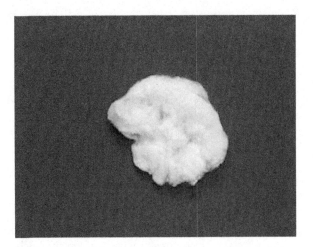

Pure nitrocellulose.

Deflagration test of nitrocellulose in slow motion.

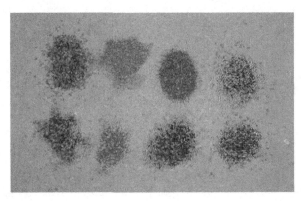

Various types of smokeless powder, consisting primarily of nitrocellulose

derstood and few safety measures were put in place. A serious explosion in July of that year killed almost two dozen workers, resulting in the immediate closure of the plant. Guncotton manufacture ceased for over 15 years until a safer procedure could be developed.*[9]

Further research indicated the importance of very careful washing of the acidified cotton. Unwashed nitrocellulose (sometimes called pyrocellulose) may spontaneously ignite and explode at room temperature, as the evaporation of water results in the concentration of unreacted acid.*[10]

The British chemist Frederick Augustus Abel developed the first safe process for guncotton manufacture, which he patented in 1865. The washing and drying times of the nitrocellulose were both extended to 48 hours and repeated eight times over. The acid mixture was changed to two parts sulfuric acid to one part nitric. Nitration can be controlled by adjusting acid concentrations and reaction temperature. Nitrocellulose is soluble in a mixture of alcohol and ether until nitrogen concentration exceeds 12%. Soluble nitrocellulose, or a solution thereof, is sometimes called collodion.*[11]

Guncotton containing more than 13% nitrogen (sometimes called insoluble nitrocellulose) was prepared by prolonged exposure to hot, concentrated acids*[11] for limited use as a blasting explosive or for warheads of underwater weapons such as naval mines and torpedoes.*[10] Safe and sustained production of guncotton began at the Waltham Abbey Royal Gunpowder Mills in the 1860s, and the material rapidly became the dominant explosive, becoming the standard for military warheads, although it remained too potent to be used as a propellant. More-stable and slower-burning collodion mixtures were eventually prepared using less-concentrated acids at lower temperatures for smokeless powder in firearms. The first practical smokeless powder made from nitrocellulose, for firearms and artillery ammunition, was invented by French chemist Paul Vieille in 1884.

Jules Verne viewed the development of guncotton with optimism. He referred to the substance several times in his novels. His adventurers carried firearms employing this substance. The most noteworthy reference is in his *From the Earth to the Moon*, in which guncotton was used to launch a projectile into space.

35.2 Nitrate film

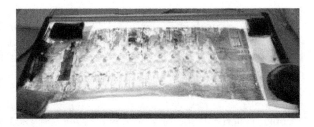

Nitrocellulose film on a light box, showing deterioration, from Library and Archives Canada collection

On May 2, 1887, Hannibal Goodwin filed a patent for "a photographic pellicle and process of producing same

35.2. NITRATE FILM

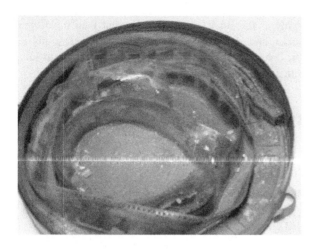

Decayed nitrate film. EYE Film Institute Netherlands.

... especially in connection with roller cameras", but the patent was not granted until 13 September 1898.*[12] In the meantime, George Eastman had already started production of roll-film using his own process.

Nitrocellulose was used as the first flexible film base, beginning with Eastman Kodak products in August, 1889. Camphor is used as a plasticizer for nitrocellulose film, often called nitrate film. Goodwin's patent was sold to Ansco, which successfully sued Eastman Kodak for infringement of the patent and was awarded $5,000,000 in 1914 to Goodwin Film.*[13]

Nitrate film was used until 1933 for X-ray films (where its flammability hazard was most acute) and for motion picture film until 1951. It was replaced by safety film with an acetate base. Nitrocellulose X-ray film ignition was the cause behind the Cleveland Clinic fire of 1929 in Cleveland, Ohio, which claimed the lives of 123 people during the fire, and a number who were rescued but died several days later due to inhalation of the toxic smoke.*[14]

The use of nitrocellulose film for motion pictures led to the requirement for fireproof projection rooms with wall coverings made of asbestos. The US Navy shot a training film for projectionists that included footage of a controlled ignition of a reel of nitrate film, which continued to burn when fully submerged in water. Unlike many other flammable materials, nitrocellulose does not need air to keep burning, as the reaction produces oxygen. Once burning, it is extremely difficult to extinguish. Immersing burning film in water may not extinguish it, and could actually increase the amount of smoke produced.*[15]*[16] Owing to public safety precautions, the London Underground forbade transport of movies on its system until well past the introduction of safety film.

Cinema fires caused by ignition of nitrocellulose film stock were the cause of the 1926 Dromcolliher cinema tragedy in County Limerick in which 48 people died and the 1929 Glen Cinema disaster in Paisley, Scotland, which killed 69 children. Today, nitrate film projection is normally highly regulated and requires extensive precautionary measures including extra projectionist health and safety training. Projectors certified to run nitrate films have many precautions, among them the chambering of the feed and takeup reels in thick metal covers with small slits to allow the film to run through. The projector is modified to accommodate several fire extinguishers with nozzles aimed at the film gate. The extinguishers automatically trigger if a piece of flammable fabric placed near the gate starts to burn. While this triggering would likely damage or destroy a significant portion of the projection components, it would prevent a fire which could cause far greater damage. Projection rooms may be required to have automatic metal covers for the projection windows, preventing the spread of fire to the auditorium. The Dryden Theatre at the George Eastman Museum is one of a few theaters in the world that is capable of safely projecting nitrate films,*[17] and regularly screens films to the public.*[18]

Nitrocellulose was found to gradually decompose, releasing nitric acid and further catalyzing the decomposition (eventually into a flammable powder). Decades later, storage at low temperatures was discovered as a means of delaying these reactions indefinitely. The great majority of films produced during the early 20th century are thought to have been lost either through this accelerating, self-catalyzed disintegration or through studio warehouse fires. Salvaging old films is a major problem for film archivists (see film preservation).

Nitrocellulose film base manufactured by Kodak can be identified by the presence of the word 'nitrate' in dark letters along one edge; the word only in clear letters on a dark background indicates derivation from a nitrate base original negative or projection print, but the film in hand itself may be a later print or copy negative, made on safety film. Acetate film manufactured during the era when nitrate films were still in use was marked 'Safety' or 'Safety Film' along one edge in dark letters. 8, 9.5, and 16 mm film stocks, intended for amateur and other nontheatrical use, were never manufactured with a nitrate base in the west, but rumors exist of 16 mm nitrate film having been produced in the former Soviet Union and/or China.*[19]

35.2.1 Replacement filmstocks

Nitrate dominated the market for professional-use 35 mm motion picture film from the industry's origins to the early 1950s. While cellulose acetate-based so-called "safety film", notably cellulose diacetate and cellulose acetate propionate, was produced in the gauge for small-scale use in niche applications (*e.g.*, printing advertisements and other short films to enable them to be sent through the mails without the need for fire safety precautions), the early generations of safety film base had two major disadvantages relative to nitrate: it was much more expensive to manufacture, and considerably less durable in repeated projection. The cost of the safety precautions associated with the use of nitrate was significantly lower than the cost of using any of the safety bases available before 1948. These drawbacks were eventually overcome with the launch of cellulose triacetate base film by Eastman Kodak in 1948.[*][20] Cellulose triacetate superseded nitrate as the film industry's mainstay base very quickly: Kodak announced the discontinuation of nitrate manufacture in February 1950.

The crucial advantage cellulose triacetate had over nitrate was that it was no more of a fire risk than paper (the stock is often erroneously referred to as "non-flam": this is not true —it is combustible, but not in as volatile or as dangerous a way as nitrate), while it almost matched the cost and durability of nitrate. It remained in almost exclusive use in all film gauges until the 1980s, when polyester/PET film began to supersede it for intermediate and release printing.[*][21]

Polyester is much more resistant to polymer degradation than either nitrate or triacetate. Although triacetate does not decompose in as dangerous a way as nitrate does, it is still subject to a process known as deacetylation, often nicknamed "vinegar syndrome" (due to the acetic acid smell of decomposing film) by archivists, which causes the film to shrink, deform, become brittle and eventually unusable. PET, like cellulose mononitrate, is less prone to stretching than other available plastics. By the late 1990s, polyester had almost entirely superseded triacetate for the production of intermediate elements and release prints.

Triacetate remains in use for most camera negative stocks because it can be "invisibly" spliced using solvents during negative assembly, while polyester film can only be spliced using adhesive tape patches or ultrasonically, both of which leave visible marks in the frame area. Also, polyester film is so strong, it will not break under tension and may cause serious damage to expensive camera or projector mechanisms in the event of a film jam, whereas triacetate film breaks easily, reducing the risk of damage. Many were opposed to the use of polyester for release prints for precisely this reason, and because ultrasonic splicers are very expensive items, beyond the budgets of many smaller theaters. In practice, though, this has not proved to be as much of a problem as was feared. Rather, with the increased use of automated long-play systems in cinemas, the greater strength of polyester has been a significant advantage in lessening the risk of a film performance being interrupted by a film break.

Despite its self-oxidizing hazards, nitrate is still regarded highly as the stock is more transparent than replacement stocks, and older films used denser silver in the emulsion. The combination results in a notably more luminous image with a high contrast ratio.[*][22]

35.3 Production

35.3.1 Guncotton

Guncotton is made by treating cotton (used as the source of cellulose) with concentrated sulfuric acid and 70% nitric acid cooled to 0 °C to produce cellulose trinitrate. While guncotton is dangerous to store, the hazards it presents can be reduced by storing it dampened with various liquids, such as alcohol. For this reason, accounts of guncotton usage dating from the early 20th century refer to "wet guncotton".

35.3.2 Nitrate film

Cellulose is treated with sulfuric acid and potassium nitrate to give cellulose mononitrate. This was used commercially as 'celluloid', a highly flammable plastic used in the first half of the 20th century for lacquers and photographic film.[*][23]

35.4 Uses

- A nitrocellulose slide, nitrocellulose membrane, or nitrocellulose paper is a sticky membrane used for immobilizing nucleic acids in southern blots and northern blots. It is also used for immobilization of proteins in western blots and atomic force microscopy[*][24] for its nonspecific affinity for amino acids. Nitrocellulose is widely used as support in diagnostic tests where antigen-antibody binding occurs, e.g., pregnancy tests, U-Albumin tests and CRP. Glycine and chloride ions make protein transfer more efficient.

- In 1846, nitrated cellulose was found to be soluble in ether and alcohol. The solution was named collodion and was soon used as a dressing for wounds.[*][25] It is still in use today in topical skin applications, such as liquid skin and in the application of salicylic acid, the active ingredient in Compound W wart remover.

- Adolph Noé developed a method of peeling coal balls using nitrocellulose.[*][26]

- In 1851, Frederick Scott Archer invented the wet collodion process as a replacement for albumen in early photographic emulsions, binding light-sensitive silver halides to a glass plate.[*][27]

- Magician's flash papers are sheets of paper or cloth made from nitrocellulose, which burn almost instantly with a bright flash, leaving no ash.

- As a medium for cryptographic one-time pads, they make the disposal of the pad complete, secure, and efficient.

- Radon tests for alpha track etches use it.

- For space flight, nitrocellulose was used by Copenhagen Suborbitals on several missions as a means of jettisoning components of the rocket/space capsule and deploying recovery systems. However, after several missions and flights, it proved not to have the desired explosive properties in a near vacuum environment.*[28]

- Nitrocellulose lacquer was used as a finish on guitars and saxophones for most of the 20th century and is still used on some current applications. Manufactured by (among others) DuPont, the paint was also used on automobiles sharing the same color codes as many guitars including Fender and Gibson brands,*[29] although it fell out of favor for a number of reasons: pollution, and the way the lacquer yellows and cracks over time.

- Nitrocellulose lacquer was also used as an aircraft dope, painted onto fabric-covered aircraft to tighten and provide protection to the material, but has been largely superseded by alternative cellulosics and other materials.

- It is also used to coat playing cards and to hold staples together in office staplers.

- Nail polish is made from nitrocellulose lacquer as it is inexpensive, dries quickly, and is not damaging to skin.

- Nitrocellulose lacquer is spin-coated onto aluminum or glass discs, then a groove is cut with a lathe, to make one-off phonograph records, used as masters for pressing or for play in dance clubs. They are referred to as acetate discs.

- Depending on the manufacturing process, nitrocellulose is esterified to varying degrees. Table tennis balls, guitar picks, and some photographic films have fairly low esterification levels and burn comparatively slowly with some charred residue.

- Guncotton, dissolved at about 25% in acetone, forms a lacquer used in preliminary stages of wood finishing to develop a hard finish with a deep lustre. It is normally the first coat applied, sanded and followed by other coatings that bond to it.

Because of its explosive nature, not all applications of nitrocellulose were successful. In 1869, with elephants having been poached to near extinction, the billiards industry offered a $10,000 prize to whomever came up with the best replacement for ivory billiard balls. John Wesley Hyatt created the winning replacement, which he created with a new material he discovered called camphored nitrocellulose—the first thermoplastic, better known as celluloid. The invention enjoyed a brief popularity, but the Hyatt balls were extremely flammable, and sometimes portions of the outer shell would explode upon impact. An owner of a billiard saloon in Colorado wrote to Hyatt about the explosive tendencies, saying that he did not mind very much personally but for the fact that every man in his saloon immediately pulled a gun at the sound.*[30]*[31] The process used by Hyatt to manufacture the billiard balls (US Patent 239,792, 1881) involved placing the mass of nitrocellulose in a rubber bag, which was then placed in a cylinder of liquid and heated. Pressure was applied to the liquid in the cylinder, which resulted in a uniform compression on the nitrocellulose mass, compressing it into a uniform sphere as the heat vaporized the solvents. The ball was then cooled and turned to make a uniform sphere. In light of the explosive results, this process was called the "Hyatt gun method".*[32]

35.5 Hazards

Collodion, a solution of nitrocellulose in ether and ethanol, is a flammable liquid.*[33]

When dry, nitrocellulose is explosive and can be ignited with heat, spark, or friction.*[33] An overheated container of dry nitrocellulose is believed to be the initial cause of the 2015 Tianjin explosions.*[34]

35.6 See also

- Cellulose

- Cordite

- Nitroglycerine

- Nitrostarch

- Potassium nitrate

- RE factor

- Smokeless powder

35.7 References

[1] *Merck Index*, 11th Edition, **8022**.

[2] http://www.dow.com/dowwolff/en/industrial_solutions/polymers/nitrocellulose/

[3] H. Braconnot (1833) "De la transformation de plusieurs substances végétales en un principe nouveau" (On the transformation of several vegetal substances into a new substance), *Annales de Chimie et de Physique*, **52** : 290-294. On page 293, Braconnot names nitrocellulose *xyloïdine*.

[4] J. Pelouze (1838) "Sur les produits de l'action de l'acide nitrique concentré sur l'amidon et le ligneux" (On the products of the action of concentrated nitric acid on starch and wood), *Comptes rendus* ···, **7** : 713-715.

[5] Jean-Baptiste Dumas, *Traité de Chimie Appliquée aux Arts* (Paris, France: Bechet Jeune, 1843), vol. 6, page 90. From page 90: *Il y a quelques années, M. Braconnot reconnut que l'acide nitrique concentré, convertit l'amidon, le ligneux, la cellulose, et quelques autres substances en un matière qu'il nomma xyloïdine, et que j'appellerai nitramidine.* (Some years ago, Mr. Braconnot recognized that concentrated nitric acid converted starch, wood, cellulose, and some other substances into a material that he called xyloïdine, and that I will call nitramidine.)

[6] Schönbein first communicated his discovery to the Naturforschende Gesellschaft of Basel, Switzerland on March 11, 1846:

- Schönbein (March 11, 1846) "Notiz über eine Veränderung der Pflanzenfaser und einiger andern organischen Substanzen" (Notice on a change of plant fibers and some other organic substances), *Bericht über die Verhandlungen der Naturforschenden Gesellschaft in Basel* (Report on the Proceedings of the Natural Science Research Society in Basel), **7** : 26-27.

- Schönbein (May 27, 1846) "Ueber Schiesswolle" (On guncotton) *Bericht über die Verhandlungen der Naturforschenden Gesellschaft in Basel*, **7** : 27.

In a letter, he subsequently communicated his discovery to the French Academy of Sciences:

- (Schönbein) (1846) "Lettre de M. Schoenbein à M. Dumas," *Comptes rendus* ···, **23** : 678-679.

[7] Itzehoer Wochenblatt, 29 October 1846, columns 1626 f.

[8] Urbanski, Tadeusz, *Chemistry and Technology of Explosives*, Pergamon Press, Oxford, 1965, Vol 1, pp 20–21.

[9] Clive Ponting (2011). *Gunpowder: An Explosive History - from the Alchemists of China to the Battlefields of Europe*. Random House.

[10] Fairfield, A. P., CDR USN. *Naval Ordnance*. Lord Baltimore Press (1921) pages 28–31.

[11] Brown, G.I. (1998). *The Big Bang: A history of Explosives*. Sutton Publishing p.132 ISBN 0-7509-1878-0

[12] U.S. Patent 610,861

[13] "Kodak Concern to Make Big Payment to Goodwin Company.", *New York Times*, March 27, 1914. Retrieved 2010-09-18. A settlement has been reached between the Goodwin Film and Camera Company and the Eastman Kodak Company concerning the suit brought in the Federal District Court by the former for an accounting of the profits derived from the sale of photographic films prepared according to the patent taken out by the late Rev. Hannibal Goodwin of Newark in 1898. The details of it have not been announced, but it is understood to provide for tile payment of a large sum of money by ...

[14] Brad Clifton , "The Cleveland Clinic X-Ray Fire of 1929," Cleveland Historical, accessed April 1, 2015, http://clevelandhistorical.org/items/show/573

[15] Health and Safety Executive leaflet/cellulose.pdf

[16] Interesting discussion on NC films.

[17] "Nitrate Film: If It Hasn't Gone Away, It's Still Here!", *Pro-Tek Vaults*. Retrieved 11 March 2016.

[18] "About the Dryden Theatre" . *George Eastman Museum*. Retrieved 11 March 2016.

[19] David Cleveland, "Don't Try This at Home: Some Thoughts on Nitrate Film, With Particular Reference to Home Movie Systems" in Roger Smither and Catherine Surowiec (eds.), *This Film is Dangerous: A Celebration of Nitrate Film*, Brussels, FIAF (2002), ISBN 978-2-9600296-0-4, p. 196

[20] Charles Fordyce et al., "Improved Safety Motion Picture Film Support" , *Journal of the SMPE*, vol. 51 (October 1948), pp. 331–350

[21] George J. van Schil, 'The Use of Polyester Film Base in the Motion Picture Industry', SMPTE Journal, vol. 89, no. 2 (February 1980), pp. 106–110.

[22] Case, Jared. "Art Talk: The Nitrate Picture Show" . Retrieved 10 March 2015.

[23] http://fliiby.com/file/208138/a7bake2p2k.html

[24] L. Kreplak et al. Atomic Force Microscopy of Mammalian Urothelial Surface. Journal of molecular biology. Volume 374, Issue 2, 23 November 2007, Pages 365–373

[25] See:

- C. F. Schoenbein (1849) "On ether glue or liquor constringens; and its uses in surgery," *The Lancet*, **1** : 289-290

- John Parker Maynard (1848) "Discovery and application of the new liquid adhesive plaster," *The Boston Medical and Surgical Journal*, **38** : 178-183.

[26] Kraus, E. J. (September 1939). "Adolf Carl Noe". *Botanical Gazette*. University of Chicago Press. **101** (1): 231. doi:10.1086/334861. JSTOR 2472034.

[27] Dr. R Leggat, A History of Photography: The Collodion Process

[28] "In Space No One Can Hear your Nitrocellulose Explode"

[29] "What is "sand damage"?".

[30] Connections, James Burke, Volume 9, "Countdown", 29:00 – 31:45, 1978

[31] United States. National Resources Committee (1941). *RESEARCH — A NATIONAL RESOURCE*. UNITED STATES GOVERNMENT PRINTING OFFICE. p. 29.

[32] Edward Chauncey Worden (1911). *Nitrocellulose Industry, Volume 2*. D. Van Nostrand Company. pp. 726–727.

[33] "Hazardous Substance Fact Sheet: Nitrocellulose" (PDF). New Jersey Department of Health.

[34] "Chinese Investigators Identify Cause Of Tianjin Explosion". Chemical & Engineering News. February 8, 2016. The immediate cause of the accident was the spontaneous ignition of overly dry nitrocellulose stored in a container that overheated

35.8 External links

- Gun Cotton at *The Periodic Table of Videos* (University of Nottingham)
- Nitrocellulose Paper Video (aka:Flash paper)
- Cellulose, nitrate (Nitrocellulose)—ChemSub Online
- How To Make Nitro-Cellulose That Works

An M13 rocket for the Katyusha launcher on display in the Musée de l'Armée: Its solid-fuel rocket motor was prepared from nitrocellulose.

A nitrocellulose membrane stained with Ponceau S dye for protein detection during western blotting

Table tennis ball, prepared from nitrocellulose (Celluloid)

Chapter 36

RDX

For other uses, see RDX (disambiguation).

RDX is the organic compound with the formula $(O_2NNCH_2)_3$. It is a white solid widely used as an explosive. Chemically, it is classified as nitramide. A more powerful explosive than TNT, it saw wide use in World War II. RDX is also known as **Research Department Formula X**.*[2]

It is often used in mixtures with other explosives and plasticizers, phlegmatizers (desensitizers). RDX is stable in storage and is considered one of the most powerful and brisant of the military high explosives.*[3]

36.1 Name

RDX is also known, but less commonly, as cyclonite, hexogen (particularly in Russian, German and German-influenced languages), T4 and chemically as cyclotrimethylenetrinitramine.*[4] In the 1930s, the Royal Arsenal, Woolwich, started investigating cyclonite to use against German U-boats that were being built with thicker hulls. The goal was an explosive more powerful than TNT. For security reasons, Britain termed cyclonite as "Research Department Explosive" (R.D.X.).*[5] The term RDX appeared in the United States in 1946.*[6] The first public reference in the United Kingdom to the name RDX, or R.D.X. to use the official title, appeared in 1948; its authors were the Managing Chemist, ROF Bridgwater, the Chemical Research and Development Department, Woolwich, and the Director of Royal Ordnance Factories, Explosives; again, it was referred to as simply RDX.*[7]

36.2 Usage

RDX was widely used during World War II, often in explosive mixtures with TNT such as Torpex, Composition B, Cyclotols, and H6. RDX was used in one of the first

Preparing to load 1,000-lb MC bombs into the bomb-bay of an Avro Lancaster B Mark III of No. 106 Squadron RAF at RAF Metheringham, prior to a major night raid on Frankfurt. The stencilled lettering around the circumference of each bomb reads "RDX/TNT"

plastic explosives. RDX is believed to have been used in many bomb plots including terrorist plots. The bouncing bomb depth charges used in the "Dambusters Raid" each contained 6,600 pounds (3,000 kg) of Torpex.*[8]

RDX forms the base for a number of common military explosives:

- Composition A: Granular explosive consisting of RDX and plasticizing wax. Such as, composition A-5 (RDX coated with 1.5% stearic acid) and composition A-3 (91% RDX coated with 9% wax)

- Composition B: Castable mixtures of 60% RDX and 40% TNT, with an extra 1% of wax added (desensitizer)

- Composition C: The original composition C was used in World War II, but there have been subsequent variations including C-2, C-3, and C-4. C-4 consists of RDX (91%), a plasticizer (which can be dioctyl adipate (DOA), diethylhexyl, or dioctyl sebacate) (5.3%), a binder, which is usually polyisobutylene (2.1%), SAE 10 non-detergent motor oil (1.6%).

- Composition CH-6: 97.5% RDX, 1.5% calcium stearate, 0.5% polyisobutylene, and 0.5% graphite.*[9]

- DBX (Depth Bomb Explosive): Castable mixture consisting of 21% RDX, 21% ammonium nitrate, 40% TNT, and 18% powdered aluminium. Developed during World War II, it was to be used in underwater munitions as a substitute for Torpex employing only half the amount of then-strategic RDX.*[3]*[10] As the supply of RDX became more adequate, the mixture was shelved.

- Cyclotol: Castable mixture of RDX (50–80%) with TNT (20–50%) designated by the amount of RDX/TNT, such as Cyclotol 70/30.

- HBX: Castable mixtures of RDX, TNT, powdered aluminium, and D-2 wax with calcium chloride.

- H-6: Castable mixture of RDX, TNT, powdered aluminum, and paraffin wax (used as a phlegmatizing agent).

- PBX: RDX is also used as a major component of many polymer-bonded explosives (PBX). RDX-based PBXs typically consist of RDX and a polymer/co-polymer binder. Examples of RDX-based PBX formulations include, but are not limited to: PBX-9007, PBX-9010, PBX-9205, PBX-9407, PBX-9604, PBXN-106, PBXN-3, PBXN-6, PBXN-10, PBXN-201, PBX-0280, PBX Type I, PBXC-116, PBXAF-108, etc.

- Semtex (trade name): Plastic demolition explosives containing RDX and PETN as major energetic components.

- Torpex: 42% RDX, 40% TNT, and 18% powdered aluminium. The mixture was designed during World War II and used mainly in underwater ordnance.

Outside military applications, RDX is also used in controlled demolition to raze structures. The demolition of the Jamestown Bridge in the US state of Rhode Island was one instance where RDX shaped charges were used to remove the span.

36.3 Chemistry

RDX is classified by chemists as a hexahydro-1,3,5-triazine derivative. The molecule adopts with a ruffled, cyclic structure similar to that of cyclohexane. The molecule has a high nitrogen content and a high O/C ratio, both of which indicate its explosive potential for formation of N_2 and CO_2.

It is obtained by treating white fuming nitric acid (WFNA) with hexamine. This nitrolysis reaction produces dinitromethane and ammonium nitrate as byproducts, as described in the following idealized reactions:*[11]

Hexamine + 10 nitric acid → RDX + dinitromethane + ammonium nitrate + 3 water

$(CH_2)_6N_4 + 10\ HNO_3 \rightarrow (CH_2\text{-}N\text{-}NO_2)_3 + 3\ CH_2(NO_3)_2 + NH_4NO_3 + 3\ H_2O$

36.3.1 Stability and explosive properties

The velocity of detonation of RDX at a density of 1.76 g/cm^3 is 8750 m/s.

It starts to decompose at about 170 °C and melts at 204 °C. At room temperature, it is very stable. It burns rather than explodes. It detonates only with a detonator, being unaffected even by small arms fire. This property makes it a useful military explosive. It is less sensitive than pentaerythritol tetranitrate (PETN). Under normal conditions, RDX has a figure of insensitivity of exactly 80 (RDX defines the reference point.).

RDX sublimates in vacuum, which limits some applications.

RDX when exploded in air has about 1.5 times the explosive power of TNT per unit weight and about 2.0 times per unit volume.*[12]*[13]

36.4 History

RDX was used by both sides in World War II. The US produced about 15,000 long tons (15,000 t) per month during WWII and Germany about 7,000 long tons (7,100 t) per month.*[14] RDX had the major advantages of possessing greater explosive power than TNT used in the First World War, and requiring no additional raw materials for its manufacture.*[14]

36.4.1 Germany

RDX was reported in 1898 by Georg Friedrich Henning, who obtained a German patent (patent No. 104280) for its manufacture by nitrolysis of hexamine (hexamethylenetetramine) with concentrated nitric acid.*[15]*[16] In this patent, the medical properties of RDX were mentioned; however, three further German patents obtained by Henning in 1916 proposed its use in

36.4. HISTORY

smokeless propellants.[15] The German military started investigating its use in 1920, referring to it as hexogen.[17] Research and development findings were not published further until Edmund von Herz,[18] described as an Austrian and later a German citizen, obtained a British patent in 1921[19] and a United States patent in 1922.[20] Both patent claims were initiated in Austria; and described the manufacture of RDX by nitrating hexamethylenetetramine.[19][20] The British patent claims included the manufacture of RDX by nitration, its use with or without other explosives, and its use as a bursting charge and as an initiator.[19] The US patent claim was for the use of a hollow explosive device containing RDX and a detonator cap containing RDX.[20] In the 1930s, Germany developed improved production methods.[17]

During the Second World War, Germany used the code names W Salt, SH Salt, K-method, the E-method and the KA-method. These names represented the identities of the developers of the various chemical routes to RDX. The W-method was developed by Wolfram in 1934 and gave RDX the code name "W-Salz". It used sulfamic acid, formaldehyde, and nitric acid.[21] SH-Salz (SH salt) was from Schnurr who developed a batch-process in 1937–38 based on nitrolysis of hexamine.[22] The K-method, from Knöffler, involved addition of ammonium nitrate to the hexamine/nitric acid process.[23] The E-method, developed by Ebele, proved to be identical to the Ross and Schiessler process described below.[24] The KA-method, also developed by Knöffler, and turned out to be identical to the Bachmann process described below.[25]

The explosive shells fired by the MK 108 cannon and the warhead of the R4M rocket, both used in Luftwaffe fighter aircraft as offensive armament, both used hexogen as their explosive base.

36.4.2 UK

In the United Kingdom (UK), RDX was manufactured from 1933 by the Research Department in a pilot plant at the Royal Arsenal in Woolwich, London, a larger pilot plant being built at the RGPF Waltham Abbey just outside London in 1939.[26][27] In 1939 a twin-unit industrial-scale plant was designed to be installed at a new 700 acres (280 ha) site, ROF Bridgwater, away from London; production of RDX started at Bridgwater on one unit in August 1941.[26][28] The ROF Bridgwater plant brought in ammonia and methanol as raw materials: the methanol was converted to formaldehyde and some of the ammonia converted to nitric acid, which was concentrated for RDX production.[7] The rest of the ammonia was reacted with formaldehyde to produce hexamine. The hexamine plant was supplied by Imperial Chemical Industries; it incorporated some features based on data obtained from the United States (US).[7] RDX was produced by continually adding hexamine and concentrated nitric acid to a cooled mixture of hexamine and nitric acid in the nitrator.[7] The RDX was purified and processed for its intended use; recovery and reuse of some methanol and nitric acid was also carried out.[7] The hexamine-nitration and RDX purification plants were duplicated (i.e. twin-unit) to provide some insurance against loss of production due to fire, explosion or air attack.[26]

The United Kingdom and British Empire were fighting without allies against Nazi Germany until the middle of 1941 and had to be self-sufficient. At that time (1941), the UK had the capacity to produce 70 long tons (71 t) (160,000 lb) of RDX per week; both Canada, an allied country and self-governing dominion within the British Empire, and the US were looked upon to supply ammunition and explosives, including RDX.[29] By 1942 the Royal Air Force's annual requirement was forecast to be 52,000 long tons (53,000 t) of RDX, much of which came from North America (Canada and the US).[28]

36.4.3 Canada

A different method of production to the Woolwich process was found and used in Canada, possibly at the McGill University Department of Chemistry. This was based on reacting paraformaldehyde and ammonium nitrate in acetic anhydride.[30] A UK patent application was made by Robert Walter Schiessler (Pennsylvania State College) and James Hamilton Ross (McGill, Canada) in May 1942; the UK patent was issued in December 1947.[31] Gilman states that the same method of production had been independently discovered by Ebele in Germany prior to Schiessler and Ross, but that this was not known by the Allies.[15][30] Urbański provides details of five methods of production, and he refers to this method as the (German) E-method.[24]

36.4.4 UK, US and Canadian production and development

At the beginning of the 1940s, the major US explosive manufacturers, E. I. du Pont de Nemours & Company and Hercules, had several decades of experience of manufacturing trinitrotoluene (TNT) and had no wish to experiment with new explosives. US Army Ordnance held the same viewpoint and wanted to continue using TNT.[32] RDX had been tested by Picatinny Arsenal in 1929 and it was regarded as too expensive and too sensitive.[29] The Navy proposed to continue using ammonium picrate.[32]

In contrast, the National Defense Research Committee (NDRC), who had visited The Royal Arsenal, Woolwich, did not share the view that new explosives were unnecessary.*[32] James B. Conant, chairman of Division B, wished to involve academic research into this area. Conant therefore set up an Experimental Explosives Research Laboratory at the Bureau of Mines, Bruceton, Pennsylvania, using Office of Scientific Research and Development (OSRD) funding.*[29]

Woolwich method

In 1941, the UK's Tizard Mission visited the US Army and Navy departments and part of the information handed over included details of the "Woolwich" method of manufacture of RDX and its stabilisation by mixing it with beeswax.*[29] The UK was asking that the US and Canada, combined, supply 220 short tons (200 t) (440,000 lb) of RDX per day.*[29] A decision was taken by William H. P. Blandy, Chief of the Bureau of Ordnance to adopt RDX for use in mines and torpedoes.*[29] Given the immediate need for RDX, the US Army Ordnance, at Blandy's request, built a plant that just copied the equipment and process used at Woolwich. The result was the Wabash River Ordnance Works run by E. I. du Pont de Nemours & Company.*[33] At that time, this works had the largest nitric acid plant in the world.*[29] The Woolwich process was expensive; it needed 11 pounds (5.0 kg) of strong nitric acid for every pound of RDX.*[34]

By early 1941, the NDRC was researching new processes.*[34] The Woolwich or direct nitration process has at least two serious disadvantages: (1) it used large amounts of nitric acid and (2) at least one-half of the formaldehyde is lost. One mole of hexamethylenetetramine could produce at most one mole of RDX.*[35] At least three laboratories with no previous explosive experience were tasked to develop better production methods for RDX; they were based at Cornell, Michigan, and Penn State universities.*[29]*[36] Werner Emmanuel Bachmann, from Michigan, successfully developed the "combination process" by combining the Canadian process with direct nitration.*[25]*[29] The combination process required large quantities of acetic anhydride instead of nitric acid in the old British "Woolwich process". Ideally, the combination process could produce two moles of RDX from each mole of hexamethylenetetramine.*[35]

The vast production of RDX could not continue to rely on the use of natural beeswax to desensitize the RDX. A substitute stabilizer based on petroleum was developed at the Bruceton Explosives Research Laboratory.*[29]

Bachmann process

The NDRC tasked three companies to develop pilot plants. They were the Western Cartridge Company, E. I. du Pont de Nemours & Company and Tennessee Eastman Company, part of Eastman Kodak.*[29] At the Eastman Chemical Company (TEC), a leading manufacturer of acetic anhydride, Werner Emmanuel Bachmann developed a continuous-flow process for RDX. RDX was crucial to the war effort and the current batch-production process was too slow. In February 1942, TEC began producing small amounts of RDX at its Wexler Bend pilot plant, which led to the US government authorizing TEC to design and build Holston Ordnance Works (H.O.W.) in June 1942. By April 1943, RDX was being manufactured there.*[37] At the end of 1944, the Holston plant and the Wabash River Ordnance Works, which used the Woolwich process, were producing 25,000 short tons (23,000 t) (50 million pounds) of Composition B per month.*[38]

The US Bachmann process for RDX was found to be richer in HMX than the United Kingdom's RDX. This later led to a RDX plant using the Bachmann process being set up at ROF Bridgwater in 1955 to produce both RDX and HMX.

36.4.5 Military compositions

The United Kingdom's intention in World War II was to use "desensitised" RDX. In the original Woolwich process, RDX was phlegmatized with beeswax, but later paraffin wax was used, based on the work carried out at Bruceton. In the event the UK was unable to obtain sufficient RDX to meet its needs, some of the shortfall was met by substituting amatol, a mixture of ammonium nitrate and TNT.*[28]

Karl Dönitz was reputed to have claimed that "an aircraft can no more kill a U-boat than a crow can kill a mole".*[39] However, by May 1942 Wellington bombers began to deploy depth charges containing Torpex, a mixture of RDX, TNT and aluminium, which had up to 50 percent more destructive power than TNT-filled depth charges.*[39] Considerable quantities of the RDX–TNT mixture were produced at the Holston Ordnance Works, with Tennessee Eastman developing an automated mixing and cooling process based around the use of stainless steel conveyor belts.*[13]

36.4.6 Terrorism

The 1993 Bombay bombings used RDX placed into several vehicles as bombs. RDX was the main component used for the 2006 Mumbai train bombings and the Jaipur bombings in 2008.*[40]*[41] It is also believed to be the explosive used in the 1999 Russian apartment bombings,*[42] 2004

Russian aircraft bombings,[43] and 2010 Moscow Metro bombings.[44]

Ahmed Ressam, the al-Qaeda Millennium Bomber, used a small quantity of RDX as one of the components in the explosives that he prepared to bomb Los Angeles International Airport on New Year's Eve 1999/2000; the combined explosives could have produced a blast forty times greater than that of a devastating car bomb.[45][46]

In July 2012, the Kenyan government arrested two Iranian nationals and charged them with illegal possession of 15 kilograms (33 pounds) of RDX. According to the Kenyan Police, the Iranians planned to use the RDX for "attacks on Israel, US, UK and Saudi Arabian targets".[47]

RDX was used to assassinate Lebanese prime minister Rafiq Hariri on February 14, 2005.[48]

36.5 Toxicity

RDX has caused convulsions (seizures) in military field personnel ingesting it, and in munition workers inhaling its dust during manufacture. The substance's toxicity has been studied for many years.[49] At least one fatality was attributed to RDX toxicity in a European munitions manufacturing plant.[50] The substance has low to moderate toxicity with a possible human carcinogen classification.[51] However, further research is ongoing and this classification may be revised by the United States Environmental Protection Agency (EPA).[52][53] Remediating RDX contaminated water supplies has proven to be successful.[54]

36.6 Biodegradation

RDX produces is degraded by the organisms in sewage sludge as well as the fungus Phanaerocheate chrysosporium.[55] Both wild and transgenic plants can phytoremediate explosives from soil and water.[56]

36.7 References

[1] "NIOSH Pocket Guide to Chemical Hazards #0169". National Institute for Occupational Safety and Health (NIOSH).

[2] The National Archives, London, DEFE 15/2406 dated September 1942, refers to this material as Research Department Formula X. Their original file reference was Explosives Report 275/2. The Research Department at Woolwich Arsenal named it thus as they invented the substance.

[3] *Department of the Army Technical Manual TM 9-1300-214: Military Explosives.* Headquarters, Department of the Army (United States).

[4] Davis, Tenney L. (1943), *The Chemistry of Powder and Explosives*, **II**, New York: John Wiley & Sons Inc., p. 396

[5] MacDonald and Mack Partnership (1984, p. 18)

[6] Baxter III 1968, pp. 27, 42, 255–259

[7] Simmons, W.H.; Forster, A.; Bowden, R. C. (August 1948), "The Manufacture of R.D.X. in Great Britain: Part II – Raw Materials and Ancillary Processes", *The Industrial Chemist*, **24**: 530–545; Simmons, W.H.; Forster, A.; Bowden, R. C. (September 1948), "The Manufacture of R.D.X. in Great Britain: Part III – Production of the Explosive", *The Industrial Chemist*, **24**: 593–601

[8] Sweetman, John (2002) *The Dambusters Raid*. London: Cassell Military Paperbacks. p. 144.

[9] Hampton, L. D. (June 15, 1960), *The Development of RDX Composition CH-6* (PDF), White Oak, MD: U. S. Naval Ordnance Laboratory, NavOrd Report 680

[10] *US Explosive Ordnance; Ordnance Pamphlet OP 1664*. **1**. Washington, D.C.: Navy Department, Bureau of Ordnance. May 28, 1947. pp. 3–4. OP 1664 states 21% "aluminum nitrate", but the immediately following text refers to ammonium nitrate.

[11] Luo, K.-M.; Lin, S.-H.; Chang, J.-G.; Huang, T.-H. (2002), "Evaluations of kinetic parameters and critical runaway conditions in the reaction system of hexamine-nitric acid to produce RDX in a non-isothermal batch reactor", *Journal of Loss Prevention in the Process Industries*, **15** (2): 119–127, doi:10.1016/S0950-4230(01)00027-4.

[12] Elderfield (1960, p. 8)

[13] Baxter III (1968, pp. 257 & 259)

[14] Urbański (1967, p. 78)

[15] Urbański (1967, pp. 77–119)

[16] DE 104280, Henning, Georg Friedrich, issued June 14, 1899

[17] Hexogen. economypoint.org. citing Gartz, Jochen (2007), *Vom griechischen Feuer zum Dynamit: eine Kulturgeschichte der Explosivstoffe* [*From Greek fire to dynamite: A cultural history of explosives*] (in German), Hamburg: E. S. Mittler & Sohn, ISBN 978-3-8132-0867-2

[18] Urbański (1967, p. 125) credits "G. C. V. Herz" for the patent, but the patentee is Edmund von Herz.

[19] GB 145791, von Herz, Edmund, "Improvements relating to Explosives", issued March 17, 1921

[20] US 1402693, von Herz, Edmund, "Explosive", issued January 3, 1922

[21] Urbański (1967, pp. 107–109)

[22] Urbański (1967, pp. 104–105)

[23] Urbański (1967, pp. 105–107)

[24] Urbański (1967, pp. 109–110)

[25] Urbański (1967, pp. 111–113)

[26] Cocroft, Wayne D. (2000), *Dangerous Energy: The archaeology of gunpowder and military explosives manufacture*, Swindon: English Heritage, pp. 210–211, ISBN 1-85074-718-0

[27] Akhavan, Jacqueline (2004), *The Chemistry of Explosives*, Cambridge, UK: Royal Society of Chemistry, ISBN 0-85404-640-2

[28] Hornby, William (1958), *Factories and Plant*, History of the Second World War: United Kingdom Civil Series, London: Her Majesty's Stationery Office; Longmans, Green and Co., pp. 112–114

[29] Baxter III (1968, pp. 253–239)

[30] Gilman, Henry (1953), "The Chemistry of Explosives", *Organic Chemistry an Advanced Treatise*, **III**, Wiley; Chapman & Hall, p. 985

[31] GB 595354, Schiessler, Robert Walter & James Hamilton Ross, "Method of Preparing 1.3.5. Trinitro Hexahydro S-Triazine", issued December 3, 1947

[32] Baxter III (1968, pp. 253–254)

[33] MacDonald and Mack Partnership (1984, p. 19)

[34] MacDonald and Mack Partnership (1984, p. 13) These pages need to be checked. Page 13 may actually be page 18.

[35] Elderfield (1960, p. 6)

[36] These were not the only laboratories to work on RDX. Gilman's 1953 account of the Ross-Schiessler method was based on unpublished work from laboratories at the Universities of Michigan, Pennsylvania, Cornell, Harvard, Vanderbilt, McGill (Canada), Bristol (UK), Sheffield (UK), Pennsylvania State College and the UK's Research Department.

[37] Bachmann, W. E.; Sheehan, John C. (1949), "A New Method of Preparing the High Explosive RDX", *Journal of the American Chemical Society*, **71** (5): 1842–1845, doi:10.1021/ja01173a092

[38] MacDonald and Mack Partnership (1984, p. 32)

[39] Baxter III (1968), p. 42

[40] Singh, Anil (October 2, 2006). "Mumbai". The Times of India.

[41] "Jaipur blasts: RDX used, HuJI suspected". *Times of India*. May 14, 2008. Retrieved May 13, 2011.

[42] "Debate on Cause of Moscow Blast Heats Up". New York Times. September 10, 1999. Retrieved November 14, 2011.

[43] "Explosive Suggests Terrorists Downed Plane, Russia Says". New York Times. August 28, 2004. Retrieved November 14, 2011.

[44] "Moscow Metro bombing masterminds 'will be destroyed'". BBC News. March 29, 2010. Retrieved April 2, 2010.

[45] U.S. Court of Appeals for the Ninth Circuit (February 2, 2010). "U.S. v. Ressam" (PDF). Retrieved February 27, 2010.

[46] "Complaint: U.S. v. Ressam" (PDF). NEFA Foundation. December 1999. Retrieved February 26, 2010.

[47] "Iranian agents in Kenya planned attacks on Israel, US, UK, Saudi Arabian targets". Washington Post. July 2, 2012. Retrieved July 2, 2012.

[48] Ronen Bergman (February 10, 2015). "The Hezbollah Connection". New York Times. Retrieved February 16, 2015.

[49] Annotated Reference Outline for the Toxicological Review of hexahydro-1,3,5-trinitro-1,3,5-triazine (RDX). U.S. Environmental Protection Agency (November 23, 2010)

[50] Schneider, N. R.; Bradley, S. L.; Andersen, M. E. (July 1976), *Toxicology of cyclotrimethylenetrinitramine (RDX): Distribution and metabolism in the rat and the miniature swine*, Scientific Report, DTIC, SR76-34; also in Toxicology and Applied Pharmacology 39(3) March 1977, doi:10.1016/0041-008X(77)90144-2

[51] Faust, Rosmarie A. (December 1994) Toxicity summary for hexahydro-1,3,5-trinitro-1,3,5-triazine (RDX). Oak Ridge National Laboratory

[52] Muhly, Robert L. (December 2001) Update on the Reevaluation of the Carcinogenic Potential of RDX. U.S. Army Center for Health Promotion and Preventive Medicine (CHPPM) "white paper"

[53] "Hexahydro-1,3,5-trinitro-1,3,5-triazine (RDX) (CASRN 121-82-4)". epa.gov. Retrieved January 1, 2014.

[54] Newell, Charles (August 2008). Treatment of RDX & HMX Plumes Using Mulch Biowalls. GSI Environmental, Inc.

[55] Hawari, J.; Beaudet, S.; Halasz, A.; Thiboutot, S.; Ampleman, G. (2000). "Microbial degradation of explosives: biotransformation versus mineralization". *Applied Microbiology and Biotechnology*. **54** (5): 605–618. doi:10.1007/s002530000445. PMID 11131384.

[56] Panz, K.; Miksch, K. (December 2012). "Phytoremediation of explosives (TNT, RDX, HMX) by wild-type and transgenic plants". *Journal of Environmental Management*. **113**: 85–92. doi:10.1016/j.jenvman.2012.08.016. PMID 22996005.

36.8 Bibliography

- Baxter III, James Phinney (1968) [1946], *Scientists Against Time* (MIT Paperback ed.), Cambridge, MA: MIT Press, ISBN 978-0-262-52012-6, OCLC 476611116

- Elderfield, Robert C. (1960), *Werner Emanual Bachmann: 1901-1951* (PDF), Washington DC: National Academy of Sciences

- MacDonald and Mack Partnership (August 1984), *Final Properties Report: Newport Army Ammunition Plant* (PDF), National Park Service, AD-A175 818

- Urbański, Tadeusz (1967), Laverton, Silvia, ed., *Chemistry and Technology of Explosives*, **III**, translated by Marian Jureck (First English ed.), Warszawa: PWN – Polish Scientific Publishers and Pergamon Press, OCLC 499857211. See also ISBN 978-0-08-010401-0.

- Urbański translation https://openlibrary.org/books/OL3160546M/Chemistry_and_technology_of_explosives, Macmillan, NY, 1964, ISBN 0-08-026206-6.

36.9 Further reading

- Agrawal, Jai Prakhash.; Hodgson, Robert Dale (2007), *Organic Chemistry of Explosives*, Wiley, ISBN 978-0-470-02967-1

- US 2680671, Bachmann, Werner E., "Method of Treating Cyclonite Mixtures", published July 16, 1943, issued June 8, 1954

- US 2798870, Bachmann, Werner E., "Method for Preparing Explosives", published July 16, 1943, issued July 9, 1957

- Cooper, Paul W. (1996), *Explosives Engineering*, New York: Wiley-VCH, ISBN 0-471-18636-8

- Hale, George C. (1925), "The Nitration of Hexamethylenetetramine", *Journal of the American Chemical Society*, **47** (11): 2754–2763, doi:10.1021/ja01688a017

- Meyer, Rudolf (1987), *Explosives* (3rd ed.), VCH Publishers, ISBN 0-89573-600-4

36.10 External links

- ADI Limited (Australia). Archive.org leads to Thales group products page that shows some military specifications.

- NLM Hazardous Substances Databank (US) – Cyclonite (RDX)

- CDC – NIOSH Pocket Guide to Chemical Hazards

- GlobalSecurity.org, *Explosives – Compositions*, Alexandria, VA: GlobalSecurity.org, retrieved September 1, 2010

- http://nla.gov.au/nla.news-article38338874, Army News (Darwin, NT), October 2, 1943, p 3. "Britain's New Explosive: Experts Killed in Terrific Blast", uses "Research Department formula X"

- http://nla.gov.au/nla.news-article42015565, The Courier-Mail (Brisbane, Qld.), September 27, 1943, p 1.

Chapter 37

Pentaerythritol tetranitrate

Pentaerythritol tetranitrate (**PETN**), also known as **PENT**, **PENTA**, **TEN**, **corpent**, **penthrite** (or —rarely and primarily in German—as **nitropenta**), is the nitrate ester of pentaerythritol, and is structurally very similar to nitroglycerin. Penta refers to the five carbon atoms of the neopentane skeleton.

PETN is one of the most powerful explosive materials known, with a relative effectiveness factor of 1.66.*[2] When mixed with a plasticizer, PETN forms a plastic explosive.*[3] Along with RDX it is the main ingredient of Semtex.

PETN is also used as a vasodilator drug to treat certain heart conditions, such as for management of angina.*[4]*[5]

37.1 History

Pentaerythritol tetranitrate was first prepared and patented in 1894 by the explosives manufacturer Rheinisch-Westfälische Sprengstoff A.G. of Cologne, Germany.*[6] The production of PETN started in 1912, when the improved method of production was patented by the German government. PETN was used by the German Military in World War I.*[7] It was also used in the MG FF/M autocannons and many other weapon systems of the Luftwaffe in World War II, specifically in the high explosive "Minengeschoß" shell.

37.2 Properties

PETN is practically insoluble in water (0.01 g/100 ml at 50 °C), weakly soluble in common nonpolar solvents such as aliphatic hydrocarbons (like gasoline) or tetrachloromethane, but soluble in some other organic solvents, particularly in acetone (about 15 g/100 g of the solution at 20 °C, 55 g/100 g at 60 °C) and dimethylformamide (40 g/100 g of the solution at 40 °C, 70 g/100 g at 70 °C). PETN forms eutectic mixtures with some liquid or molten aromatic nitro compounds, e.g. trinitrotoluene (TNT) or tetryl. Due to its highly symmetrical structure, PETN is resistant to attack by many chemical reagents; it does not hydrolyze in water at room temperature or in weaker alkaline aqueous solutions. Water at 100 °C or above causes hydrolysis to dinitrate; presence of 0.1% nitric acid accelerates the reaction.

The chemical stability of PETN is of interest, because of the presence of PETN in aging weapons. A review has been published.*[8] Neutron radiation degrades PETN, producing carbon dioxide and some pentaerythritol dinitrate and trinitrate. Gamma radiation increases the thermal decomposition sensitivity of PETN, lowers melting point by few degrees Celsius, and causes swelling of the samples. Like other nitrate esters, the primary degradation mechanism is the loss of nitrogen dioxide; this reaction is autocatalytic. Studies were performed on thermal decomposition of PETN.*[9]

In the environment, PETN undergoes biodegradation. Some bacteria denitrate PETN to trinitrate and then dinitrate, which is then further degraded. PETN has low volatility and low solubility in water, and therefore has low bioavailability for most organisms. Its toxicity is relatively low, and its transdermal absorption also seems to be low.*[1] It poses a threat for aquatic organisms. It can be degraded to pentaerythritol by iron.*[10]

37.3 Production

Production is by the reaction of pentaerythritol with concentrated nitric acid to form a precipitate which can be recrystallized from acetone to give processable crystals.*[11]

Variations of a method first published in a US Patent

2,370,437 by Acken and Vyverberg (1945 to Du Pont) forms the basis of all current commercial production.

PETN is manufactured by numerous manufacturers as a powder, or together with nitrocellulose and plasticizer as thin plasticized sheets (e.g. Primasheet 1000 or Detasheet). PETN residues are easily detectable in hair of people handling it.[12] The highest residue retention is on black hair; some residues remain even after washing.[13][14]

37.4 Explosive use

Pentaerythritol tetranitrate before crystallization from acetone

The most common use of PETN is as an explosive with high brisance. It is more difficult to detonate than primary explosives, so dropping or igniting it will typically not cause an explosion (at atmospheric pressure it is difficult to ignite and burns relatively slowly), but is more sensitive to shock and friction than other secondary explosives such as TNT or tetryl.[11][15] Under certain conditions a deflagration to detonation transition can occur.

It is rarely used alone, but primarily used in booster and bursting charges of small caliber ammunition, in upper charges of detonators in some land mines and shells, and as the explosive core of detonation cord.[16] PETN is the least stable of the common military explosives, but can be stored without significant deterioration for longer than nitroglycerin or nitrocellulose.[17]

During World War II, PETN was most importantly used in exploding-bridgewire detonators for the atomic bombs. These exploding-bridgewire detonators gave more precise detonation, compared with primacord. PETN was used for these detonators because it was safer than primary explosives like lead azide; while it was sensitive, it would not detonate below a threshold amount of energy.[18] Exploding bridgewires containing PETN remain used in current nuclear weapons. In spark detonators, PETN is used to avoid the need for primary explosives; the energy needed for a successful direct initiation of PETN by an electric spark ranges between 10–60 mJ.

Its basic explosion characteristics are:

- Explosion energy: 5810 kJ/kg (1390 kcal/kg), so 1 kg of PETN has the energy of 1.24 kg TNT.

- Detonation velocity: 8350 m/s (1.73 g/cm^3), 7910 m/s (1.62 g/cm^3), 7420 m/s (1.5 g/cm^3), 8500 m/s (pressed in a steel tube)

- Volume of gases produced: 790 dm^3/kg (other value: 768 dm^3/kg)

- Explosion temperature: 4230 °C

- Oxygen balance: −6.31 atom -g/kg

- Melting point: 141.3 °C (pure), 140–141 °C (technical)

- Trauzl lead block test: 523 cm^3 (other values: 500 cm^3 when sealed with sand, or 560 cm^3 when sealed with water)

- Critical diameter (minimal diameter of a rod that can sustain detonation propagation): 0.9 mm for PETN at 1 g/cm^3, smaller for higher densities (other value: 1.5 mm)

37.4.1 In mixtures

PETN is used in a number of compositions. It is a major ingredient of the Semtex plastic explosive. It is also used as a component of pentolite, a 50/50 blend with TNT. The XTX8003 extrudable explosive, used in the W68 and W76 nuclear warheads, is a mixture of 80% PETN and 20% of Sylgard 182, a silicone rubber.[19] It is often phlegmatized by addition of 5–40% of wax, or by polymers (producing polymer-bonded explosives); in this form it is used in some cannon shells up to 30 mm caliber, though unsuitable for higher calibers. It is also used as a component of some gun propellants and solid rocket propellants. Nonphlegmatized PETN is stored and handled with approximately 10% water content. PETN alone cannot be cast as it explosively decomposes slightly above its melting point, but it can be mixed with other explosives to form castable mixtures.

PETN can be initiated by a laser.[20] A pulse with duration of 25 nanoseconds and 0.5–4.2 joules of energy from a Q-switched ruby laser can initiate detonation of a PETN surface coated with a 100 nm thick aluminium layer in less than half of a microsecond.

PETN has been replaced in many applications by RDX, which is thermally more stable and has a longer shelf life.*[21] PETN can be used in some ram accelerator types.*[22] Replacement of the central carbon atom with silicon produces Si-PETN, which is extremely sensitive.*[23]*[24]

37.4.2 Terrorist use

Main articles: Shoe Bomber, 2009 Christmas Day bomb plot, and 2010 cargo plane bomb plot

In the 1980 Paris synagogue bombing.

In 1983, the "Maison de France" house in Berlin was brought to a near-total collapse by the detonation of 24 kilograms (53 lb) of PETN by terrorist Johannes Weinrich.*[25]

In 1999, Alfred Heinz Reumayr used PETN as the main charge for his fourteen improvised explosive devices that he constructed in a thwarted attempt to damage the Trans-Alaska Pipeline System.

In 2001, al-Qaeda member Richard Reid, the "Shoe Bomber", used PETN in the sole of his shoe in his unsuccessful attempt to blow up American Airlines Flight 63 from Paris to Miami.*[14]*[26] He had intended to use the solid triacetone triperoxide (TATP) as a detonator.*[15]

In 2009, PETN was used in an attempt by al-Qaeda in the Arabian Peninsula to murder the Saudi Arabian Deputy Minister of Interior Prince Muhammad bin Nayef, by Saudi suicide bomber Abdullah Hassan al Asiri. The target survived and the bomber died in the blast. The PETN was hidden in the bomber's rectum, which security experts described as a novel technique.*[27]*[28]*[29]

On December 25, 2009, PETN was found in the underwear of Umar Farouk Abdulmutallab, the "Underwear bomber", a Nigerian with links to al-Qaeda in the Arabian Peninsula.*[30] According to US law enforcement officials,*[31] he had attempted to blow up Northwest Airlines Flight 253 while approaching Detroit from Amsterdam.*[32] Abdulmutallab had tried, unsuccessfully, to detonate approximately 80 grams (2.8 oz) of PETN sewn into his underwear by adding liquid from a syringe;*[33] however, only a small fire resulted.*[15]

In the al-Qaeda in the Arabian Peninsula October 2010 cargo plane bomb plot, two PETN-filled printer cartridges were found at East Midlands Airport and in Dubai on flights bound for the US on an intelligence tip. Both packages contained sophisticated bombs concealed in computer printer cartridges filled with PETN.*[34]*[35] The bomb found in England contained 400 grams (14 oz) of PETN, and the one found in Dubai contained 300 grams (11 oz) of PETN.*[35] Hans Michels, professor of safety engineering at University College London, told a newspaper that 6 grams (0.21 oz) of PETN—"around 50 times less than was used—would be enough to blast a hole in a metal plate twice the thickness of an aircraft's skin".*[36] In contrast, according to an experiment conducted by a BBC documentary team designed to simulate Abdulmutallab's Christmas Day bombing, using a Boeing 747 plane, even 80 grams of PETN was not sufficient to materially damage the fuselage.*[37]

37.4.3 Detection

In the wake of terrorist PETN bomb plots, an article in *Scientific American* noted PETN is difficult to detect because it does not readily vaporize into the surrounding air.*[34] The *Los Angeles Times* noted in November 2010 that PETN's low vapor pressure makes it difficult for bomb-sniffing dogs to detect.*[14]

Many technologies can be used to detect PETN,*[38] some of which have been implemented in public screening applications, primarily for air travel. PETN is one of the explosive chemicals typically of interest in that area, and it belongs to a family of common nitrate-based explosive chemicals which can often be detected by the same tests.

One detection system in use at airports involves analysis of swab samples obtained from passengers and their baggage. Whole-body imaging scanners that use radio-frequency electromagnetic waves, low-intensity X-rays, or T-rays of terahertz frequency that can detect objects hidden under clothing are not widely used because of cost, concerns about the resulting traveler delays, and privacy concerns.*[39]

Both parcels in the 2010 cargo plane bomb plot were x-rayed without the bombs being spotted.*[40] Qatar Airways said the PETN bomb "could not be detected by x-ray screening or trained sniffer dogs".*[41] The Bundeskriminalamt received copies of the Dubai x-rays, and an investigator said German staff would not have identified the bomb either.*[40]*[42] New airport security procedures followed in the U.S., largely to protect against PETN.*[14]

37.5 Medical use

Like nitroglycerin (glyceryl trinitrate) and other nitrates, PETN is also used medically as a vasodilator in the treatment of heart conditions.*[4]*[5] These drugs work by releasing the signaling gas nitric oxide in the body. The heart medicine *Lentonitrat* is nearly pure PETN.*[43]

Monitoring of oral usage of the drug by patients has been performed by determination of plasma levels of several of its hydrolysis products, pentaerythritol dinitrate, pentaerythritol mononitrate and pentaerythritol, in plasma using gas chromatography-mass spectrometry."[44]

37.6 See also

- Erythritol tetranitrate
- Pentaerythritol
- RDX
- RE factor

37.7 References

[1] "Wildlife Toxicity Assessment for pentaerythritol tetranitrate" (PDF). U.S. Army Center for Health Promotion and Preventive Medicine. November 2001

[2] "PETN (Pentaerythritol tetranitrate)". Retrieved March 29, 2010.

[3] John Childs (1994). "Explosives" (Google Books extract). *A dictionary of military history and the art of war*. ISBN 978-0-631-16848-5.

[4] "New Drugs". *Can Med Assoc J*. **80** (12): 997–998. 1959. PMC 1831125. PMID 20325960.

[5] Manuchair S. Ebadi (1998). *CRC desk reference of clinical pharmacology* (Google Books excerpt). p. 383. ISBN 978-0-8493-9683-0.

[6] See:
- Deutsches Reichspatent 81,664 (1894).
- Bruno Thieme, "Process of making nitropentaerythrit." U.S. patent no. 541,899 (filed: November 13, 1894 ; issued: July 2, 1895).
- Peter O. K. Krehl. *History of Shock Waves, Explosions and Impact* ... (Berlin, Germany: Springer-Verlag, 2009), p. 405.
- Tadeusz Urbański with Władysław Ornaf and Sylvia Laverton, trans., *Chemistry and Technology of Explosives*, vol. 2 (Oxford, England: Permagon Press, 1965), p. 175.

[7] See:
- German Patent 265,025 (1912)
- Stettbacher, Alfred (1933). *Die Schiess- und Sprengstoffe* (2. völlig umgearb. Aufl. ed.). Leipzig: Barth. p. 459.

[8] M. F. Foltz. "Aging of Pentaerythritol Tetranitrate (PETN)" (PDF). Lawrence Livermore National Laboratory

[9] Thermal decomposition of PENT and HMX over a wide temperature range by V.N. German et al.

[10] Li Zhuang, Lai Gui & Robert W. Gillham (2008). "Degradation of Pentaerythritol Tetranitrate (PETN) by Granular Iron". *Environ. Sci. Technol.* **42** (12): 4534–9. doi:10.1021/es7029703. PMID 18605582.

[11] Jacques Boileau, Claude Fauquignon, Bernard Hueber, Hans H. Meyer (2005). "Explosives". *Ullmann's Encyclopedia of Industrial Chemistry*. Weinheim. Wiley-VCH. doi:10.1002/14356007.a10_143.pub2

[12] Winslow, Ron. (December 29, 2009) A Primer in PETN – WSJ.com. *The Wall Street Journal*. Retrieved 2010-02-08.

[13] Oxley, Jimmie C.; Smith, James L.; Kirschenbaum, Louis J.; Shinde, Kajal. P.; Marimganti, Suvarna (2005). "Accumulation of Explosives in Hair". *Journal of Forensic Sciences*. **50**: 1. doi:10.1520/JFS2004545.

[14] Bennett, Brian (November 24, 2010). "PETN: The explosive that airport security is targeting". *Los Angeles Times*. Tribune Washington Bureau. Retrieved July 19, 2015.

[15] Kenneth Chang (December 27, 2009). "Explosive on Flight 253 Is Among Most Powerful". *The New York Times*.

[16] "Primacord Technical Information" (PDF). Dyno Nobel. Archived from the original (PDF) on July 10, 2011. Retrieved April 22, 2009.

[17] PETN (chemical compound) – Britannica Online Encyclopedia. *Encyclopædia Britannica*. Retrieved February 8, 2010.

[18] Lillian Hoddeson; Paul W. Henriksen; Roger A. Meade; Catherine L. Westfall; Gordon Baym; Richard Hewlett; Alison Kerr; Robert Penneman; Leslie Redman; Robert Seidel (2004). *A Technical History of Los Alamos During the Oppenheimer Years, 1943–1945* (Google Books excerpt). pp. 164–173. ISBN 978-0-521-54117-6.

[19] Information Bridge: DOE Scientific and Technical Information – Sponsored by OSTI. Osti.gov (November 23, 2009). Retrieved 2010-02-08.

[20] Tarzhanov, V. I.; Zinchenko, A. D.; Sdobnov, V. I.; Tokarev, B. B.; Pogrebov, A. I.; Volkova, A. A. (1996). "Laser initiation of PETN". *Combustion, Explosion, and Shock Waves*. **32**: 454. doi:10.1007/BF01998499.

[21] US Army – Encyclopedia of Explosives and Related Items, vol.8

[22] Simulation of ram accelerator with PETN layer, Arkadiusz Kobiera and Piotr Wolanski, XXI ICTAM, August 15–21, 2004, Warsaw, Poland

[23] Wei-Guang Liu; et al. (2009). "Explanation of the Colossal Detonation Sensitivity of Silicon Pentaerythritol Tetranitrate (Si-PETN) Explosive" (PDF). *J. Am. Chem. Soc.* **131** (22): 7490–1. doi:10.1021/ja809725p. PMID 19489634.

[24] Computational Organic Chemistry » Si-PETN sensitivity explained. Comporgchem.com (July 20, 2009). Retrieved 2010-02-08.

[25] "Article detailing attack on Maison de France in Berlin (German)". *Der Spiegel*. December 13, 1999. Retrieved November 4, 2010.

[26] "'Shoe bomb suspect 'did not act alone'". BBC News. January 25, 2002. Retrieved April 22, 2009.

[27] "Saudi suicide bomber hid IED in his anal cavity". *Homeland Security Newswire*. September 9, 2009

[28] Andrew England (November 1, 2010). "Bomb clues point to Yemeni terrorists". *Financial Times*.

[29] "Saudi Bombmaker Key Suspect in Yemen Plot". CBS News. November 1, 2010. Retrieved November 2, 2010.

[30] "Al Qaeda Claims Responsibility for Attempted Bombing of U.S. Plane". FOX News Network. December 28, 2009. Retrieved December 29, 2009.

[31] "Criminal Complaint" (PDF). *The Huffington Post*. Retrieved November 4, 2010.

[32] "Investigators: Northwest Bomb Plot Planned by al Qaeda in Yemen". ABC News. December 26, 2009. Retrieved December 26, 2009.

[33] Explosive in Detroit terror case could have blown hole in airplane, sources say *The Washington Post*. Retrieved February 8, 2010.

[34] Greenemeier, Larry. "Exposing the Weakest Link: As Airline Passenger Security Tightens, Bombers Target Cargo Holds". *Scientific American*. Retrieved November 3, 2010.

[35] Shane, Scott; Worth, Robert F. (November 1, 2010). "Early Parcels Sent to U.S. Were Eyed as Dry Run". *The New York Times*.

[36] "Parcel bombs could rip 50 planes in half". *India Today*. Retrieved November 3, 2010.

[37] "'Underwear Bomber' Could not have Blown Up Plane". Discovery. March 10, 2010. Retrieved November 16, 2010.

[38] Committee on the Review of Existing and Potential Standoff Explosives Detection Techniques, National Research Council, Existing and Potential Standoff Explosives Detection Techniques, National Academies Press, Washington, D.C., 2004, p. 77

[39] "Equipment to detect explosives is available". *The Washington Post*. Retrieved February 8, 2010.

[40] "Foiled Parcel Plot: World Scrambles to Tighten Air Cargo Security". *Der Spiegel*. Retrieved November 2, 2010.

[41] "Q&A: Air freight bomb plot". BBC News. October 30, 2010. Retrieved November 3, 2010.

[42] "Passenger jets carried Dubai bomb". Al Jazeera. Retrieved November 1, 2010.

[43] Russek H. I. (1966). "The therapeutic role of coronary vasodilators: glyceryl trinitrate, isosorbide dinitrate, and pentaerythritol tetranitrate.". *American Journal of the Medical Sciences*. **252** (1): 9–20. doi:10.1097/00000441-196607000-00002. PMID 4957459.

[44] R. Baselt, *Disposition of Toxic Drugs and Chemicals in Man*, 8th edition, Biomedical Publications, Foster City, CA, 2008, pp. 1201–1203.

37.8 Further reading

- Cooper, Paul (1997). *Explosives Engineering*. Weinheim: Wiley-VCH. ISBN 0-471-18636-8.

37.9 External links

- Media related to Pentaerythritol tetranitrate at Wikimedia Commons

Chapter 38

HMX

For other uses, see HMX (disambiguation).

HMX, also called **octogen**, is a powerful and relatively insensitive nitroamine high explosive, chemically related to RDX. Like RDX, the compound's name is the subject of much speculation, having been variously listed as High Melting eXplosive, Her Majesty's eXplosive, High-velocity Military eXplosive, or High-Molecular-weight rdX.[1]

The molecular structure of HMX consists of an eight-membered ring of alternating carbon and nitrogen atoms, with a nitro group attached to each nitrogen atom. Because of its high molecular weight, it is one of the most potent chemical explosives manufactured, although a number of newer ones, including HNIW and ONC, are more powerful.

38.1 Production

HMX is more complicated to manufacture than most explosives and this confines it to specialist applications. It may be produced by nitration of hexamine in the presence of acetic anhydride, paraformaldehyde and ammonium nitrate. RDX produced using the Bachmann Process usually contains 8–10% HMX.[2]

38.2 Applications

Also known as cyclotetramethylene-tetranitramine, tetrahexamine tetranitramine, or octahydro-1,3,5,7-tetranitro-1,3,5,7-tetrazocine, HMX was first made in 1930. In 1949 it was discovered that HMX can be prepared by nitrolysis of RDX. Nitrolysis of RDX is performed by dissolving RDX in a 55% HNO_3 solution, followed by placing the solution on a steambath for about six hours.[3] HMX is used almost exclusively in military applications, including as the detonator in nuclear weapons, in the form of polymer-bonded explosive, and as a solid rocket propellant.

HMX is used in melt-castable explosives when mixed with TNT, which as a class are referred to as "octols". Additionally, polymer-bonded explosive compositions containing HMX are used in the manufacture of missile warheads and armor-piercing shaped charges.

HMX is also used in the process of perforating the steel casing in oil and gas wells. The HMX is built into a shaped charge that is detonated within the wellbore to punch a hole through the steel casing and surrounding cement out into the hydrocarbon bearing formations. The pathway that is created allows formation fluids to flow into the wellbore and onward to the surface.

The Hayabusa 2 space probe will use HMX to excavate a hole in an asteroid in order to access material that has not been exposed to the solar wind.[4]

38.2.1 Toxicity

At present, the information needed to determine if HMX causes cancer is insufficient. Due to the lack of information, EPA has determined that HMX is not classifiable as to its human carcinogenicity.[5]

The available data on the effects on human health of exposure to HMX are limited. HMX causes CNS effects similar to those of RDX, but at considerably higher doses. In one study, volunteers submitted to patch testing, which produced skin irritation. Another study of a cohort of 93 workers at an ammunition plant found no hematological, hepatic, autoimmune, or renal diseases. However, the study did not quantify the levels of exposure to HMX.

HMX exposure has been investigated in several studies on animals. Overall, the toxicity appears to be quite low. HMX is poorly absorbed by ingestion. When applied to the dermis, it induces mild skin irritation but not delayed contact sensitization. Various acute and subchronic neurobehavioral effects have been reported in rabbits and rodents, including ataxia, sedation, hyperkinesia, and convulsions. The chronic effects of HMX that have been documented through animal studies include decreased hemoglobin, increased serum alkaline phosphatase, and decreased albumin. Pathological changes were also observed in the animals' livers and kidneys. No data are available concerning the possible reproductive, developmental, or carcinogenic effects of HMX.*[2]*[6] HMX is considered the least toxic amongst TNT and RDX.*[7] Remediating HMX contaminated water supplies has proven to be successful.*[8]

38.3 Biodegradation

Both wild and transgenic plants can phytoremediate explosives from soil and water.*[9]

38.4 See also

- 2,4,6-Tris(trinitromethyl)–1,3,5-triazine
- 4,4'-Dinitro-3,3'-diazenofuroxan (DDF)
- Heptanitrocubane (HNC)
- HHTDD
- Octanitrocubane (ONC)
- RE factor

38.5 Notes

[1] Cooper, Paul W., *Explosives Engineering*, New York: Wiley-VCH, 1996. ISBN 0-471-18636-8

[2] John Pike (1996-06-19). "Nitramine Explosives". Globalsecurity.org. Retrieved 2012-05-24.

[3] WE Bachmann, JC Sheehan (1949). "A New Method of Preparing the High Explosive RDX1". *Journal of the American Chemical Society*, 1949 (5):1842–1845.

[4] Saiki, Takanao; Sawada, Hirotaka; Okamoto, Chisato; Yano, Hajime; Takagi, Yasuhiko; Akahoshi, Yasuhiro; Yoshikawa, Makoto (2013). "Small carry-on impactor of Hayabusa2 mission". *Acta Astronautica*. **84**: 227. Bibcode:2013AcAau..84..227S. doi:10.1016/j.actaastro.2012.11.010.

[5] "Octahydro-1,3,5,7-tetranitro-1,3,5,7-tetr... (HMX) (CASRN 2691-41-0) | IRIS | US EPA." EPA. Environmental Protection Agency, n.d. Web. 15 Nov. 2012.

[6] "Fact Sheets". Mmr-iagwsp.org. Retrieved 2012-05-24.

[7] "Information Bridge: DOE Scientific and Technical Information - Sponsored by OSTI" (PDF). Osti.gov. Retrieved 2012-05-24.

[8] Newell, Charles. "Treatment of RDX & HMX Plumes Using Mulch Biowalls." ESTCP Project ER-0426. 2008.

[9] Panz K; Miksch K (December 2012). "Phytoremediation of explosives (TNT, RDX, HMX) by wild-type and transgenic plants". *Journal of Environmental Management*. **113**: 85–92. doi:10.1016/j.jenvman.2012.08.016. PMID 22996005.

38.6 References

- Cooper, Paul W. (1996). *Explosives Engineering*. New York: Wiley-VCH. ISBN 0-471-18636-8. OCLC 34409473. Retrieved 9 June 2014.

- Urbanski, Tadeusz (1967). *Chemistry and Technology of Explosives*. Vol. III. Warszawa: Polish Scientific Publishers.

Chapter 39

C-4 (explosive)

C-4 or **Composition C-4** is a common variety of the plastic explosive family known as Composition C. The British version of the explosive is known as **PE-4** (Plastic Explosive). C-4 is composed of explosives, plastic binder, plasticizer to make it malleable, and usually a marker or odorizing taggant chemical.

C-4 has a texture similar to modeling clay and can be molded into any desired shape. C-4 is stable and an explosion can only be initiated by the combination of extreme heat and shock wave from a detonator.

39.1 Characteristics and uses

39.1.1 Composition

The Composition C-4 used by the United States Armed Forces contains 91% RDX ("Research Department Explosive", an explosive nitroamine), 5.3% dioctyl sebacate (DOS) or dioctyl adipate (DOA) as the plasticizer (to increase the plasticity of the explosive), 2.1% polyisobutylene (PIB, a synthetic rubber) as the binder, and 1.6% of a mineral oil often called "process oil." Instead of "process oil," low-viscosity motor oil is used in the manufacture of C-4 for civilian use.*[1]

Technical data according to the Department of the Army follows.*[2]

Manufacture

C-4 is manufactured by combining the above ingredients with binder dissolved in a solvent. Once the ingredients have been mixed, the solvent is extracted through drying and filtering. The final material is a solid with a dirty white to light brown color, a putty-like texture similar to modeling clay, and a distinct smell of motor oil.*[2]*[3]*[4]

Depending on its intended usage and on the manufacturer, there are differences in the composition of C-4. For example, a 1990 U.S. Army technical manual stipulated that Class IV composition C-4 consists of 89.9±1% RDX, 10±1% polyisobutylene, and 0.2±0.02% dye that is itself made up of 90% lead chromate and 10% lamp black.*[2] RDX classes A, B, E, and H are all suitable for use in C-4. Classes are measured by granulation.*[5]

The substitution of ethylene glycol (found in anti-freeze as used in automotive cooling systems) in place of the plastic binder prevents its freezing and the composition remains pliable under all environmental conditions.

The manufacturing process for Composition C-4 specifies that wet RDX and plastic binder are added in a stainless steel mixing kettle. This is called the aqueous slurry-coating process.*[6] The kettle is tumbled to obtain a homogeneous mixture. This mixture is wet and must be dried after transfer to drying trays. Drying with forced air for 16 hours at 50°C to 60°C is recommended to eliminate excess moisture.*[2]*:198

39.1.2 Detonation

C-4 is very stable and insensitive to most physical shocks. C-4 cannot be detonated by a gunshot or by dropping it onto a hard surface. It does not explode when set on fire or exposed to microwave radiation.*[7] Detonation can only be initiated by a combination of extreme heat and a shockwave, such as when a detonator inserted into it is fired.*[3] When detonated, C-4 rapidly decomposes to release nitrogen and carbon oxides as well as other gasses.*[3] The gasses expand at an explosive velocity of 8,092 m/s (26,550 ft/s).*[8]

A major advantage of C-4 is that it can easily be moulded into any desired shape to change the direction of the resulting explosion.*[3]*[9]

A detonation within a blast resistant trash receptacle using a large C-4 explosive charge.

C-4 packaged as standard size M112 demolition charges. Sometimes 16 blocks of M112 are used to create a M183 demolition charge assembly.

39.1.3 Form

Military grade C-4 is commonly packaged as the M112 demolition block. The demolition charge M112 is a rectangular block of Composition C-4 approximately 2 inches by 1.5 inches and 11 inches long, weighing 1.25 lb (0.57 kg).[10][11] The M112 is wrapped in a sometimes olive color Mylar-film container with a pressure-sensitive adhesive tape on one surface.[12][13]

The M112 demolition blocks of C-4 are commonly manufactured into the M183 "demolition charge assembly",[11] which consists of 16 M112 block demolition charges and four priming assemblies packaged inside military Carrying Case M85. The M183 is used to breach obstacles or demolish large structures where larger satchel charges are required. Each priming assembly includes a five- or twenty-foot length of detonating cord assembled with detonating cord clips and capped at each end with a booster. When the charge is detonated, the explosive is converted into compressed gas. The gas exerts pressure in the form of a shock wave, which demolishes the target by cutting, breaching, or cratering.[10]

Other forms include the mine-clearing line charge (MICLIC) and M18A1 Claymore Mine.[6]

39.1.4 Safety

Further information: Explosives safety and Safety testing of explosives

Composition C-4 exists in the US Army Hazardous Components Safety Data Sheet on sheet number 00077.[14]:323

Impact tests done by the US military indicate composition C-4 is less sensitive than composition C-3 and is fairly insensitive. The insensitivity is attributed to using a large amount of binder in its composition. A series of shots were fired at vials containing C-4 in a test referred to as "the rifle bullet test". Only 20 percent of the vials burned, and none exploded. While C-4 passed the Army's bullet impact and fragment impact tests at ambient temperature, it did in fact fail the shock stimulus, sympathetic detonation and shaped charge jet tests.[6]

Additional tests were done including the "pendulum friction test", which measured a five-second explosion temperature of 263 °C to 290 °C. The minimum initiating charge required is 0.2 grams of lead azide or 0.1 grams of tetryl.

The results of 100 °C heat test are: 0.13 percent loss in the first 48 hours, no loss in the second 48 hours, and no explosions in 100 hours. The vacuum stability test at 100 °C yields 0.2 cubic centimeters of gas in 40 hours. Composition C-4 is essentially nonhygroscopic.[2]

The shock sensitivity of C-4 can be further reduced by how fine the nitramine particles are. The finer they are the better they help to absorb and suppress shock. Using 3-nitrotriazol-5-one (NTO), or 1,3,5-triamino-2,4,6-trinitrobenzene (TATB) (available in two particle sizes (5 μm, 40 μm)), as a substitute for RDX, is also able to improve stability to thermal, shock, and impact/friction stimulus; however, TATB is not cost-effective, and NTO is more difficult to use in the manufacturing process.[6]

Sensitivity test values

Sensitivity test values reported by the US Army follow.[14]:311, 314

Source variation

C-4 produced for use by the U.S. military, commercial C-4 (also produced in the United States), and C-4 (otherwise known as PE-4) from England each have their own unique properties and are not identical. The analytical techniques of time-of-flight secondary ion mass spectrometry and X-ray photoelectron spectroscopy have been demonstrated to discriminate finite differences in different C-4 sources. Chemical, morphological structural differences, and variation in atomic concentrations are detectable and definable.[15]

39.2 Analysis

39.2.1 Toxicity

C-4 has toxic effects on humans when ingested. Within a few hours multiple generalized seizures, vomiting, and changes in mental activity occur.[16] A strong link to central nervous dysfunction is observed.[17] If ingested, patients may be administered a dose of active charcoal to absorb some of the toxins, and haloperidol intramuscularly and diazepam intravenously to help the patient control seizures until it has passed. RDX, the primary component of C-4, is known to be a possible human carcinogen.[18] However, ingesting small amounts of C-4 is not known to cause any long-term impediment.[19]

39.2.2 Investigation

If C-4 is marked with a taggant, such as DMNB, it can be detected with an explosive vapor detector before it has been detonated.[20]

A variety of methods for explosive residue analysis may be used to identify C-4. These include optical microscope examination and scanning electron microscopy for unreacted explosive, chemical spot tests, thin-layer chromatography (TLC), X-ray crystallography, and infrared spectroscopy for products of the explosive chemical reaction. Small particles of C-4 may be easily identified by mixing with thymol crystals and a few drops of sulfuric acid. The mixture will become rose colored upon addition of a small quantity of ethyl alcohol.[21]

RDX has a high birefringence, and the other components

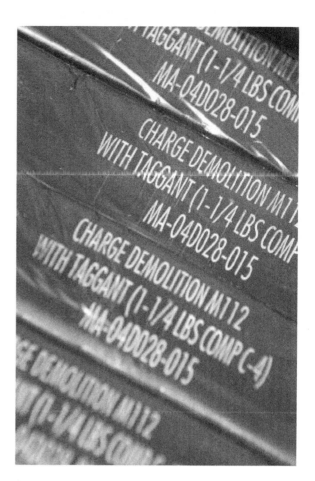

Wrapping on packaged C-4 indicate that it has been tagged for easier detection. Even if no taggant is used, sophisticated forensic means can still be employed to identify the presence of C-4.

commonly found in C-4 are generally isotropic; this makes it possible for forensic science teams to detect trace residue on fingertips of individuals who may have recently been in contact with the compound. However, positive results are highly variable and the mass of RDX can range between 1.7 and 130 ng, each analysis must be individually handled using magnifying equipment. The cross polarized light images obtained from microscopic analysis of the fingerprint are analyzed with gray-scale thresholding[22] to improve contrast for the particles. The contrast is then inverted in order to show dark RDX particles against a light background. Relative numbers and positions of RDX particles have been measured from a series of 50 fingerprints left after a single contact impression.[23]

Military and commercial C-4 are blended with different oils. It is possible to distinguish these sources by analyzing this oil by high-temperature gas chromatography–mass spectrometry. The oil and plasticizer must be separated from the C-4 sample, typically by using a non-polar organic solvent such as pentane followed by solid phase extraction of the plasticizer on silica. This method of analysis is limited by manufacturing variation and methods of distribution.*[1]

39.3 History

39.3.1 Development

C-4 is a member of the Composition C family of chemical explosives. Variants have different proportions and plasticisers and include composition C-2, composition C-3, and composition C-4.*[24] The original material was developed by the British during World War II, and standardised as Composition C when introduced to US service. It was replaced by Composition C-2 around 1943, and later redeveloped around 1944 as Composition C-3. The toxicity of C-3 was reduced, the concentration of RDX was increased, it improved safety of usage and storage. Research on a replacement for C-3 was begun prior to 1950, but the new material, C-4, did not begin pilot production until 1956.*[14]*:125 C-4, was submitted for patent as "Solid Propellant and a Process for its Preparation" March 31, 1958 by the Phillips Petroleum Company.*[25]

39.3.2 Vietnam War

U.S. soldiers during the Vietnam War era would sometimes use small amounts of C-4 as a fuel for heating rations as it will deflagrate unless detonated with a primary explosive.*[3] However, burning C-4 produces poisonous fumes, and soldiers are warned of the dangers of personal injury when using the plastic explosive.*[26]

Amongst field troops in Vietnam it became common knowledge that ingestion of a small amount of C-4 would produce a "high" similar to that of ethanol.*[19] Others would ingest C-4, commonly obtained from a Claymore mine, to induce temporary illness in hopes of being sent on sick leave.*[27]

39.4 Use in terrorism

Terrorist groups have used C-4 worldwide. C-4 has been used in terrorism and insurgency related to Middle Eastern crises, but also in domestic terrorism and state terrorism.

Composition C-4 is recommended in al-Qaeda's traditional curriculum of explosives training.*[4] In October 2000, the group used C-4 to attack the USS *Cole*, killing 17 sailors.*[28] In 1996, Saudi Hezbollah terrorists used C-4 to blow up the Khobar Towers, a U.S. military housing complex in Saudi Arabia.*[29] Composition C-4 has also been used in improvised explosive devices by Iraqi insurgents.*[4]

Homemade C-4 is a popular subject amongst domestic anarchist terrorists in the United States*[30] and is the subject of a chapter in the original *The Anarchist Cookbook* which details how to separate RDX from Composition-4.*[31] Ammonium nitrate is referenced as the anarchists "homemade C-4", and many do-it-yourself books list several explosive formulations derived from it, with detailed instructions as to the proper grade of AN to purchase. Prepared by reacting ammonia and nitric acid, it is widely available to the public as a fertilizer. In 1986 over 11 billion pounds of ammonium nitrate were produced in the U.S.*[32]

In 1987, North Korean agents used C-4 as part of their operation to bomb Korean Air Flight 858.*[33]

39.5 See also

- Bomb
- Composition B
- Fuse
- Polymer-bonded explosive
- RE factor
- Semtex
- Use forms of explosives

39.6 References

[1] Reardon, Michelle R.; Bender, Edward C. (2005). "Differentiation of Composition C4 Based on the Analysis of the Process Oil". *Journal of Forensic Sciences*. Ammendale, MD: Bureau of Alcohol, Tobacco, Firearms, and Explosives, Forensic Science Laboratory. **50** (3): 1–7. doi:10.1520/JFS2004307. ISSN 0022-1198.

[2] Headquarters, U.S. Department of the Army (25 Sep 1990), *Department of the Army Technical Manual – Military Explosives* (PDF).

[3] Harris, Tom. "How C-4 Works". *How Stuff Works*. HowStuffWorks. Retrieved 14 July 2014.

[4] "Introduction to Explosives" (PDF). *C4: Characteristics, Properties, and Overview*. U.S. Department of Homeland Security. pp. 4–5. Retrieved 18 July 2014.

[5] Headquarters, U.S. Department of the Army (25 Sep 1990), *Department of the Army Technical Manual – Military Explosives* (PDF), pp. 8–37–38 (124–125).

39.6. REFERENCES

[6] Owens, Jim. "Recent Developments in Composition C-4: Towards an Alternate Binder and Reduced Sensitivity" (PDF). Holston Army Ammunition Plant: BAE Systems OSI.

[7] Nagy, Brian. "Grosse Point Blank Microwave C4 Mercury Switch". Carnegie Mellon University. Retrieved 14 July 2014.

[8] "C4 product page". Ribbands Explosives

[9] Nordin, John. "Explosives and Terrorists". The First Responder. AristaTek. Retrieved 14 July 2014.

[10] Pike, J. "Explosives - Compositions". GlobalSecurity.org. Retrieved 14 July 2014.

[11] Use of Mine, Antitank: HE, Heavy, M15 as a Substitute for Charge Assembly Demolition, M37 Or M183. Headquarters, Department of the Army. 1971.

[12] "M112" (PDF). American Ordnance. Retrieved 19 July 2014.

[13] "Military Explosives". ATF Law Enforcement Guide to Explosives Incident Reporting (PDF). Bureau of Alcohol, Tobacco, Firearms, and Explosives. Retrieved 15 July 2014.

[14] Headquarters, U.S. Department of the Army (25 Sep 1990). Department of the Army Technical Manual – Military Explosives (PDF). pp. A–13 (323).

[15] Mahoney, Christine M.; Fahey, Albert J.; Steffens, Kristen L.; Benner, Bruce A.; Lareau, Richard T. "Characterization of Composition C4 Explosives using Time-of-Flight Secondary Ion Mass Spectrometry and X-ray Photoelectron Spectroscopy". Analytical Chemistry. 82 (17): 7237–7248. doi:10.1021/ac101116r.

[16] Stone, William J.; Paletta, Theodore L.; Heiman, Elliott M.; Bruce, John I.; Knepshield, James H. (December 1969). "Toxic Effects Following Ingestion of C4 Plastic Explosive". Arch Intern Med. 124 (6): 726–730. doi:10.1001/archinte.1969.00300220078015.

[17] Woody, Robert C.; Kearns, Gregory L.; Brewster, Marge A.; Turley, Charles P.; Sharp, Gregory B.; Lake, Robert S. (1986). "The Neurotoxicity of Cyclotrimethylenetrinitramine (RDX) in a Child: A Clinical and Pharmacokinetic Evaluation". Clinical Toxicology. 24 (4): 305–319. doi:10.3109/15563658608992595.

[18] http://cira.ornl.gov/documents/RDX.pdf

[19] K Fichtner, MD (May 2002). "A plastic explosive by mouth". Journal of the Royal Society of Medicine. U.S. Army Hospital, Camp Bondsteel, Kosovo. 95 (5): 251–252. doi:10.1258/jrsm.95.5.251. C4 contains 90% cyclotrimethylenetrinitramine (RDX)

[20] Committee on Marking, Rendering Inert, and Licensing of Explosive Materials; National Research Council; Division on Engineering and Physical Sciences; Commission on Physical Sciences, Mathematics, and Applications (27 May 1998). Containing the Threat from Illegal Bombings:: An Integrated National Strategy for Marking, Tagging, Rendering Inert, and Licensing Explosives and Their Precursors. National Academies Press. p. 46. ISBN 978-0-309-06126-1.

[21] Allman, Jr., Robert. "Explosives". chemstone.net. Retrieved 19 July 2014.

[22] Brown, Lew. "Thresholding in Imaging Particle Analysis (A four part series)" (PDF). www.particleimaging.com. ParticleImaging.com. Retrieved 19 July 2014.

[23] Verkouteren, Jennifer R.; Coleman, Jessica L.; Cho, Inho. "Automated Mapping of Explosives Particles in Composition C-4 Fingerprints" (PDF). Journal of Forensic Sciences. 55 (2): 334–340. doi:10.1111/j.1556-4029.2009.01272.x.

[24] Rudolf Meyer; Josef Köhler; Axel Homburg (Sep 2007). Explosives. Wiley-VCH. p. 63. ISBN 978-3-527-31656-4.

[25] D, G.E. "US Patent 3,018,203". Google Patents. Retrieved 15 July 2014.

[26] "Chapter 1: Military Explosives". FM 3-34.214 (FM 5-250) Explosives and Demolitions (PDF). Washington, DC: U.S. Department of the Army. 27 August 2008. p. 6. Composition C4 explosive is poisonous and dangerous if chewed or ingested; its detonation or burning produces poisonous fumes.

[27] Herr, Michael (1977). Dispatches. Knopf. ISBN 9780679735250.

[28] Whitaker, Brian (21 August 2003). "Bomb type and tactics point to al-Qaida". The Guardian. London: Guardian Media Group. Retrieved July 11, 2009.

[29] Ashcroft, John (21 June 2001). "Attorney General, on Khobar Towers Indictment" (Press release).

[30] "4 anarchists sentenced in Cleveland bridge bomb plot". Dec 6, 2012. Retrieved 16 July 2014.

[31] Bergman, William Powell. With a prefatory note on anarchism today by P. M. (2002). "137 Reclamation of RDX from C-4 Explosives". The Anarchist Cookbook. El Dorado, Ariz.: Ozark Press. ISBN 0-9623032-0-8.

[32] Oxley, Jimmie C. NON-TRADITIONAL EXPLOSIVES: POTENTIAL DETECTION PROBLEMS (PDF). Kingston, RI: Department of Chemistry, University of Rhode Island. pp. 6–7. Retrieved 18 July 2014.

[33] McBeth, John (March 12, 2014). "Asia's long history of carnage in the air". Asia Times Online. Retrieved July 20, 2014.

39.7 External links

- HowStuffWorks article
- The Original Anarchist's Cookbook Ch. 137.Reclamation of RDX from C-4 Explosives by the Jolly Roger
- Encyclopedia of Explosives and Related Items
- US Army Technical Manual: Military Explosives

Chapter 40

Gunpowder

For other uses, see Gunpowder (disambiguation).
This article is about the early firearm propellant. For modern firearm propellants, see Gun propellant and Smokeless powder.

Gunpowder, also known as **black powder**, is the ear-

Black powder for muzzleloading rifles and pistols in FFFG granulation size. U.S. Quarter (diameter 24 mm) for comparison.

liest known chemical explosive. It is a mixture of sulfur, charcoal, and potassium nitrate (saltpeter). The sulfur and charcoal act as fuels, and the saltpeter is an oxidizer.[1][2] Because of its burning properties and the amount of heat and gas volume that it generates, gunpowder has been widely used as a propellant in firearms and as a pyrotechnic composition in fireworks. Formulations used in blasting rock (such as in quarrying) are called **blasting powder**. Gunpowder is mainly used in older guns now because the propellants used today are too powerful and could break the already fragile barrels.

Gunpowder was invented in the 9th century in China,[3][4] and the earliest record of a written formula for gunpowder appears in the 11th century Song dynasty text, *Wujing Zongyao*.[5] This discovery led to the invention of fireworks and the earliest gunpowder weapons in China. In the centuries following the Chinese discovery, gunpowder weapons began appearing in the Muslim world, Europe, and India. The technology spread from China through the Middle East or Central Asia, and then into Europe.[6] The earliest Western accounts of gunpowder appear in texts written by English philosopher Roger Bacon in the 13th century.[7]

Gunpowder is assigned the UN number UN0027 and has a hazard class of 1.1D. It has a flash point of approximately 427–464 °C (801–867 °F). The specific flash point may vary based on the specific composition of the gunpowder. Gunpowder's specific gravity is 1.70–1.82 (mercury method) or 1.92–2.08 (pycnometer), and it has a pH of 6.0–8.0.[8]

Gunpowder is classified as a low explosive because of its relatively slow decomposition rate and consequently low brisance. Low explosives deflagrate (i.e., burn) at *subsonic* speeds, whereas high explosives detonate, producing a supersonic wave. Ignition of the powder packed behind a bullet must generate enough pressure to force it from the muzzle at high speed, but not enough to rupture the gun barrel. Gunpowder thus makes a good propellant, but is less suitable for shattering rock or fortifications. Gunpowder was widely used to fill artillery shells and in mining and civil engineering to blast rock until the second half of the 19th century, when the first high explosives were put into use. Gunpowder is no longer used in modern explosive military warheads, nor is it used as main explosive in mining operations due to its cost relative to that of newer alternatives such as ammonium nitrate/fuel oil (ANFO).[9] Black powder is still used as a delay element in various munitions where its slow-burning properties are valuable.

40.1 History of gunpowder

Main article: History of gunpowder
Further information: History of the firearm

Early Chinese rocket

A Mongol bomb thrown against a charging Japanese samurai during the Mongol invasions of Japan after founding the Yuan Dynasty, 1281.

The mainstream scholarly consensus is that gunpowder was invented in China, spread through the Middle East, and then into Europe,*[6] although there is a dispute over how much the Chinese advancements in gunpowder warfare influenced later advancements in the Middle East and Europe.*[10]*[11] The spread of gunpowder across Asia from China is widely attributed to the Mongols. One of the first examples of Europeans encountering gunpowder and firearms is at the Battle of Mohi in 1241. At this battle the Mongols not only used gunpowder in early Chinese firearms but in the earliest grenades as well.

A major problem confronting the study of the early history of gunpowder is ready access to sources close to the events described. Often enough, the first records potentially describing use of gunpowder in warfare were written several centuries after the fact, and may well have been colored by the contemporary experiences of the chronicler.*[12] It is also difficult to accurately translate original alchemy texts, especially medieval Chinese texts that try to explain phenomena through metaphor, into modern scientific language with rigidly defined terminology. The translation difficulty has led to errors or loose interpretations bordering on artistic licence.*[13]*[14] Early writings potentially mentioning gunpowder are sometimes marked by a linguistic process where old words acquired new meanings.*[15] For instance, the Arabic word *naft* transitioned from denoting naphtha to denoting gunpowder, and the Chinese word *pào* evolved from meaning catapult to referring to cannon.*[16] According to science and technology historian Bert S. Hall: "It goes without saying, however, that historians bent on special pleading, or simply with axes of their own to grind, can find rich material in these terminological thickets." *[17]

40.1.1 China

Further information: Wujing Zongyao, Four Great Inventions, List of Chinese inventions, and Heilongjiang hand cannon

Saltpeter was known to the Chinese by the mid-1st cen-

Yuan Dynasty hand cannon dated to 1288.

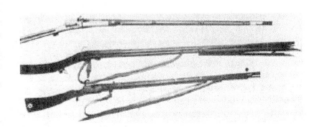

Chinese Ming Dynasty (1368-1644) matchlock firearms

tury AD and there is strong evidence of the use of saltpeter and sulfur in various largely medicinal combinations.*[18] A Chinese alchemical text dated 492 noted saltpeter burnt with a purple flame, providing a practical and reliable means of distinguishing it from other inorganic salts, thus enabling alchemists to evaluate and compare purification techniques; the earliest Latin accounts of saltpeter purification are dated after 1200.*[19]

The first reference to the incendiary properties of such mixtures is the passage of the *Zhenyuan miaodao yaoliie*, a

40.1. HISTORY OF GUNPOWDER

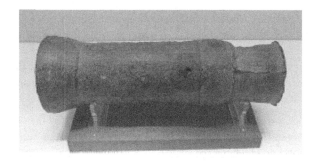

Yuan Dynasty bronze hand cannon from 1332 at th (c. 808); it describes mixing six parts sulfur to six parts saltpeter to one part birthwort herb (which would provide carbon).[20]

- Formula for gunpowder in 1044 *Wujing zongyao* part I vol 12
- Instruction for fire bomb in *Wujing zongyao*
- Fire bomb
- Fire grenade
- Proto-cannon from the Ming Dynasty text *Huolongjing*
- Land mine from the Ming Dynasty text *Huolongjing*
- Fire arrow rocket launcher from the *Wujing zongyao*

40.1.2 Middle East

Main articles: Inventions in the Islamic world and Alchemy and chemistry in Islam

The Muslims acquired knowledge of gunpowder some time

The Sultani Cannon, a very heavy bronze breech-loading cannon of type used by Ottoman Empire in the conquest of Constantinople, in 1453.

Taoist text tentatively dated to the mid-9th century:*[19] "Some have heated together sulfur, realgar and saltpeter with honey; smoke and flames result, so that their hands and faces have been burnt, and even the whole house where they were working burned down." *[21] The Chinese word for "gunpowder" is Chinese: 火药/火藥; pinyin: *huō yào* /xuo yaʊ/, which literally means "Fire Medicine";*[22] however this name only came into use some centuries after the mixture's discovery.*[23] During the 9th century, Taoist monks or alchemists searching for an elixir of immortality had serendipitously stumbled upon gunpowder.*[6]*[24] The Chinese wasted little time in applying gunpowder to the development of weapons, and in the centuries that followed, they produced a variety of gunpowder weapons, including flamethrowers, rockets, bombs, and land mines, before inventing guns as a projectile weapon.*[25] Archaeological evidence of a hand cannon has been excavated in Manchuria dated from the late 13th century*[26] and the shells of explosive bombs have been discovered in a shipwreck off the shore of Japan dated from 1281, during the Mongol invasions of Japan.*[27]

The Chinese "Wu Ching Tsung Yao" (*Complete Essentials from the Military Classics*), written by Tseng Kung-Liang between 1040–1044, provides encyclopedia references to a variety of mixtures that included petrochemicals—as well as garlic and honey. A slow match for flame throwing mechanisms using the siphon principle and for fireworks and rockets is mentioned. The mixture formulas in this book do not contain enough saltpeter to create an explosive however; being limited to at most 50% saltpeter, they produce an incendiary.*[28] The *Essentials* was however written by a Song dynasty court bureaucrat, and there is little evidence that it had any immediate impact on warfare; there is no mention of gunpowder use in the chronicles of the wars against the Tanguts in the 11th century, and China was otherwise mostly at peace during this century. The first chronicled use of "fire spears" (or "fire lances") is at the siege of De'an in 1132 by Song forces against the Jin.*[29]

between 1240 and 1280, by which time the Syrian Hasan al-Rammah had written, in Arabic, recipes for gunpowder, instructions for the purification of saltpeter, and descriptions of gunpowder incendiaries. Gunpowder arrived in the Middle East, possibly through India, from China. This is implied by al-Rammah's usage of "terms that suggested he derived his knowledge from Chinese sources" and his references to saltpeter as "Chinese snow" (Arabic: ثلج الصين *thalj al-ṣīn*), fireworks as "Chinese flowers" and rockets as "Chinese arrows".*[30] However, because al-Rammah attributes his material to "his father and forefathers", al-Hassan argues that gunpowder became prevalent in Syria and Egypt by "the end of the twelfth century or the beginning of the thirteenth".*[31] Persians called saltpeter "Chinese salt" (Persian: نمک چینی) *namak-i chīnī*)*[32]*[33]*[34][35][36] or "salt from Chinese salt marshes" (نمک شوره چینی *namak-i shūra-yi chīnī*).*[37]*[38]

Al-Hassan claims that in the Battle of Ain Jalut of 1260, the Mamluks used against the Mongols in "the first cannon in

A picture of a 15th-century Granadian cannon from the book Al-izz wal rifa'a.

history" gunpowder formula with near-identical ideal composition ratios for explosive gunpowder.*[31] Other historians urge caution regarding claims of Islamic firearms use in the 1204-1324 period as late medieval Arabic texts used the same word for gunpowder, *naft*, that they used for an earlier incendiary, naphtha.*[12]*[16] Khan claims that it was invading Mongols who introduced gunpowder to the Islamic world*[39] and cites Mamluk antagonism towards early musketeers in their infantry as an example of how gunpowder weapons were not always met with open acceptance in the Middle East.*[40] Similarly, the refusal of their Qizilbash forces to use firearms contributed to the Safavid rout at Chaldiran in 1514.*[40]

1840 drawing of a gunpowder magazine near Tehran, Persia. Gunpowder was extensively used in the Naderian Wars.

The earliest surviving documentary evidence for the use of the hand cannon, considered the oldest type of portable firearm and a forerunner of the handgun, are from several Arabic manuscripts dated to the 14th century.*[41] Al-Hassan argues that these are based on earlier originals and that they report hand-held cannons being used by the Mamluks at the Battle of Ain Jalut in 1260.*[31]

Hasan al-Rammah included 107 gunpowder recipes in his text *al-Furusiyyah wa al-Manasib al-Harbiyya* (*The Book of Military Horsemanship and Ingenious War Devices*), 22 of which are for rockets. If one takes the median of 17 of these 22 compositions for rockets (75% nitrates, 9.06% sulfur, and 15.94% charcoal), it is nearly identical to the modern reported ideal gunpowder recipe of 75% potassium nitrate, 10% sulfur, and 15% charcoal.*[31]

The state-controlled manufacture of gunpowder by the Ottoman Empire through early supply chains to obtain nitre, sulfur and high-quality charcoal from oaks in Anatolia contributed significantly to its expansion between the 15th and 18th century. It was not until later in the 19th century when the syndicalist production of Turkish gunpowder was greatly reduced, which coincided with the decline of its military might.*[42]

40.1.3 Mainland Europe

Several sources mention Chinese firearms and gunpowder weapons being deployed by the Mongols against European forces at the Battle of Mohi in 1241.*[43]*[44]*[45] Professor Kenneth Warren Chase credits the Mongols for introducing into Europe gunpowder and its associated weaponry.*[46]

C. F. Temler interprets Peter, Bishop of Leon, as reporting the use of cannons in Seville in 1248.*[47]

In Europe, one of the first mentions of gunpowder use appears in a passage found in Roger Bacon's *Opus Maius* and *Opus Tertium* in what has been interpreted as being firecrackers. The most telling passage reads: "We have an example of these things (that act on the senses) in [the sound and fire of] that children's toy which is made in many [diverse] parts of the world; i.e., a device no bigger than one's thumb. From the violence of that salt called saltpeter [together with sulfur and willow charcoal, combined into a powder] so horrible a sound is made by the bursting of a thing so small, no more than a bit of parchment [containing it], that we find [the ear assaulted by a noise] exceeding the roar of strong thunder, and a flash brighter than the most brilliant lightning." *[7] In the early 20th century, British artillery officer Henry William Lovett Hime proposed that another work tentatively attributed to Bacon, *Epistola de Secretis Operibus Artis et Naturae, et de Nullitate Magiae* contained an encrypted formula for gunpowder. This claim has been disputed by historians of science including Lynn Thorndike, John Maxson Stillman and George Sarton and by Bacon's editor Robert Steele, both in terms of authenticity of the work, and with respect to the decryption method.*[7] In any case, the formula claimed to have been decrypted (7:5:5 saltpeter:charcoal:sulfur) is not useful for firearms use or even firecrackers, burning slowly and producing mostly smoke.*[48]*[49]

40.1. HISTORY OF GUNPOWDER

Cannon forged in 1667 at the Fortin de La Galera, Nueva Esparta, Venezuela.

The *Liber Ignium*, or *Book of Fires*, attributed to Marcus Graecus, is a collection of incendiary recipes, including some gunpowder recipes. Partington dates the gunpowder recipes to approximately 1300.*[50] One recipe for "flying fire" (*ingis volatilis*) involves saltpeter, sulfur, and colophonium, which, when inserted into a reed or hollow wood, "flies away suddenly and burns up everything." Another recipe, for artificial "thunder", specifies a mixture of one pound native sulfur, two pounds linden or willow charcoal, and six pounds of saltpeter.*[51] Another specifies a 1:3:9 ratio.*[51]

Some of the gunpowder recipes of *De Mirabilibus Mundi* of Albertus Magnus are identical to the recipes of the *Liber Ignium*, and according to Partington, "may have been taken from that work, rather than conversely." *[52] Partington suggests that some of the book may have been compiled by Albert's students, "but since it is found in thirteenth century manuscripts, it may well be by Albert." *[52] Albertus Magnus died in 1280.

German Franciscan monk named Berthold Schwarz, who likely read Bacon's works, is credited with introducing the recipe in Germany, thus earning it the German name *Schwarzpulver*, which translates literally into English as *Black powder*.

A major advance in manufacturing began in Europe in the late 14th century when the safety and thoroughness of incorporation was improved by wet grinding: liquid, such as distilled spirits or perhaps the urine of wine-drinking bishops*[53] was added during the grinding-together of the ingredients and the moist paste dried afterwards. (The principle of wet mixing to prevent the separation of dry ingredients, invented for gunpowder, is used today in the pharmaceutical industry.*[54]) It was also discovered that if the paste was rolled into balls before drying the resulting gunpowder absorbed less water from the air during storage and traveled better. The balls were then crushed in a mortar by the gunner immediately before use, with the old problem of uneven particle size and packing causing unpredictable results.

Büchsenmeysterei : von Geschoß, Büchsen, Pulver, Salpeter und Feurwergken, 1531

If the right size particles were chosen, however, the result was a great improvement in power. Forming the damp paste into *corn*-sized clumps by hand or with the use of a sieve instead of larger balls produced a product after drying that loaded much better, as each tiny piece provided its own surrounding air space that allowed much more rapid combustion than a fine powder. This "corned" gunpowder was from 30% to 300% more powerful. An example is cited where 34 pounds of serpentine was needed to shoot a 47-pound ball, but only 18 pounds of corned powder.*[53] The optimum size of the grain depended on its use; larger for large cannon, finer for small arms. Larger cast cannons were easily muzzle-loaded with corned powder using a long-handled ladle. Corned powder also retained the advantage of low moisture absorption, as even tiny grains still had much less surface area to attract water than a floury powder.

During this time, European manufacturers also began regularly purifying saltpeter, using wood ashes containing potassium carbonate to precipitate calcium from their dung liquor, and using ox blood, alum, and slices of turnip to clarify the solution.*[53]

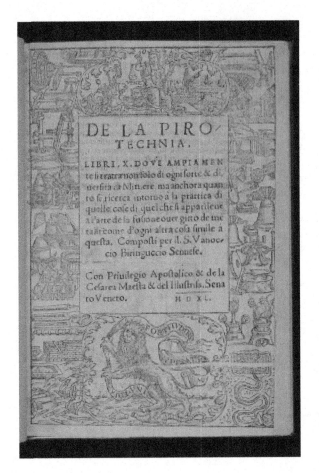

De la pirotechnia, *1540*

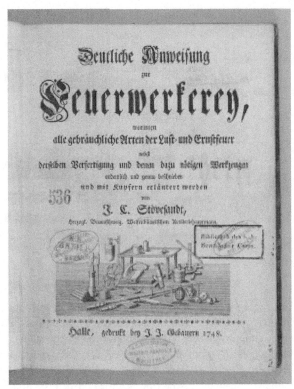

Deutliche Anweisung zur Feuerwerkerey, *1748*

Gunpowder-making and metal-smelting and casting for shot and cannon fee was closely held by skilled military tradesmen, who formed guilds that collected dues, tested apprentices, and gave pensions. "Fire workers" were also required to craft fireworks for celebrations of victory or peace.

During the Renaissance, two European schools of pyrotechnic thought emerged, one in Italy and the other at Nuremberg, Germany. The German printer and publisher Christiaan Egenolff adapted an earlier work on pyrotechnics from manuscript to print form, publishing his *Büchsenmeysterei* in 1529 and reprinting it in 1531. Now extremely rare, the book discusses the manufacturing of gunpowder, the operation of artillery and the rules of conduct for the gunsmith.*[55]

In Italy, Vannoccio Biringuccio, born in 1480, was a member of the guild *Fraternita di Santa Barbara* but broke with the tradition of secrecy by setting down everything he knew in a book titled *De la pirotechnia*, written in vernacular. It was published posthumously in 1540, with 9 editions over 138 years, and also reprinted by MIT Press in 1966.*[53]

By the mid-17th century fireworks were used for entertainment on an unprecedented scale in Europe, be-ing popular even at resorts and public gardens.*[56] With the publication of *Deutliche Anweisung zur Feuerwerkerey* (1748), methods for creating fireworks were sufficiently well-known and well-described that "Firework making has become an exact science." *[57] In 1774 Louis XVI ascended to the throne of France at age 20. After he discovered that France was not self-sufficient in gunpowder, a Gunpowder Administration was established; to head it, the lawyer Antoine Lavoisier was appointed. Although from a bourgeois family, after his degree in law Lavoisier became wealthy from a company set up to collect taxes for the Crown; this allowed him to pursue experimental natural science as a hobby.*[58]

Without access to cheap Indian saltpeter (controlled by the British), for hundreds of years France had relied on saltpetermen with royal warrants, the *droit de fouille* or "right to dig", to seize nitrous-containing soil and demolish walls of barnyards, without compensation to the owners.*[59] This caused farmers, the wealthy, or entire villages to bribe the petermen and the associated bureaucracy to leave their buildings alone and the saltpeter uncollected. Lavoisier instituted a crash program to increase saltpeter production, revised (and later eliminated) the *droit de fouille*, researched best refining and powder manufacturing methods, instituted management and record-keeping, and established pricing that encouraged private investment in works. Although saltpeter from new Prussian-style putrefaction works had not been produced yet (the process taking about 18 months), in only a year France had gunpowder to export. A chief beneficiary of this surplus was the American Revolution. By careful testing and adjusting the proportions and grinding time, powder from mills such as at Essonne outside Paris became the best in the world by 1788, and inexpensive.*[59]*[60]

40.1.4 Britain and Ireland

The old Powder or Pouther magazine dating from 1642, built by order of Charles I, Irvine, North Ayrshire, Scotland

Gunpowder production in Britain appears to have started in the mid 14th century with the aim of supplying the English Crown.*[61] Records show that, in England, gunpowder was being made in 1346 at the Tower of London; a powder house existed at the Tower in 1461; and in 1515 three King's gunpowder makers worked there.*[61] Gunpowder was also being made or stored at other Royal castles, such as Portchester. By the early 14th century, according to N.J.G. Pounds's study *The Medieval Castle in England and Wales*, many English castles had been deserted and others were crumbling. Their military significance faded except on the borders. Gunpowder had made smaller castles useless.*[62]

Henry VIII of England was short of gunpowder when he invaded France in 1544 and England needed to import gunpowder via the port of Antwerp in what is now Belgium.*[61]

The English Civil War (1642–1645) led to an expansion of the gunpowder industry, with the repeal of the Royal Patent in August 1641.*[61]

Two British physicists, Andrew Noble and Frederick Abel, worked to improve the properties of black powder during the late 19th century. This formed the basis for the Noble-Abel gas equation for internal ballistics.*[63]

The introduction of smokeless powder in the late 19th century led to a contraction of the gunpowder industry. After the end of World War I, the majority of the United Kingdom gunpowder manufacturers merged into a single company, "Explosives Trades limited"; and number of sites were closed down, including those in Ireland. This company became Nobel Industries Limited; and in 1926 became a founding member of Imperial Chemical Industries. The Home Office removed gunpowder from its list of *Permitted Explosives*; and shortly afterwards, on 31 December 1931, the former Curtis & Harvey's Glynneath gunpowder factory at Pontneddfechan, in Wales, closed down, and it was demolished by fire in 1932.*[64]

Gunpowder storing barrels at Martello tower in Point Pleasant Park

The last remaining gunpowder mill at the Royal Gunpowder Factory, Waltham Abbey was damaged by a German parachute mine in 1941 and it never reopened.*[65] This was followed by the closure of the gunpowder section at the Royal Ordnance Factory, ROF Chorley, the section was closed and demolished at the end of World War II; and ICI Nobel's Roslin gunpowder factory, which closed in 1954.*[65]*[66]

This left the sole United Kingdom gunpowder factory at ICI Nobel's Ardeer site in Scotland; it too closed in October 1976.*[65] Since then gunpowder has been imported into the United Kingdom. In the late 1970s/early 1980s gunpowder was bought from eastern Europe, particularly from what was then the German Democratic Republic and former Yugoslavia.

40.1.5 India

In the year 1780 the British began to annex the territories of the Sultanate of Mysore, during the Second Anglo-Mysore War. The British battalion was defeated during the Battle of Guntur, by the forces of Hyder Ali, who effectively utilized Mysorean rockets and rocket artillery against the closely massed British forces.

Gunpowder and gunpowder weapons were transmitted to India through the Mongol invasions of India.*[67]*[68] The Mongols were defeated by Alauddin Khilji of the Delhi Sultanate, and some of the Mongol soldiers remained in northern India after their conversion to Islam.*[68] It was written in the *Tarikh-i Firishta* (1606–1607) that Nasir ud din Mahmud the ruler of the Delhi Sultanate presented the envoy of the Mongol ruler Hulegu Khan with a dazzling pyrotechnics display upon his arrival in Delhi in 1258. Nasir ud din Mahmud tried to express his strength as a ruler and tried to ward off any Mongol attempt similar to the Siege of Baghdad (1258).*[69] Firearms known as *top-o-tufak* also existed in many Muslim kingdoms in India by as early as 1366.*[69] From then on the employment of gunpowder warfare in India was prevalent, with events such as the "Siege of Belgaum" in 1473 by Sultan Muhammad Shah Bahmani.*[70]

The shipwrecked Ottoman Admiral Seydi Ali Reis is known to have introduced the earliest type of matchlock weapons, which the Ottomans used against the Portuguese during the Siege of Diu (1531). After that, a diverse variety of firearms, large guns in particular, became visible in Tanjore, Dacca, Bijapur, and Murshidabad.*[71] Guns made of bronze were recovered from Calicut (1504)- the former capital of the Zamorins*[72]

The Mughal emperor Akbar mass-produced matchlocks for the Mughal Army. Akbar is personally known to have

Mughal Emperor Shah Jahan, hunting deer using a matchlock as the sun sets in the horizon.

shot a leading Rajput commander during the Siege of Chittorgarh.*[73] The Mughals began to use bamboo rockets (mainly for signalling) and employ sappers: special units that undermined heavy stone fortifications to plant gunpowder charges.

The Mughal Emperor Shah Jahan is known to have introduced much more advanced matchlocks, their designs were a combination of Ottoman and Mughal designs. Shah Jahan also countered the British and other Europeans in his province of Gujarāt, which supplied Europe saltpeter for use in gunpowder warfare during the 17th century.*[74] Bengal and Mālwa participated in saltpeter production.*[74] The Dutch, French, Portuguese, and English used Chhapra as a center of saltpeter refining.*[74]

Ever since the founding of the Sultanate of Mysore by Hyder Ali, French military officers were employed to train the Mysore Army. Hyder Ali and his son Tipu Sultan were the first to introduce modern cannons and muskets, their army was also the first in India to have official uniforms. During the Second Anglo-Mysore War Hyder Ali and his son Tipu Sultan unleashed the Mysorean rockets at their

40.1.6 Indonesia

The Javanese Majapahit Empire was arguably able to encompass much of modern-day Indonesia due to its unique mastery of bronze smithing and use of a central arsenal fed by a large number of cottage industries within the immediate region. Documentary and archeological evidence indicate that Arab or Indian traders introduced gunpowder, gonnes, muskets, blunderbusses, and cannons to the Javanese, Acehnese, and Batak via long established commercial trade routes around the early to mid 14th century.*[76] Portuguese and Spanish invaders were unpleasantly surprised and even outgunned on occasion.*[77] The resurgent Singhasari Empire overtook Sriwijaya and later emerged as the Majapahit whose warfare featured the use of fire-arms and cannonade.*[78] Circa 1540, the Javanese, always alert for new weapons found the newly arrived Portuguese weaponry superior to that of the locally made variants. Javanese bronze breech-loaded swivel-guns, known as meriam, or erroneously as lantaka, was used widely by the Majapahit navy as well as by pirates and rival lords. The demise of the Majapahit empire and the dispersal of disaffected skilled bronze cannon-smiths to Brunei, modern Sumatra, Malaysia and the Philippines lead to widespread use, especially in the Makassar Strait.

Saltpeter harvesting was recorded by Dutch and German travelers as being common in even the smallest villages and was collected from the decomposition process of large dung hills specifically piled for the purpose. The Dutch punishment for possession of non-permitted gunpowder appears to have been amputation.*[79] Ownership and manufacture of gunpowder was later prohibited by the colonial Dutch occupiers.*[76] According to a colonel McKenzie quoted in Sir Thomas Stamford Raffles, *The History of Java* (1817), the purest sulfur was supplied from a crater from a mountain near the straits of Bali.*[78]

40.2 Manufacturing technology

For the most powerful black powder, meal powder, a wood charcoal, is used. The best wood for the purpose is Pacific willow,*[80] but others such as alder or buckthorn can be used. In Great Britain between the 15th and 19th centuries charcoal from alder buckthorn was greatly prized for gunpowder manufacture; cottonwood was used by the American Confederate States.*[81] The ingredients are reduced in

Edge-runner mill in a restored mill, at Eleutherian Mills

particle size and mixed as intimately as possible. Originally this was with a mortar-and-pestle or a similarly operating stamping-mill, using copper, bronze or other non-sparking materials, until supplanted by the rotating ball mill principle with non-sparking bronze or lead. Historically, a marble or limestone edge runner mill, running on a limestone bed, was used in Great Britain; however, by the mid 19th century this had changed to either an iron-shod stone wheel or a cast iron wheel running on an iron bed.*[82] The mix was dampened with alcohol or water during grinding to prevent accidental ignition. This also helps the extremely soluble saltpeter to mix into the microscopic nooks and crannies of the very high surface-area charcoal.

Around the late 14th century, European powdermakers first began adding liquid during grinding to improve mixing, reduce dust, and with it the risk of explosion.*[83] The powder-makers would then shape the resulting paste of dampened gunpowder, known as mill cake, into corns, or grains, to dry. Not only did corned powder keep better because of its reduced surface area, gunners also found that it was more powerful and easier to load into guns. Before long, powder-makers standardized the process by forcing mill cake through sieves instead of corning powder by hand.

The improvement was based on reducing the surface area of a higher density composition. At the beginning of the 19th century, makers increased density further by static pressing. They shoveled damp mill cake into a two-foot square box, placed this beneath a screw press and reduced it to $\frac{1}{2}$ its volume. "Press cake" had the hardness of slate. They broke the dried slabs with hammers or rollers, and sorted the granules with sieves into different grades. In the United States, Eleuthere Irenee du Pont, who had learned the trade from Lavoisier, tumbled the dried grains in rotating barrels to round the edges and increase durability during shipping and handling. (Sharp grains rounded off in transport, producing fine "meal dust" that changed the burning properties.)

Another advance was the manufacture of kiln charcoal by distilling wood in heated iron retorts instead of burning it in earthen pits. Controlling the temperature influenced the power and consistency of the finished gunpowder. In 1863, in response to high prices for Indian saltpeter, DuPont chemists developed a process using potash or mined potassium chloride to convert plentiful Chilean sodium nitrate to potassium nitrate.*[84]

The following year (1864) the Gatebeck Low Gunpowder Works in Cumbria (Great Britain) started a plant to manufacture potassium nitrate by essentially the same chemical process.*[85] This is nowadays called the 'Wakefield Process', after the owners of the company. It would have used potassium chloride from the Staßfurt mines, near Magdeburg, Germany, which had recently become available in industrial quantities.*[86]

During the 18th century, gunpowder factories became increasingly dependent on mechanical energy.*[87] Despite mechanization, production difficulties related to humidity control, especially during the pressing, were still present in the late 19th century. A paper from 1885 laments that "Gunpowder is such a nervous and sensitive spirit, that in almost every process of manufacture it changes under our hands as the weather changes." Pressing times to the desired density could vary by a factor of three depending on the atmospheric humidity.*[88]

40.3 Composition and characteristics

The term *black powder* was coined in the late 19th century, primarily in the United States, to distinguish prior gunpowder formulations from the new smokeless powders and semi-smokeless powders, in cases where these are not referred to as cordite. Semi-smokeless powders featured bulk volume properties that approximated black powder, but had significantly reduced amounts of smoke and combustion products. Smokeless powder has different burning properties (pressure vs. time) and can generate higher pressures and work per gram. This can rupture older weapons designed for black powder. Smokeless powders ranged in color from brownish tan to yellow to white. Most of the bulk semi-smokeless powders ceased to be manufactured in the 1920s.*[89]*[90]*[91]

Black powder is a granular mixture of

- a nitrate, typically potassium nitrate (KNO_3), which supplies oxygen for the reaction;
- charcoal, which provides carbon and other fuel for the reaction, simplified as carbon (C);
- sulfur (S), which, while also serving as a fuel, lowers the temperature required to ignite the mixture, thereby increasing the rate of combustion.

Potassium nitrate is the most important ingredient in terms of both bulk and function because the combustion process releases oxygen from the potassium nitrate, promoting the rapid burning of the other ingredients.*[92] To reduce the likelihood of accidental ignition by static electricity, the granules of modern black powder are typically coated with graphite, which prevents the build-up of electrostatic charge.

Charcoal does not consist of pure carbon; rather, it consists of partially pyrolyzed cellulose, in which the wood is not completely decomposed. Carbon differs from ordinary charcoal. Whereas charcoal's autoignition temperature is relatively low, carbon's is much greater. Thus, a black powder composition containing pure carbon would burn similarly to a match head, at best.*[93]

The current standard composition for the black powders that are manufactured by pyrotechnicians was adopted as long ago as 1780. Proportions by weight are 75% potassium nitrate (known as saltpeter or saltpetre), 15% softwood charcoal, and 10% sulfur.*[82] These ratios have varied over the centuries and by country, and can be altered somewhat depending on the purpose of the powder. For instance, power grades of black powder, unsuitable for use in firearms but adequate for blasting rock in quarrying operations, are called blasting powder rather than gunpowder with standard proportions of 70% nitrate, 14% charcoal, and 16% sulfur; blasting powder may be made with the cheaper sodium nitrate substituted for potassium nitrate and proportions may be as low as 40% nitrate, 30% charcoal, and 30% sulfur.*[94] In 1857, Lammot du Pont solved the main problem of using cheaper sodium nitrate formulations when he patented DuPont "B" blasting powder. After manufacturing grains from press-cake in the usual way, his process tumbled the powder with graphite dust for 12 hours. This formed a graphite coating on each grain that reduced its ability to absorb moisture.*[95]

Neither the use of graphite nor sodium nitrate was new. Glossing gunpowder corns with graphite was already an accepted technique in 1839,*[96] and sodium nitrate-based blasting powder had been made in Peru for many years using the sodium nitrate mined at Tarapacá (now in Chile).*[97] Also, in 1846, two plants were built in southwest England to make blasting powder using this sodium nitrate.*[98] The idea may well have been brought from Peru by Cornish miners returning home after completing their contracts. Another suggestion is that it was William Lobb, the planthunter, who recognised the possibilities of sodium nitrate during his travels in South America. Lammot du Pont would have known about the use of graphite and probably also knew about the plants in south-west England. In his patent he was careful to state that his claim was for the combination of graphite with sodium nitrate-based powder, rather than for either of the two individual technologies.

French war powder in 1879 used the ratio 75% saltpeter, 12.5% charcoal, 12.5% sulfur. English war powder in 1879 used the ratio 75% saltpeter, 15% charcoal, 10% sulfur.*[99] The British Congreve rockets used 62.4% saltpeter, 23.2% charcoal and 14.4% sulfur, but the British Mark VII gunpowder was changed to 65% saltpeter, 20% charcoal and 15% sulfur.*[100] The explanation for the wide variety in formulation relates to usage. Powder used for rocketry can use a slower burn rate since it accelerates the projectile for a much longer time—whereas powders for weapons such as flintlocks, cap-locks, or matchlocks need a higher burn rate to accelerate the projectile in a much shorter distance. Cannons usually used lower burn rate powders, because most would burst with higher burn rate powders.

40.4 Serpentine

The original dry-compounded powder used in 15th-century Europe was known as "Serpentine", either a reference to Satan*[101] or to a common artillery piece that used it.*[102] The ingredients were ground together with a mortar and pestle, perhaps for 24 hours,*[102] resulting in a fine flour. Vibration during transportation could cause the components to separate again, requiring remixing in the field. Also if the quality of the saltpeter was low (for instance if it was contaminated with highly hygroscopic calcium nitrate), or if the powder was simply old (due to the mildly hygroscopic nature of potassium nitrate), in humid weather it would need to be re-dried. The dust from "repairing" powder in the field was a major hazard.

Loading cannons or bombards before the powder-making advances of the Renaissance was a skilled art. Fine powder loaded haphazardly or too tightly would burn incompletely or too slowly. Typically, the breech-loading powder chamber in the rear of the piece was filled only about half full, the serpentine powder neither too compressed nor too loose, a wooden bung pounded in to seal the chamber from the barrel when assembled, and the projectile placed on. A carefully determined empty space was necessary for the charge to burn effectively. When the cannon was fired through the touchhole, turbulence from the initial surface combustion caused the rest of the powder to be rapidly exposed to the flame.*[102]

The advent of much more powerful and easy to use *corned* powder changed this procedure, but serpentine was used with older guns into the 17th century.*[103]

40.5 Corning

For gunpowder to explode effectively, the combustible ingredients must be reduced to the smallest possible particle sizes, and be as thoroughly mixed as possible. Once mixed, however, for better results in a gun, makers discovered that the final product should be in the form of individual dense grains that spread the fire quickly from grain to grain, much as straw or twigs catch fire more quickly than a pile of sawdust.

Primarily for safety reasons, size reduction and mixing is done while the ingredients are damp, usually with water. After 1800, instead of forming grains by hand or with sieves, the damp *mill-cake* was pressed in molds to increase its density and extract the liquid, forming *press-cake*. The pressing took varying amounts of time, depending on conditions such as atmospheric humidity. The hard, dense product was broken again into tiny pieces, which were separated with sieves to produce a uniform product for each purpose: coarse powders for cannons, finer grained powders for muskets, and the finest for small hand guns and priming.*[103] Inappropriately fine-grained powder often caused cannons to burst before the projectile could move down the barrel, due to the high initial spike in pressure.*[104] *Mammoth* powder with large grains, made for Rodman's 15-inch cannon, reduced the pressure to only 20 percent as high as ordinary cannon powder would have produced.*[105]

In the mid-19th century, measurements were made determining that the burning rate within a grain of black powder (or a tightly packed mass) is about 0.20 fps, while the rate of ignition propagation from grain to grain is around 30 fps, over two orders of magnitude faster.*[103]

40.6 Modern types

Modern corning first compresses the fine black powder meal into blocks with a fixed density (1.7 g/cm^3).*[106] In the United States, gunpowder grains were designated F (for fine) or C (for coarse). Grain diameter decreased with a larger number of Fs and increased with a larger number of Cs, ranging from about 2 mm (0.08 in) for 7F to 15 mm (0.6 in) for 7C. Even larger grains were produced for artillery bore diameters greater than about 17 cm (6.7 in). The standard DuPont *Mammoth* powder developed by Thomas Rodman and Lammot du Pont for use during the American Civil War had grains averaging 0.6 inches (15 mm) in diameter with edges rounded in a glazing barrel.*[105] Other versions had grains the size of golf and tennis balls for use in 20-inch (51 cm) Rodman guns.*[107] In 1875 DuPont introduced *Hexagonal* powder for large artillery, which was pressed using shaped plates with a small center core—about 1.5 inches (3.8 cm) diameter, like a wagon wheel nut, the center hole widened as the grain burned.[108] By 1882 German makers also produced hexagonal grained powders of a similar size for artillery.[108]

By the late 19th century manufacturing focused on standard grades of black powder from Fg used in large bore rifles and shotguns, through FFg (medium and small-bore arms such as muskets and fusils), FFFg (small-bore rifles and pistols), and FFFFg (extreme small bore, short pistols and most commonly for priming flintlocks).[109] A coarser grade for use in military artillery blanks was designated A-1. These grades were sorted on a system of screens with oversize retained on a mesh of 6 wires per inch, A-1 retained on 10 wires per inch, Fg retained on 14, FFg on 24, FFFg on 46, and FFFFg on 60. Fines designated FFFFFg were usually reprocessed to minimize explosive dust hazards.[110] In the United Kingdom, the main service gunpowders were classified RFG (rifle grained fine) with diameter of one or two millimeters and RLG (rifle grained large) for grain diameters between two and six millimeters.[107] Gunpowder grains can alternatively be categorized by mesh size: the BSS sieve mesh size, being the smallest mesh size, which retains no grains. Recognized grain sizes are Gunpowder G 7, G 20, G 40, and G 90.

Owing to the large market of antique and replica black-powder firearms in the US, modern gunpowder substitutes like Pyrodex, Triple Seven and Black Mag3[111] pellets have been developed since the 1970s. These products, which should not be confused with smokeless powders, aim to produce less fouling (solid residue), while maintaining the traditional volumetric measurement system for charges. Claims of less corrosiveness of these products have been controversial however. New cleaning products for black-powder guns have also been developed for this market.[109]

40.7 Other types of gunpowder

Besides black powder, there are other historically important types of gunpowder. "Brown gunpowder" is cited as composed of 79% nitre, 3% sulfur, and 18% charcoal per 100 of dry powder, with about 2% moisture. Prismatic Brown Powder is a large-grained product the Rottweil Company introduced in 1884 in Germany, which was adopted by the British Royal Navy shortly thereafter. The French navy adopted a fine, 3.1 millimeter, not prismatic grained product called *Slow Burning Cocoa* (SBC) or "cocoa powder". These brown powders reduced burning rate even further by using as little as 2 percent sulfur and using charcoal made from rye straw that had not been completely charred, hence the brown color.[108]

Lesmok powder was a product developed by DuPont in 1911,[112] one of several semi-smokeless products in the industry containing a mixture of black and nitrocellulose powder. It was sold to Winchester and others primarily for .22 and .32 small calibers. Its advantage was that it was believed at the time to be less corrosive than smokeless powders then in use. It was not understood in the U.S. until the 1920s that the actual source of corrosion was the potassium chloride residue from potassium chlorate sensitized primers. The bulkier black powder fouling better disperses primer residue. Failure to mitigate primer corrosion by dispersion caused the false impression that nitrocellulose-based powder caused corrosion.[113] Lesmok had some of the bulk of black powder for dispersing primer residue, but somewhat less total bulk than straight black powder, thus requiring less frequent bore cleaning.[114] It was last sold by Winchester in 1947.

40.8 Sulfur-free gunpowder

Burst barrel of a muzzle loader pistol replica, which was loaded with nitrocellulose powder instead of black powder and could not withstand the higher pressures of the modern propellant

The development of smokeless powders, such as cordite, in the late 19th century created the need for a spark-sensitive priming charge, such as gunpowder. However, the sulfur content of traditional gunpowders caused corrosion problems with Cordite Mk I and this led to the introduction of a range of sulfur-free gunpowders, of varying grain sizes.[65] They typically contain 70.5 parts of saltpeter and 29.5 parts of charcoal.[65] Like black powder, they were produced in different grain sizes. In the United Kingdom, the finest grain was known as *sulfur-free mealed powder* (*SMP*). Coarser grains were numbered as sulfur-free gunpowder (SFG n): 'SFG 12', 'SFG 20', 'SFG 40' and 'SFG 90', for example; where the number represents the smallest BSS sieve mesh size, which retained no grains.

Sulfur's main role in gunpowder is to decrease the ignition temperature. A sample reaction for sulfur-free gunpowder would be

$$6\ KNO_3 + C_7H_4O \rightarrow 3\ K_2CO_3 + 4\ CO_2 + 2\ H_2O + 3\ N_2$$

40.9 Combustion characteristics

A simple, commonly cited, chemical equation for the combustion of black powder is

$$2 KNO_3 + S + 3 C \rightarrow K_2S + N_2 + 3 CO_2.$$

A balanced, but still simplified, equation is:[115]

$$10 KNO_3 + 3 S + 8 C \rightarrow 2 K_2CO_3 + 3 K_2SO_4 + 6 CO_2 + 5 N_2.$$

Although charcoal's chemical formula varies, it can be summed up by its empirical formula: C_7H_4O. Therefore, a more accurate equation of the decomposition of regular black powder with sulfur is:

$$6 KNO_3 + C_7H_4O + 2 S \rightarrow K_2CO_3 + K_2SO_4 + K_2S + 4 CO_2 + 2 CO + 2 H_2O + 3 N_2$$

Black powder without sulfur gives:

$$10 KNO_3 + 2 C_7H_4O \rightarrow 5 K_2CO_3 + 4 CO_2 + 5 CO + 4 H_2O + 5 N_2$$

However, gunpowder does not burn as a single reaction, so the byproducts are not easily predicted. One study showed that it produced (in order of descending quantities) 55.91% solid products: potassium carbonate, potassium sulfate, potassium sulfide, sulfur, potassium nitrate, potassium thiocyanate, carbon, ammonium carbonate and 42.98% gaseous products: carbon dioxide, nitrogen, carbon monoxide, hydrogen sulfide, hydrogen, methane, 1.11% water.

Black powder made with less-expensive and more plentiful sodium nitrate (in appropriate proportions) works just as well but is more hygroscopic than powders made from potassium nitrate—popularly known as saltpeter. Because *corned* black powder grains made with saltpeter are less affected by moisture in the air, they can be stored unsealed without degradation by humidity. Muzzleloaders have been known to fire after hanging on a wall for decades in a loaded state, provided they remained dry. By contrast, black powder made with sodium nitrate must be kept sealed to remain stable.

Gunpowder contains 3 megajoules per kilogram and contains its own oxidant. For comparison, the specific energy of TNT is 4.7 megajoules per kilogram, and the specific energy of gasoline is 47.2 megajoules per kilogram (though gasoline requires an oxidant, so an optimized gasoline and O_2 mixture contains 10.4 megajoules per kilogram). Gunpowder is a low explosive, so it does not detonate but rather deflagrates. Since it contains its own oxidizer and additionally burns faster under pressure, its combustion is capable of bursting containers such as shell, grenade, or improvised "pipe bomb" or "pressure cooker" casings to form shrapnel.

40.9.1 Advantages

In quarrying, high explosives are generally preferred for shattering rock. However, because of its low brisance, black powder causes fewer fractures and results in more usable stone compared to other explosives, making black powder useful for blasting monumental stone such as granite and marble. Black powder is well suited for blank rounds, signal flares, burst charges, and rescue-line launches. Black powder is also used in fireworks for lifting shells, in rockets as fuel, and in certain special effects.

40.9.2 Disadvantages

Black powder has a low energy density compared to modern "smokeless" powders, and thus to achieve high energy loadings, large amounts of black powder are needed with heavy projectiles. Black powder also produces thick smoke as a byproduct, which in military applications may give a soldier's location away to an enemy observer and may also impair aiming for additional shots.

Combustion converts less than half the mass of black powder to gas. The rest ends up as a thick layer of soot inside the barrel. In addition to being a nuisance, the residue from burnt black powder is hygroscopic and with the addition of moisture absorbed from the air, this residue forms a caustic substance. The soot contains potassium oxide or sodium oxide that turns into potassium hydroxide, or sodium hydroxide, which corrodes wrought iron or steel gun barrels. Black powder arms must be well cleaned both inside and out to remove the residue. The matchlock musket or pistol (an early gun ignition system), as well as the flintlock would often be unusable in wet weather, due to powder in the pan being exposed and dampened. Because of this unreliability, soldiers carrying muskets, known as musketeers, were armed with additional weapons such as swords or pikes. The bayonet was developed to allow the musket to be used as a pike, thus eliminating the need for the soldier to carry a secondary weapon.

40.9.3 Transportation

The United Nations Model Regulations on the Transportation of Dangerous Goods and national transportation authorities, such as United States Department of Transportation, have classified gunpowder (black powder) as a *Group*

A: *Primary explosive substance* for shipment because it ignites so easily. Complete manufactured devices containing black powder are usually classified as *Group D: Secondary detonating substance, or black powder, or article containing secondary detonating substance*, such as firework, class D model rocket engine, etc., for shipment because they are harder to ignite than loose powder. As explosives, they all fall into the category of Class 1.

40.10 Other uses

Besides its use as an explosive, gunpowder has been occasionally employed for other purposes; after the Battle of Aspern-Essling (1809), the surgeon of the Napoleonic Army Larrey, lacking salt, seasoned a horse meat bouillon for the wounded under his care with gunpowder.[116][117] It was also used for sterilization in ships when there was no alcohol.

Jack Tars (British sailors) used gunpowder to create tattoos when ink wasn't available, by pricking the skin and rubbing the powder into the wound in a method known as traumatic tattooing.[118]

Christiaan Huygens experimented with gunpowder in 1673 in an early attempt to build an internal combustion engine, but he did not succeed. Modern attempts to recreate his invention were similarly unsuccessful.

Fireworks use gunpowder as lifting and burst charges, although sometimes other more powerful compositions are added to the burst charge to improve performance in small shells or provide a louder report. Most modern firecrackers no longer contain black powder.

Beginning in the 1930s, gunpowder or smokeless powder was used in rivet guns, stun guns for animals, cable splicers and other industrial construction tools.[119] The "stud gun" drove nails or screws into solid concrete, a function not possible with hydraulic tools. See powder-actuated tool. Shotguns have been used to eliminate persistent material rings in operating rotary kilns (such as those for cement, lime, phosphate, etc.) and clinker in operating furnaces, and commercial tools make the method more reliable.[120]

Near London in 1853, Captain Shrapnel demonstrated a method for crushing gold-bearing ores by firing them from a cannon into an iron chamber, and "much satisfaction was expressed by all present". He hoped it would be useful on the goldfields of California and Australia. Nothing came of the invention, as continuously-operating crushing machines that achieved more reliable comminution were already coming into use.[121]

40.11 See also

- Ballistics
- Berthold Schwarz
- Black powder substitute
- Bulk loaded liquid propellants
- Faversham explosives industry
- Gunpowder magazine
- Gunpowder Plot
- Gunpowder warfare
- History of gunpowder
- Technology of the Song dynasty

40.12 References

[1] Jai Prakash Agrawal (2010). *High Energy Materials: Propellants, Explosives and Pyrotechnics.* Wiley-VCH. p. 69. ISBN 978-3-527-32610-5.

[2] David Cressy, *Saltpeter: The Mother of Gunpowder* (Oxford University Press, 2013)

[3] "Who Built It First?". *History.com*.

[4] Anne Marie Helmenstine, Ph.D. "Gunpowder Facts, History and Description". *About.com Education*.

[5] Chase 2003:31 : "the earliest surviving formulas for gunpowder can be found in the Wujing zongyao, a military work from around 1040"

[6] Buchanan 2006, p. 2 "With its ninth century AD origins in China, the knowledge of gunpowder emerged from the search by alchemists for the secrets of life, to filter through the channels of Middle Eastern culture, and take root in Europe with consequences that form the context of the studies in this volume."

[7] Joseph Needham; Gwei-Djen Lu; Ling Wang (1987). *Science and civilisation in China, Volume 5, Part 7.* Cambridge University Press. pp. 48–50. ISBN 978-0-521-30358-3.

[8] Owen Compliance Services. "Black Powder" (PDF). *Material Safety Data Sheet*. Retrieved 31 August 2014.

[9] Hazel Rossotti (2002). *Fire: Servant, Scourge, and Enigma.* Courier Dover Publications. pp. 132–137. ISBN 978-0-486-42261-9.

[10] Jack Kelly *Gunpowder: Alchemy, Bombards, and Pyrotechnics: The History of the Explosive that Changed the World,* Perseus Books Group: 2005, ISBN 0-465-03722-4, ISBN 978-0-465-03722-3, 272 pages

[11] St. C. Easton: "Roger Bacon and his Search for a Universal Science", Oxford (1962)

[12] Gábor Ágoston (2005). *Guns for the sultan: military power and the weapons industry in the Ottoman Empire.* Cambridge University Press. p. 15. ISBN 978-0-521-84313-3.

[13] Ingham-Brown, George (1989) *The Big Bang: A History of Explosives*, Sutton Publishers, ISBN 0-7509-1878-0, ISBN 978-0-7509-1878-7, page vi

[14] Kelly, Jack (2005) *Gunpowder: Alchemy, Bombards, and Pyrotechnics: The History of the Explosive that Changed the World*, Perseus Books Group, ISBN 0-465-03722-4, ISBN 978-0-465-03722-3, page 22

[15] Bert S. Hall, "Introduction, 1999" pp. xvi–xvii to the reprinting of James Riddick Partington (1960). *A history of Greek fire and gunpowder.* JHU Press. ISBN 978-0-8018-5954-0.

[16] Peter Purton (2009). *A History of the Late Medieval Siege, 1200–1500.* Boydell & Brewer. pp. 108–109. ISBN 978-1-84383-449-6.

[17] Bert S. Hall, "Introduction, 1999" p. xvii to the reprinting of James Riddick Partington (1960). *A history of Greek fire and gunpowder.* JHU Press. ISBN 978-0-8018-5954-0.

[18] Buchanan. "Editor's Introduction: Setting the Context", in Buchanan 2006.

[19] Chase 2003:31–32

[20] Lorge, Peter A. (2008). *The Asian military revolution, 1300-2000 : from gunpowder to the bomb* (1. publ. ed.). Cambridge: Cambridge University Press. p. 32. ISBN 978052160954-8.

[21] Kelly 2004:4

[22] *The Big Book of Trivia Fun*, Kidsbooks, 2004

[23] Peter Allan Lorge (2008). *The Asian military revolution: from gunpowder to the bomb.* Cambridge University Press. p. 18. ISBN 978-0-521-60954-8

[24] Needham 1986, p. 7 "Without doubt it was in the previous century, around +850, that the early alchemical experiments on the constituents of gunpowder, with its self-contained oxygen, reached their climax in the appearance of the mixture itself."

[25] Chase 2003:1 "The earliest known formula for gunpowder can be found in a Chinese work dating probably from the 800s. The Chinese wasted little time in applying it to warfare, and they produced a variety of gunpowder weapons, including flamethrowers, rockets, bombs, and land mines, before inventing firearms."

[26] Chase 2003:1

[27] Delgado, James (February 2003). "Relics of the Kamikaze". *Archaeology.* Archaeological Institute of America. **56** (1).

[28] Chase 2003:31

[29] Peter Allan Lorge (2008). *The Asian military revolution: from gunpowder to the bomb.* Cambridge University Press. pp. 33–34. ISBN 978-0-521-60954-8

[30] Kelly 2004:22 'Around year 1240, Arabs acquired knowledge of saltpeter ("Chinese snow") from the East, perhaps through India. They knew of gunpowder soon afterward. They also learned about fireworks ("Chinese flowers") and rockets ("Chinese arrows"). Arab warriors had acquired fire lances before year 1280. Around that same year, a Syrian named Hasan al-Rammah wrote a book that, as he put it, "treats of machines of fire to be used for amusement or for useful purposes." He talked of rockets, fireworks, fire lances, and other incendiaries, using terms that suggested he derived his knowledge from Chinese sources. He gave instructions for the purification of saltpeter and recipes for making different types of gunpowder.'

[31] Hassan, Ahmad Y. "Transfer of Islamic Technology to the West: Part III". *History of Science and Technology in Islam.*

[32] Peter Watson (2006). *Ideas: A History of Thought and Invention, from Fire to Freud.* HarperCollins. p. 304. ISBN 978-0-06-093564-1. The first use of a metal tube in this context was made around 1280 in the wars between the Song and the Mongols, where a new term, chong, was invented to describe the new horror...Like paper, it reached the West via the Muslims, in this case the writings of the Andalusian botanist Ibn al-Baytar, who died in Damascus in 1248. The Arabic term for saltpetre is 'Chinese snow' while the Persian usage is 'Chinese salt'.28

[33] Cathal J. Nolan (2006). *The age of wars of religion, 1000–1650: an encyclopedia of global warfare and civilization.* Volume 1 of Greenwood encyclopedias of modern world wars. Greenwood Publishing Group. p. 365. ISBN 0-313-33733-0. Retrieved 2011-11-28. In either case, there is linguistic evidence of Chinese origins of the technology: in Damascus, Arabs called the saltpeter used in making gunpowder "Chinese snow," while in Iran it was called "Chinese salt." Whatever the migratory route

[34] Oliver Frederick Gillilan Hogg (1970). *Artillery: its origin, heyday, and decline.* Archon Books. p. 123. The Chinese were certainly acquainted with saltpetre, the essential ingredient of gunpowder. They called it Chinese Snow and employed it early in the Christian era in the manufacture of fireworks and rockets.

[35] Oliver Frederick Gillilan Hogg (1963). *English artillery, 1326–1716: being the history of artillery in this country prior to the formation of the Royal Regiment of Artillery.* Royal Artillery Institution. p. 42. The Chinese were certainly acquainted with saltpetre, the essential ingredient of gunpowder. They called it Chinese Snow and employed it early in the Christian era in the manufacture of fireworks and rockets.

[36] Oliver Frederick Gillilan Hogg (1993). *Clubs to cannon: warfare and weapons before the introduction of gunpowder*

(reprint ed.). Barnes & Noble Books. p. 216. ISBN 1-56619-364-8. Retrieved 2011-11-28. The Chinese were certainly acquainted with saltpetre, the essential ingredient of gunpowder. They called it Chinese snow and used it early in the Christian era in the manufacture of fireworks and rockets.

[37] Partington, J. R. (1960). *A History of Greek Fire and Gunpowder* (illustrated, reprint ed.). JHU Press. p. 335. ISBN 0801859549. Retrieved 2014-11-21.

[38] Needham, Joseph; Yu, Ping-Yu (1980). Needham, Joseph, ed. *Science and Civilisation in China: Volume 5, Chemistry and Chemical Technology, Part 4, Spagyrical Discovery and Invention: Apparatus, Theories and Gifts*. Volume 5. Contributors Joseph Needham, Lu Gwei-Djen, Nathan Sivin (illustrated, reprint ed.). Cambridge University Press. p. 194. ISBN 052108573X. Retrieved 2014-11-21.

[39] Khan 1996

[40] Khan 2004:6

[41] *Ancient Discoveries, Episode 12: Machines of the East*, History Channel, 2007 (Part 4 and Part 5)

[42] Nelson, Cameron Rubaloff (2010-07). Manufacture and transportation of gunpowder in the Ottoman Empire: 1400-1800 M.A. Thesis.

[43] William H. McNeill (1992). *The Rise of the West: A History of the Human Community*. University of Chicago Press. p. 492. ISBN 0-226-56141-0. Retrieved 29 July 2011.

[44] Michael Kohn (2006), *Dateline Mongolia: An American Journalist in Nomad's Land*, RDR Books, p. 28, ISBN 1-57143-155-1, retrieved 29 July 2011

[45] Robert Cowley (1993). Robert Cowley, ed. *Experience of War* (reprint ed.). Random House Inc. p. 86. ISBN 0-440-50553-4. Retrieved 29 July 2011.

[46] Kenneth Warren Chase (2003). *Firearms: a global history to 1700* (illustrated ed.). Cambridge University Press. p. 58. ISBN 0-521-82274-2. Retrieved 29 July 2011.

[47] C. F. Temler, *Historische Abhandlungen der Koniglichen Gesellschaft der Wissenschaften zu Kopenhagen ... ubersetzt ... von V. A. Heinze*, Kiel, Dresden and Leipzig, 1782, i, 168, as cited in Partington, p. 228, footnote 6.

[48] Joseph Needham; Gwei-Djen Lu; Ling Wang (1987). *Science and civilisation in China, Volume 5, Part 7*. Cambridge University Press. p. 358. ISBN 978-0-521-30358-3.

[49] Bert S. Hall, "Introduction, 1999" p. xxiv to the reprinting of James Riddick Partington (1960). *A history of Greek fire and gunpowder*. JHU Press. ISBN 978-0-8018-5954-0.

[50] Partington 1960:60

[51] Partington 1960:48–49, 54

[52] Partington 1960:82–83

[53] Kelly 2004, p.61

[54] Molerus, Otto. "History of Civilization in the Western Hemisphere from the Point of View of Particulate Technology, Part 2," Advanced Powder Technology 7 (1996): 161-66

[55] "Early printing, 15th and 16th century" (PDF). *Asher Rare Books*. Retrieved 4 May 2015.

[56] Microsoft Encarta Online Encyclopedia 2007 Archived 31 October 2009.

[57] Philip, Chris (1988). *A bibliography of firework books : works on recreative fireworks from the sixteenth to the twentieth century*. Dingmans Ferry, Pa.: American Fireworks News. ISBN 978-0929931005.

[58] In 1777 Lavoisier named *oxygen*, which had earlier been isolated by Priestley; the realization that saltpeter contained this substance was fundamental to understanding gunpowder.

[59] Kelly 2004, p.164

[60] Metzner, Paul (1998), *Crescendo of the Virtuoso: Spectacle, Skill, and Self-Promotion in Paris during the Age of Revolution*, University of California Press

[61] Cocroft 2000, "Success to the Black Art!". Chapter 1

[62] Ross, Charles. *The Custom of the Castle: From Malory to Macbeth*. Berkeley: University of California Press, c1997. pages 131-130

[63] The Noble-Abel Equation of State: Thermodynamic Derivations for Ballistics Modelling

[64] Pritchard, Tom; Evans, Jack; Johnson, Sydney (1985), *The Old Gunpowder Factory at Glynneath*, Merthyr Tydfil: Merthyr Tydfil & District Naturalists' Society

[65] Cocroft 2000, "The demise of gunpowder" . Chapter 4

[66] MacDougall, Ian (2000). *'Oh, ye had to be careful' : personal recollections by Roslin gunpowder mill and bomb factory workers*. East Linton, Scotland: Tuckwell Press in association with the European Ethnological Research Centre and the Scottish Working People's History Trust. ISBN 1-86232-126-4.

[67] Iqtidar Alam Khan (2004). *Gunpowder And Firearms: Warfare In Medieval India*. Oxford University Press. ISBN 978-0-19-566526-0.

[68] Iqtidar Alam Khan (25 April 2008). *Historical Dictionary of Medieval India*. Scarecrow Press. p. 157. ISBN 978-0-8108-5503-8.

[69] Khan 2004:9–10

[70] Khan 2004:10

[71] Partington (Johns Hopkins University Press edition, 1999), 225

40.12. REFERENCES

[72] Partington (Johns Hopkins University Press edition, 1999), 226

[73] "Mughal Matchlock", *YouTube*.

[74] "India." Encyclopædia Britannica. Encyclopedia Britannica 2008 Ultimate Reference Suite. Chicago: Encyclopedia Britannica, 2008.

[75] "rocket and missile system." Encyclopædia Britannica. Encyclopædia Britannica 2008 Ultimate Reference Suite. Chicago: Encyclopædia Britannica, 2008.

[76] Dipanegara, P. B. R. Carey, *Babad Dipanagara: an account of the outbreak of the Java war, 1825-30 : the Surakarta court version of the Babad Dipanagara with translations into English and Indonesian* volume 9: Council of the M.B.R.A.S. by Art Printing Works; 1981.

[77] Atsushi, Ota (2006). *Changes of regime and social dynamics in West Java : society, state, and the outer world of Banten, 1750-1830*. Leiden: Brill. ISBN 90-04-15091-9.

[78] Thomas Stamford Raffles, *The History of Java*, Oxford University Press, 1965 (originally published in 1817), ISBN 0-19-580347-7

[79] Raffles, Thomas Stamford (1978). *The History of Java* ([Repr.]. ed.). Kuala Lumpur: Oxford University Press. ISBN 0-19-580347-7.

[80] US Department of Agriculture (1917). *Department Bulleting No. 316: Willows: Their growth, use, and importance*. The Department. p. 31.

[81] Kelly 2004, p.200

[82] Earl 1978, Chapter 2: The Development of Gunpowder

[83] Kelly 2004:60–63

[84] Kelly 2004, p.199

[85] Jecock, Marcus; Dunn, Christopher; et al. (2009). "Gatebeck Low Gunpowder Works and the Workers' Settlements of Endmoor and Gatebeck, Cumbria". *Research Department Report Series*. English Heritage. 63-2009. ISSN 1749-8775.

[86] Heller, Cornelia (December 2009). "Stassfurt" (PDF). *STASSFURT - FAD*. Ministry of Regional Development and Transport Saxony-Anhalt. p. 10. Retrieved 27 May 2015.

[87] Frangsmyr, Tore, J. L. Heilbron, and Robin E. Rider, editors *The Quantifying Spirit in the Eighteenth Century*. Berkeley: University of California Press, c. 1990. http://ark.cdlib.org/ark:/13030/ft6d5nb455/ p. 292.

[88] C.E. Munroe (1885) "Notes on the literature of explosives no. VIII", Proceedings of the US Naval Institute, no. XI, p. 285

[89] "Swiss Handguns 1882".

[90] Blackpowder to Pyrodex and Beyond by Randy Wakeman at Chuck Hawks

[91] The History and Art of Shotshells by Jon Farrar, Nebraskaland Magazine

[92] Buchanan, "Editor's Introduction: Setting the Context", in Buchanan 2006, p. 4.

[93] Black Powder Recipes, Ulrich Bretscher

[94] Julian S. Hatcher, *Hatcher's Notebook*, Military Service Publishing Company, 1947. Chapter XIII Notes on Gunpowder, pages 300-305.

[95] Kelly 2004, p.218

[96] "Some Account of Gunpowder", *The Saturday Magazine*, 422, supplement: 33–40, January 1839.

[97] Wisniak, J. J.; Garcés, I. (September 2001). "The Rise and Fall of the Salitre (Sodium Nitrate) Industry". *Indian Journal of Chemical Technology*: 427–438.

[98] Ashford, Bob (2016). "A New Interpretation of the Historical Data on the Gunpowder Industry in Devon and Cornwall". *J. Trevithick Soc.* Camborne, Cornwall: The Trevithick Society. 43: 65–73.

[99] Book title Workshop Receipts Publisher William Clowes and Son limited Author Ernest Spon. Date 1 August 1873.

[100] *GunpowderTranslation*. Academic. Retrieved 2014-08-31.

[101] Cathal J. Nolan (2006), *The age of wars of religion, 1000-1650: an encyclopedia of global warfare and civilization*, Greenwood Publishing Group, p. 365. ISBN 978-0-313-33733-8

[102] Kelly 2004, p58

[103] John Francis Guilmartin (2003). *Gunpowder & galleys: changing technology & Mediterranean warfare at sea in the 16th century*. Conway Maritime Press. pp. 109–110 and 298–300. ISBN 0851779514.

[104] T.J. Rodman (1861), *Reports of experiments on the properties of metals for cannon and the qualities of cannon powder*, p. 270

[105] Kelly 2004, p.195

[106] Tenney L. Davis (1943). *The Chemistry of Powder and Explosives* (PDF). p. 139.

[107] Brown, G.I. (1998) *The Big Bang: A history of Explosives* Sutton Publishing pp.22 & 32 ISBN 0-7509-1878-0

[108] Kelly 2004, p.224

[109] Rodney James (2011). *The ABCs of Reloading: The Definitive Guide for Novice to Expert* (9 ed.). Krause Publications. pp. 53–59. ISBN 978-1-4402-1396-0.

[110] Sharpe, Philip B. (1953) *Complete Guide to Handloading* Funk & Wagnalls p.137

[111] Wakeman, Randy. "Blackpowder to Pyrodex and Beyond". Retrieved 31 August 2014.

[112] "LESMOK POWDER".

[113] Julian S. Hatcher, *Hatcher's Notebook*, Stackpole Books, 1962, Chapter XIV, Gun Corrosion and Ammunition Developments, pages 346-349.

[114] Wakeman, Randy. "Blackpowder to Pyrodex and Beyond".

[115] Flash! Bang! Whiz!, University of Denver

[116] Parker, Harold T. (1983). *Three Napoleonic battles.* (Repr., Durham, 1944. ed.). Durham, NC: Duke Univ. Pr. p. 83. ISBN 0-8223-0547-X.

[117] Larrey is quoted in French at Dr Béraud, *Études Hygiéniques de la chair de cheval comme aliment*, Musée des Familles (1841-42).

[118] Rediker, Marcus (1989). *Between the devil and the deep blue sea : merchant seamen, pirates, and the Anglo-American maritime world, 1700-1750* (1st pbk. ed.). Cambridge: Cambridge University Press. p. 12. ISBN 9780521379830.

[119] *Popular Science*.

[120] "MasterBlaster System". Remington Products.

[121] *Mining Journal* 22 January 1853, p. 61

- Benton, Captain James G. (1862). *A Course of Instruction in Ordnance and Gunnery* (2 ed.). West Point, New York: Thomas Publications. ISBN 1-57747-079-6.

- Brown, G. I. (1998). *The Big Bang: A History of Explosives*. Sutton Publishing. ISBN 0-7509-1878-0.

- Buchanan, Brenda J., ed. (2006). *Gunpowder, Explosives and the State: A Technological History*. Aldershot: Ashgate. ISBN 0-7546-5259-9.

- Chase, Kenneth (2003). *Firearms: A Global History to 1700*. Cambridge University Press. ISBN 0-521-82274-2.

- Cocroft, Wayne (2000). *Dangerous Energy: The archaeology of gunpowder and military explosives manufacture*. Swindon: English Heritage. ISBN 1-85074-718-0.

- Crosby, Alfred W. (2002). *Throwing Fire: Projectile Technology Through History*. Cambridge University Press. ISBN 0-521-79158-8..

- Earl, Brian (1978). *Cornish Explosives*. Cornwall: The Trevithick Society. ISBN 0-904040-13-5..

- al-Hassan, Ahmad Y. "Gunpowder Composition for Rockets and Cannon in Arabic Military Treatises In Thirteenth and Fourteenth Centuries". *History of Science and Technology in Islam*.

- Johnson, Norman Gardner. "explosive". *Encyclopædia Britannica*. Chicago: Encyclopædia Britannica Online.

- Kelly, Jack (2004). *Gunpowder: Alchemy, Bombards, & Pyrotechnics: The History of the Explosive that Changed the World*. Basic Books. ISBN 0-465-03718-6.

- Khan, Iqtidar Alam (1996). "Coming of Gunpowder to the Islamic World and North India: Spotlight on the Role of the Mongols". *Journal of Asian History*. **30**: 41–5.

- Khan, Iqtidar Alam (2004). "Gunpowder and Firearms: Warfare in Medieval India". Oxford University Press. doi:10.1086/ahr.111.3.817.

- Needham, Joseph (1986). "Science & Civilisation in China" (PDF). V:7: The Gunpowder Epic. Cambridge University Press. ISBN 0-521-30358-3.

- Norris, John (2003). *Early Gunpowder Artillery: 1300-1600*. Marlborough: The Crowood Press. ISBN 9781861266156.

- Partington, J.R. (1960). *A History of Greek Fire and Gunpowder*. Cambridge, UK: W. Heffer & Sons.

- Partington, James Riddick; Hall, Bert S. (1999). *A History of Greek Fire and Gunpowder*. Baltimore: Johns Hopkins University Press. doi:10.1353/tech.2000.0031. ISBN 0-8018-5954-9.

- Urbanski, Tadeusz (1967). "Chemistry and Technology of Explosives". **III**. New York: Pergamon Press.

40.13 External links

- Gun and Gunpowder
- The Origins of Gunpowder
- Cannons and Gunpowder
- Oare Gunpowder Works, Kent, UK
- Royal Gunpowder Mills

40.13. EXTERNAL LINKS

- The DuPont Company on the Brandywine A digital exhibit produced by the Hagley Library that covers the founding and early history of the DuPont Company powder yards in Delaware

- "Ulrich Bretschler's Gunpowder Chemistry page".

- Video Demonstration of the Medieval Siege Society's Guns, Including showing ignition of gunpowder

- Black Powder Recipes

- "Dr. Sasse's investigations (and others) found via search at US DTIC.MIL These contain scientific studies of BP properties and details of measurement techniques.".

Chapter 41

Flash powder

Flash powder is a pyrotechnic composition, a mixture of oxidizer and metallic fuel, which burns quickly and if confined produces a loud report. It is widely used in theatrical pyrotechnics and fireworks (namely salutes, e.g., cherry bombs, M-80s, firecrackers, and cap gun shots) and was once used for flashes in photography.

Examples of theatrical binary flash powders. Note the shared oxidizer (A) powder for some types of fuels (B).

Different varieties of flash powder are made from different compositions; most common are potassium perchlorate and aluminium powder. Sometimes, sulphur is included in the mixture to increase the sensitivity. Early formulations used potassium chlorate instead of potassium perchlorate.

Flash powder compositions are also used in military pyrotechnics when production of large amount of noise, light, or infrared radiation is required, e.g. missile decoy flares and stun grenades.

41.1 Mixtures

Normally, flash powder mixtures are compounded to achieve a particular purpose. These mixtures range from extremely fast-burning mixtures designed to produce a maximum audio report, to mixtures designed to burn slowly and provide large amounts of illumination, to mixtures that were formerly used in photography.

41.1.1 Aluminium and chlorate

Because of the above-mentioned instability, the combination of aluminium powder and potassium chlorate is a poor choice for flash powder that is to be stored for more than a very short period of time. For that reason, it has been largely replaced by the potassium perchlorate mixtures. Chlorate mixes are used when cost is the overriding concern because potassium chlorate is less expensive than perchlorate. It is critically important to exclude sulphur and any acidic components from these mixtures. Sometimes a few percent of bicarbonate buffer is added to the mixture to ensure the absence of acidic impurities.

$$6\ KClO_3 + 10\ Al \rightarrow 3\ K_2O + 5\ Al_2O_3 + 3\ Cl_2$$

The composition is approximately 70% $KClO_3$: 30% Al by weight for the reactants of the above stoichiometrically balanced equation.

41.1.2 Aluminium - nitrate with sulphur

This composition, usually in a ratio of 5 parts potassium nitrate, to 3 parts aluminium powder, to 2 parts sulphur, is especially popular with hobbyists. It is not very quick-burning, unless exceptionally fine ingredients are used. Although it incorporates sulphur, it is in fact fairly stable, sustaining multiple hits from a hammer onto a hard surface. Adding 2% of its weight with boric acid is reputed to significantly increase stability and shelf life, through resistance to dampening through ambient humidity. Other ratios such as 6 KNO3/3 Al/2 S and 5 KNO3/2 Al/3 S also exist and work. All ratios have similar burn times and strength, although 5 KNO3/3 Al/2 S seems to be dominant.

$$2\,KNO_3 + 4\,Al + S \rightarrow K_2S + N_2 + 2\,Al_2O_3$$

The composition is approximately 59% KNO_3 : 31.6% Al : 9.4% S by weight for the reactants of the above stoichiometrically balanced equation.

For best results, "German Dark" aluminium should be used, with airfloat sulphur, and finely ball milled pure potassium nitrate. The finished mixture should never be ball milled together.

41.1.3 Aluminium and perchlorate

Aluminium powder and potassium perchlorate are the only two components of the pyrotechnic industry standard flash powder. It provides a great balance of stability and power, and is the composition used in most commercial exploding fireworks.

The balanced equation for the reaction is:

$$6\,KClO_4 + 14\,Al \rightarrow 3\,K_2O + 7\,Al_2O_3 + 3\,Cl_2$$

Although not stoichiometrically balanced, a ratio of seven parts potassium perchlorate to three parts dark pyro aluminium is the composition used by most pyrotechnicians. However, a ratio of 2 mass units potassium perchlorate to 1 mass unit dark pyro aluminium is closer to stoichiometric, and may produce a louder report.

For best results, the aluminium powder should be "Dark Pyro" grade, with a flake particle shape, and a particle size of fewer than 10 micrometres. The $KClO_4$ should be in powder form, free from clumps. It can be sieved through a screen, if necessary, to remove any clumps prior to use. The particle size of the perchlorate is not as critical as that of the aluminium component, as much less energy is required to decompose the $KClO_4$ than is needed to melt the aluminium into the liquid state required for the reaction.

Although this composition is fairly insensitive, it should be treated with care and respect. Hobbyist pyrotechnicians usually use a method called *diapering*, in which the materials are poured separately onto a large piece of paper, which is then alternately lifted at each corner to roll the composition over itself and mix the components. Some amateur pyrotechnicians choose to mix the composition by shaking in a closed paper container, as this is much quicker and more effective than diapering. One method of mixing flash is to put the components in the final device and handling the device will mix the flash powder. Paper/cardboard is chosen over other materials such as plastic as a result of its favorable triboelectric properties.

Large quantities should never be mixed in a single batch. Large quantities are not only more difficult to handle safely, but they place innocent bystanders within the area at risk. In the event of accidental ignition, debris from a multiple-pound flash powder explosion can be thrown hundreds of feet with sufficient force to kill or injure. (Note: 25 grams of mixture is enough to explode in open air without constraint other than air pressure.)

No matter the quantity, care must always be taken to prevent any electrostatic discharge or friction during mixing or handling, as these may cause accidental ignition.

41.1.4 Magnesium and nitrate

Another flash composition common among amateurs consists of magnesium powder and potassium nitrate. Other metal nitrates have been used, including barium and strontium nitrates. Compositions using nitrate and magnesium metal have been used as photographic flash powders almost since the invention of photography. Potassium nitrate/magnesium flash powder must be mixed and used immediately and not stored due to its tendency of self-ignition

$$2\,KNO_3 + 5\,Mg \rightarrow K_2O + N_2 + 5\,MgO$$

The composition is approximately 50% KNO3 : 50% Mg by weight for the reactants of the above stoichiometrically balanced equation. Below is the same reaction but invlolving barium nitrate.

$$Ba(NO_3)_2 + 5\,Mg \rightarrow BaO + N_2 + 5\,MgO$$

Mixtures designed to make reports are substantially different from mixtures designed for illumination. A stoichiometric ratio of three parts KNO_3 to two parts Mg is close to ideal and provides the most rapid burn. The magnesium powder should be smaller than 200 mesh, though up to 100 mesh will work. The potassium nitrate should be impalpable dust. This mixture is popular in amateur pyrotechnics because it is insensitive and relatively safe as such things go.

For photographic use, mixtures containing magnesium and nitrates are made much more fuel rich. The excess magnesium is volatilized by the reaction and burns in air providing additional light. In addition, the higher concentration of fuel results in a slower burn, providing more of a "poof" and less of a "bang" when ignited. A formula from 1917 specifies 5 parts of magnesium to 6 parts of barium nitrate for a stoichiometry of nine parts fuel to one part oxidizer."[1] Modern recreations of photographic flash powders may avoid the use of barium salts because of their toxic nature. A mixture of five parts 80 mesh magnesium to one part of potassium nitrate provides a good white flash without being too violent. Fuel rich flash powders are also used in theatrical flash pots.

Magnesium based compositions degrade over long periods of time, as magnesium does not form a passivating oxide coating, meaning the metallic Mg will slowly react with atmospheric oxygen and moisture. In military pyrotechnics involving magnesium fuels, external oxygen can be excluded by using hermetically sealed canisters. Commercial photographic flash powders are sold as two-part mixtures, to be combined immediately before use.

41.1.5 Magnesium and PTFE

A flash composition designed specifically to generate flares that are exceptionally bright in the infrared portion of the spectrum use a mixture of pyro-grade magnesium and powdered polytetrafluoroethylene. These flares are used as decoys from aircraft that might be subject to heat-seeking missile fire.

$$2n\ Mg + (C_2F_4)_n \rightarrow 2n\ MgF_2\ (s) + 2n\ C\ (s)$$

41.1.6 Antimony trisulfide and chlorate

This mixture, and similar mixtures sometimes containing pyro aluminium have been used since the early 1900s for small "Black Cat" style paper firecrackers. Its extremely low cost makes it popular among manufacturers of low-grade fireworks in China. Like all mixtures containing chlorates, it is extremely sensitive to friction, impact and ESD, and is considered unsafe in pyrotechnic devices that contain more than a few tens of milligrams of the mixture.

$$18\ KClO_3 + 5\ Sb_2S_3 \rightarrow 5\ Sb_2O_3 + 15\ SO_2 + 9\ K_2O + 9\ Cl_2$$

This mixture is not highly energetic, and in at least some parts of the United States, firecrackers containing 50 mg or less of this mixture are legal as consumer fireworks.

41.2 Safety and handling

Flash powders even within intended usages often release explosive force of deadly capacity. Nearly all widely used flash powder mixtures are sensitive to shock, friction and electrostatic discharge. In certain mixtures, it is not uncommon for this sensitivity to spontaneously change over time, or due to change in the environment, or to other unknowable factors in either the original manufacturing or in real-world storage. Additionally, accidental contaminants such as strong acids or sulphur compounds can sensitise them even more. Because flash powder mixtures are so easy to initiate, there is potentially a high risk of accidental explosions which can inflict severe blast/fragmentation injuries, e.g. blindness, explosive amputation, permanent maiming, or disfigurement. Fatalities have occurred. The various flash powder compositions should therefore not be handled by anyone who is unfamiliar with their properties, or the handling techniques required to maintain safety. Flash powder and flash powder devices pose exceptionally high risks to children, who typically cannot understand the danger and may be less adept with safe handling techniques. As a result, children tend to suffer more severe injuries than adults.

Flash powders—especially those that use chlorate—are often highly sensitive to friction, heat/flame and static electricity. A spark of as little as 0.1–10 millijoules can set off certain mixtures. Certain formulations prominent in the underground press contain both sulphur and potassium chlorate. These mixtures are especially shock and friction sensitive and in many applications should be considered unpredictable. Modern pyrotechnic practices call for never using sulphur in a mix containing chlorate salts.

Some flash powder formulations (those that use single-digit micrometre flake aluminium powder or fine magnesium powder as their fuel) can self-confine and explode in small quantities. This makes flash powder dangerous to handle, as it can cause severe hearing damage and amputation injury even when sitting in the open. Self-confinement occurs when the mass of the pile provides sufficient inertia to allow high pressure to build within it as the mixture reacts. This is referred to as 'inertial confinement', and it is not to be confused with a detonation.

Flash powder of any formulation should not be mixed in large quantities by the amateur pyrotechnician. Beginners should start with sub-gram quantities, and refrain from making large devices. Flash powder should only be made at the site at which it will be used. Additionally, the mixture should be made immediately before use. When mixed, the transportation, storage, usage, various possession, and illegal "firearms" laws (including felonies) may come into effect that do not apply to the unmixed or pre-assembled components.

41.3 See also

- Pyrotechnic initiator
- Sprengel explosive
- Thermite
- Black powder
- Lycopodium powder

41.4 References

[1] Watkins, *The Photographic Journal of America*, Vol. 54, 1917, Philadelphia, p. 384

41.5 External links

- Flash Powder—Three different types of Flash powder

Chapter 42

Ammonal

Ammonal is an explosive made up of ammonium nitrate and aluminium powder. Not to be confused with T-ammonal which contains trinitrotoluene as well to increase properties such as brisance.

The ammonium nitrate functions as an oxidizer and the aluminium as fuel. The use of the relatively cheap ammonium nitrate and aluminium makes it a replacement for pure TNT.

The mixture is affected by humidity because ammonium nitrate is highly hygroscopic. Ammonal's ease of detonation depends on fuel and oxidizer ratios, 95:5 ammonium nitrate and aluminum being fairly sensitive, however not very oxygen balanced. Even copper metal traces are known to sensitize bulk amounts of ammonium nitrate and further increase danger of spontaneous detonation during a fire, most likely due to the formation of tetramines. More oxygen balanced mixtures are not easily detonated, requiring a fairly substantial shock, though it remains more sensitive than trinitrotoluene and C-4.

The detonation velocity of ammonal is approximately 4,400 metres per second or 9,842 miles per hour.

42.1 History

From early 1916, the British Army employed ammonal for their mines during World War I, starting with the Hawthorn Ridge mine during the Battle of the Somme, and reaching a zenith in the mines in the Battle of Messines which were exploded on 7 June 1917 at the start of the Third Battle of Ypres (also known as the Battle of Passchendaele). Several of the mines in the Battle of Messines contained 30,000 lbs (over 13.6 tonnes) of ammonal, and others contained 20,000 lbs (over 9 tonnes). The joint explosion of the ammonal mines beneath the German lines at Messines created 19 large craters, killing 10,000 German soldiers in one of the largest non-nuclear explosions in history. Not all of the mines laid by the British Army at Messines were detonated, however. Two mines were not ignited in 1917 because they had been abandoned before the battle, and four were outside the area of the offensive. On 17 July 1955, a lightning strike set off one of these four latter mines. There were no human casualties, but one cow was killed. Another of the unused mines is believed to have been found in a location beneath a farmhouse,*[1] but no attempt has been made to remove it.

Ammonal used for military mining purposes was generally contained within metal cans or rubberised bags to prevent moisture ingress problems. The composition of ammonal used at Messines was 65% ammonium nitrate, 17% aluminium, 15% trinitrotoluene (TNT), and 3% charcoal.*[2] Ammonal remains in use as an industrial explosive. Typically, it is used for quarrying or mining purposes.

ETA, a Basque separatist organisation, used 250 kg of ammonal in a car bomb in its attack on the Zaragoza barracks on 11 December 1987 in Zaragoza, Spain.

42.2 Proportions

An ammonal mixture previously used in hand grenades and shells has the proportions (by mass):*[3]

- ammonium nitrate 58.6%
- aluminum powder 21%
- charcoal 2.4%
- TNT 18%

42.3 See also

- Amatol
- BLU-82 "Daisy Cutter"
- Tritonal

42.4 References

[1] Tweedie, N. (2004-01-12). "Farmer who is sitting on a bomb". *The Daily Telegraph*. Retrieved 2010-05-17.

[2] Brown, G. I. (1998). *The Big Bang: A History of Explosives*. Sutton Publishing. p. 163. ISBN 0-7509-1878-0.

[3] Chamberlain, J. S. (1921). *A Textbook of Organic Chemistry*, Philadelphia: P. Blankiston's Son & Co. p. 534. OCLC 245530036. Retrieved 2010-05-17.

Chapter 43

Armstrong's mixture

Armstrong's mixture is a highly sensitive primary explosive. Its primary ingredients are red phosphorus and strong oxidizer, such as potassium chlorate and potassium perchlorate. Sulfur and calcium carbonate might be present in small amounts, though other additives are also used. Commercially, Armstrong's mixture is used in extremely small quantities on the paper caps in toy cap guns[1] and in party poppers.

It has also been considered a suitable mixture for the primer used in guns after boron carbide has been added.[2]

43.1 Safety considerations

Because of its sensitivity to shock, friction and flame, Armstrong's mixture is an extremely dangerous explosive. Only about 10 mg of it is used per item of consumer fireworks. Depending on composition, conditions and quantity, Armstrong's mixture can explode violently in an enclosed space.[3]

43.2 References

[1] J. B. Calvert. "Flash! Bang! Whiz!: An introduction to propellants, explosives, pyrotechnics and fireworks". Archived from the original on 15 November 2006. Retrieved 2006-11-11.

[2] US patent 3973502, Charles R Olsen, "Tube primer", issued 1976-08-10

[3] John Donner. "Impact Firecrackers" (PDF). Retrieved 2006-11-11.

Chapter 44

Sprengel explosive

Sprengel explosives are a generic class of materials invented by Hermann Sprengel in the 1870s.[*][1] They consist of stoichiometric mixtures of strong oxidisers and reactive fuels, mixed just prior to use in order to enhance safety. Either the oxidiser or the fuel, or both, should be a liquid to facilitate mixing, and intimate contact between the materials for a fast reaction rate.

Sprengel suggested nitric acid, nitrates and chlorates as oxidisers, and nitroaromatics (e.g. nitrobenzene) as fuels. Other Sprengel explosives used at various times include charcoal with liquid oxygen (an oxyliquit), "Rackarock", and ANFO ammonium nitrate (oxidiser) mixed with a fuel oil (fuel), normally diesel kerosene or nitromethane. Eventually ANFO supplanted all others because its oxidiser was the safest, and - due to its widespread use as a fertiliser in agriculture - also the cheapest.

"**Rackarock**" consisted of potassium chlorate and nitrobenzene. It was provided in the form of permeable cartridges of the chlorate, which were placed in wire baskets and dipped in the nitrobenzene for a few seconds before use. For underwater use, it could be provided in cans instead. It was famously used in the massive submarine demolition of a navigational hazard in Long Island Sound in 1885. The charge of over a hundred tonnes of explosive (laid in tunnels 20 metres below sea level) destroyed approximately 600,000 tonnes of rock, and created a wave 30 m high.

44.1 See also

- Cheddite
- Oxyliquit
- Panclastite

44.2 References

[1] Messel, Rudolph (1907). *Hermann Johann Philipp Sprengel. Journal of the Chemical Society.* **91**. pp. 661 – 663.

Chapter 45

ANFO

Ammonium nitrate prills used in ANFO at a potash mine by the K+S AG

25 kg (55 lb) sacks containing ANFO

ANFO (or **AN/FO**, for **ammonium nitrate/fuel oil**) is a widely used bulk industrial explosive mixture.

It consists of 94% porous prilled ammonium nitrate (NH_4NO_3) (AN) that acts as the oxidizing agent and absorbent for the fuel and 6% number 2 fuel oil (FO).[1]

ANFO has found wide use in coal mining, quarrying, metal mining, and civil construction in undemanding applications where the advantages of ANFO's low cost and ease of use matter more than the benefits offered by conventional industrial explosives, such as water resistance, oxygen balance, high detonation velocity, and performance in small diameters. ANFO is also widely used in avalanche hazard mitigation.[2]

It accounts for an estimated 80% of the 2.7×10^9 kg (6×10^9 lb) of explosives used annually in North America.[3]

The press and other media have used the term ANFO loosely and imprecisely in describing IEDs, in cases of **fertilizer bombs** (see Malicious use below).[4]

The use of ANFO originated in the 1950s.[5]

45.1 Chemistry

ANFO under most conditions is blasting cap–insensitive, so it is classified as a blasting agent[6] and not a high explosive;[7] it decomposes through detonation rather than deflagration with a moderate velocity of about 3,200 m/s in 130 mm (5 in) diameter, unconfined, at ambient temperature. It is a tertiary explosive consisting of distinct fuel and oxidizer phases, and requires confinement for efficient detonation and brisance.

Because it is cap-insensitive, it generally requires a primer,[8] also known as a booster (e.g., one or two sticks of dynamite is historically used, or in more recent times Tovex or cast boosters of pentolite (TNT)/PETN or similar compositions) to ensure continuation of the detonation wave-train.[9]

The chemistry of ANFO detonation is the reaction of ammonium nitrate with a long-chain alkane (C_nH_{2n+2}) to form nitrogen, carbon dioxide, and water. In an ideal stoichiometrically balanced reaction, ANFO is composed of about 94.3% AN and 5.7% FO by weight. The normal ratio recommended is 2 U.S. quarts of fuel oil per 50 pounds of ammonium nitrate (80 ml/kg). In practice, a slight excess of fuel oil is added, i.e., 2.5 to 3 quarts of fuel oil per 50 pounds of ammonium nitrate (100 to 125 ml/kg), as underdosing results in reduced performance while overdosing merely results in more post-blast fumes.*[10] When detonation conditions are optimal, the aforementioned gases are the only products. In practical use, such conditions are impossible to attain, and blasts produce moderate amounts of toxic gases such as carbon monoxide and nitrogen oxides (NO_x).

Variants of ANFO using diesel fuel, kerosene, coal dust, racing fuel, or even molasses in place of the red diesel (№ 2 fuel oil) have been used as a source of carbon, and finely powdered aluminium in the mixture will sensitise it to detonate more readily.

45.2 Industrial use

Charging a hole with ANFO for rock blasting

Ammonium nitrate is widely used as a fertilizer in the agricultural industry. It is also found in instant cold packs. In many countries, its purchase and use are restricted to buyers who have obtained the proper license. This restriction is primarily because it is an attractive and simple component used in the production of bombs.

In the mining industry, the term ANFO specifically describes a mixture of solid ammonium nitrate prills and heating oil. In this form, it has a bulk density of about 840 kg/m^3. The density of individual prills is about 1300 kg/m^3, while the density of pure crystalline ammonium nitrate is 1700 kg/m^3. AN prills used for explosive applications are physically different from fertilizer prills: the former contain around 20% air. These versions of ANFO are generally called explosives-grade, low density, or industrial-grade ammonium nitrate. These voids are necessary to sensitize ANFO: they create so-called "hot spots".*[11] Finely powdered aluminium can be added to ANFO to increase both sensitivity and energy; however, this has fallen out of favor due to cost. Other additions include perlite, chemical gassing agents, or glass air bubbles to create these voids.*[12]

AN is highly hygroscopic, readily absorbing water from air. It is dangerous when stored in humid environments, as any absorbed water interferes with its explosive function. AN is also water-soluble. When used in wet mining conditions, considerable effort must be taken to dewater boreholes.

Other explosives based on the ANFO chemistry exist; the most commonly used are emulsions. They differ from ANFO in the physical form the reactants take. The most notable properties of emulsions are water resistance and higher bulk density.

The popularity of ANFO is largely attributable to its low cost and high stability. In most jurisdictions, ammonium nitrate need not be classified as an explosive for transport purposes; it is merely an oxidizer. Many mines prepare ANFO on-site using the same diesel fuel that powers their vehicles, although heating oil, which is nearly identical, may cost less than diesel fuel due to lower fuel tax. Many fuels can theoretically be used; the low volatility and cost of fuel oil makes it ideal.

45.3 In popular culture

The Discovery Channel show *MythBusters* commonly used ANFO (with the help of detonation professionals), especially in episode 26: "Salsa Escape, Cement Removal" and episode 125: "Knock Your Socks Off" as well as the series finale when they not only blew up a recreational vehicle, but recreated the most iconic explosion in the show's history when they used 5001 pounds of ANFO to blow up a cement truck.

It was used by Jim Caviezel's character in the 2006 film *Déjà Vu* in a domestic terrorism attack.

In the book *The Third Day, The Frost* by John Marsden, ANFO is used to blow up Cobblers Bay.

In a sub-plot of the book *Executive Orders* by Tom Clancy, anarchists make a truck bomb filled with ANFO but are caught before reaching their target.

In the book *Battle Royale* by Koshun Takami, students who attempt to bomb a school use ANFO.

In the movie *The Dark Knight* by Christopher Nolan, The Joker uses the compound to hold two ferries hostage, and tries to make the people on each ferry detonate the other ferry.

In Stephen King's novel *Desperation*, novelist Johnny Marinville prevents the rest of the group from going forward, and proceeds to blow up the Pit and the *ini* inside with the ANFO, sacrificing himself.

It is often mentioned and used by protagonist Vic in NOS4A2 by Joe Hill.

45.4 Disasters

Main article: Ammonium nitrate disasters

Unmixed ammonium nitrate can decompose explosively and has been responsible for several industrial disasters, including the 1947 Texas City disaster in Texas City, Texas, the 2004 Ryongchon disaster in North Korea, and the 2013 West Fertilizer Company explosion in West, Texas. Environmental hazards include eutrophication in confined waters and nitrate/gas oil contamination of ground or surface water.[13]

45.5 Malicious use

ANFO was first used maliciously in 1970 by student protesters at the University of Wisconsin–Madison, who learned how to make and use ANFO from a Wisconsin Conservation Department booklet entitled *Pothole Blasting for Wildlife*,[10][14] resulting in the Sterling Hall bombing.

The ANFO car bomb was adopted by the Provisional IRA in 1972 and, by 1973, the Troubles were consuming 47,000 lb of ammonium nitrate for the majority of bombs.[15] The IRA detonated an ANFO truck bomb on Bishopsgate in London in 1993, killing one and causing £350 million in damage. It has also seen use by groups such as the Revolutionary Armed Forces of Colombia and ETA. In 1992, Shining Path perpetrated the Tarata bombing in Lima, Peru using two ANFO truck bombs.

A more sophisticated variant of ANFO (ammonium nitrate with nitromethane as the fuel called ANNM) was used in the 1995 Oklahoma City bombing.

The Shijiazhuang bombings (Chinese: 靳如超爆炸案 or 石家庄"3·16" 特大爆炸案) rocked the city of Shijiazhuang, China, on 16 March 2001. A total of 108 people were killed, and 38 others injured when, within a short time, several ANFO bombs exploded near four apartment buildings, and were characterized by China scholar Andrew Scobell as perhaps the worst terrorist act in the history of the People's Republic of China.

Improvised bombs made with agricultural-grade AN are less sensitive and less efficient than the explosive-grade variety. In November 2009, a ban on ammonium sulfate, ammonium nitrate, and calcium ammonium nitrate fertilizers was imposed in the former Malakand Division – comprising the Upper Dir, Lower Dir, Swat, Chitral and Malakand districts of the North West Frontier Province (NWFP) of Pakistan, by the NWFP government, following reports that those chemicals were used by militants to make explosives.

In April 2010, police in Greece confiscated 180 kg of ANFO and other related material stashed in a hideaway in the Athens suburb of Kareas. The material was believed to be linked to attacks previously carried out by the "Revolutionary Struggle" terrorist group.

In January 2010, President Hamid Karzai of Afghanistan also issued a decree banning the use, production, storage, purchase, or sale of ammonium nitrate, after an investigation showed militants in the Taliban insurgency had used the substance in bomb attacks.[16][17][18]

On 22 July 2011, an aluminium powder-enriched ANNM explosive, with total size of 950 kg (150 kg of aluminum powder), increasing demolition power by 10-30% over plain ANFO, was used in the Oslo bombing.[19][20]

On 13 April 2016, two suspected IRA members were stopped in Dublin with 67kg of ANFO[21]

45.6 ANNM

Ammonium nitrate and nitromethane (ANNM) is one of the most powerful improvised types of AN-based explosives. The relative effectiveness factor of ANNM varies depending on the mix, but does not exceed 1 (annmal = RE 1-1.1). ANNM usually contains a 60:40 (kinepak) mix of AN and NM (60% ammonium nitrate, 40% nitromethane by mass), though this results in a wet slurry. Sometimes, more AN is added to reduce liquidity and make it easier to store and handle, as well as providing an oxygen-balanced mix. ANNM is also more sensitive to shock than standard ANFO and is therefore easier to detonate. When ANNM detonates, the primary products are H_2O, CO_2 and N_2, but NO_x and other toxic gases are inevitably formed because of a negative oxygen balance. The balanced equation is as follows:

$$3NH_4NO_3 + 2CH_3NO_2 \rightarrow 4N_2 + 2CO_2 + 9H_2O$$

Depending on the detonation impetus (for example a #6 versus a #10 detonator), the products of the detonation can be decidedly unstoichiometric.

45.7 References

[1] Cook, Melvin A. (1974). *The Science of Industrial Explosives*. IRECO Chemicals. p. 1. ASIN B0000EGDJT.

[2] Cook, Melvin A. (1974). *The Science of Industrial Explosives*. IRECO Chemicals. p. 2. ASIN B0000EGDJT.

[3] Edward M. Green (June 2006). "Explosives regulation in the USA" (PDF). *Industrial Materials* (465): 78. Retrieved 3 March 2013.

[4] Jo Thomas (29 September 1997). "Jury to Be Picked in 2d Oklahoma Bomb Trial". *The New York Times*. Retrieved 3 March 2013.

[5] Encyclopædia Britannica

[6] Cook, Melvin A. (1974). *The Science of Industrial Explosives*. IRECO Chemicals. p. 16. ASIN B0000EGDJT.

[7] "Explosives and blasting agents". Occupation Safety & Health Administration. Retrieved March 3, 2013.

[8] *Blasters' Handbook 15th Edition*. E. I. du Pont de Nemours & Company. 1969. pp. 64–68. ASIN B000JM3SD0.

[9] "Explosives - ANFO (Ammonium Nitrate - Fuel Oil)". GlobalSecurity.org. Retrieved 3 March 2013.

[10] Mathiak, Harold A. (1965). *Pothole Blasting for Wildlife*. Wisconsin Conservation Department, Madison, Wisconsin 53701. p. 11.

[11] It was found by the IRA, in response to using low-brisance AN fertilizers, that "hot spots" can be created by blending powdered sugar into the ANFO mixture, effectively sensitizing the mixture to mining-standard prilled ammonium nitrate effectiveness in which the interaction of the detonation front with a spherical void concentrates energy. Blasting-grade AN prills are typically between 0.9 and 3.0 mm in diameter.

[12] Michael Karmis (2001). *Mine Health and Safety Management*. Society for Mining Metallurgy. ISBN 978-0873352000.

[13] P. Cosgrove. Ammogex Material Safety Data Sheet, Document No: HS-MSDS-03, Irish Industrial Explosives Ltd

[14] Mike Davis (2007). *Buda's Wagon: A Brief History of the Car Bomb*. New York: Verso. p. 53. ASIN B005DI9UVO. ISBN 1844671321. LCCN 2007274127..

[15] Henry Stanhope (8 November 1974). "The will to blow the lid off Ulster still remains strong". *The Times*. London.

[16] "Afghanistan bans chemical used to make bombs; protesters denounce killings". *Times Union*. Albany, N.Y. Archived from the original on 7 June 2010.

[17] "Afghanistan bans chemical used to make bombs". *The Guardian*. AP Foreign. 22 January 2010. Retrieved 3 March 2013.

[18] Dexter Filkins (11 November 2009). "Bomb Material Cache Uncovered in Afghanistan". *The New York Times*. Retrieved 3 March 2013.

[19] Stina Åshildsdatter Grolid; Unni Eikeseth (25 July 2011). "Slik virket trykkbølgen etter bomben" [Such seemed the shock wave after the bomb] (in Norwegian). NRK. Retrieved 28 July 2011.

[20] Stigset, Marianne; Kremer, Josiane; Treloar, Stephen (27 July 2011). "Police in Norway Extend Terror Probe Across Europe After Breivik Attacks". *Bloomberg*.

[21] Daniel Hickey (13 April 2016). "Two men appear in court charged with possession of 150kg of homemade explosives". *Irish Independent*. Dublin. Retrieved 16 April 2016.

45.8 External links

-
- Video of ANFO being used at an open pit mine
- Video showing detonation of a 5 kg ANFO charge
- Securing Ammonium Nitrate: Using Lessons Learned in Afghanistan to Protect the Homeland from IEDs: Hearing before the Subcommittee on Cybersecurity, Infrastructure Protection, and Security Technologies of the Committee on Homeland Security, House of Representatives, One Hundred Twelfth Congress, Second Session, 12 July 2012

Chapter 46

Cheddite

Cheddite is a class of explosive materials that were originally manufactured in the town of Chedde in Haute-Savoie, France in the early twentieth century. Closely related to Sprengel explosives, cheddites consisted of a high proportion of inorganic chlorates mixed with nitroaromatics (e.g. nitrobenzene or dinitrotoluene) plus a little paraffin or castor oil as a moderant for the chlorate. Several different types were made, and they were principally used in quarrying. Due to availability of ingredients and easy production process it was also the most common explosive material manufactured by the Polish Underground State in occupied Poland during World War II; it was used for production of the R wz. 42 and Filipinka hand grenades.

Since the 1970s, Cheddite is the commercial name for an explosive compound used as an explosive primer for shotgun cartridges. It contains 90% potassium chlorate, 7% paraffin, 3% petroleum jelly, and traces of carbon black.

46.1 See also

- Sprengel explosive
- Boxer Primer

Chapter 47

Oxyliquit

An **oxyliquit**, also called **liquid air explosive** or **liquid oxygen explosive**, is an explosive material which is a mixture of liquid oxygen (LOX) with a suitable fuel, such as carbon (as lampblack), or an organic chemical (e.g. a mixture of soot and naphthalene), wood meal, or aluminium powder or sponge. These fuels have the ability to absorb liquid oxygen amounts several times their own weight. It is a class of Sprengel explosives.

47.1 Properties

Oxyliquits have numerous advantages. They are inexpensive to make, can be initiated by a safety fuse, and in case of a misfire, the oxygen evaporates quickly, rendering the charge quite safe in a short period of time. The first large scale deployment took place in 1899 during the building of the Simplon Tunnel, in the form of cartridges filled with diatomaceous earth soaked with petroleum, or an absorbent cork charcoal, dipped in liquid oxygen immediately before use. In another modification, the cartridge is filled with liquid oxygen after placement in the borehole.

One of the disadvantages of oxyliquits is that, once mixed, they are sensitive to sparks, shock, and heat, in addition to reported cases of spontaneous ignition. The power relative to weight is high, but the density is low, so the brisance is low as well. Ignition by a fuse alone is sometimes unreliable. The charge should be detonated within 5 minutes of soaking, but even after 15 minutes it may be capable of exploding, even though weaker and with production of carbon dioxide.

An oxyliquit explosive can be accidentally made by spilling liquid oxygen on tarmac during filling high-altitude airplane systems. The pavement then can become sufficiently explosive to be initiated by walking on it; the oxygen evaporates soon, though.

At first, liquid air, self-enriched by standing (nitrogen has a lower boiling point and evaporates preferentially) was used, but pure liquid oxygen gives better results.

A mixture of lampblack and liquid oxygen was measured to have detonation velocity of 3,000 m/s, and 4 to 12% more strength than dynamite. However, the flame it makes has too long duration to be safe in possible presence of explosive gases, so oxyliquits found their use mostly in open quarries and strip mining.

47.2 History

The explosive properties of these mixtures were discovered in Germany in 1895 by Prof. Carl von Linde, a developer of a successful machine for liquefaction of gases, who named them oxyliquits.

In 1930, over 3 million pounds of liquid oxygen were used for this purpose in Germany alone, and additional 201,466 lb (91,383 kg) were consumed by British quarries. The accident rate was lower than with conventional explosives. However, the Dewar flasks the LOX was stored in occasionally exploded, which was caused by iron impurities in the activated carbon serving as trace gas absorbent in the insulation vacuum layer in the flask, which caused spontaneous ignition in case of LOX leak into the enclosed space.

Use of oxyliquits during World War II was low, as there was a plentiful supply of nitrates obtained from synthetic ammonia.

Due to the complicated machinery required for manufacture of liquid oxygen, oxyliquit explosives were used mostly only where their consumption was high. In the United States, some such locations were the strip mines in coal mining areas of the Midwest. Its consumption peaked in 1953 with 10,190 tons, but then decreased until zero in 1968, when it was totally replaced with even cheaper ANFO.

47.3 Fiction

Oxyliquit explosive was prepared *ad hoc* from sugar and liquid oxygen from an oxygen bottle to blast a hole in a collapsed cave in Stanisław Lem's 1951 novel *The Astronauts*. The same device was used in Andy Weir's novel *The Martian* to cause the intentional depressurization of a spaceship by blasting the airlock door.

47.4 External links

- Google Groups, alt.engr.explosives old literature on Oxyliquit - alt.engr.explosives
- Liquid Oxygen Explosives Page seems to be broken. Archived version on the Internet Archive.

Chapter 48

Panclastite

Panclastites are a class of Sprengel explosives similar to oxyliquits. They were first suggested in 1881 by Eugène Turpin, a French chemist. They are a mixture of liquid dinitrogen tetroxide serving as oxidizer with a suitable fuel, e.g. carbon disulfide, in the 3:2 volume ratio. Other fuel being used is nitrobenzene.*[1] Possible alternative fuels are e.g. nitrotoluene, gasoline, nitromethane, or halocarbons.

Panclastites are shock-sensitive and difficult to handle, requiring their mixing immediately before use; also the dinitrogen tetroxide is highly corrosive and explodes in contact with some chemicals. Despite their brisance and detonation velocity being comparable with TNT, panclastites have virtually no use today.

During World War I, due to shortages of other explosives, French used some panclastite-class mixtures, which they called **anilites**, in small aircraft bombs. The mixing of the chemicals was triggered by airflow spinning a propeller on the nose of the bomb after it was dropped, mixing the previously separated chemicals inside. The resulting mixture was so sensitive the bombs did not need a fuze to explode on impact.

In the 1880s, Germans were testing torpedoes with panclastite warhead. Carbon disulfide and nitrogen tetroxide were stored in separate glass compartments, which were broken when the torpedo was launched and the chemicals mixed, and later were detonated by a contact fuse.

48.1 References

[1] "Re: Panclastite". Newsgroup: alt.engr.explosives. 1998-06-30. Usenet: 6natdcsqa1@news01.btx.dtag.de.

48.2 External links

- The Journal of the Society of Chemical Industry. April 29, 1886: NOTE ON SO-CALLED "PANCLASTITE." BY H. SPRENGEL, PH.D., F.R.S.

48.3 Text and image sources, contributors, and licenses

48.3.1 Text

- **Explosive material** *Source:* https://en.wikipedia.org/wiki/Explosive_material?oldid=742212235 *Contributors:* AxelBoldt, The Epopt, Bryan Derksen, The Anome, Koyaanis Qatsi, XJaM, Rmhermen, Karen Johnson, Ghakko, Roadrunner, Ray Van De Walker, Jtoomim, Rmrf1024, Heron, Stevertigo, Dwmyers, Patrick, Mtmsmile, JohnOwens, Michael Hardy, Odin~enwiki, Collabi, Ixfd64, Gbleem, Looxix~enwiki, Ahoerstemeier, Andrewa, Julesd, Mulad, Hollgor, Denni, IceKarma, Big Bob the Finder, Stormie, Pakaran, Johnleemk, Riddley, Gentgeen, Robbot, MrJones, 1984, Korath, WormRunner, Securiger, Lowellian, Mayooranathan, Stewartadcock, Tobycat, Hadal, Ddstretch, Buster2058, Centrx, Smjg, DocWatson42, Tom harrison, TorreFernando, Everyking, No Guru, Snowdog, Leonard G., Yekrats, Eequor, Solipsist, Bobblewik, Edcolins, Mobius, Bacchiad, Gadfium, Calm, Gdr, Xmnemonic, Knutux, Beland, Jossi, Jasco, Sam Hocevar, Chadernook, Neutrality, Deglr6328, Metahacker, Oskar Sigvardsson, Freakofnurture, Venu62, Diagonalfish, Discospinster, Rich Farmbrough, Guanabot, Cacycle, Paulr~enwiki, ArnoldReinhold, Xezbeth, Bender235, Hapsiainen, SElefant, MisterSheik, Pt, Sietse Snel, Triona, Femto, Peter M Gerdes, Truthflux, Hurricane111, Ypacarai, Peter Eedy, Kjkolb, Codeman~enwiki, Haham hanuka, Hooperbloob, Glaucus, Ocohen, Jumbuck, Freako, Jérôme, Mrzaius, Alansohn, Sherurcij, Sl, ABCD, ScooterSES, Mac Davis, Alex '05, Katefan0, Bart133, Wtmitchell, Leoadec, Amorymeltzer, Shoefly, SteinbDJ, Gene Nygaard, KTC, Oleg Alexandrov, Woohookitty, ScottDavis, LeeJacksonKing, GregorB, Graham87, Deltabeignet, Canderson7, Ketiltrout, Rjwilmsi, CustardJack, WoodenTaco, The Engineer~enwiki, Salix alba, Vegaswikian, Sango123, Kevinpcoles, Editdroid, FlaBot, Mishuletz, Chanting Fox, HERMiT cRAB, Gurch, Simishag, Alphachimp, Esoterica, YurikBot, RobotE, Midgley, RussBot, Bergsten, Yyy, Shaddack, Rsrikanth05, David R. Ingham, Thatoneguy, Welsh, Megapixie, Icelight, Pyrotec, Misza13, Alex43223, Dbfirs, Kkmurray, The Spith, Georgewilliamherbert, 21655, Lt-wiki-bot, Closedmouth, Arthur Rubin, Tdangkhoa, Reyk, Wikiwawawa, Tierce, Kungfuadam, ToolmAKER, Segv11, Mardus, Eog1916, Yvwv, SmackBot, Nihonjoe, Reedy, Royalguard11, McGeddon, Pgk, Tbonnie, Jrockley, Delldot, Sam8, Cessator, Boris Barowski, W!B:, Edgar181, Gilliam, Ohnoitsjamie, Hmains, Cabe6403, Rmosler2100, Armeria, Chris the speller, Robroy114, Snori, Deli nk, Uthbrian, CSWarren, Audriusa, Yidisheryid, Thisisbossi, Zazpot, Rrburke, Mugaliens, MilitaryTarget, Hoof Hearted, RolandR, A.R., Copysan, Pilotguy, Srikeit, John, Jidanni, Vgy7ujm, Kipala, LWF, Tim Q. Wells, Goodnightmush, Scetoaux, Nobunaga24, BillFlis, Kelusky m, Anonymous anonymous, Novangelis, Acetylcholine, D1000, Asyndeton, Scoops-uk, Hitwhereithurts, JMK, Vxkitty, Justjohnny, Exander, Tawkerbot2, Stifynsemons, CRGreathouse, CmdrObot, Anakata, NickW557, ShelfSkewed, MarsRover, Fortran~enwiki, Mattbuck, Gogo Dodo, Adolphus79, Pascal.Tesson, Tawkerbot4, Roberta F., Nabokov, Viridae, Marek69, Mikeeg555, Uruiamme, Dawnseeker2000, EdJogg, AntiVandalBot, Seaphoto, Tmopkisn, Dylan Lake, Sbarnard, Canadian-Bacon, MikeLynch, JAnDbot, Leuko, RastaKins, Airbreather, Goldenfool, Robsavoie, Magioladitis, Bongwarrior, VoABot II, Foochar, Bubba hotep, Gabriel Kielland, Allstarecho, JaGa, WLU, Locewtus, Nopira, Gwern, MartinBot, CliffC, Zouavman Le Zouave, KTo288, Wiki Raja, Captain panda, Ckielstra, Jmm6f488, Ali, Rjsheehan, Uncle Dick, Tdadamemd, It Is Me Here, Lionmaster15, Notreallydavid, Daniblanco, Belovedfreak, Vanished user 39948282, YKgm, Nehpetskenawi, Xnuala, Cactus Guru, Jameslwoodward, Sześćsetsześćdziesiątsześć, TXiKiBoT, Oshwah, Nicholasnice, Slysplace, Jaws 321, Davidbooth, StillTrill, Logon88, SQL, Cantiorix, MajorHazard, MCTales, Seresin, Worldidol, Symane, The cov, SieBot, Schmoop, Cae prince, Arda Xi, Flyer22 Reborn, Smruss2000, Redmarkviolinist, Sr4delta, AMbot, Hamiltondaniel, Wikidaily2, ClueBot, Foxj, The Thing That Should Not Be, Lawrence Cohen, Ndenison, VQuakr, Jmn100, Niceguyedc, MARKELLOS, Auntof6, 12wert, Iyaayas, Ktr101, Excirial, Apelbaum, Socrates2008, Jusdafax, Anon lynx, Evertw, DJSparky, EhJJ, ChrisHodgesUK, Thewellman, Saenzc, Meske, Slayer41, Sgt. Salt, Mdeby, DumZiBoT, InternetMeme, XLinkBot, Spitfire, Mattyrigby00, P30Carl, WikHead, WikiDao, Skyhawk0005, Model122, Thebestofall007, Blackspotw, Addbot, Jmcinerney6, Fyrael, NjardarBot, Image151, Jlt1995, Numbo3-bot, Tide rolls, Lightbot, Zorrobot, Legobot, Luckas-bot, Yobot, II MusLiM HyBRiD II, Bdog9121, Nallimbot, AnomieBOT, Materialscientist, The High Fin Sperm Whale, Straight-shooter(42), Xqbot, G1235711, Nickkid5, Ryzer777, J04n, RibotBOT, Horst Emscher, GhalyBot, A.amitkumar, Bekus, FrescoBot, Pillcrow, Remotelysensed, Justsail, Crazychinchilla, Sea King 27, Redrose64, Rdxshubham, I dream of horses, A412, Calmer Waters, V.narsikar, Wikitanvir, Jujutacular, Full-date unlinking bot, Jauhienij, TobeBot, LCE1506, Lotje, Yopure, DARTH SIDIOUS 2, Mean as custard, Bhawani Gautam, NitricAcidandTHC, EmausBot, Kwm0707, GoingBatty, Tommy2010, ScienceRulez, Ronk01, ZéroBot, Fæ, DoesNotFollow, Wayne Slam, ChemMater, Sbmeirow, Donner60, Ego White Tray, Nmaxcom, ChuispastonBot, Ebehn, Whoop whoop pull up, Gwen-chan, ClueBot NG, Corsava, Gilderien, Stevenxlead, Explosives101, O.Koslowski, LightBringer, Widr, Mitch9harry, Lynxx2, Explodo-nerd, Justinbkay, Mr.Chow69, 11bo53, SodaAnt, Aisteco, Phoenixia1177, Samwalton9, Hghyux, Mdann52, Aginwald, ChrisGualtieri, FoCuSandLeArN, Openflower, SFK2, محمد شعيب, T42N24T, Reatlas, Icemanwcs, Soham, Jaybird7of9, OvidNaso, Kahtar, BHBrunt, Lizia7, DudeWithAFeud, Monkbot, Jbodenman, Uboa297, Trolludaily, Gokarting54, Caealn, Aoroundlake, DarkerChild, DreamWeaver87, KasparBot, James Hare (NIOSH), Khriswithhomies, Tegh420curry, Baking Soda, Razgriz51, Tamara Tloftibē, Melinda Muckson and Anonymous: 522

- **Explosion** *Source:* https://en.wikipedia.org/wiki/Explosion?oldid=740012003 *Contributors:* Bryan Derksen, The Anome, Karen Johnson, Peterlin~enwiki, Patrick, Dominus, Ixfd64, Mdebets, Ahoerstemeier, Mac, Glenn, Smack, Reddi, Tempshill, Kukuri, Jni, Robbot, Cdang, ChrisO~enwiki, Mushroom, Tea2min, Jordon Kalilich, Dbenbenn, DavidCary, Tom harrison, Bkonrad, Bensaccount, Solipsist, Wmahan, Alexf, LiDaobing, Antandrus, Oneiros, Icairns, Joyous!, Sonett72, Ta bu shi da yu, Archer3, Discospinster, Rich Farmbrough, Westendgirl, Paul August, Violetriga, FirstPrinciples, MBisanz, Hayabusa future, Tom, C1k3, Triona, Orlady, Bobo192, Smalljim, Orbst, Viriditas, Bert Hickman, Kjkolb, Darwinek, PassW0rd, Alansohn, Anthony Appleyard, Oasisbob, Tek022, Andrewpmk, Tezeti, Redfarmer, Kfitzgib, Mysdaao, Wtshymanski, Cal 1234, Shoefly, Bsadowski1, Blaxthos, Ataru, Camw, BeenBeren, Uncle G, WadeSimMiser, Bhound89, Trice25, Eternalsleeper, Tutmosis, RedxelaSinnak, BD2412, Rjwilmsi, Brucelee, The Engineer~enwiki, Vegaswikian, Krash, The wub, Dar-Ape, FlaBot, G Clark, Gold Stur, Latka, Crazycomputers, Nivix, Ahipple, Gurch, DiamondDave~enwiki, Alphachimp, BradBeattie, Narvalo, Scimitar, Chobot, DVdm, WillMcC, Ahpook, Hall Monitor, EamonnPKeane, YurikBot, Extraordinary Machine, RussBot, Rxnd, Red Slash, Stephenb, Kyorosuke, NawlinWiki, Robbie314, Eriethonan, Badagnani, NickBush24, Gerben49~enwiki, Darker Dreams, Bmdavll, Stevenwmccrary58, Ospalh, Gadget850, Bota47, Wknight94, Vortigern, FF2010, Zzuuzz, Silverhorse, Closedmouth, Aeon1006, Fram, RenamedUser jaskldjslak904, Paul Erik, Ghazer~enwiki, Yvwv, SmackBot, Alan Pascoe, Bobet, Slashme, KnowledgeOfSelf, Proficient, C.Fred, KocjoBot~enwiki, Edgar181, Xaosflux, Yamaguchi 先生, PeterSymonds, Pzavon, Gilliam, Ohnoitsjamie, Hmains, Skizzik, Martial Law, Squiddy, Chris the speller, Bluebot, Bidgee, SchfiftyThree, Stevage, Deli nk, DHN-bot~enwiki, Egsan Bacon, John Hyams, MadameArsenic, Darthgriz98, Rrburke, Storm05, COMPFUNK2, Jumping cheese, CanDo, Downwards, Dreadstar, DMacks, Hrimfaxi, Pilotguy, TenPoundHammer, SashatoBot, ArglebargleIV, Robomaeyhem, Soap, Euchiasmus, Peterlewis, IronGargoyle, Optakeover, Mets501, Ryulong, Acetylcholine, Xionbox, BranStark, ILovePlankton, Iridescent, Charliemeyers, Walton One, Twas Now, Hyperman 42, Lindsey8417, Tawkerbot2, Daniel5127, LMcBrutus, JForget, Makeem-

48.3. TEXT AND IMAGE SOURCES, CONTRIBUTORS, AND LICENSES

lighter, Ilikefood, Mika1h, WeggeBot, INVERTED, Michaelas10, Gogo Dodo, Mysernnm, Daniel J. Leivick, Gproud, Doug Weller, Nabokov, Danogo, UberScienceNerd, EnglishEfternamn, Thijs!bot, Epbr123, Kablammo, N5iln, Mojo Hand, Marek69, John254, StudentJCase, Escarbot, I already forgot, AntiVandalBot, Luna Santin, CZmarlin, TimVickers, Chaosman, Farosdaughter, Salgueiro~enwiki, Dallas84, Mcgillismusic, JAnDbot, Husond, MER-C, Time3000, Kerotan, Hey girlz, Bongwarrior, VoABot II, JamesBWatson, Kevinmon, Mtd2006, Boffob, Justanother, LorenzoB, DerHexer, Esanchez7587, WLU, Mczech1111, Tserton, DancingPenguin, MartinBot, Mabahandula, Arjun01, Foraminifera, Viking10, AlexiusHoratius, Fusion7, Jargon777, LedgendGamer, Tgeairn, J.delanoy, Rgoodermote, Adavidb, Tdadamemd, Barts1a, Kataiaveno, 2IzSz, McSly, Gurchzilla, Igotthecool, Youngjim, Bobianite, Abridger, Juliancolton, CardinalDan, Zeltar, Signalhead, Hugo999, Vranak, X!, VolkovBot, Cireshoe, AInoktaBOT, Aesopos, Philip Trueman, TXiKiBoT, Oshwah, Technopat, Qxz, Someguy1221, GIJoe fan113, Plus-media, Cremepuff222, Maxim, Lejarrag, Crypu, Mathero98, Kali97, Lamro, THOMASNATOR, Enviroboy, Why Not A Duck, Chenzw, Twooars, AlleborgoBot, Logan, Metalmario128, Agent 918, Jxw13, Matt Gerber, JieBot, CuPo, VVVBot, Mungo Kitsch, The way, the truth, and the light, Big Dazz, Arda Xi, Flyer22 Reborn, Radon210, Wilson44691, TragicallySuave, Steven Crossin, Greatrobo76, Biali95, Billa2101, 9ot icGull, Duolih65, Wuhwuzdat, Anyeverybody, 19Edgar5, ClueBot, LAX, Strider12233, The Thing That Should Not Be, Jan1nad, Drmies, Uncle Milty, SuperHamster, Niceguyedc, Chicmagnet920, Shustov, Excirial, Quercus basaseachicensis, Jusdafax, CrazyChemGuy, Anon lynx, Tomeasy, Reperspliter, Floydrox, Vivio Testarossa, Cenarium, Firstwesleyfan, Russianchica, Redthoreau, Thehelpfulone, Aitias, SoxBot III, NERIC-Security, XLinkBot, Rror, Onehundredtrillion, Nepenthes, Facts707, Ickyice, Vianello, WikiOverdose, Addbot, Some jerk on the Internet, Tcncv, Jatinshome, Ronhjones, Fieldday-sunday, Sexdude101, Gbelter, Vishnava, CanadianLinuxUser, NjardarBot, Download, Dudemeister1234, Tyranlord, AndersBot, Tongeh, Kyle1278, West.andrew.g, Ya2020, Jane819, AshleyX3, Tide rolls, Smeagol17, Krano,   , Bartledan, Frehley, Luckas-bot, Yobot, Happyboy3, Thatgains, Beeswaxcandle, CinchBug, A Stop at Willoughby, AnomieBOT, KDS4444, DemocraticLuntz, Jim1138, AdjustShift, Kingpin13, Materialscientist, The High Fin Sperm Whale, Citation bot, Belasted, Capricorn42, Jmundo, Abigail-Abernathy, Fred the leprechaun, Omar77, 78.26, Zubair93, GNRY09, Neil Clancy, Boi.haha, Interstellar Man, BoomerAB, Joshu2449, FrescoBot, Doolijo6, Sky Attacker, MetalMan01, Flamingeagles, Skymath, Hotelexplosion, Dr.hippy2, Phallicmonster, Tetraedycal, DivineAlpha, Citation bot 1, Telamonz, Pinethicket, Duckmanhoop, Explocontrol, SpaceFlight89, Minno72, Σ, Stephen234, Reconsider the static, Hay202, TobeBot, PiRSquared17, Zkr34m0, Diannaa, Vanished user aoiowaiuyr894isdik43, Adi4094, Suffusion of Yellow, Ufailbad, Shpriggs, RjwilmsiBot, TeleportingLizard, DASHBot, EmausBot, Az29, AnonymousHippopotomus, Naraic101, Socerguy89, Tommy2010, OMFGHAXOR, Wikipelli, Erpert, 15turnsm, Ratcat97, ZéroBot, DistillSpirit, Shuipzv3, Ricobro400, Aeonx, EWikist, Caspertheghost, AManWithNoPlan, Smartmannnm, L Kensington, Damirgraffiti, Bomazi, TYelliot, ClueBot NG, Noothernames, Mauvekapibara, Sam.owns, Peace Maker AI, Ultramegachicken, MajorWheezy, Widr, PowerFiddle, Mimik531, Zaxcord, Noahcallaghan, Wbm1058, Heildisney, Nilballa, Boomermankid666, Cookiemonster56, Lowercase sigmabot, BG19bot, WallEwilson, Doyouknowmeh28, Blake Burba, Alf.laylah.wa.laylah, MusikAnimal, JacobTrue, Solomon7968, Mark Arsten, Blahone1, Altaïr, Supernerd11, Mnfcp, Ricordisamoa, Hurricanefan24, Glaciafox, Kriskkiscool, Anbu121, Hyperpanda42, David.moreno72, Th4n3r, Udderfly, ChrisGualtieri, Chrisvelnet, Nicolas due, Lugia2453, Frosty, Rudivittori, Clagghead, GidenFTW, Telfordbuck, Cor Ferrum, GrieferHellYea, Reatlas, Fmc47, Leemans1015, Inkorbin, Eyesnore, Froglich, Blaziken1324, Glaisher, Zenibus, Califragic, Ginsuloft, D Eaketts, GreenGoldfish17, Wikieditor1002lel, The Red Morrigan, XPluvah, FriendlyCaribou, Mootisma, Everybody is an idiot, I the great and powerful one, AlvaroMolina, Explosivepoop, Devwebtel, Vgtfrynhgfhjrjgfejgr, Xlvii435, Lbgold00, KasparBot, ThatAwesomePenguin, CAPTAIN RAJU, WoPower, Jeffable101 and Anonymous: 573

- **Explosive weapon** Source: https://en.wikipedia.org/wiki/Explosive_weapon?oldid=681637658 Contributors: GCarty, Anthony Appleyard, BD2412, Jrtayloriv, Thomasnash, Neelix, Rmoyes, N5iln, Legaiaflame, Goodvac, XLinkBot, Yobot, Materialscientist, J04n, Coltsfan, Mark Schierbecker, Shadowjams, Hillarin, Butterzopf, Toilet10293847566574839201, Gob Lofa, ChrisGualtieri, XXzoonamiXX and Anonymous: 8

- **Fuel** Source: https://en.wikipedia.org/wiki/Fuel?oldid=740803630 Contributors: Derek Ross, Andre Engels, Rmhermen, Ben-Zin~enwiki, Heron, Ewen, Edward, Patrick, Ahoerstemeier, Stan Shebs, Mac, Angela, Александър, Glenn, Sugarfish, Tpbradbury, Taxman, Shantavira, Twang, Robbot, Moriori, Academic Challenger, Hadal, Sterlingda, Mushroom, Centrx, Bensaccount, Yekrats, Sundar, Zoney, Avala, Jackol, Kandar, Utcursch, Antandrus, Icairns, Sam Hocevar, Discospinster, Zaheen, Rich Farmbrough, Clawed, Vsmith, Florian Blaschke, User2004, Roybb95~enwiki, Leandros, Mani1, ESkog, Kbh3rd, RJHall, Hayabusa future, Shanes, Femto, Bobo192, Viriditas, Cmdrjameson, Solar, MPerel, Jumbuck, LtNOWIS, Mo0, Arthena, SlimVirgin, Walkerma, Danaman5, Computerjoe, Dennis Bratland, Smokeala, KelisFan2K5, JeffTK, Novacatz, Woohookitty, RHaworth, Trwh~enwiki, Rocastelo, MONGO, Kralizec!, Wayward, Yesukai, JohnJohn, Ashmoo, BD2412, RadioActive~enwiki, Sjö, Sjakkalle, Rjwilmsi, Vary, Vegaswikian, RobertG, AdnanSa, Margosbot~enwiki, Acefitt, Mongreilf, King of Hearts, Chobot, DVdm, Banaticus, YurikBot, Wavelength, Andrea Ronza, RussBot, Stephenb, Rsrikanth05, Salsb, Wimt, NawlinWiki, Grafen, StarTrekkie, Hogne, Cholmes75, Tony1, Kkmurray, Nlu, FF2010, Deltastyle, Closedmouth, BorgQueen, JLaTondre, Caballero1967, Erudy, Pankkake, Amalthea, SmackBot, Blue520, Edgar181, Gilliam, Skizzik, Anwar saadat, Chris the speller, Lazyquasar~enwiki, Octahedron80, Darth Panda, Can't sleep, clown will eat me, TheGerm, Addshore, SundarBot, Wizardman, Mion, Will Beback, John, Mbeychok, Minna Sora no Shita, Bjankuloski06en~enwiki, Michael miceli, Fender5, Nwwaew, Onionmon, Vinccecate, Hu12, OnBeyondZebrax, Exander, Kthemank, Tawkerbot2, Fvasconcellos, Mikiemike, Asm79, Stebulus, Asknine, Gogo Dodo, Longhornsg, Wikipediarules2221, RottweilerCS, Omicronpersei8, Khamar, JamesAM, Epbr123, Pajz, Ajwt2, AndrewDressel, Gralo, John254, X201, JustAGal, Radio Guy, Ambarawa~enwiki, Escarbot, AntiVandalBot, CodeWeasel, Paste, Nseidm1, Danger, North Shoreman, Dallas84, JAnDbot, Husond, Hydro, Arch dude, .Absolution., Steveprutz, Acroterion, Ecki~enwiki, Bongwarrior, VoABot II, Rich257, Brusegadi, Catgut, MetsBot, 28421u2232nfenfcenc, Alistarecho, Beagel, Johnbrownsbody, Oroso, Hdt83, Twigletmac, Anaxial, Keith D, R'n'B, J.delanoy, Rgoodermote, Extransit, Icseaturtles, AtholM, Engineer shoaib, Belovedfreak, KylieTastic, Fr33kman, Wikieditor06, ABF, Pparazorback, Mercurish, Philip Trueman, TXiKiBoT, KeithRoss, Plenumchamber~enwiki, Yilloslime, Melsaran, Anthrcer, PDFbot, Wiae, Madhero88, Roland Kaufmann, RandomXYZb, Synthebot, 'Altermike, Enviroboy, Monty845, Tiddly Tom, Speed Air Man, Kazanrao, Krawi, Caltas, Matthew Yeager, Flyer22 Reborn, Tiptoety, Oda Mari, OKBot, LidiaFourdraine, Explicit, Tanvir Ahmmed, ClueBot, NickCT, Ψ−113μ, HalsTireCentreAdBot, Jlglex, Erik Musbach, Fuelie, Excirial, Jusdafax, Sun Creator, Okiefromokla, Aitias, 20percent, Bc biranavi, SilvonenBot, Alexius08, Cpt.madman, Addbot, ERK, Willking1979, DOI bot, Betterusername, Atethnekos, Theleftorium, CarsracBot, Froggabbiggle, Azx2, Tide rolls, Lightbot, OC Ripper, Zorrobot, Luckas-bot, Anon mouse14, Wikipedian2, Synchronism, AnomieBOT, Galoubet, 9258fahsflkh917fas, Materialscientist, Danno uk, Citation bot, Xqbot, Addihockey10, JimVC3, Capricorn42, Anna Frodesiak, Callumpuffy, Enigmatist23, Shadowjams, Tobby72, Sebastiangarth, NCS2004, Chunyee12, Citation bot 1, XxTimberlakexx, Pinethicket, I dream of horses, Cameron marical, 10metreh, Calmer Waters, Turian, TobeBot, Lotje, Tbhotch, Reach Out to the Truth, Minimac, DARTH SIDIOUS 2, Mean as custard, Animalmad122, EmausBot, Dcirovic, K6ka, Bxtrby, ZéroBot, Fæ, Akshat.mundra, Pioner70, H3llBot, Makecat, L Kensington, U25, Donner60, Subrata Roy, ChuispastonBot, Sven Manguard, Petrb, ClueBot NG, Satellizer, Artybald, Teddles206, Frietjes, Widr, Morgan Riley, Helpful Pixie Bot, HMSSolent, KD888, John Cummings, Dan653,

Mark Arsten, Aranea Mortem, Writ Keeper, ارزن گ, Shaun, Huzefamohammed, ChrisGualtieri, ZappaOMati, None but shining hours, Ekren, MadGuy7023, JYBot, EleriWall, Frosty, Analogous89, Telfordbuck, C5st4wr6ch, Hasana12367, Eachandall, PhantomTech, Johnscotaus, DavidLeighEllis, Haminoon, Achmad Fahri, Hasan Kheireddine, UY Scuti, Thenextneo42, FrB.TG, JaconaFrere, Gaerteuth, Monkbot, TheTechnicLord, TranquilHope, TheMagikCow, Bnomedia2014, AlmostBatman, Kumar.nura, Esquivalience, Zortwort, Srghcguccuyucugcuyvyu, Swissjman, KasparBot, Oluwa2Chainz, Carbon zenith, Taco400, Jetfuel6969, 800a.dCaveman, Quickstrike, Newt1986, CLCStudent, Beyond Bozo, Klaus Schmidt-Rohr, GreenC bot, Bender the Bot and Anonymous: 454

- **Oxidizing agent** Source: https://en.wikipedia.org/wiki/Oxidizing_agent?oldid=740773759 Contributors: Dwmyers, Netizen, Lowellian, Bensaccount, Zeimusu, Chiu frederick, Maximaximax, H Padleckas, Poccil, Vsmith, ESkog, Reinyday, Arcadian, Kappa, Alphax, Nhandler, Benjah-bmm27, Kmill, Wtmitchell, Cburnett, Skatebiker, Username314, V8rik, Ctdunstan, HappyCamper, Ffaarr, Gurch, Dalef, Physchim62, Chobot, YurikBot, Member, Grafen, Kkmurray, Lt-wiki-bot, Reyk, AGToth, Itub, Hydrogen Iodide, Thunderboltz, Alksub, Edgar181, Gilliam, Ohnoitsjamie, Bluebot, Sixsous~enwiki, Bduke, Mark Riehm, Ajaxkroon, Subcreature, WinstonSmith, Smokefoot, Clean Copy, Drphilharmonic, Scharks, Danilcha, J. Finkelstein, Chrisch, Newone, Jamesy, RSido, Nczempin, WeggeBot, Grein, Asknine, Al Lemos, Morgana The Argent, Paul from Michigan, Shirt58, Jj137, Kainino, JAnDbot, Avjoska, Grimlock, Fiaworldrally, Ben Ram, SJP, Philip Trueman, TXiKiBoT, BotKung, Brianga, Gerakibot, Nopetro, Aruton, Steven Crossin, Naganaresh, Ernest P. Worrell, Mario Žamić, ClueBot, The Thing That Should Not Be, Sabri76, LarryMorseDCOhio, Versus22, Sami Lab, Siripswich, Addbot, Kongr43gpen, Jncraton, Favonian, ScAvenger, Yobot, Ptbotgourou, TaBOT-zerem, The Earwig, EryZ, GB fan, Xqbot, Br77rino, SassoBot, Louperibot, Pinethicket, Fuzbaby, Tinton5, Jauhienij, Johnnycpis, Wikiredox, Babizhet, Jeffrd10, Unbitwise, Ripchip Bot, EmausBot, Dcirovic, JSquish, Fintelia, Chemicalinterest, I10neorg, Whoop whoop pull up, ClueBot NG, Topper917, JohnSRoberts99, Curb Chain, Todan~enwiki, Swierdo, Mark Arsten, GoShow, EuroCarGT, Dexbot, ThunderSkunk, Frosty, The Ocean, NawlinWikiIsAnAssHat, Vindrop, Matiia, KasparBot and Anonymous: 185

- **Explosive booster** Source: https://en.wikipedia.org/wiki/Explosive_booster?oldid=735586581 Contributors: Bryan Derksen, Cimon Avaro, Peat, DocWatson42, Leonard G., Dan Gardner, Geni, Plugwash, Helix84, A2Kafir, Vegaswikian, Willemo, Groyolo, Lambiam, Tim Q. Wells, Nabokov, Thijs!bot, QuiteUnusual, Chill doubt, SieBot, Malcolmxl5, Stonejag, ClueBot, Addbot, FrescoBot, ChuispastonBot, M11rtinb and Anonymous: 13

- **Explosive train** Source: https://en.wikipedia.org/wiki/Explosive_train?oldid=723034452 Contributors: Delirium, GRAHAMUK, Riddley, LX, Dave6, Karn, Hooperbloob, A2Kafir, Blaxthos, Woohookitty, Descendall, Vegaswikian, SmackBot, Mibo, Tim Q. Wells, JossBuckle Swami, Anon lynx, Misha Vargas, Erik9bot, Jeremymclain and Anonymous: 11

- **Detonation velocity** Source: https://en.wikipedia.org/wiki/Detonation_velocity?oldid=680709374 Contributors: Tom harrison, Linuxlad, Anthony Appleyard, Shoefly, Kenyon, GregorB, Rjwilmsi, Vegaswikian, Theshibboleth, GeeJo, NickBush24, Ospalh, SmackBot, Reedy, Jrockley, Kevin Ryde, DHN-bot~enwiki, Lambiam, Tim Q. Wells, Esurnir, RSido, John Bastien, Uruiamme, Chill doubt, Jv9mmm, Idioma-bot, Kilmersan, Francis Flinch, SieBot, Wolfch, Anon lynx, Dthomsen8, Addbot, Luckas-bot, Yobot, ArthurBot, Brane.Blokar, LucienBOT, Wikitanvir, کاشف عقیل, Armando-Martin, ZéroBot, Virtualiter, BarrelProof, Primergrey, B.Laxmi.Venkatesh and Anonymous: 20

- **Sensitivity (explosives)** Source: https://en.wikipedia.org/wiki/Sensitivity_(explosives)?oldid=687386485 Contributors: Robsavoie, Fratrep, JLBot, Anon lynx, 7, Kruusamägi, Addbot, LarryJeff, Yobot, Xqbot, Twirligig, Dinamik-bot and Helpful Pixie Bot

- **Use forms of explosives** Source: https://en.wikipedia.org/wiki/Use_forms_of_explosives?oldid=719356259 Contributors: Apoc2400, Rjwilmsi, Vegaswikian, Georgewilliamherbert, Kvng, Rifleman 82, Gwen Gale, Yobot, RjwilmsiBot, BG19bot, EricEnfermero, Sharib Ahmad Khan, Flyboy38 and Anonymous: 7

- **Combustibility** Source: https://en.wikipedia.org/wiki/Combustibility?oldid=738543023 Contributors: Kku, Beland, Hooperbloob, Kolbasz, Chobot, DinosaursLoveExistence, Bejnar, 16@r, Mets501, Ahering@cogeco.ca, Iridescent, STBot, J.delanoy, MrBell, Oshwah, Flyer22 Reborn, Simmsa, ClueBot, Addbot, AnomieBOT, Daniele Pugliesi, Mopcop, ArthurBot, Jan van der Loos, FrescoBot, Salvio giuliano, Unreal7, BattyBot, Cyberbot II, Dark Silver Crow, PassinggTimee, SheikhTheBaby, GreenC bot and Anonymous: 18

- **Flammability** Source: https://en.wikipedia.org/wiki/Flammability?oldid=736272227 Contributors: Michael Hardy, Kku, Taxman, Academic Challenger, Texture, Macrakis, Beland, Setokaiba, Oskar Sigvardsson, Alistair1978, DaveGorman, Giraffedata, Pharos, Jérôme, Anthony Appleyard, Isaac, Suruena, Shoefly, Vuo, Skatebiker, Gene Nygaard, A D Monroe III, OwenX, Lost.goblin, Shreevatsa, Ekem, Dionyziz, V8rik, Hnandrew, Pjetter, XP1, FutureNJGov, Rockingbeat, Zimbabweed, YurikBot, Jimp, RussBot, Tetzcatlipoca, Bhny, Alynna Kasmira, Welsh, Nick C, Zwobot, Bayerischermann, BorgQueen, NeilN, SmackBot, KnowledgeOfSelf, Edgar181, Catalysto, Chris the speller, Hibernian, SquarePeg, Charles Nguyen, Cybercobra, Metta Bubble, MatthewBChambers, Kukini, Attys, Kuru, IsaacD, Jim Derby, Mbeychok, 16@r, Werdan7, Hramat, Ahering@cogeco.ca, Wizard191, Iridescent, Ale jrb, Kevin McE, The Font, Mircea.Vutcovici, Dgw, Tdw, Silentghost, Jon C., James086, Echo7tango, AntiVandalBot, Leuko, Roleplayer, VoABot II, Bubba hotep, Lenticel, Leyo, MrBell, Minesweeper.007, Beanbread, WinterSpw, VolkovBot, Panserbjørn, Anna Lincoln, Yillosime, Chrishibbard7, Raymondwinn, Venny85, Kilmer-san, Tomaxer, TheXenocide, Jauerback, SE16, LeadSongDog, Oxymoron83, Lohengrin1991, Correogsk, Piononno, Richard David Ramsey, Martarius, ClueBot, Binksternet, PipepBot, The Thing That Should Not Be, Binkleyz, Otolemur crassicaudatus, Reedy172, Puppy8800, DragonBot, Grahamlaws, Doprendek, Apparition11, EdChem, Addbot, Njsustain, TutterMouse, TheFreeloader, KaiKemmann, Il MusLiM HyBRiD Il, Tempodivalse, AnomieBOT, Dinesh smita, Materialscientist, Xqbot, Batticdoor, Tomas62, Shadowjams, FrescoBot, PigFlu Oink, Geoffreybernardo, Pinethicket, I dream of horses, TobeBot, Dinamik-bot, Vancouver Outlaw, Reaper Eternal, TreacherousWays, Monzac, Lucas Thoms, PJinBoston, ZéroBot, Unreal7, ClueBot NG, Cntras, Widr, JohnSRoberts99, Skoben, Isaac1207zeede, Mogism, Ashima sengupta, Mikayé, Littlefischie, Starfirefv603, Wscribner, Fangirl143 and Anonymous: 139

- **Deflagration** Source: https://en.wikipedia.org/wiki/Deflagration?oldid=741146594 Contributors: The Anome, Docu, Riddley, Robbot, Jredmond, Rtfisher, ElBenevolente, Xanzzibar, BenFrantzDale, Tom harrison, Tagishsimon, DragonflySixtyseven, Varuna, Ayeroxor, ProhibitOnions, Wtshymanski, Derktar, Firien, AndrewWatt, Strait, YurikBot, Victor falk, SmackBot, BluePlatypus, Edgar181, Pzavon, J Darnley, Henning Makholm, Tim Q. Wells, 16@r, Thijs!bot, Uruiamme, TimVickers, Forensicengineer, JAnDbot, Igodard, Albmont, Allstarecho, CommonsDelinker, Screen111, Idioma-bot, Shiggity, MikeChE, Qxz, Strappado~enwiki, Steven J. Anderson, Kilmer-san, Pablomdo, AlleborgoBot, Anon lynx, Deltaway, Addbot, Yobot, AnomieBOT, ArthurBot, Xqbot, Δζ, Remotelysensed, RedBot, Dcirovic, ClueBot NG, Stevenxlead, A szu, Bakunen, AFLmcgill, Ssscienccce, Athomeinkobe, Me, Myself, and I are Here, Meteor sandwich yum, Gargamol2000, KasparBot and Anonymous: 43

48.3. TEXT AND IMAGE SOURCES, CONTRIBUTORS, AND LICENSES

- **Detonation** *Source:* https://en.wikipedia.org/wiki/Detonation?oldid=740790925 *Contributors:* Patrick, Docu, Zoicon5, IceKarma, E23~enwiki, Rm, Omegatron, Elwoz, Riddley, Altenmann, Mushroom, Tom harrison, Leonard G., PFHLai, Sonett72, Gcanyon, O'Dea, Discospinster, Avriette, Igorivanov~enwiki, JJJJust, Brian0918, RJHall, Darwinek, Linuxlad, Anthony Appleyard, Oasisbob, Hu, Splintax, Trice25, M412k, Deltabeignet, Yurik, Rjwilmsi, Motorhead, Taichi, David R. Ingham, Catharticflux, Zwobot, Georgewilliamherbert, Cæruleum, Bernd in Japan, SmackBot, Man with two legs, Pzavon, Mibo, Brainfood, Tim Q. Wells, 16@r, BillFlis, Acetylcholine, NaBUru38, Richard Keatinge, Future Perfect at Sunrise, Gproud, Nabokov, Rcgy, Thijs!bot, Uruiamme, Orionus, Chill doubt, JAnDbot, Wasell, Albmont, Tiuks, Bieb, CommonsDelinker, Social tamarisk, Nwbeeson, Gracz54, Jeff G., TXiKiBoT, Reodor, SalJyDieBoereKomLei, Cwkmail, Hac13, Dolphin51, Mahendri, Murtarius, EMBaero, Shniken1, TimBilly1224, Wprth, 7, Kodster, Addbot, Donhoraldo, Cesiumfrog, Yobot, Donfbreed, OneAhead, AnomieBOT, Materialscientist, Citation bot, ArthurBot, Jeffrey Mall, Nagualdesign, Michael Nettleton, Gopherite, Vicenarian, Musicneologist, Dinamik-bot, Diannaa, Olawlor, Humble bin khalid, EmausBot, John of Reading, Lalacy, Coathpapercurric, Dcjrovic, ZéroBot, Druzhnik, AManWithNoPlan, DASHBotAV, Whoop whoop pull up, ClueBot NG, Astatine211, MerlIwBot, Bibcode Bot, Bakunen, Dough34, Gactrzult, Bender the Bot and Anonymous: 60

- **Brisance** *Source:* https://en.wikipedia.org/wiki/Brisance?oldid=707953552 *Contributors:* Gutsul, Riddley, Tom harrison, Finn-Zoltan, Decoy, Passw0rd, Pzoot, Shoefly, Alvis, TotoBaggins, GregorB, Vegaswikian, Wegsjac, YurikBot, Shaddack, Neilbeach, Sliggy, SmackBot, Geoff B. Armeria, Yaf, Fuhghettaboutit, Tim Q. Wells, Mikael V, Peripitus, Nabokov, Deflective, Magioladitis, V-Man737, Notreallydavid, Idiomabot, MajorHazard, Sevela.p, SieBot, K. Takeda~enwiki, DrK82, NillaGoon, PixelBot, Kruusamägi, Addbot, Mr0t1633, Lightbot, Knight2fly, Luckas-bot, AnomieBOT, Jim1138, LittleWink, Jfmantis, Armando-Martin, CarloMartinelli, Cyberbot II, Froglich, Evensteven, Vebinford and Anonymous: 21

- **Pressure** *Source:* https://en.wikipedia.org/wiki/Pressure?oldid=741234628 *Contributors:* AxelBoldt, Magnus Manske, Mav, Bryan Derksen, Zundark, The Anome, Tarquin, Cable Hills, Peterlin~enwiki, DavidLevinson, Jdpipe, Heron, Patrick, Infrogmation, Smelialichu, Michael Hardy, Tim Starling, Pit~enwiki, Fuzzie, GTBacchus, Delirium, Minesweeper, Egil, Mkweise, Ellywa, Ahoerstemeier, Mac, Александр, Glenn, Smack, GRAHAMUK, Halfdan, Ehn, Emperorbma, RodC, Charles Matthews, Jay, Pheon, DJ Clayworth, Tpbradbury, Jimbreed, Omegatron, Fvw, Robbot, Hankwang, Pigsonthewing, Chris 73, R3m0t, Peak, Merovingian, Bkell, Moink, Hadal, UtherSRG, Aetheling, Cronian~enwiki, Tea2min, Giftlite, Smjg, Harp, Wolfkeeper, Tom harrison, Herbee, Mark.murphy, Wwoods, Michael Devore, Bensaccount, Thierryc, Jackol, Simian, Gadium, Lst27, Anoopm, Ackerleytng, Jossi, DragonflySixtyseven, Johnflux, Icairns, Zfr, Sam Hocevar, Lindberg G Williams Jr, Urhixidur, Peter bertok, Sonett72, ELApro, Rich Farmbrough, Guanabot, Vsmith, Sam Derbyshire, Mani1, Paul August, MarkS, SpookyMulder, LemRobotry, Calair, Pmcm, Lankiveil, Joanjoc~enwiki, Shanes, Sietse Snel, RoyBoy, Spoon!, Bobo192, Marco Polo, Fir0002, Meggar, Duk, LeonardoGregianin, Evgeny, Foobaz, Dungodung, La goutte de pluie, Unused000701, MPerel, Hooperbloob, Musiphil, Alansohn, Brosen~enwiki, Dbeardsl, Jeltz, Goldom, Kotasik, Katana, PAR, Malo, Snowolf, Velella, Ish ishwar, Shoefly, Gene Nygaard, ZakuSage, Oleg Alexandrov, Reinoutr, Armando, Pol098, Commander Keane, Keta, Wocky, Isnow, Crucis, Gimboid13, Palica, FreplySpang, NebY, Koavf, Isaac Rabinovitch, RayC, Tawker, Daano15, Yamamoto Ichiro, FlaBot, Gurch, AlexCovarrubias, Takometer, Yggdrasilsroot, Srleffler, Ahunt, Chobot, DVdm, YurikBot, Zaidpjd~enwiki, Jimp, Spaully, Ytrottier, SpuriousQ, Stephenb, Gaius Cornelius, Yyy, Alex Bakharev, Bovineone, Wimt, NawlinWiki, Wiki alf, Test-tools~enwiki, Kdkeller, Dhollm, Moe Epsilon, Alex43223, JHCaufield, Scottfisher, Deeday-UK, FF2010, Light current, Johndburger, Redgolpe, HereToHelp, Tonyho, RG2, Protero, NeilN, ChemGardener, SmackBot, RDBury, Blue520, KocjoBot~enwiki, Jrockley, Gilliam, Skizzik, Jamie C, Bluebot, Audacity, NCurse, MK8, Oli Filth, MalafayaBot, SchfiftyThree, Complexica, Kourd, DHN-bot~enwiki, Colonies Chris, Zven, Suicidalhamster, Can't sleep, clown will eat me, DHeyward, Fiziker, JonHarder, Yidisheryid, Fuhghettaboutit, Tvaughn05, Bowlhover, Nakon, Kntrabssi, Dreadstar, Smokefoot, Drphilharmonic, Sadi Carnot, Ronaz, Cookie90, Sashato-Bot, Finejon, Dbtfz, Carnby, Gobonobo, Middlec, Tktktk, Mbeychok, BLUE, Chodorkovskiy, Pflatau, MarkSutton, Willy turner, Waggers, Peter Horn, Hgrobe, Shoeofdeath, Wjejskenewr, CharlesM, Courcelles, Tawkerbot2, Bstepp99, Petr Matas, Zakian49, Fnfal, WeggeBot, Gerhardt m, Cydebot, Fnlayson, Gogo Dodo, Rracecarr, Dancter, Odie5533, AndersFeder, Bookgrrl, Karuna8, Epbr123, Bot-maru, LeBofSportif, Headbomb, Marek69, Iviney, Greg L, Oreo Priest, Porqin, AntiVandalBot, Garbagecansrule, Opelio, Credema, Adz 619, B7582, JAnDbot, Hemingrubbish, MER-C, Nthep, Marsey04, Hello32020, Andonic, Easchiff, Magioladitis, Bongwarrior, VoABot II, JNW, Rivertorch, Midgrid, Dirac66, Chris G, DerHexer, Waninge, Yellowing, Mania112, Ashishbhatnagar72, Wikianon, Seba5618, MartinBot, Rob0571, LedgendGamer, J.delanoy, Trusilver, Piercetheorganist, Mike.lifeguard, Gzkn, Lantonov, Salih, Mikael Häggström, Yadevol, Warut, Belovedfreak, Cmichael, Fylwind, SlightlyMad, M bastow, TraceyR, Idioma-bot, VolkovBot, Trebacz, Martin Cole, Philip Trueman, Dbooksta, TXiKiBoT, Oshwah, Zidonuke, Malinaccier, Ranmamaru, Hqb, JayC, Qxz, Anna Lincoln, Jetforme, Martin451, From-cary, Zondi, Greg searle, Krushia, Vincent Grosskopf, Neparis, Admkushwaha, EJF, SieBot, Coffee, Springbreak04, Tresiden, Caltas, Arda Xi, AlonCoret, Flyer22 Reborn, Tiptoety, Antzervos, Oxymoron83, Sr4delta, Lightmouse, The Valid One, OKBot, Vituzzu, StaticGull, Anchor Link Bot, TheGreatMango, Geoff Plourde, Dolphin51, Denisarona, Xjwiki, Faithlessthewonderboy, Codyfinke6, ClueBot, LAX, The Thing That Should Not Be, Uxorion, Jan1nad, Smichr, Drmies, Mild Bill Hiccup, Wolvereness, Orthoepy, Liempt, DragonBot, Djr32, Excirial, SubstanceDx99, Joa po, Nigelleelee, Lartoven, Sun Creator, L1f07bscs0035, JamieS93, Razorflame, Plasmic Physics, Versus22, SoxBot III, Uri2~enwiki, Rvoorhees, Antti29, XLinkBot, BodhisattvaBot, FactChecker1199, TZGreat, Gotta catch 'em all yo, Gonfer, Fxzboy, WikiDao, Jpfru2, Addbot, AVand, Some jerk on the Internet, Vanished user kksudfijekkdfjlrd, Betterusername, Sir cumalot, Seán Travers, Ronhjones, Fieldday-sunday, Adrian147, CanadianLinuxUser, Fluffernutter, Morning277, Glane23, Favonian, Jasper Deng, 84user, Tide rolls, Lightbot, Cesiumfrog, Ralf Roletschek, Superboy112233, Jarble, HerculeBot, Snaily, Legobot, Luckas-bot, Yobot, Ht686rg90, AnomieBOT, DemocraticLuntz, Daniele Pugliesi, Sfaefaol, Jim1138, AdjustShift, Rudolf.hellmuth, Kingpin13, Nyanhtoo, Flewis, Bluerasberry, Materialscientist, Felyza, GB fan, LilHelpa, Jemandwicca, Xqbot, Transity, .45Colt, Jeffrey Mall, Wyklety, Gap9551, Time501, GrouchoBot, Derintelligente, ChristopherKingChemist, Mathonius, Energybender, Shadowjams, Keo Ross Sangster, Aaron Kauppi, SD5, Inveracious, BoomerAB, GliderMaven, Pascaldulieu, FrescoBot, LucienBOT, Tlork Thunderhead, BenzolBot, Jamesooders, Haein45, Pinethicket, I dream of horses, HRoestBot, Calmer Waters, Hamtechperson, Jschnur, RedBot, Marcmarroquin, Pbsouthwood, Jujutacular, Bgpaulus, Jonkerz, Navidh.ahmed, Vrenator, Darsie42, Jeffrd10, DARTH SIDIOUS 2, Onel5969, Mean as custard, DRAGON BOOSTER, Newty23125, William Shi, EmausBot, Tommy2010, Wikipelli, Dcirovic, K6ka, Thecheesykid, JSquish, Shuipzv3, Empty Buffer, Hazard-SJ, Quondum, Talyor Will, Morgankevinj, Perseus, Son of Zeus, Tls60, Orange Suede Sofa, RockMagnetist, DASHBotAV, 28bot, ClueBot NG, Jack Greenmaven, Mythicism, This lousy T-shirt, Neeraj1997, Cj005257, Frietjes, Jessica-NJITWILL, Braincricket, Angelo Michael, Widr, Christ1013, Rectangle546, Becarlson, Analwarrior, Wiki13, ElphiBot, Joydeep, Saurabhbaptista, Franz99, YVSREDDY, Cky2250, Matt Hayter, Shikhar1089, 李邦凯, Kasamasa, Anujjjj, Mrt3366, Jack No1, Shyncat, Avengingbandit, Forcez, JYBot, Librscorp, Mysterious Whisper, Superduck463, Frosty, Sriharsh1234, The Anonymouse, Reatlas, Resolution3.464, Paikrishnan, Masterbait123, Jasualcomni, DavidLeighEllis, Montyv, PanDaGirl, FizykLJF, Wyn.junior, Mahusha, Trackteur, Johnnprince203, Bog snorkeller, Crystallized-carbon, Jokeop, Gladamas, Alicemitchellweddingpressure, Esquivalience, Engmeas, KasparBot, JJMC89, CAPTAIN RAJU, Christofferekman, Vishrut Malik, Sharasque, Harmon758, Aditi Tripathi09, Gulercetin, BlueUndigo13, Daniel kenneth, Mizaan Shamaun and Anonymous: 783

- **Blasting cap** *Source:* https://en.wikipedia.org/wiki/Blasting_cap?oldid=741908067 *Contributors:* Heron, Julesd, Andres, Big Bob the Finder, Gwrede, DocWatson42, Bobblewik, Icairns, Nickptar, Fluzwup, Ibagli, Bender235, Kbh3rd, Harald Hansen, Duk, Kjkolb, A2Kafir, Mac Davis, Woohookitty, Linas, Bratsche, Trlovejoy, Ewlyahoocom, Aspro, YurikBot, FrenchIsAwesome, Fabartus, Gaius Cornelius, Shaddack, Brandon, Scs, Kkmurray, Georgewilliamherbert, Cynthia Bennett, SmackBot, Geoff B, Chris the speller, Snori, Halen~enwiki, AK7, Hvn0413, MikeLieman, Chetvorno, Mamanakis, Anakata, Bubblematrix, Rifleman 82, Nabokov, Dawnseeker2000, JAnDbot, Glrx, Uncle Dick, Dawright12, Balajijagadesh, MajorHazard, Bentogoa, Sfan00 IMG, Anon lynx, PixelBot, DJSparky, Addbot, GargoyleBot, Lightbot, Surv1v411st, Kopiersperre, Devper94, EmausBot, Rails, Thewolfchild, ClueBot NG, Helpful Pixie Bot, SolidLemonsoup, ShamanSommerfeld, SkateTier, SQMeaner, Bombacity and Anonymous: 54

- **Percussion cap** *Source:* https://en.wikipedia.org/wiki/Percussion_cap?oldid=740493912 *Contributors:* Andre Engels, Ray Van De Walker, Patrick, Notheruser, Jonik, Patrick0Moran, VikOlliver, Pibwl, Buster2058, DocWatson42, Ryanrs, Tom harrison, Lefty, Mcapdevila, Per Honor et Gloria, Bobblewik, Jrdioko, Edcolins, Jmueller71, Phil1988, AliveFreeHappy, Rama, Vsmith, GoClick~enwiki, Primalchaos, Mac Davis, TaintedMustard, GraemeLeggett, FlaBot, MacRusgail, Chobot, Benvenuto, YurikBot, 4C~enwiki, Tdevries, Hellbus, Hydrargyrum, Shaddack, Asams10, DisambigBot, Nick Michael, SmackBot, Hux, Chris the speller, Jprg1966, Yaf, Derekbridges, Petlif, Xmastree, BillFlis, SubSeven, MargyL, Nabokov, Aldis90, Thijs!bot, Dawnseeker2000, Noclevername, Chill doubt, Brain40, Thernlund, Mike Searson, Adamdaley, Robertgreer, NLW, Steel1943, VolkovBot, Rei-bot, CanOfWorms, One half 3544, Telecineguy, MCTales, Paul J Williams, SieBot, Cwkmail, Antonio Lopez, WikiBotas, Martarius, Counterparry, The Thing That Should Not Be, Jan1nad, Nick19thind, Socrates2008, Evertw, Wikirey2, SchreiberBike, Thewellman, DumZiBoT, Nukes4Tots, Addbot, Bahamut Star, Lightbot, Quantumobserver, Ricce, Legobot, Luckasbot, Yobot, KamikazeBot, AnomieBOT, Archon 2488, Xqbot, Gbchaosmaster, RibotBOT, Gruß Tom, Morgan5219, FrescoBot, Surv1v411st, Oktanyum, Techhead7890, Holly25, Samuraiantiqueworld, Sonicyouth86, AvocatoBot, Kendall-K1, MathewTownsend, BigPadge94, Historyphysics, Khazar2, SQMeaner, Bender the Bot and Anonymous: 44

- **Shock wave** *Source:* https://en.wikipedia.org/wiki/Shock_wave?oldid=741807794 *Contributors:* Ed Poor, Branden, Stevertigo, Lir, Nealmcb, Michael Hardy, Liftarn, Gbleem, Wiersma, Egil, Angela, Julesd, Nikai, Charles Matthews, Doradus, Furrykef, Omegatron, Twang, Zandperl, Bkell, Moink, Robinh, PBP, Wjbeaty, Giftlite, Wolfkeeper, Dratman, Bit~enwiki, Mboverload, Gracefool, Mateuszica, Pgan002, Karol Langner, Imjustmatthew, Sonett72, Deglr6328, Zowie, Gschmidt, FT2, Quietly, Femto, Cmdrjameson, Kjkolb, Linuxlad, Anthony Appleyard, Chris McFeely, ליאיר, Echuck215, Hohum, Cburnett, Daquake, Raygirvan, Woohookitty, PatGallacher, Polyparadigm, Tabletop, GregorB, Magister Mathematicae, Thierry Dugnolle~enwiki, Lasunncty, JIP, Rjwilmsi, SeanMack, Colin Holgate, Arnero, RexNL, Kolbasz, Tardis, LeCire~enwiki, Deklund, Ahpook, YurikBot, Wavelength, Retaggio, Hairy Dude, RussBot, Hellbus, Stephenb, Shaddack, Trovatore, Prickus, Eudoxie, Light current, Reyk, Sean Whitton, BorgQueen, AKAF, SmackBot, Betacommand, Bluebot, Egg plant, Rrburke, Dreadstar, RichAromas, Just plain Bill, Andrei Stroe, MegaHasher, Jaganath, Peterlewis, J Crow, BillFlis, Tac2z, Antwan718, Ace Class Shadow, Hu12, Ranny1, CmdrObot, Krauss, Nabokov, Obrian7, Settles1, Thijs!bot, Headbomb, Gerry Ashton, Davidhorman, Genick, AntiVandalBot, Rdupre, Wasell, DeMongo, LorenzoB, WLU, Philryan, Mythealias, R'n'B, CommonsDelinker, J.delanoy, Trusilver, Rlsheehan, Captain Infinity, Rteeter, Coppertwig, Nat682, Josephmpowers, Idioma-bot, Cuzkatzimhut, ABF, AresAndEnyo, A4bot, Rei-bot, USferdinand, Piperh, Ourli, Spiral5800, MajorHazard, Nibios, SieBot, Oxymoron83, Muhends, ClueBot, EMBaero, Binksternet, AnnEditor, Ariadacapo, AirdishStraus, Robert Skyhawk, Jefflayman, Estirabot, Wprlh, NatLongley, Fastily, Jovianeye, LaaknorBot, Glane23, Zorrobot, س.م., Luckas-bot, Yobot, Kilom691, IW.HG, AnomieBOT, Kaesmaruf, Citation bot, ArthurBot, Nickkid5, NOrbeck, GrouchoBot, RibotBOT, P s public, FrescoBot, BUY ME A WII OR I'LL CALL 911, Deathfly7, D'ohBot, Citation bot 1, Pinethicket, Jordgette, ଶରଭ, Mean as custard, Snegtrail, Kingjohnv, Jamesshtiu, EmausBot, Octaazacubane, Laketown, Wikfr, Idealpaul, Hang Li Po, Ego White Tray, Mikhail Ryazanov, FrEteGi, ClueBot NG, Delusion23, Go Phightins!, Bibcode Bot, BG19bot, Guy vandegrift, Trevayne08, Sentient Rover, David.moreno72, Wikiflew, Mechknight117, CuriousMind01, Albina-belenkaya, 93, Slenderman45454, Epicgenius, Mk85 2, Eyesnore, IRWillis, Laidbackuser, Tusharkants, Ballistic studies, Jocelyn Parent Optical Designer, Monkbot, KasparBot, GoldCar, Lancerts, Mechanysics, IndianEngineer1980 and Anonymous: 158

- **Binary explosive** *Source:* https://en.wikipedia.org/wiki/Binary_explosive?oldid=713900348 *Contributors:* The Anome, Lowellian, Daveydweeb, SpuriousQ, SmackBot, Mdd4696, JoshuaZ, Frigo, Sarahj2107, Idioma-bot, UnitedStatesian, Lamro, Errata13, PixelBot, CassidyJones, XLinkBot, Addbot, Fraggle81, R8etgj8er9threth888ht and Anonymous: 15

- **Improvised explosive device** *Source:* https://en.wikipedia.org/wiki/Improvised_explosive_device?oldid=741294899 *Contributors:* The Anome, Edward, Ixfd64, Kosebamse, Tregoweth, Jpatokal, GCarty, Mulad, Bomberben, Robertb-dc, Furrykef, Ironman419, HarryHenryGebel, Dbabbitt, ChrisO~enwiki, UtherSRG, Mushroom, Wayland, PBP, Mattflaschen, Tea2min, Buster2058, Centrx, MathKnight, Fastfission, Karn, Niteowlneils, Zoney, Bobblewik, Antandrus, Beland, Balcer, Jeremykemp, Kingal86, Johan Elisson, Discospinster, Avriette, Pmsyyz, Rama, Sriram, Dbachmann, Bender235, Kbh3rd, Palm dogg, Dalf, Smalljim, Hooverbag, Adrian~enwiki, Giraffedata, Alansohn, Walter Görlitz, Geo Swan, ליאור, DGedye, Mac Davis, Malo, Hohum, Wtmitchell, Bagradian, M3tainfo, Bobbyandck, Arcas2000, Ceyockey, Novacatz, Woohookitty, LOL, Apokrif, Kglavin, Bbatsell, Jdorney, Stefanomione, Descendall, BD2412, MC MasterChef, Rjwilmsi, Amire80, ElKevbo, Brighterorange, Williamborg, Edbrown05~enwiki, Ysangkok, Nivix, Esoterica, VolatileChemical, Bgwhite, Cactus.man, The Rambling Man, YurikBot, Hairy Dude, Jimp, Rxnd, Anonymous editor, Briaboru, Limulus, Gaius Cornelius, Pseudomonas, Bovineone, Anomalocaris, Bachrach44, Badagnani, Kyle Barbour, Tullie, Sandstein, De Administrando Imperio, GraemeL, Tomj, Vicarious, Tierce, GMan552, GrinBot~enwiki, DocendoDiscimus, Crystallina, Fightindaman, Scolaire, SmackBot, Kerekesk, Verne Equinox, CMD Beaker, Mdd4696, Gjs238, Kintetsubuffalo, Scott Paeth, Geoff B, Aixroot, Mauls, ERcheck, Chris the speller, Thumperward, Snori, Torzsmokus, Hgrosser, DéRahier, BobJones, Jmlk17, Jumping cheese, Neutralizer~enwiki, Nakon, Mini-Geek, Zero Gravity, Only, Drphilharmonic, WhosAsking, Fcleve, Rory096, Polihale, AThing, Teneriff, John, Fremte, Ckatz, BillFlis, Noah Salzman, InedibleHulk, Therealhazel, Norm mit, OnBeyondZebrax, Iridescent, Joseph Solis in Australia, P tasso, Micropsia, Haroldandkumar, Whaiaun, Rhetth, Frank Lofaro Jr., ChrisCork, Lahiru k, Owen214, CmdrObot, NinjaKid, Ilikefood, Im.a.lumberjack, Mak Thorpe, WeggeBot, Joakimekstrom, Gogo Dodo, ANTIcarrot, Difluoroethene, Nabokov, Thijs!bot, Ante Aikio, Hervegirod, Amjaabc, Denverjeffrey, Ph.L, AntiVandalBot, JHFTC, Jim whitson, Karoma, Darklilac, Spencer, Tomertomer, Erxnmedia, Peter Harriman, DagosNavy, MER-C, EKindig, Snowolfd4, Ryan4314, Lawitkin, Acroterion, 808, TommyDaniels, Bakilas, Parsecboy, VoABot II, Father Goose, Soulbot, Ed!, Parous, Hifrommike65, Claymoney, Dili, Pokemogu, Tracer9999, Raoulduke47, CliffC, Lav-25, Jim.henderson, Rettetast, Kokanee, R'n'B, Snozzer, Trusilver, Jcbohorquez, Anirvanroy, A Nobody, Cannibalicious!, Andrewhelling, Olegwiki, Gimpmask, Eodcoin, Bonadea, Xiahou, CardinalDan, RJASE1, WWGB, Wikieditor06, WFinegan, 28bytes, Jmrowland, Bnkausik,

FergusM1970, Mercurywoodrose, Tr-the-maniac, Dchall1, Jackfork, Wiae, Robert1947, Wstodd, Meters, MajorHazard, Finnrind, 4wajzkd02, WereSpielChequers, Unregistered.coward, HyperrealORnot, Boooooom, Andrewjlockley, SeiteNichtGefunden, Bbolen, Oxymoron83, Henry Delforn (old), Harry-, Lisatwo, Dravecky, ZH Evers, Hamiltondaniel, Mrkf650, ImageRemovalBot, BrutusCirrus, Twinsday, ClueBot, The Thing That Should Not Be, Amrithraj, Wraithful, Drmies, Mild Bill Hiccup, Niceguyedc, Nanobear~enwiki, Mspraveen, Ernstblumberg, Rleedsi, Excirial, CohesionBot, WikiWhereTo, Tweetlebeetle367, Sun Creator, Arjayay, Legacypac, Ngebendi, Iohannes Animosus, Redthoreau, Gundersen53, Rui Gabriel Correia, Jellyfish dave, Aitias, Terminator484, Berean Hunter, DumZiBoT, CaptainVideo890, XLinkBot, Little Mountain 5, Dave1185, Addbot, Professor Calculus, CanadianLinuxUser, Tide rolls, OlEnglish, Jarble, Smallroach, Yobot, PMLawrence, Apophenic, Tim Wister, AnomieBOT, Ulric1313, Dicttrshp, Materialscientist, GB fan, LilHelpa, Blrosenberg, GrouchoBot, JanDeFietser, Glic16, Shadowjams, Baldeadly, FrescoBot, Surv1v4l1st, HPUPIXKID, Intelligentsium, I dream of horses, Stalia.f, RiceCholo, Jabberjawjapan, SpaceFlight89, RadXman, Penusofnazarethpart2, Turian, Auledas, Ruzihm, ArchiveCamelaeigus, Lotje Boarwkrv, IRISZOOM, DARTH SIDIOUS 2, RjwilmsiBot, No.TBI, Misconceptions2, Belomorkanal, Envirodan, Fig eater, Emilschnoor, Stormchaser89, Wikipelli, Jessica hhu, Italia2006, MadJunkie, Midas02, Spøketse, H3llBot, EWikist, Amitabh1986, Natalie84, Donner60, Insomnia, CharlieEchoTango, Whoop whoop pull up, ClueBot NG, Battlesnake1, BryanGross, Vacation9, Sudip2118, The Master of Mayhem, Moto67, Helpful Pixie Bot, Dinarsad, Droopy1943, Shaven23, RustyHarlequin, Kjveeley, BG19bot, Blake Burba, Mossesb43, MusikAnimal, Opky, VoiceOfreason, Harizotoh9, ProudIrishAspie, Minsbot, Crumblord, Arigoldberg, BattyBot, Tutelary, Cyberbot II, ChrisGualtieri, ZappaOMati, 86steveD, MathKnight-at-TAU, Tandrum, Pushkarv, IjonTichyIjonTichy, Dexbot, Mogism, Makecat-bot, GentleDjinn, DJStarrfish, NiteshRijhwani, EvergreenFir, DavidLeighEllis, Babitaarora, Oranjelo100, Jknifemanager, Asfandyarxxx, Monkbot, SantiLak, Stacie Croquet, MRD2014, Julietdeltalima, MindRail, Roncopio47, Zcobb, Parsley Man, Emilyg568, GreenC bot, Camoedup and Anonymous: 479

- **Insensitive munition** Source: https://en.wikipedia.org/wiki/Insensitive_munition?oldid=731351505 Contributors: RickK, Danhash, Dr Gangrene, Rjwilmsi, Pleiotrop3, NSR, Arado, Gaius Cornelius, Shaddack, Retired username, IceCreamAntisocial, Georgewilliamherbert, SmackBot, Marc Kupper, Rcbutcher, Kevin W., Thijs!bot, Widefox, Chill doubt, Lklundin, Nave.notnilc, The1marauder, Jerryobject, Svick, CohesionBot, Socrates2008, Holothurion, Addbot, Trappist the monk, RjwilmsiBot, WikitanvirBot, Dcirovic, Sth8-NJITWILL, AOP39, Helpful Pixie Bot, Monkbot and Anonymous: 13

- **Chemical explosive** Source: https://en.wikipedia.org/wiki/Chemical_explosive?oldid=739079692 Contributors: Bryan Derksen, Bearcat, Wtmitchell, Malcolma, Chris the speller, DinosaursLoveExistence, AnomieBOT, Ego White Tray, Sven Manguard, ClueBot NG, Rileyccarlson and Anonymous: 9

- **Nuclear explosive** Source: https://en.wikipedia.org/wiki/Nuclear_explosive?oldid=596707919 Contributors: AxelBoldt, Mav, Bryan Derksen, The Anome, Patrick, Darkwind, Palmpilot900, Dino, Tempshill, Lowellian, Fastfission, Sladen, Eagleamn, Hohum, DV8 2XL, Limulus, Leo Lazauskas, Meiers Twins, SmackBot, Reedy, Judgesurreal777, Twin Suns, Travelbird, Emax0, Francisdurham, Tiddly Tom, Legobot, MaxDel, Bomazi, ClueBot NG, MyNameWasTaken and Anonymous: 13

- **Nuclear weapon** Source: https://en.wikipedia.org/wiki/Nuclear_weapon?oldid=742291972 Contributors: AxelBoldt, Magnus Manske, TwoOneTwo, Trelvis, The Epopt, Dreamyshade, Sodium, ClaudeMuncey, Ansible, Eloquence, Mav, Wesley, Bryan Derksen, Robert Merkel, The Anome, Tarquin, AstroNomer, Taw, Manning Bartlett, Ed Poor, Alex.tan, AdamW, Andre Engels, Ted Longstaffe, Youssefsan, Arvindn, Rmhermen, Toby Bartels, SJK, Little guru, Roadrunner, Ray Van De Walker, SimonP, Maury Markowitz, Zoe, Graft, FlorianMarquardt, Hephaestos, Soulpatch, Tedernst, Olivier, Patrick, RTC, Infrogmation, JohnOwens, Michael Hardy, GABaker, Modster, Cprompt, DopefishJustin, Dante Alighieri, Norm, Dominus, Ixfd64, Bcrowell, Frank Shearar, Cameron Dewe, TakuyaMurata, GTBacchus, Dori, Eric119, Minesweeper, Alfio, Ronabop, Mkweise, Ellywa, Ahoerstemeier, Anders Feder, Snoyes, Angela, Kingturtle, Erzengel, BigFatBuddha, Aarchiba, Ugen64, Glenn, Djmutex, Vzbs34, Susurrus, Jiang, Oliezekat, Alex756, [212] Mxn, Ilyanep, Lommer, Conti, Pizza Puzzle, Rami Neudorfer, Trevor Lawson, Ehn, Vroman, Jengod, Malbi, Ec5618, Jonadab~enwiki, Timwi, David Newton, Dino, Jefelex, Daniel Quinlan, Jfeckstein, Fuzheado, Andrewman327, WhisperToMe, Zoicon5, Jessel, DJ Clayworth, Haukurth, Tpbradbury, Maximus Rex, E23~enwiki, Pacific1982, Saltine, Kaal, Nv8200pa, Tempshill, Zero0000, Omegatron, Babbler, Thue, Bevo, Xevi~enwiki, Shizhao, Topbanana, Toreau, Vaceituno, Stormie, Raul654, Pstudier, Bcorr, Jusjih, Johnleemk, Finlay McWalter, Skybunny, Owen, Stargoat, Jni, Riddley, Robbot, Ke4roh, Sander123, Astronautics~enwiki, ChrisO~enwiki, Nabeel, Fredrik, Kizor, PBS, Chris 73, Chocolateboy, Kadin2048, Romanm, Arkuat, Securiger, Lowellian, Ukuk~enwiki, Merovingian, Sverdrup, Rfc1394, Academic Challenger, SchmuckyTheCat, Texture, Meelar, Yacht, Rhombus, Bkell, Mervyn, Hadal, Victor, LX, TPK, Tsavage, Seth Ilys, Diberri, Dina, David Gerard, SimonMayer, Ancheta Wis, Alexwcovington, Benji Franklyn, DocWatson42, Christopher Parham, Oberiko, Mat-C, Sj, Kim Bruning, Inter, Tom harrison, Lupin, Ferkelparade, Fastfission, Dersen, Zigger, Karn, Peruviantlama, Everyking, No Guru, Jacob1207, Anville, Perl, Curps, Electric goat, Bensaccount, Cantus, Mike40033, Guanaco, Tom-, Jherico, Zhen Lin, Gracefool, MRubenzahl, Steven jones, Matt Crypto, Chrissmith, Bobblewik, Deus Ex, Golbez, Kandar, DontMessWithThis, Christopherlin, Hob, Stevietheman, Barneyboo, Gadfium, Knutux, LiDaobing, Sonjaaa, Quadell, Fangz, Antandrus, Tom the Goober, Beland, Estel~enwiki, Apox~enwiki, PDH, Armaced, Jossi, CaribDigita, Rdsmith4, OwenBlacker, Mitaphane, Woofles, Tothebarricades.tk, Daniel11, Mysidia, Bk0, Tyler McHenry, Anirvan, Creidieki, Neutrality, Imjustmatthew, Karl Dickman, Deglr6328, Mtnerd, Barnaby dawson, Trevor MacInnis, Zaf, Mormegil, Rfl, Freakofnurture, N328KF, Venu62, Nimbulan, DanielCD, Discospinster, Rich Farmbrough, Rhobite, FiP, Jpk, Silence, Chowells, Prateep, Dsadinoff, Xezbeth, Ponder, Ioliver, Mani1, Pavel Vozenilek, Aardark, Paul August, Stereotek, SpookyMulder, Night Gyr, Bender235, ESkog, Kaisershatner, Danny B-), Hapsiainen, Brian0918, El C, Chairboy, Aude, Shanes, Sietse Snel, RoyBoy, Triona, Bookofjude, Deanos, DarkArctic, Jburt1, Balok, Adambro, Bobo192, Smalljim, BrokenSegue, Duk, Viriditas, Serialized, Vortexrealm, Kormoran, Jag123, Scott Ritchie, Jojit fb, Kjkolb, BM, Townmouse, Bawolff, PeterisP, Naturenet, Daf, WikiLeon, Rje, Pschemp, MPerel, Sam Korn, Haham hanuka, Ral315, Ylwsub68, Nsaa, Jakew, HasharBot~enwiki, OGoncho, Jumbuck, Stephen G. Brown, Alansohn, Gary, Tablizer, Uncle.bungle, SnowFire, Mo0, 119, Atlant, Rd232, Mr Adequate, Keenan Pepper, Trainik, Joshbaumgartner, Rwoodsco, Andrew Gray, Lord Pistachio, Lectonar, MarkGallagher, Zippanova, SlimVirgin, Lightdarkness, Sligocki, Garfield226, InShaneee, Dark Shikari, Hgrenbor, Hu, Malo, Idont Havaname, Bart133, GregLindahl, Hohum, Snowolf, Melaen, ClockworkSoul, Super-Magician, Evil Monkey, Ramius, Cal 1234, RainbowOfLight, Randy Johnston, Sciurinæ, Mikeo, Pethr, Vuo, Ianblair23, DV8 2XL, LordAmeth, Stepheno, Gene Nygaard, Redvers, Admiral Valdemar, HenryLi, Dan100, Tr00st, GreatGatsby, Crosbiesmith, Feezo, Itinerant, MickWest, Sylvain Mielot, Boothy443, Reinoutr, OwenX, Woohookitty, Jannex, GrouchyDan, JarlaxleArtemis, Superstring, Jersyko, Guy M, PatGallacher, James Kemp, Nvinen, TomTheHand, Namenko, JeremyA, MONGO, Nakos2208~enwiki, Tabletop, Cabhan, Firien, Bluemoose, GregorB, M412k, Petwil, Atomicarchive, Wayward, Volkz, Smartech~enwiki, Christopher Thomas, Dysepsion, GSlicer, Johndoe85839, Graham87, JiMidnite, Deltabeignet, Magister Mathematicae, Kalmia, MC MasterChef, Ligar~enwiki, Kbdank71, FreplySpang, Josh Parris, Gorrister, Rjwilmsi, Joefu, George Burgess, Phileas, Panoptical, Mystalic, Bill37212, Hibernianters, Linuxbeak, JHMM13, Tawker, Mred64, Oblivious, Ligulem, CQJ, Frenchman113,

The wub, DoubleBlue, ATLBeer, Sango123, Yamamoto Ichiro, Lcolson, Titoxd, FlaBot, Mirror Vax, RobertG, Ground Zero, A scientist, Nihiltres, Josh~enwiki, TheMelenchukSmell, Crazycomputers, Survivor, JIMBO WALES, Subterfuge~enwiki, RexNL, Gurch, Ayla, Jimbo D. Wales, RobyWayne, SweBrainz, KFP, OrbitOne, Cause of death, Jfiling, Pchors, King of Hearts, Scimitar, Chobot, Hatch68, Theo Pardilla, GangofOne, Bgwhite, Digitalme, Dj Capricorn, Simesa, NSR, Gwernol, Peter Grey, Loco830, UkPaolo, The Rambling Man, YurikBot, Wavelength, TexasAndroid, Dimimimon4, Extraordinary Machine, Sceptre, Blightsoot, Hairy Dude, Jimp, RussBot, Arado, Red Slash, John Quincy Adding Machine, Majin Gojira, Anonymous editor, Splash, Alavena, Stalmannen, Anders.Warga, Anomaly1, 0nizuka the Great, Cmk5b, Akamad, CambridgeBayWeather, Shaddack, Bisqwit, Sweetwilliams, GeeJo, Bullzeye, Finbarr Saunders, David R. Ingham, PaulGarner, Shanel, NawlinWiki, SEWilcoBot, Wiki alf, Ceremony1968, Harrisale, WAS, Jaxl, Milo99, Robchurch, JDoorjam, Nick, Ragesoss, Anetode, Dmoss, PhilipO, Misza13, Grafikm fr, Lomn, LarryMac, Aaron Schulz, Karl Meier, DeadEyeArrow, Psy guy, Kander, Superiority, Essexmutant, Mtu, Mgnbar, Saric, FF2010, Newagelink, Georgewilliamherbert, Vonfraginoff, Enormousdude, Ali K, Lt-wiki-bot, Gtdp, Ageekgal, Theda, Jwissick, Fang Aili, Adilch, Nemu, Dspradau, Rhallanger, GraemeL, JoanneB, TBadger, CWenger, JLaTondre, Garion96, AGToth, Gorgan almighty, David Biddulph, Jack Upland, Junglecat, RG2, Mikedogg, GrinBot~enwiki, Airconswitch, Dkasak, Vreddy92, Nick-D, Sam Weber, BiH, Jade Knight, DVD R W, Kf4bdy, Marquez~enwiki, NetRoller 3D, Luk, Sycthos, Bigcheesegs, Sardanaphalus, Joshbuddy, A bit iffy, SmackBot, Looper5920, YellowMonkey, Mattarata, Tarret, Prodego, KnowledgeOfSelf, Royalguard11, Hydrogen Iodide, Melchoir, Jhartshorn, Unyoyega, Pgk, C.Fred, Bomac, Neptunius, Davewild, Wikedpedia~enwiki, CMD Beaker, Alksub, Delldot, Desk003, Sam8, Ajm81, AnOddName, Vilerage, Aivazovsky, Nscheffey, Wittylama, Alex earlier account, Gaff, Xaosflux, Yamaguchi 先生, Zvonsully, Aksi great, Gilliam, The Gnome, Ppntori, Andy M. Wang, Psiphiorg, Afa86, The monkeyhate, Saros136, Chris the speller, Master Jay, Payam81, SlimJim, Persian Poet Gal, Lordkazan, Thumperward, Emt147, Silly rabbit, Hibernian, Imaginaryoctopus, Croquant, Sbharris, Darth Panda, A. B., Mikker, Cigale, Gsp8181, Dinnyy, Royboycrashfan, PeRshGo, Zsinj, Rogermw, Dethme0w, Can't sleep, clown will eat me, Jahiegel, Милан Јелисавчић, Jorvik, HoodedMan, Markkasan, Skidude9950, Nixeagle, OOODDD, Korinkami, Prmacn, Addshore, Interfector, Joema, Mrdempsey, Khoikhoi, WhereAmI, Digitize, Jumping cheese, Iapetus, Khukri, Makemi, Engwar, Nakon, Savidan, Loannes, Kevlar67, Shadow1, Dreadstar, Mini-Geek, Lcarscad, Polonium, TCorp, DMacks, Dlamini, Daniel4004, Kotjze, Whiplashxe, Edgeris, Daniel.Cardenas, Pilotguy, Prasi90, ピ—ロ, Ohconfucius, Kuzaar, Nmnogueira, WikiWitch, Rory096, Harryboyles, AAA765, Zahid Abdassabur, Dbtfz, Kreb Dragonrider, Kuru, John, HellecticMojo, Buchanan-Hermit, J 1982, Xu3w3nan, Kipala, Amenzix, Lazylaces, Sir Nicholas de Mimsy-Porpington, JorisvS, Minna Sora no Shita, Captain-Vindaloo, Zarniwoot, Gevalt, JohnWittle, Scetoaux, Jaywubba1887, Syra987, Ckatz, Kkken, Slakr, Werdan7, Stwalkerster, Shangrilaista, Tasc, Mr Stephen, Nitro-X, InedibleHulk, Waggers, SandyGeorgia, Mets501, Java 109, Spook`, Unnamed01, Ryulong, Serlin, Ryanjunk, Gary Jacobsen, Balderdash707, Aktako, Kenny&becca, Iridescent, K, Hydra Rider, Aspuar, CapitalR, Esurnir, Aeons, Dublan, Aaron DT, Civil Engineer III, Thebigone45, Morgan Wick, Tawkerbot2, Brian53199, Dlohcierekim, Chetvorno, Zaphody3k, Benfranklinlover, Penguincornguy, ERAGON, Vikram.raja, JForget, Pigstinky, Ale jrb, Sir Vicious, TheHerbalGerbil, Pools200, Scohoust, Iced Kola, JohnCD, Grimgor79, Randalllin, 5-HT8, GHe, Dgw, Toropop, Adrienhocky16, Evilhairyhamster, Avillia, Hipdog11, Qwertyman4444, Borislav Dopudja, TJDay, PC supergeek, Abeg92, Ryan, Tkloumo, Jeffdb123, UncleBubba, Gogo Dodo, HPaul, Travelbird, Deathmak, Llort, A Softer Answer, Give Peace A Chance, Pascal.Tesson, Nate74, Noohgodno, Tawkerbot4, Roberta F., Optimist on the run, Kingthwomp, Kansas Sam, Omicronpersei8, Bascombe2, UberScienceNerd, EvocativeIntrigue, FrancoGG, Mathpianist93, Epbr123, Daa89563, PolaroidKiss, Forsaken88, Tairen125, Corsair18, Jedibob5, Sagaciousuk, Mansoorhabib, Drift~enwiki, Mojo Hand, Afitillidie13, Louis Waweru, West Brom 4ever, John254, Bobblehead, Pavel from Russia, CST, Cj67, Geostar1024, Pcbene, RamanVirk, Nick Number, Mm11, SebastianSalceek, Thedarkestshadow, Dawnseeker2000, Escarbot, Bilbobjoe, Dagingsta, Supran, KrakatoaKatie, Ialsoagree, AntiVandalBot, Yonatan, Gioto, Luna Santin, Settersr, Seaphoto, Sobaka, Opelio, Chairman Meow, Quintote, Doc Tropics, Paste, Pokemeharder, Robzz, Sweart1, Dr who1975, Arclem, Jj137, Postlewaight, Dylan Lake, LibLord, Farosdaughter, EP111, MrBill, VonV, Aliwalla, MishMich, Lorethal, Canadian-Bacon, Bigjimr, JAnDbot, Najeb, Husond, Fidelfair, FidelFair, MER-C, Skomorokh, Mark Grant, Nthep, Instinct, Arnegrim, Seddon, Rearete, Hello32020, Ribonucleic, Tengfred, Andonic, Roleplayer, TAnthony, Fluffy the Cotton Fish, LittleOldMe, Yahel Guhan, Brandox1, Magioladitis, Pedro, Bongwarrior, VoABot II, Edwardmking, Nyq, Weser, Trnj2000, Carom, J mcandrews, Ben515, Redaktor, Bfiene, Akmoilan, Avicennasis, Gblay, Bubba hotep, Animum, Adrian J. Hunter, Allstarecho, A3nm, Cpl Syx, Tokino, Spellmaster, Vssun, Glen, DerHexer, JaGa, Fulvius~enwiki, Khalid Mahmood, Hans Moravec, Saganaki-, Philbj, Tuviya, Stevepaget, FisherQueen, Leaderofearth, Hdt83, MartinBot, Mornock, Racepacket, Ninestrokes, Arjun01, One of them, Rettetast, Mschel, Nono64, PrestonH, Kentucho, Headmaster2008, MnM2324, Napalmdeth~enwiki, Zephyr21, RockMFR, Zarathura, Limongi, J.delanoy, Pharaoh of the Wizards, Loongyh, Bogey97, Hacbarton, Leaflet, Maurice Carbonaro, Fleiger, Mike.lifeguard, Menew22, Yucki8aby, Octevious, Thaurisil, Rahzvel, Sfgamfan, Tdadamemd, John11479, Aym710, Daedalus CA, Icseaturtles, Bot-Schafter, Nosfartu, Ncmvocalist, McSly, Ninjadeath, L'Aquatique, Grumpyapp, Sheahae, Reichner1000, AllanDeGroot, Pyrospirit, Detah, RenniePet, NewEnglandYankee, ChineseGoldFarmer, DadaNeem, Skrelk, Malerin, Halfvamp, Nikobro, Hrishie, Xecog, Bloodvayne, MetsFan76, Billyx1337x, Asdfasdf321, Antepenultimate, Morimura, Nukeitup2, Vanished user 39948282, Gemini1980, Natl1, Waterfox1, Cs302b, Useight, MissAtomicbomb, StoptheDatabaseState, Awesomeman42, Hmsbeagle, Phr0gor, Pistonhonda4, Idioma-bot, Wikieditor06, ACSE, Dansen3008, Happy guy of happyness, Eleron123, Mattybobo, X!, Cdmajava, JoshBuck123456789, Spartan 2.0, Nucwikigirl, VolkovBot, CN111111111, TreasuryTag, CWii, Johnfos, ABF, Jeff G., Indubitably, Lbunker, Stopping Power, HJ32, Soliloquial, Vulgarkid, Barneca, Flintsparkler, Jomorepinch, Oshwah, Xavier-Green, GimmeBot, Solracm 021, SeanNovack, Maximillion Pegasus, Baldusi, Dj stone, TommyKiwi, Dchall1, Karmos, Something915, Qxz, DavidSaff, Noob wikipedian, Billy1223billy, Bloigen, Don4of4, Destroyer 2943, LeaveSleaves, Heidi, Seb az86556, UnitedStatesian, Arigato1, Cremepuff222, Hooduphodium, Mazarin07, Tybluesum, Buffs, Sparkyrob, Feudonym, Cantiorix, Falcon8765, Tompkins818, Turgan, -ross616-, Burntsauce, Babilingbaboon, Dustybunny, Afonsecajames, NPguy, AlleborgoBot, Funeral, 682635q, Kampking13, MattW93, Worship cindy, LOTRrules, SieBot, Dusti, ShiftFn, Sonicology, Tiddly Tom, Scarian, SheepNotGoats, Jacotto, Awesome Truck Ramp, RJaguar3, Triwbe, Mcygan123, Calabraxthis, Lexicog, Bootha, Aprudhomme, Arda Xi, Dattebayo321, Keilana, Tiptoety, Oda Mari, Arbor to SJ, PeaveyStrat5, Chridd, Lagrange613, Games14pmw, Lanzarotemaps, Oxymoron83, Antonio Lopez, Byrialbot, Faradayplank, AngelOfSadness, Steven Crossin, Lightmouse, RW Marloe, Tombomp, Megansmith18, Harry the Dirty Dog, Jackal242, RouterIncident, Anchor Link Bot, Mygerardromance, Trashbird1240, Vanished User 8902317830, Nn123645, Khilon, SaltyForth123, Mr. Granger, Smashville, Twinsday, Utergar~enwiki, Beeblebrox, MBK004, ClueBot, LAX, GorillaWarfare, Xilften, Snigbrook, Foxj, The Thing That Should Not Be, Ub3r n00ber, Wxyz334, Kafka Liz, Rjd0060, Dioneces, RomeijnLand II, Mickwaca, Chessy999, Rise Above the Vile, Arakunem, Magnoliasltd, Inventors, VQuakr, Cube lurker, NiD.29, Ventusa, Sasuke9031, Niceguyedc, Piledhigheranddeeper, Switchcraft, Auntof6, Ludoman, Monobi, PixelBot, Wilsone9, Zaharous, Esbboston, Ice Cold Beer, L.tak, PhySusie, Xpolygraphrightnowx, Kaiba, Dekisugi, Warrior4321, Thehelpfulone, Shimerdron, La Pianista, AbJ32, Light show, Aprock, Thingg, 9Nak, Aitias, Zilliput, Kyle2131, DJ Sturm, Party, Mahmoud-Megahid, XLinkBot, Javieranfispatria, Curby4, Gorillawataru, Bfgoobla, Lopper304, Altair1453, Bahman15, Duncan, Enigma 3, CDOG13, Osingh, Nepenthes, Lolkok, Ay nako, Atombombfootball, Dbev69, Batman278, Cstorm462, JinJian, ZooFari, Vqors, JCDenton2052, Dabobsta123, Shoemaker's Holiday, Twoolf1,

48.3. TEXT AND IMAGE SOURCES, CONTRIBUTORS, AND LICENSES

Bobfran, EEng, HexaChord, Wierd al 101, Pamejudd, F-22G10, Spico1, Mbodnar101, Addbot, Cxz111, Manuel Trujillo Berges, Uruk2008, Dante4, Betterusername, CycloneGU, Irroy, Ronhjones, Mww113, Leszek Jańczuk, Black sheep997, Download, Bassbonerocks, Szooper99, Punkrockpiper, Favonian, AtheWeatherman, LinkFA-Bot, Jaydec, Joomple, Immortal Horrors or Everlasting Splendors, Amjsjc, 84user, VASANTH S.N., Erutuon, Lightbot, Krano, Apteva, Meisam, Luckas-bot, TheSuave, Yobot, 2D, Therimjob, Tohd8BohaithuGh1, TaBOT-zerem, II MusLiM HYBRiD II, Amirobot, Paepaok, DJ LoPaTa, THEN WHO WAS PHONE?, Santryl, Sorruno, WisdomFromIntrospect, Ayrton Prost, IW.HG, KNLR, Eric-Wester, AnomieBOT, Floquenbeam, VX, Jim1138, IRP, Galoubet, JackieBot, Piano non troppo, Jhjh112, Gc9580, Poiu18894012, Utric1313, Sousapaloosa, Masterj89, Omg a llama, Flewis, Geord0, Materialscientist, Senio eilliw, Archaeopteryx, Citation bot, Opuntiaspliur, churknorris, Neurolysis, Unh20050, Tylermweeks, Taikah, Andyconda, Chrisxmas, Dude4747, Andrewtol546, Wufei05, Ezietsman, Bobandbulider1, Ahloahlo, Parthian Scribe, Aqbui, LukeJocko5, W27138, Funnyediting, Guythatedits, Xcaliber14, Chair7, Capricorn42, Weeeeeman, Austin+mariah, Mackbot1234, Mastarhon, Kschultz15, Liquidnitrogen5000, Gobooognaaaa, Probox1595, Djholio, Ferman2727, Peaser2009, TheGunn, Kdmoss, Livrocaneca, Ricoswavez, Cockopops, Chongo713, Jordoboy123, Jhickey04, Berkeley0000, Tootladclay666, Jack conway2, ProtectionTaggingBot, ChillyMD, Kroack, Chainmaster, Surv1v411st, Tobby72, Trinity54, Kyteto, MathFacts, HJ Mitchell, L1ttleTr33, Operation Fiscal Jackhammer, PasswordUsername, Bambuway, Louperibot, Citation bot 1, Mimzy1990, Jonesey95, Shiva Khanal, Cos-tr, Yutsi, Fui in terra aliena, Redbeanpaste, Rotblats09, Lwiki222, Cnwilliams, Pit0001, Lightlowemon, FoxBot, TobeBot, Mercy11, Trappist the monk, Comet Tuttle, Himypiedie, Grantbonn, Mr.98, Vera.tetrix, DARTH SIDIOUS 2, RjwilmsiBot, TjBot, Jackehammond, Bhawani Gautam, Beyond My Ken, Mandolinface, DASHBot, EmausBot, John of Reading, Nima1024, Manga28, Docman500, Mk5384, Boundarylayer, Tisane, Challisrussia, Neifdude, Dcirovic, Somerwind, The Blade of the Northern Lights, JSquish, ERRORHUNT, John Cline, Quasihuman, Josve05a, Fintelia, Nicolas Eynaud, AvicAWB, Zloyvolsheb, Wikfr, Confession0791, Brandmeister, Hudson Stern, L Kensington, MonoAV, Keithgneild, Hidenori watanave, Kc0wir, Thewolfchild, Cn7abc, Tussna, Poolatino12, Hookemhornsgannon, ClueBot NG, AlbertBickford, Catlemur, Georgepauljohnringo, Spikesjb, Buktaodord, Snotbot, XHawkz, Comonline, Popcornduff, Tholme, Bibcode Bot, The lost library, Neptune's Trident, MangoWong, Usefulchanges, Lazord00d, Cadiomals, Altaïr, Trevayne08, Eesoov, DPL bot, Polmande, 220 of Borg, TheGoodBadWorst, BattyBot, R3venans, Netherzone, FiveFourTwo, Cyberbot II, ChrisGualtieri, Jray310, SD5bot, John M. DiNucci, Ryay32, JY-Bot, Dexbot, 311S, XXzoonamiXX, Evildoer187, NagOc 945, Reatlas, Joeinwiki, Ninjaboos, Hermes 1900s, A Certain Lack of Grandeur, Godofwar1016050, Atotalstranger, Limnalid, Barjimoa, Rotaryphone111, Bennett Graff, Monkbot, Trackteur, Gronk Oz, Mhhossein, Davearthurs, Breedentials, TheGuyWhoHasAUsername, Atvica, Joshlabroski, Kymako, Mj thenovelatre, KenTancwell, KasparBot, Hulk576, Rightkeatsboom, Overtime.Editor, Ihsanturk, GoldCar, Wikkileaker, GreenC bot, AnimosityAnimalEdits, I2padams and Anonymous: 1775

- **Chemical energy** Source: https://en.wikipedia.org/wiki/Chemical_energy?oldid=741372039 Contributors: Ed Poor, Lir, Andrewman327, Bensaccount, Eequor, ESkog, Kjkolb, WadeSimMiser, Rjwilmsi, TexasAndroid, NawlinWiki, Eog1916, Gilliam, Skizzik, PureRED, Colonies Chris, RProgrammer, Rrburke, Gobonobo, Bendzh, Shinryuu, Black and White, Urdna, Scepbot, Bongwarrior, Jorfer, Jevansen, Bonadea, SoCalSuperEagle, VolkovBot, Sporti, Falcon8765, Kbrose, Laoris, Flyer22 Reborn, Oda Mari, SPACKlick, Capitalismojo, Anee jose, WickerGuy, Coinmanj, Forbes72, Mifter, Addbot, Some jerk on the Internet, Shakiestone, Legobot, Luckas-bot, Yobot, AnomieBOT, Materialscientist, LilHelpa, RockManQ, Mathonius, Shadowjams, Pepper, DivineAlpha, Pinethicket, 10metreh, Serols, SkyMachine, FoxBot, Vrenator, MrX, Jeffrd10, EmausBot, WikitanvirBot, RA0808, Dcirovic, ZéroBot, Josve05a, Jay-Sebastos, Brandmeister, Usb10, 28bot, ClueBot NG, Rtucker913, Djax1000, MerlIwBot, NuclearEnergy, Calabe1992, DBigXray, Wasbeer, Jimbo41197, Benzband, News Historian, Rainto~enwiki, Lover gurl steelers3, Th4n3r, Tinkietink, ChrisGualtieri, GoShow, LHcheM, Webclient101, Poppendavid, Stewwie, FallingGravity, Quenhitran, Shanepelletier, 7Sidz, Rhysrhys321, JonathanHopeThisIsUnique, Eteethan, Salinagomes101, Urawosome, Reddy23, Klaus Schmidt-Rohr and Anonymous: 137

- **Explosives engineering** Source: https://en.wikipedia.org/wiki/Explosives_engineering?oldid=702966103 Contributors: Rjwilmsi, Vegaswikian, Zath42, Georgewilliamherbert, NeilN, Audry2, Funandtrvl, Addbot, Luckas-bot, Bobmack89x, RjwilmsiBot, ClueBot NG, Tideflat, Rezabot, Subhashkarki and Anonymous: 6

- **Explosives safety** Source: https://en.wikipedia.org/wiki/Explosives_safety?oldid=739125407 Contributors: Klemen Kocjancic, Chris radcliff, RJFJR, Vegaswikian, Kurt, Wavelength, Pyrotec, Ageekgal, SmackBot, Jared555, DinosaursLoveExistence, Rory096, Tim Q. Wells, Beefyt, Ioannes Pragensis, Jonest, J.delanoy, Brazilian Man, WereSpielChequers, Paulhen, Auntof6, Iyaayas, Excirial, Socrates2008, Anon lynx, AnomieBOT, Anti bones, Bihco, Eugene-elgato, FrescoBot, Explocontrol, Topper82~enwiki, RjwilmsiBot, Chouster, Yellowpolkadot, 烤麵包機, Emaha, Elliott007kf, BattyBot, Jc86035, Becker.larry, Kevinmeakes, Colonel Wilhelm Klink and Anonymous: 15

- **Sellier & Bellot** Source: https://en.wikipedia.org/wiki/Sellier_%26_Bellot?oldid=715686715 Contributors: Woohookitty, Stronghow, BD2412, Boris Barowski, Chris the speller, Aida CZ, Nabokov, MaxBrains, Squids and Chips, Iaroslavvs, Addbot, Tsange, Luckas-bot, Yobot, AnomieBOT, Surv1v411st, DrilBot, Lotje, IRISZOOM, PhnomPencil, Filedelinkerbot and Anonymous: 14

- **Strength (explosive)** Source: https://en.wikipedia.org/wiki/Strength_(explosive)?oldid=544437092 Contributors: Vegaswikian, Shaddack, Tim Q. Wells, MajorHazard, Kruusamägi, Addbot and Anonymous: 1

- **Gurney equations** Source: https://en.wikipedia.org/wiki/Gurney_equations?oldid=738484840 Contributors: Hohum, GregorB, Vegaswikian, Georgewilliamherbert, SmackBot, Tim Q. Wells, Quibik, Headbomb, GrahamHardy, MajorHazard, FrescoBot, Citation bot 1, RjwilmsiBot, Josve05a, Tradedia, Monkbot and Anonymous: 3

- **Nitroglycerin** Source: https://en.wikipedia.org/wiki/Nitroglycerin?oldid=738705433 Contributors: AxelBoldt, Magnus Manske, TwoOneTwo, Kpjas, Marj Tiefert, Mav, Bryan Derksen, Tarquin, Koyaanis Qatsi, Taral, Rjstott, XJaM, Drbug, Heron, Leandrod, RTC, Michael Hardy, JakeVortex, Ixfd64, Fwappler, Ellywa, Ahoerstemeier, CatherineMunro, Александър, Cyan, Cherkash, GCarty, CarlKenner, Ilyanep, Raven in Orbit, PaulinSaudi, Stismail, WhisperToMe, Munford, Jakenelson, Furrykef, Tero~enwiki, Ed g2s, Floydian, Fvw, David.Monniaux, Gentgeen, Pigsonthewing, Fredrik, Donreed, Gandalf61, Merovingian, Henrygb, DrachenFyre, Sunray, Hadal, Rucky, Diberri, Lysy, Centrx, Graeme Bartlett, Ksheka, Nunh-huh, TorreFernando, No Guru, TomViza, Wikibob, Eequor, Foobar, Bobblewik, ChicXulub, Chowbok, Gadfium, Alexf, Yath, Antandrus, Ddhix 2002, GeoGreg, MishaChan, JeffreyN, Cynical, Edsanville, Jutta, Oskar Sigvardsson, Guanabot, Cacycle, Vsmith, Alistair1978, Night Gyr, JemeL, Bender235, Kbh3rd, Violetriga, El C, Bobo192, BM, TheProject, Hagerman, Nsaa, Matthewcieplak, Drf5n, Alansohn, Anthony Appleyard, Dtsang, Benjah-bmm27, AzaToth, Swift, Benna, Yuckfoo, Stephan Leeds, RainbowOfLight, Magicjigpipe, Kazvorpal, Stemonitis, Boothy443, OwenX, Woohookitty, Garylhewitt, TigerShark, EnSamulili, Extremebob, JeremyA, Rickjpelleg, Lensovet, Grace Note, GregorB, Gimboid13, Ajshm, Graham87, DePiep, Rjwilmsi, Wikiboth, Soakologist, Bhadani, SNIyer12, Ground Zero, Nihiltres, Chanting Fox, RexNL, Gurch, Terrace4, Physchim62, Chobot, DVdm, Mhking, YurikBot, Mikalra, RussBot, Jeffhoy, WAvegetarian,

Stephenb, Gaius Cornelius, Shaddack, GeeJo, NawlinWiki, Grafen, Pyrotec, Nucleusboy, IDude 101, Georgewilliamherbert, StuRat, Imaninjapirate, CharlesHBennett, ArielGold, Nippoo, HlynurT, That Guy, From That Show!, Yakudza, SmackBot, Hkhenson, Reedy, NaiPiak, C.Fred, AndyZ, Speight, Kilo-Lima, KocjoBot~enwiki, Edgar181, Hmains, Fogster, Ajsh, Billyhart, Chris the speller, Qwasty, Bartimaeus, Thumperward, MalafayaBot, Dlohcierekim's sock, DHN-bot~enwiki, Sbharris, Mladifilozof, Yaf, GreatMizuti, The tooth, DinosaursLoveExistence, Jumping cheese, Ambix, Nakon, Pistolen08, MartinRe, Chrylis, Acdx, Jóna Þórunn, Wossi, Nasz, John, Goodnightmush, Beetstra, Cratylus3, Spydercanopus, Cyanidesandwich, Naaman Brown, BananaFiend, Civil Engineer III, Túrelio, Chovain, Pathosbot, Tawkerbot2, VinceB, CalebNoble, ViruValge, Wikipeedio, JForget, Scirocco6, NickW557, Neelix, Phatom87, Vectro, Shano85, Rifleman 82, JFreeman, Ibanix, Christian75, Roberta F., Crum375, Thijs!bot, Epbr123, Wikidenizen, CTZMSC3, I already forgot, AntiVandalBot, Seaphoto, Ian Donaldson, JAnDbot, Xhienne, Niagara, Wasell, Venusnair, Bongwarrior, VoABot II, Arie Inbar~enwiki, Jnb, GODhack~enwiki, Tremilux, Uberhobo, Cpl Syx, Enquire, Exigence, ChemNerd, Jay Litman, Leyo, Snozzer, Em Mitchell, Wikiman232, Paranomia, Bogey97, Anas Salloum, Uncle Dick, Xris0, Gzkn, Doktor Musmatta, KylieTastic, Vranak, VolkovBot, AlnoktaBOT, Philip Trueman, Fsdjflsadjfklsdjfkls, DoorsAjar, TXiKiBoT, Toll booth, Rei-bot, Armithiren, NGfan, Ferengi, Contusion, MajorHazard, 51fifty, Doc James, AlleborgoBot, Xchsxbigxmike, KILROY KILROY, SieBot, Sonicology, Moonriddengirl, The Overlooker, Wing gundam, JetLover, Redmarkviolinist, Oxymoron83, Maryamico, Alex.muller, Anchor Link Bot, Landry0, Chem-awb, ClueBot, Arunsingh16, LukeTheSpook, Shinkolobwe, Medos2, Dogriggr, Thingg, Plasmic Physics, Burner0718, MelonBot, AlanM1, Hookemdustin, DaL33T, Coltona12, Anturiaethwr, WikHead, SilvonenBot, WikiDao, Arturo57, Addbot, Macbethy, SpillingBot, Chamal N, Chzz, ChenzwBot, Incredibleman007, Lineface, Äppelmos~enwiki, Tide rolls, BrianKnez, Legobot, Luckasbot, Yobot, Quinyu, CheMoBot, Actionarms, AnomieBOT, Popezilla, Materialscientist, 90 Auto, Citation bot, Quebec99, Smiththr, Jmundo, حسن على البط, Srich32977, Pmlineditor, GrouchoBot, Wojtow, Locobot, Brutaldeluxe, Nebojsapajkic, GNRY09, Dinamyte, Some standardized rigour, Pepper, Vinithehat, Pies765, Woodenchemist, In the midst of a dream, Pinethicket, Jonesey95, MondalorBot, Wikitanvir, Jomanted, Σ, BogBot, Ahu1959, Someman64, Grammarxxx, Jynto, DARTH SIDIOUS 2, Ritchie123, RjwilmsiBot, Pansypower, Ripchip Bot, Buzz007, Skamecrazy123, EmausBot, WikitanvirBot, Ch0411, Gfoley4, Slightsmile, Wikipelli, HiW-Bot, ZéroBot, Fæ, Caspertheghost, AManWithNoPlan, Mayur, VictorianMutant, JonRichfield, Louisajb, Debu334, ClueBot NG, Smm201'0, Tsk351, MarB23, Widr, NickCalan, Nao1958, Theopolisme, Redtool, Helpful Pixie Bot, JohnSRoberts99, Curb Chain, Explodo-nerd, Jeffrey997, Mikkellhf, MusikAnimal, JSCleveland, Zedshort, ProudIrishAspie, Pratyya Ghosh, ElliotGrey, GoShow, TylerDurden8823, 00AgentBond93, Dexbot, Hmainsbot1, Mogism, JZNIOSH, Makecat-bot, Project Osprey, FairyTale'sEnd, Ugog Nizdast, HamiltonFromAbove, Brainiacal, DudeWithAFeud, Baqeri, Medgirl131, Oleaster, Ommiki, Emily Temple-Wood (NIOSH), Emeldir, KasparBot, This is for an experament, Cal.Potaka, Baking Soda, Marvellous Spider-Man and Anonymous: 516

- **Acetone peroxide** Source: https://en.wikipedia.org/wiki/Acetone_peroxide?oldid=735301385 Contributors: AxelBoldt, Bryan Derksen, The Anome, Rmhermen, Collabi, Evanherk, Karada, Bdonlan, Rossami, GCarty, Ww, Stone, Gentgeen, Robbot, ChrisO~enwiki, Securiger, Lowellian, Texture, Seth Ilys, Cordell, Centrx, DocWatson42, Thorne, Lupin, MSGJ, Ich, Markus Kuhn, Mellum, Breadmanpaul, Brockert, VampWillow, Darrien, Ato, Chowbok, Knutux, Beland, MacGyverMagic, Ddhix 2002, DragonflySixtyseven, GeoGreg, Kar98, Iantresman, Tsemii, Ukexpat, Hillel, Abdull, Jayjg, Poccil, Helohe, Rhobite, Penis-breath, Mykhal, Sum0, Plugwash, El C, J-Star, Mh26, ClementSeveillac, Sommerfeld, Gerweck, Mo0, Keenan Pepper, Benjah-bmm27, ABCD, Swift, BRW, Fdedio, Vuo, Ceyockey, Markaci, Crosbiesmith, The Brain, Rickjpelleg, Astanhope, Descendall, V8rik, NoPuzzleStranger, DePiep, Rjwilmsi, Joe Decker, PinchasC, HappyCamper, Toresbe, Margosbot~enwiki, Ysangkok, Bubbleboys, Karelj, Zaphood, Jaraalbe, Skoosh, Peter Grey, YurikBot, RobotE, Arado, Polverone, Hede2000, JamieMcCarthy, Gaius Cornelius, Yyy, Shaddack, Trious, Pseudomonas, GeeJo, Annabel, Trimoor, Millsey, D. Wu, Kivulu, Davemck, El Pollo Diablo, Cerejota, Terrified, Phillprice, JetlagMk2, Jezzabr, Tetracube, JereKrischel, Rbirkby, TheMadBaron, Modify, Femmina, Bluezy, Borisbaran, SmackBot, IddoGenuth, KocjoBot~enwiki, AndreasJS, Chaosfeary, Edgar181, R no, Chris the speller, Bluebot, Snori, Salvor, RoysonBobson, Scott3, Rrburke, Anthon.Eff, Jumping cheese, Cybercobra, Zen611, Smokefoot, Clean Copy, Polonium, DMacks, Jóna Þórunn, Vinaiwbot~enwiki, Ohconfucius, John, JohnCub, Kashmiri, Majorclanger, SimonasWikiBotLT~enwiki, Yms, Beetstra, Rev-san, 2T, Therealhazel, Foolishben, Unangst, MightyWarrior, Geo8rge, Seven of Nine, Chrisahn, Cydebot, UncleBubba, Doug Weller, Cancun771, Tapir Terrific, AntiVandalBot, Luna Santin, Randomproof, Gdo01, Stuzzelin, Epeefleche, Quentar~enwiki, VoABot II, Misheu, Pixel ;-), Chris451a, Nick Cooper, DerHexer, InvertRect, Seba5618, ChemNerd, Jim.henderson, Nono64, Lilac Soul, Matt57, Rrostrom, Boghog, Stan J Klimas, Notreallydavid, Matt18224, DadaNeem, Akeron, VolkovBot, Douglas Bradford Oliver, Unixtastic, TXiKiBoT, Broadbot, Benrr101, Ephix, Lamro, !dea4u, Insanity Incarnate, OMCV, 4wajzkd02, Cwkmail, Ketone16, Escaper2007, Lightmouse, Chem-awb, Drpeter 2000, ProkopHapala, EPadmirateur, Maxmc1027, Duckhunter123, Mild Bill Hiccup, Michał Sobkowski, Alexbot, MinnieRae~enwiki, Ltnemo2000, Sun Creator, Maxmc1028, Greenport, Vojtěch Dostál, Addbot, Goorky, DOI bot, Kman543210, Incredibleman007, Mfhulskemper, Luckas-bot, Yobot, CheMoBot, AnomieBOT, Cubansmoothie, Materialscientist, LovesMacs, LilHelpa, Gymnophoria, Belasted, Tomdo08, Jü, حسن على البط, Broluo, Eugene-elgato, Eframgoldberg, River.crab.hk, Citation bot 1, DrilBot, Pinethicket, ShadowRangerRIT, Trappist the monk, RjwilmsiBot, Uanfala, DASHBot, EmausBot, WikitanvirBot, Parkywiki, Gecg, GoingBatty, Westley Turner, Frank-Wilcox, Fred Gandt, MajorVariola, Djapa84, Mu4963, Diverjohn2u, Zlhu.int, MrCleanOut, Whoop whoop pull up, Bjohns86, Sreenathvijayan, Onanoff, Teodret, Helpful Pixie Bot, Explodo-nerd, Wikih101, Matbury, BattyBot, Cyberbot II, Berudagon, Leprof 7272, Orchsoccer, I am One of Many, American In Brazil, RNLockwood, Paul2520, Methylated603, VexorAbVikipædia, Mzasso, Alekssobolewski, ThaCazador and Anonymous: 235

- **Trinitrotoluene** Source: https://en.wikipedia.org/wiki/Trinitrotoluene?oldid=741302009 Contributors: Magnus Manske, TwoOneTwo, Trelvis, Bryan Derksen, Tarquin, AstroNomer, Rjstott, Andre Engels, Zoe, Topory, Patrick, JohnOwens, Tim Starling, Hdpigott, Tannin, Mkweise, Ahoerstemeier, Александър, Jll, Netsnipe, GCarty, Stone, Doradus, Big Bob the Finder, Furrykef, Indefatigable, Prisonblues, Pollinator, Mjmcb1, Riddley, Rogper~enwiki, Gentgeen, Pigsonthewing, Fredrik, Donreed, Moncrief, Securiger, Ojigiri~enwiki, Catbar, Neckro, Tea2min, Alexwcovington, Centrx, Giftlite, TorreFernando, Fatal error, Curps, Stern~enwiki, Eequor, Matt Crypto, Lakefall~enwiki, Bobblewik, JE, J. 'mach' wust, Antandrus, AlexanderWinston, Icairns, Tail, Sam Hocevar, Edsanville, Oknazevad, TheObtuseAngleOfDoom, Rich Farmbrough, Mani1, JemeL, Dolda2000, Bender235, CanisRufus, Kwamikagami, Sietse Snel, Bobo192, Pearle, Schnolle, Andrewpmk, Benjah-bmm27, ABCD, Ciceroni, Walkerma, Melaen, Shogun~enwiki, Cal 1234, Alfvaen, Shoefly, Gene Nygaard, Kazvorpal, Kitch, Dan100, Gosgood, Alvis, Mel Etitis, TigerShark, LOL, Ikescs, Kosher Fan, JeremyA, Rickjpelleg, Sir Lewk, Ebradford, Christopher Thomas, Eluchil, Tslocum, Graham87, DePiep, Rjwilmsi, PinchasC, HappyCamper, Maxim Razin, FlaBot, SiriusB, Nihiltres, Tom Y8s, Klosterdev, Meeve, Ichudov, Physchim62, DVdm, Roboto de Ajvol, YurikBot, SpuriousQ, RadioFan, Hydrargyrum, Shaddack, GeeJo, Bullzeye, Shanel, Buster79, Shaun F, Lexicon, Pyrotec, DeadEyeArrow, Wknight94, Fiaschi~enwiki, Flooey, Georgewilliamherbert, Lt-wiki-bot, Hstoffels, Fang Aili, JoanneB, David Biddulph, Erik J, Mdwyer, GrinBot~enwiki, Nippoo, CIreland, SmackBot, InverseHypercube, AnOddName, Edgar181, DrKyle, IW4, Gilliam, Rmosler2100, Chris the speller, Uthbrian, DHN-bot~enwiki, Tsca.bot, Shalom Yechiel, Braydie Haskell, DChiuch, LMF5000, MartinRe, Smokefoot, Vina-

48.3. TEXT AND IMAGE SOURCES, CONTRIBUTORS, AND LICENSES

iwbot~enwiki, Ronaz, Ugur Basak Bot~enwiki, SashatoBot, Esrever, DO11.10, John, General lzation, LWF, Reepnorp, Bjankuloski06en~enwiki, NongBot~enwiki, IronGargoyle, MarkSutton, BillFlis, Beetstra, Ryulong, MTSbot~enwiki, Galactor213, Politepunk, Civil Engineer III, Mr3641, MightyWarrior, Eastlaw, JForget, PorthosBot, Le poulet noir, Lmcelhiney, Phatom87, Rifleman 82, ST47, Chasingsol, CostelId, Nabokov, Crum375, Thijs!bot, Opabinia regalis, Nemesis 961, Klaas1978, LeeNapier, John254, RickinBaltimore, Hcobb, Bob the Wikipedian, ZosoSG, Fildon, AntiVandalBot, Widefox, Grouchy Chris, LibLord, Chill doubt, Saltbekeeper, Res2216firestar, DagosNavy, JAnDbot, Deflective, Telamonian, Hut 8.5, Jerkajerka, Jonnyd001, VoABot II, JNW, Fabrictramp, Lenschulwitz, Spellmaster, Cliff smith, ChemNerd, NReitzel, Captain panda, Trusilver, Boghog, Mike.lifeguard, Tdadamemd, AntiSpamBot, Spinach Dip, HazyM, MartinBotIII, Pdcook, Funandtrvl, AlnoktaBOT, Doeagle meany, Fluoborate, Anonymous Dissident, JhsBot, Bob12345678987654321, Raymondwinn, Wiae, Lejarrag, Dralexander, Curtisross, Falcon8765, Cvf-ps, Fanatix, Ian Glenn, SieBot, Kumawen, Caltas, Cwkmail, Wing gundam, Wateva101, Flyer22 Reborn, Darth Metus, JSpung, Zariya, Lightmouse, SMakabwe, Fratrep, Galaplox, Maelgwnbot, StaticGull, Chem awb, ChiIE, ClueBot, The Thing That Should Not Be, Pekelney, DragonBot, Estirabot, Razorflame, Thewellman, La Pianista, Isenouthe, DerBorg, Fswd~enwiki, InternetMeme, Mottoman101, JCrowTNT, Rreagan007, Alexius08, Navy Blue, Erikhansson1, Addbot, Uruk2008, DOI bot, Ronhjones, Vchorozopoulos, CanadianLinuxUser, Derfsta, Jim10701, Download, LaaknorBot, CarsracBot, ChenzwBot, Naidevinci, Numbo3-bot, Kasey23, Pietrow, HerculeBot, Luckas-bot, Yobot, Ptbotgourou, CheMoBot, AnomieBOT, Kristen Eriksen, Jim1138, Piano non troppo, Theseeker4, Flewis, Alexikoua, Bluerasberry, Mahmudmasri, Materialscientist, The High Fin Sperm Whale, Citation bot, ArthurBot, Primalmu, Xqbot, Genryls24, Capricorn42, .45Colt, Andoof3476, Srich32977, Habowh43, Smallman12q, Mike Dill~enwiki, Imveracious, HighFlyingFish, Vinceouca, Citation bot 1, Nirmos, I dream of horses, Jonesey95, RedBot, Pikiwyn, Tcrboyscout, Jauhienij, Vrenator, Xor4200, Reach Out to the Truth, Jfmantis, Onel5969, EmausBot, Boundarylayer, GoingBatty, Dcirovic, Bamyers99, Yor.tima, Isarra, Uaintgotnothinonme, Jevarah, Donner60, Bomazi, The chemistds, Louisajb, Gmt2001, Xonqnopp, ClueBot NG, Pashihiko, Smm201`0, Soulhearth99, DieSwartzPunkt, Helpful Pixie Bot, ?oygul, JohnSRoberts99, Wertyu739, Calabe1992, Eating People, Dan653, TheMan4000, Bluedog123321, Emaha, Shea150, Hansen Sebastian, Sfarney, Mediran, JZNIOSH, Lugia2453, Boomzzz, Project Osprey, Blm93, MarchOrDie, AshFR, Lemnaminor, RomanM82, Howicus, 1YlGC6dsynvm, Froglich, CensoredScribe, Killerboy30, Greenteamcomm, William.prewett, NottNott, Sam Sailor, DudeWithAFeud, Momo04169.yale, Ak47281, Monkbot, Hgdhfdtdyewru.u, Locked522, Cyrej, Christina M. Joseph, Emily Temple-Wood (NIOSH), Emeldir, Marktw8ne, SQMeaner, DaethBreath86, KasparBot, Dynablock, Renamed user jC6jAXNBCg, Mixermasher11, Jimmymorogoro, Illuminatieye 25, Boy if you dont, Bananman and Anonymous: 372

- **Nitrocellulose** *Source:* https://en.wikipedia.org/wiki/Nitrocellulose?oldid=741589786 *Contributors:* Magnus Manske, Bryan Derksen, Malcolm Farmer, Maury Markowitz, Tim Starling, Ellywa, Ronz, CatherineMunro, Julesd, Scott, GCarty, [212], Lee M, Kat, Stone, Doradus, Taxman, Renato Caniatti~enwiki, Oaktree b, David.Monniaux, Twang, Riddley, Gentgeen, Robbot, Romanm, Naddy, Securiger, Lowellian, Walloon, Centrx, DocWatson42, Pretzelpaws, Tom harrison, Wyss, Bensaccount, Rchandra, Bobblewik, Database~enwiki, Manuel Anastácio, Girolamo Savonarola, Sonett72, AliveFreeHappy, Vsmith, Fluzwup, CanisRufus, Imoen, Dennis Brown, Bobo192, Longhair, Mdhowe, Dillee1, Djspiewak, Gerweck, Sherurcij, Philip Cross, Keenan Pepper, Benjah-bmm27, Linmhall, Sobolewski, Yurivict, Kznf, Pol098, Kelisi, Lensovet, Bkwillwm, Arden, Deltabeignet, DePiep, Jimbsagwa, FlaBot, SportsMaster, Siddhant, YurikBot, Shaddack, Janke, Pyrotec, Sfnhltb, Bozoid, Zirland, IceCreamAntisocial, Jwissick, SMcCandlish, Thephotoplayer, ChemGardener, SmackBot, Emoscopes, Rojomoke, Brossow, Edgar181, Yamaguchi 先生, Ohnoitsjamie, Chris the speller, DanF, MalafayaBot, Rcbutcher, Yaf, Wxxvi, Drphilharmonic, PhilipB, J306, LWF, Peterlewis, BillFlis, Beetstra, MIckStephenson, Courcelles, PaddyM, Egor, Scigatt, CRGreathouse, Jason Olshefsky, Agathman, Sabolsky, Green451, Cydebot, Quibik, Dipics, Argymeg, Omicronpersei8, Rbanzai, Thijs!bot, Thomprod, Widefox, Barneyg, LDGE, Edokter, Canadiana, Gcm, Plantsurfer, Lisle45, Belg4mit, Daarznieks, Markus451, WLU, Mczech1111, Editman4321, Conquerist, ChemNerd, NReitzel, R'n'B, Mikek999, Siryendor, McDScott, Dorgan, Num1dgen, Djflem, AlnoktaBOT, Blueknife09, Ragemanchoo, Liko81, Piperh, Broadbot, Andy Dingley, Lamro, NickScalan, Neparis, SieBot, Calliopejen1, Jmowreader, Cwkmail, Fyrverkarn~enwiki, OKBot, TX55, Denisarona, Chemawb, Binksternet, Shjacks45, Piledhigheranddeeper, Mr Accountable, Somno, Flightsoffancy, PixelBot, Thewellman, AnimalLover323, Little Mountain 5, SilvonenBot, Addbot, Goorky, Non-dropframe, EjsBot, PaulPadfield66, Ironholds, Jim10701, Nuberger13, Luckas-bot, Yobot, Legobot II, CheMoBot, Pyrorocketman, Retro00064, Lukeowens, Rubinbot, Captain Quirk, Materialscientist, The High Fin Sperm Whale, Eumolpo, Xqbot, Anthony Chiu, Jü, Srich32977, FrescoBot, WackoZacho, Riventree, MChrisThom, Nixiebunny, Wicker1, Chenopodiaceous, Metricmike, MolBioMan, RedBot, Serols, Σ, BluefieldWV, Seahorseruler, Jfmantis, IronyCrusader, Benjamin soelberg, MonoALT, A930913, Noodleki, Donner60, ChuispastonBot, Pkisme, The chemistds, Outsidedog, Whoop whoop pull up, ClueBot NG, Davidlooser, JordoCo, Ryan Vesey, Helpful Pixie Bot, Vmelkon, Urgeroute, YorkshireBryn, Amolbot, Logo3801, BattyBot, Stantan, Kschultz23, Patriciab99, Aclyde1, Monochrome Monitor, Yorkmba99, Hansmuller, Gravuritas, Mortelltalking, Trackteur, Jacob Graham17, Wordsman Dude, Alekssobolewski, Clevelandeph, Thishuman, Compassionate727, JAIU GDAHB, Bender the Bot, JChMathae and Anonymous: 178

- **RDX** *Source:* https://en.wikipedia.org/wiki/RDX?oldid=735566246 *Contributors:* TwoOneTwo, Bryan Derksen, The Anome, Ray Van De Walker, Thosp, Tannin, Karada, Shimmin, Ahoerstemeier, Zannah, Александър, GCarty, [212], JidGom, Mulad, Stone, Dysprosia, Uninvited-Company, Riddley, Phil Boswell, Gentgeen, ChrisO~enwiki, Peak, Romanm, Lowellian, Sverdrup, Rorro, Rsduhamel, Centrx, DocWatson42, Ryanrs, BenFrantzDale, Leonard G., Soren.harward, Gdr, Knutux, HorsePunchKid, Gunnar Larsson, Rdsmith4, Maximaximax, Balcer, Klemen Kocjancic, Deglr6328, Rob cowie, Brianhe, Rich Farmbrough, Cacycle, Alistair1978, Bender235, Kwamikagami, Robotje, Jericho4.0, Matt Britt, Passw0rd, Mrzaius, Anthony Appleyard, Wdfarmer, Malo, TaintedMustard, Mixer, Gene Nygaard, Drbreznjev, RandomWalk, Alvis, Mark K. Jensen, Pol098, Wrath0fb0b, JeremyA, Rickjpelleg, Paradon, Nosmo, GregorB, SDC, BD2412, DePiep, Mendaliv, Krymson, Rjwilmsi, Jaybeeunix, Onagrus, Ligulem, FlaBot, Dusty78, Physchim62, Bgwhite, Skoosh, YurikBot, Hede2000, Okedem, Yyy, Shaddack, Varnav, GeeJo, Kerry Raymond, DavidConrad, Megapixie, Pyrotec, Someones life, WAS 4.250, Georgewilliamherbert, NorsemanII, Marketdiamond, Arthur Rubin, David Biddulph, DasBub, SmackBot, Edgar181, Grant Janzen, Marc Kupper, Chris the speller, Kurykh, Hibernian, Moshe Constantine Hassan Al-Silverburg, Oni Ookami Alfador, DHN-bot~enwiki, Darth Panda, Sgt Pinback, Trekphiler, Gothmog.es, Vprajkumar, Jeborr, RandomP, Smokefoot, The PIPE, John, CoolKoon, BillFlis, Beetstra, G patkar, SkyWalker, CmdrObot, Derek17719346, Treviboy, Rifleman 82, Myscrnnm, Costelld, Tawkerbot4, Nabokov, Arb, EWAdams, Headbomb, Zhochaka, Nick Number, CTZMSC3, Rees11, AntiVandalBot, WerWil, JAnDbot, Epeefleche, Mildly Mad, Dclegcounsel, Girx, Nono64, FANSTARbot, Bob657, Notreallydavid, Trumpet marietta 45750, C1010, Whiteandnerdy52, HazyM, Magiaaron, George.Hutchinson, Al.locke, TXiKiBoT, Rei-bot, Tockeg, Broadbot, Wiae, Tri400, Clfranklin4, Tmaull, Lamro, Michael Frind, SieBot, Flyer22 Reborn, Lightmouse, Sram1986, Galaplox, Msjayhawk, ClueBot, Mike Warns, Michal Sobkowski, Pekelney, Jotterbot, Rror, JCrowTNT, Shred-69, DaL33T, DOI bot, Fyrael, Cst17, Chempedia, Alandeus, Lightbot, ﻋﻠﯽ, Zorrobot, Legobot, Gth-au, Yobot, Bunnyhop11, CheMoBot, Partha1022, Mr T (Based), Crisstoph, AnomieBOT, Rubinbot, Jim1138, Materialscientist, Citation bot, Stanislao Avogadro, ArthurBot, Xqbot, Robert H Berlin, Tomdo08, FrescoBot, Riventree, HJ Mitchell, Woodenchemist, Citation bot 1, Jean-François Clet, Jhog1978, MastiBot, Dinamik-bot, Oracleofottawa, RjwilmsiBot, Craxyxarc, Dbanzye, Boundarylayer, ScienceRulez, ZéroBot, Redhanker, MajorVariola, Kweckzilber, Frigotoni, MaGa, Snubcube, Whoop whoop pull up, ClueBot NG, Sreenathvijayan, Widr, Helpful Pixie Bot, Explodo-nerd, BG19bot, 220 of Borg, Euryklon, Shisha-Tom, Anbu121, Cyberbot II, Webclient101, Mogism, JZNIOSH, Radiotrefoil, Martin.buttolph, Wuerzele, Evano1van, CensoredScribe, NottNott, Finnusertop, Juhuyuta, Davmacbea, Kurian george2, Emily Temple-Wood (NIOSH), KasparBot, Stewi101015, GreenC bot and Anonymous: 224

- **Pentaerythritol tetranitrate** Source: https://en.wikipedia.org/wiki/Pentaerythritol_tetranitrate?oldid=739134754 Contributors: AxelBoldt, TwoOneTwo, Bryan Derksen, Rmrf1024, Poor Yorick, GCarty, Mulad, Dino, Stone, Riddley, Gentgeen, Goethean, Romanm, Bkell, Mattflaschen, Matt Gies, Centrx, DocWatson42, Mintleaf~enwiki, BigBen212, Bobblewik, Chowbok, Aramgutang, Quota, GreenReaper, Dbaron, Rich Farmbrough, Edibobb, Michael Zimmermann, Night Gyr, Bender235, Arcadian, Gar37bic, Mh26, Anthony Appleyard, Benjah-bmm27, Wtmitchell, TaintedMustard, Gene Nygaard, Pol098, Rickjpelleg, Marudubshinki, Mandarax, A Train, DePiep, Rjwilmsi, Vegaswikian, FlaBot, SiriusB, Nihiltres, Physchim62, YurikBot, Jimp, Yyy, Shaddack, GeeJo, Daveswagon, Anomalocaris, Johann Wolfgang, Megapixie, Brian Crawford, Deeday-UK, Georgewilliamherbert, Tanet, Poppy, Wechselstrom, JDspeeder1, DasBub, Nippoo, User24, SmackBot, Stepa, Edgar181, MalafayaBot, DHN-bot~enwiki, Can't sleep, clown will eat me, Jumping cheese, Ambix, DMacks, Risker, John, Buchanan-Hermit, Krbvroc1, Beetstra, Kelreth, Hu12, Tarchon, Geo8rge, Jbenjamin, Edward Vielmetti, Scott.medling, Rifleman 82, Nabokov, Ante Aikio, Headbomb, Dtgriscom, Pap3rw8, Marokwitz, Tjmayerinsf, JEH, NapoliRoma, Epeefleche, Wasell, GODhack~enwiki, CliffC, ChemNerd, Glrx, Nono64, Leyo, RockMFR, Slash, Boghog, Ian McGrady, Cogorno, RenniePet, GDW13, HazyM, DorganBot, VolkovBot, TXiKiBoT, Oshwah, Nablad, Billgordon1099, Docbob49, Northfox, Cwkmail, Anilmuthineni, Taggard, Galaplox, Sindala, Wjemather, Msjayhawk, Wantnot, NickCT, Binksternet, EoGuy, Pwitham, AirdishStraus, PixelBot, Hasteur, Aitias, Addbot, Willking1979, DOI bot, Wickey-nl, EjsBot, Cuaxdon, Nessunome, Download, Tassedethe, Lightbot, Zorrobot, Luckas-bot, Yobot, Enemyunknown, CheMoBot, Anypodetos, AnomieBOT, Shootbamboo, Shlomster, Materialscientist, Citation bot, Stanislao Avogadro, GnawnBot, Xqbot, TracyMcClark, Br77rino, Mlpearc, GrouchoBot, FrescoBot, Riventree, Poison Oak, Victor Victoria, DaBlazesUSay, Itu, Never21, Diannaa, Jynto, Stroppolo, Bernd.Brincken, RjwilmsiBot, Welby7, WikitanvirBot, CAMASS, Rbaselt, Dcirovic, H3llBot, The chemistds, Davey2010, Louisajb, ClueBot NG, Rand21, Helpful Pixie Bot, Explodo-nerd, Cyberbot II, Scrappo55, Dough34, Monkbot, 718281828wk, Medgirl131, VexorAbVikipædia, Emeldir, Alekssobolewski, GreenC bot and Anonymous: 151

- **HMX** Source: https://en.wikipedia.org/wiki/HMX?oldid=734929446 Contributors: Bryan Derksen, Rmrf1024, Jll, GCarty, Big Bob the Finder, Jose Ramos, Gentgeen, Donreed, Altenmann, Sverdrup, Centrx, DocWatson42, Gcanyon, Cacycle, Bender235, Evand, Sietse Snel, Avitek~enwiki, Anthony Appleyard, Raymond, Benjah-bmm27, Yuckfoo, Gene Nygaard, Woohookitty, JeremyA, Rickjpelleg, DePiep, Rjwilmsi, FlaBot, Physchim62, Chobot, Roboto de Ajvol, YurikBot, Yyy, GeeJo, DavidConrad, Georgewilliamherbert, SmackBot, Reedy, Sam8, Edgar181, Chris the speller, Bluebot, DHN-bot~enwiki, Trekphiler, Derek R Bullamore, Smokefoot, Kalathalan, Vgy7ujm, BillFlis, Beetstra, Martinp23, CRGreathouse, Jaeger5432, Rifleman 82, Nabokov, Thijs!bot, Seaphoto, Txomin, Epeefleche, MSBOT, .anacondabot, J.delanoy, Troubleinozark, VolkovBot, Rei-bot, Lamro, Yone Fernandes, Chem-awb, Wikijens, Puppy8800, Anon lynx, JCrowTNT, Addbot, Chempedia, Download, Qjim, Lightbot, Xxxx00, Yobot, CheMoBot, Materialscientist, Stanislao Avogadro, Xqbot, Nirmos, Jonesey95, Hmxt2, Octaazacubane, Boundarylayer, Dcirovic, ZéroBot, AlexKiaChung, Whoop whoop pull up, ClueBot NG, Zandrow, Gluonman, Khazar2, CensoredScribe, OccultZone, KasparBot and Anonymous: 40

- **C-4 (explosive)** Source: https://en.wikipedia.org/wiki/C-4_(explosive)?oldid=741953316 Contributors: Bryan Derksen, Ant, Ixfd64, DropDeadGorgias, Julesd, Jll, Cimon Avaro, Jeandré du Toit, Tobias Conradi, Oaktree b, AnthonyQBachler, Riddley, Misterrick, Lowellian, Puckly, DrachenFyre, Rebrane, Pps, Kent Wang, Xanzzibar, Tea2min, DocWatson42, Tom harrison, Brian Kendig, Crag, SoWhy, Gdr, Quadell, Antandrus, Blazotron, Wikster E, Ary29, Kaustuv, Imroy, Discospinster, Sladen, Ioliver, Bender235, Aude, Martey, Smalljim, Tronno, Alansohn, Mduvekot, Monado, Mac Davis, YDZ, Hohum, Snowolf, Hadlock, TaintedMustard, Mikeo, Kaiser matias, Henry W. Schmitt, Gene Nygaard, RandomWalk, Vashti, GregorB, Kralizec!, Jon Harald Søby, Sin-man, Knidu, Rjwilmsi, Miserlou, Oo64eva, FlaBot, Kolbasz, Monkeyfoo, Benlisquare, ColdFeet, YurikBot, Npgallery, Pigman, Hellbus, Stephenb, Rsrikanth05, Neilbeach, Kimchi.sg, Randomekewaka, IUJHJS-DHE, Merman, Megapixie, Ospalh, DGJM, Gadget850, Vlad, Sandman1142, MarkBrooks, Virogtheconq, NormDor, Sandstein, Yonidebest, Zzuuzz, Ninly, KGasso, Ray Chason, Dubbya9, Pavan.maddamsetti, Victor falk, Attilios, SmackBot, EvilCouch, Hydrogen Iodide, Chairman S., Gilliam, Indium, Chris the speller, Tree Biting Conspiracy, Fluri, Hibernian, DHN-bot~enwiki, Audriusa, Anabus, Abaddon314159, Jasca Ducato, VMS Mosaic, Pax85, Khoikhoi, Jmlk17, Berensflame, Mr Minchin, OutRIAAge, NickPenguin, Pilotguy, Kukini, Isequals, Spinolio, Phinn, John, Heimstern, LWF, Berek Halfhand, Linnell, NongBot~enwiki, Ckatz, BillFlis, Illythr, Anthonypants, Metalrobot, Anonymous anonymous, Kevg, Sifaka, EPO, Muhand, Civil Engineer III, Chetverno, Flubeca, Atomobot, Spacemars88, Will Pittenger, Alexey Feldgendler, Jesse Viviano, Derek17719346, Hydraton31, Chrishans, Nabokov, Ward3001, Khamar, Thijs!bot, Epbr123, Lanky, Gamer007, Headbomb, Marek69, WikiSlasher, AntiVandalBot, Amdkillsintel, Seaphoto, Fireice, Husond, CombatWombat42, Lan Di, SeanCollins, Reign of Toads, .anacondabot, Io Katai, Bakilas, Bongwarrior, Jacce, GODhack~enwiki, Thernlund, Herit, Inhumandecency, Patherfinder, SwedishPsycho, MartinBot, BlackPocket, Death Blade 182, Keith D, Glrx, Mitchx3, Snozzer, Smokizzy, Tgeairn, Slash, J.delanoy, Trusilver, Ginsengbomb, Fuzza409, Jeepday, Destructo 087, Atropos235, STBotD, Animals370, Num1dgen, CardinalDan, Xinhin, Lights, ABF, Jeff G., AlnoktaBOT, Philip Trueman, TXiKiBoT, Rei-bot, BwDraco, VNCCC, StillTrill, Natg 19, Onore Baka Sama, David Condrey, P1h3r1e3d13, Ryguy1994, MajorHazard, Jjdon, EmxBot, SieBot, TJRC, Godofdaydreams, XkamkikazeX, Raazui, VVVBot, Jsc83, Caltas, Bushsux, Yintan, Keilana, Flyer22 Reborn, James.Denholm, Jharris815, JSpung, Allmightyduck, Android Mouse Bot 3, Csloomis, Galaplox, C4blows, Mygearadromance, Tegrenath, ClueBot, Narom, VQuakr, User5802, Zl1vette, Puppy8800, Excirial, Alexbot, Anon lynx, Eeekster, Muenda, Nuclear-Warfare, Proxy User, Stungravy, El bot de la dieta, Versus22, Prav.nj, Ophello, Spitfire, Rror, Mitch Ames, WikHead, Addbot, Freakmighty, Jojhutton, Fyrael, Quiteone 129, DougsTech, SunDragon34, Tiago Morbus Sá, Fieldday-sunday, Fluffernutter, Glane23, Chzz, Getmoreatp, 5 albert square, Binder1, Tide rolls, Lightbot, Apteva, Kurtis, Luckas-bot, Yobot, THEN WHO WAS PHONE?, Backslash Forwardslash, AnomieBOT, Dude340, Dah 144 144, Rubinbot, Jim1138, Minicoop500, Tacticalassasin1, Materialscientist, KittenX3, 90 Auto, 45Factoid44, Madalibi, Armbrust, Armyjoe, Prunesqualer, Wikipediiaa, Shadowjams, Erik9, FrescoBot, Surv1v4l1st, The Grim Killer, Ktm3121, DivineAlpha, Pinethicket, GreenpeaceUbuntuMan, Jonesey95, Tom.Reding, Jschnur, SpaceFlight89, K-carsten, Trappist the monk, Red91, Unique.kevin, Tbhotch, Enemyfish, Forenti, WikitanvirBot, Ncsr11, RA0808, Tommy2010, Dcirovic, K6ka, Famicus, ZéroBot, John Cline, Illegitimate Barrister, Josve05a, Traxs7, Bananaman626, AvicAWB, AManWithNoPlan, Joshkb01, ChesterTheBear, Brandmeister, Tomásdearg92, JeffBengtson, Mineallmine12, Rocketrod1960, Ebehn, Mjbmrbot, Petrb, Fghtre, ClueBot NG, Sreenathvijayan, MelbourneStar, BarrelProof, Cntras, Widr, Extremeness, Frapps, DBigXray, Da5id403, Northamerica1000, CSJJ104, Duxwing, BattyBot, EuroCarGT, FoCuSandLeArN, Hacker226, Frosty, Redalert2fan, 93, Theo's Little Bot, William2001, Flat Out, Michael breeden, Melody Lavender, SymmetricalMegalomania, Finnuser-

48.3. TEXT AND IMAGE SOURCES, CONTRIBUTORS, AND LICENSES 219

top, Retartist, Filedelinkerbot, McGill64, Ceosad, Frogonlilypad, CodyLeePeeSee, JamalAlnuaman, Kylerooni, C4Pro98, JJMC89, CAPTAIN RAJU, Allthefoxes, IsaacR22, Rhdzxjtsr and Anonymous: 503

- **Gunpowder** *Source:* https://en.wikipedia.org/wiki/Gunpowder?oldid=742235611 *Contributors:* Derek Ross, Mav, Bryan Derksen, Timo Honkasalo, The Anome, Malcolm Farmer, Ted Longstaffe, Chuckhoffmann, Rmhermen, Johan Dahlin, William Avery, Roadrunner, Ray Van De Walker, Ewen, Hephaestos, Olivier, RTC, Liftarn, Ixfd64, Evanherk, Shoaler, Delirium, Ahoerstemeier, Snoyes, Notheruser, Julesd, Jll, Glenn, Error, Evercat, Lommer, Hollgor, Fuzheado, WhisperToMe, Timc, Patrick0Moran, Furrykef, SEWilco, Quoth-22, Riddley, Robbot, Moriori, Donreed, Pjbwl, F3meyer, Yelyos, Romanm, Naddy, Securiger, Mayooranathan, Llavigne, Rhombus, Mervyn, Hadal, Robinh, SoLando, Buster2058, Centrx, DocWatson42, MPF, Fennec, Jpta~enwiki, Wolfkeeper, Tom harrison, Bradeos Graphon, Everyking, Lefty, Dratman, Joconnor, Yekrats, Per Honor et Gloria, Brockert, Arconada, Softjada, Aulundi~o, Piotrus, Feline Avenger, 1297, Oknazevad, Klemen Kocjancic, Syvanen, Maikel, Adashiel, Trevor MacInnis, Canterbury Tail, Running, Grstain, Mike Rosoft, Freakofnurture, Auroranorth, Random contributor, Discospinster, Brianhe, Rich Farmbrough, Cnwb, FiP, Vsmith, YUL89YYZ, LindsayH, Bender235, Brian0918, Syp, El C, Kross, Sietse Snel, Dennis Brown, Nickj, Femto, Jpgordon, Adambro, Bobo192, Stesmo, Ypacarai, Harald Hansen, John Vandenberg, Sukiari, Haham hanuka, Ral315, Kierano, Krellis, Jonathunder, Nsaa, Nkedel, Ranveig, Red Winged Duck, Alansohn, Gary, LtNOWIS, Keenan Pepper, Sjschen, Dachannien, Sl, Tocky, Zerofoks, Hu, Snowolf, Wtmitchell, Vedantm, Velella, Max rspct, RainbowOfLight, Mikeo, Dragunova, Gunter, Sleigh, Zootm, Fyrefiend, Adrian.benko, RyanGerbil10, Hijiri88, Zntrip, Bobrayner, Woobookitty, LOL, Bullenwächter, BillC, ^demon, MONGO, Kelisi, Bluemoose, Arrkhal, Male1979, Frankie1969, Gimboid13, Gisling, Graham87, BD2412, Qwertyus, Hiram K Hackenbacker, WoodenTaco, MZMcBride, Vegaswikian, Yug, Crucible Guardian, Lotu, JamesEG, Yamamoto Ichiro, Rangek, FayssalF, Helpful Dave, Cowabunga5587, Old Moonraker, Dan Guan, Musical Linguist, Jamiecampbell, Mark83, Gurch, Nuge, TeaDrinker, Tardis, Silivrenion, Benjwong, Butros, Chobot, Antiuser, Bgwhite, Ahpook, NSR, Benvenuto, Gwernol, Wavelength, Hairy Dude, RussBot, GLaDOS, Nesbit, Akamad, Stephenb, Gaius Cornelius, Ksyrie, Yyy, Shaddack, GeeJo, Wikimachine, David R. Ingham, NawlinWiki, ENeville, Wiki alf, Cassw, Dialectric, Chick Bowen, Rjensen, Texboy, Pyrotec, Cholmes75, JFD, Raven4x4x, Ospalh, Dbtirs, Kyle Barbour, IslandGyrl, Rwalker, Zephalis, Dv82matt, Avalon, FF2010, Calcwatch, Blurble, Pfft Bot~enwiki, Chase me ladies, I'm the Cavalry, Closedmouth, E Wing, Jmackaerospace, Chris Brennan, Smileyface11945, Fram, Mhenriday, Caballero1967, Dynamaniac, Aliens, Kungfuadam, Appleseed, TLSuda, Limkopi, NeilN, Appleby, Nick Michael, Prantasa, SmackBot, Mangoe, Haza-w, SinisterOwl, Au And Cs, Reedy, KnowledgeOfSelf, Deon Steyn, Pgk, Deiaemeth, Jagged 85, Davewild, RedSpruce, Delldot, Cessator, Fnfd, TharkunColl, Commander Keane bot, Xaosflux, Thuringius, Gilliam, Ohnoitsjamie, Hmains, OldsVistaCruiser, Ajpappal, Chris the speller, Bluebot, TimBentley, Movementarian, Bk22, Bduke, Ingestre, Thumperward, Snori, Freedom skies, Kamosuke, SchfiftyThree, Hibernian, MARVEL~enwiki, AtmanDave, Cloj, TheLeopard, Baby Jane, Sbharris, Gracenotes, Zachorious, MaxSem, Halen~enwiki, Xchbla423, Onceler, Famspear, Yaf, Jayanthv86, Can't sleep, clown will eat me, Ammarshaker, RandyKaelber, Ioscius, Onorem, Jennica, Gurps npc, Yidisheryid, Rrburke, Pinkaos, Allan McInnes, Steven X, Aldaron, Regnator, Emre D., Granla, D97rolph, Nakon, TedE, Knowitalloriginal, DMacks, Romanski, Cbriens, Bidabadi~enwiki, Isequals, Fabexplosive, Deepred6502, Chitoryu12, SkippyUK, Yakbasser, Jandcott, 5aret, John, Ergative rlt, AmiDaniel, J 1982, Kipala, Ocanter, LWF, Ishmaelblues, AllStarZ, Peterlewis, Cwiki, Mofomojo, Beetstra, Ehheh, Fedallah, Sob666, RememberMe?, Intranetusa, Naaman Brown, Jose77, Peyre, Sifaka, Phuzion, Krispos42, ILovePlankton, Wjejskenewr, Walton One, Spudstud, Blehfu, Courcelles, Jamesy, Tawkerbot2, ChrisCork, Falconus, Scarecrow Repair, Aaronak, Eiorgiomugini, Scohoust, Papermaker, Basawala, GHe, Kylu, Sangrito, Dgw, MarsRover, Moreschi, WongFeiHung, OracleGuy, Kribbeh, ProfessorPaul, Cydebot, =Axiom=, Meno25, Clayoquot, Gogo Dodo, Ttiotsw, SquareWave, Studerby, Odie5533, B, Tawkerbot4, Nabokov, FastLizard4, Rehcsif, Briantw, Editor at Large, EngineerShorty, Gimmetrow, Rosser1954, Generalmiaow, Wandalstouring, Epbr123, Leedeth, CynicalMe, Hugo.arg, Watersoftheoasis, RevolverOcelotX, Lawiseman, Marek69, NorwegianBlue, James086, Kungfujoe, Southernstar, CharlotteWebb, Nick Number, Sakkout, Wikidenizen, Dawnseeker2000, Natalie Erin, Mentifisto, AntiVandalBot, Royhills, Seaphoto, Sobaka, Sion8, Opelio, Paste, Mary Mark Ockerbloom, Fayenatic london, RSekulovich, Darklilac, Chill doubt, Yellowdesk, Ravimpillay, Trappist, Student Driver, MikeLynch, Kariteh, JAnDbot, Bugna19, DuncanHill, Plantsurfer, Tosayit, Medconn, Matthew Fennell, Arch dude, Lisle45, Sigurd Dragon Slayer, Joycedula, Ccrrccrr, Mrflip, NSR77, Gavia immer, Acroterion, Penubag, Magioladitis, Jaysweet, Kreecher, Bongwarrior, VoABot II, Mondebleu, Cowrider, JamesBWatson, Think outside the box, Joachimv, Thernlund, Animum, 28421u2232nfenfcenc, Cpl Syx, Vssun, DerHexer, JaGa, Pyrochem, Khalid Mahmood, Gun Powder Ma, Lost tourist, Hdt83, MartinBot, CliffC, Arjun01, Keith D, Jay Litman, Glrx, R'n'B, CommonsDelinker, RockMFR, BJ Axel, J.delanoy, Nev1, Kimse, Uncle Dick, Dbiel, 12dstring, Siryendor, Polenth, BrokenSphere, Katalaveno, McSly, Son of More, Jeepday, Chanman121, NewEnglandYankee, Fountains of Bryn Mawr, Serge925, Chasw0405, SJP, Bobianite, Ontarioboy, Joshua Isaac, Juliancolton, DH85868993, Vanished user 39948282, HighKing, Idioma-bot, NatePhysics, Chaos forge5, Meiskam, Malik Shabazz, Thomas.W, Johan1298~enwiki, ABF, Peter Bell, Firstorm, Soliloquial, Philip Trueman, Oshwah, Ambush14, Technopat, Ann Stouter, ElinorD, GcSwRhIc, Crohnie, Someguy1221, Taceo, Steven J. Anderson, Corvus cornix, Ferengi, Meatwaggon, Colteh, Wikieditor12, LeaveSleaves, Raymondwinn, BotKung, Markboltres, David Condrey, Terrymacro, Katimawan2005, Njn, Osho-Jabbe, SQL, Cantiorix, Ccashell, SpicyDragonZ, Imheretohelppeople, Imheretohelppeople2, Master of the Orichalcos, Socksysquirrel, Nibios, Bobo The Ninja, Palaeovia, Praefectorian, Helpmecomeon, Dark Dragon Sword, PericlesofAthens, Fsda, Moerou toukon, Mxc140, Okme123, Biscuittin, Lylefor, StAnselm, Coffee, Ttony21, Tiddly Tom, Dough4872, Scarian, WereSpielChequers, Basketball forev, Dawn Bard, GrooveDog, Philportman, Keilana, Adabow, Flyer22 Reborn, Jjw, Oda Mari, JSpung, Oxymoron83, Antonio Lopez, John fromer, Hello71, Steven Crossin, Lightmouse, Ealdgyth, Alex.muller, Mátyás, Billyg, Bake hi, Kgdsaxfnb, Mygerardromance, Tinglepal, PlantTrees, DRTllbrg, Asher196, Faithlessthewonderboy, IAC-62, ClueBot, Swamptortoise, Binksternet, Hustvedt, Micky750k, Ideal gas equation, The Thing That Should Not Be, RashersTierney, Sevilledade, NiD.29, J8079s, Eclectic hippie, Tallman77777, Blanchardb, Starstylers, Bwolf77, Excirial, Jusdafax, Eeekster, The Founders Intent, Alpha Ralpha Boulevard, NuclearWarfare, Peter.C, Frozen4322, SchreiberBike, Thewellman, Teraldthecat, PaintedWombat, Thingg, Error − 128, Nelsen98, DJ Sturm, Balmacaan, SoxBot III, Kirkite, Bravissimo594, InternetMeme, XLinkBot, Aaron north, Spitfire, Gonzonoir, Dark Mage, Rror, LeheckaG, P30Carl, Facts707, Grmike, NellieBly, Mitter, Flash111, Badgernet, Subversive.sound, JinJian, EEng, HexaChord, Ryanjstephenson, SireMarshall, Addbot, Proofreader77, Vero.Verite, Willking1979, Manuel Trujillo Berges, AVand, Some jerk on the Internet, Vtria 08, Guoguo12, DougsTech, C3r4, Fieldday-sunday, Vishnava, Fluffernutter, Benjamin Trovato, Jim10701, MrOllie, Download, SrAtoz, Chamal N, Glane23, Bassbonerocks, West.andrew.g, Bwrs, Tide rolls, Pietrow, Krano, Teles, MrMontag, Yobot, DerechoReguerraz, Senator Palpatine, Rsquire3, Il MusLiM HyBRiD Il, Usedwake, PMLawrence, THEN WHO WAS PHONE?, KirkCliff2, AnomieBOT, Kristen Eriksen, 1exec1, Jim1138, Galoubet, Royote, AdjustShift, Brerose, Kingpin13, Materialscientist, The High Fin Sperm Whale, Eumolpo, MidnightBlueMan, GB fan, ArthurBot, Quebec99, Beny898, Addihockey10, JimVC3, Timmyshin, BritishWatcher, Ubcule, Santista1982, J04n, Cwchng, Abce2, Mark Schierbecker, Nx, 78.26, Luciandrei, Lyabes31, Shadowjams, WebCiteBOT, Muffinstastenice, SD5, Bobbobbob12333, A.amitkumar, Celuici, Depictionimage, FrescoBot, Riventree, Tranletuhan, Lookatthis, VS6507, Recognizance, OgreBot, Citation bot 1, Neyagawa, Pinethicket, Boulaur, Edderso, Abductive, Lesath, Hard Sin, Maria Chady, Jschnur, Ezhuttukari, Serols, Meaghan, Mikespedia, Miguel Escopeta, SkyMachine, IVAN3MAN,

Escribblings, FoxBot, Ollo2301, Vrenator, Reaper Eternal, Diannaa, Eric615, DARTH SIDIOUS 2, Olawlor, Cathardic, Wideg3cko, Mean as custard, Bethanyy104, RjwilmsiBot, Limequat, RG104, Ripchip Bot, Jackehammond, Bhawani Gautam, Hajatvrc, NerdyScienceDude, Rolfthecat, Slon02, CalicoCatLover, Skamecrazy123, EmausBot, John of Reading, Orphan Wiki, WikitanvirBot, Annette.whitehurst, Dewritech, Vlazov, GuyFawlks, Peaceoutpeop, Syncategoremata, GoingBatty, KevinCurator, RenamedUser01302013, NotAnonymous0, Bettymnz4, Bridgeboy4, ZxxZxxZ, Mo ainm, Brandonhab, Slightsmile, Tommy2010, Winner 42, Wikipelli, Dcirovic, K6ka, Rmelonides, Lucas Thoms, Tanner Swett, A2soup, Knight1993, Mekong mainstream, Shuipzv3, Lateg, EdMcCorduck, Pookpok, ChembioMajor, Spartanassassian, MajorVariola, Limasenla, EHFOH, Wayne Slam, Labnoor, Calvin Lourdes He, Lord Psyko Jo, Donner60, Inka 888, Interloper2, ElockidAlternate, ChuispastonBot, Kristian Lindahl, DASHBotAV, Wikiwind, E. Fokker, Petrb, KYO888, Awewe, ClueBot NG, Gareth Griffith-Jones, GnollChieftain, Jojororo, LogX, Micah702, Bulldog73, JesseW900, DieSwartzPunkt, Widr, Rurik the Varangian, DingwenLi, Platonicmaria, MerlIwBot, RafikiSykes, Secret of success, Helpful Pixie Bot, ?oygul, Raffinate2, Mr. Credible, Calabe1992, Gob Lofa, DaveRossetti, Neogovernment, Justinbkay, BG19bot, Toakase, George Ponderevo, Eladynnus, Registreernu, Kangaroopower, PhnomPencil, MongolWiki, Mysterytrey, MusikAnimal, Unclenick01, Crazedpsyc, Kendall-K1, Cold Season, Red Rover112, Mark Arsten, NoopsterXD, Mughal Lohar, Twads12345, Paulitzer, ASCIIn2Bme, Sridhar100000, Assar, Zedshort, JellyJoy1234, Achowat, Lieutenant of Melkor, Piasecki, BattyBot, Troll98, Troll998, Pratyya Ghosh, Lebaige, ChrisGualtieri, Khazar2, Eoxenford, نفـی‌روز اردوواالل, Dexbot, Alexwang65, Mysterious Whisper, TehPlaneFreak, Wikimalkindy, Dravyn, Lugia2453, Frosty, Hair, Fox2k11, T42N24T, Bethymcq, CklDHsbi6, Rajmaan, Scottdudefun, Reatlas, AllenY99, PinkAmpersand, Epicgenius, MasterSpellcaster, Pnta-pntb, Garicula, Garicula2, Debouch, Harlem Baker Hughes, WalkAndTalk, Mjfantom, Ruzzer123, Garicula0, Ugog Nizdast, Qubist, Garicula20, Khanate General, Makerekam, Quenhitran, Drtilford, Lucker423, Museumgoing, Sepamu92, Antrocent, Monkbot, Horseless Headman, Thetoadoftruth123456, Wilsondylan319, Yourmom12334, Ivan's Hella Swag, Csuzxbfdfbage, TerryAlex, Dippydop, Urow3nd2, Fuckoffjew, TrackerAR, Gladamas, Yprpyqp, YeOldeGentleman, Bscvbsdghdfg, Sweg12345678, Ad bros, KasparBot, Adam9007, Username3.10, Chrisjgsb, Anthracenedione, MichaelNg69, KSFT, Thelachlank, CAPTAIN RAJU, Tommyschuelkeandsabrina, Dcornell0103, Wiki5012, Qzd, Bjobjoska, Dazany13, Abdullah strong habeeb, Destroy626, Cheesebugerlord69 and Anonymous: 1335

- **Flash powder** *Source:* https://en.wikipedia.org/wiki/Flash_powder?oldid=741271228 *Contributors:* Jaknouse, RTC, Julesd, Stone, Riddley, DocWatson42, 23skidoo, Ncurses, Gerweck, Zenosparadox, Tom12519, Swmcd, Zanturaeon, Firebug, Physchim62, King of Hearts, Ekstasis, YurikBot, Hede2000, Shaddack, Tobybuk, Katieh5584, Groyolo, SmackBot, Reedy, Edgar181, Ohnoitsjamie, Chris the speller, KirbyWallace, Snori, Suicidalhamster, AK7, Can't sleep, clown will eat me, MJP87, Tim Q. Wells, Mgiganteus1, RomanSpa, Ian Dalziel, Jamesy, Tawkerbot2, Willancs, JohnCD, WeggeBot, TJDay, Zomic13, Nabokov, CLSwiki, TimVickers, MaxBrains, VoABot II, LafinJack, Kingofthemorning, Pyrochem, MartinBot, NReitzel, Chasw0405, Cremepuff222, BotKung, WereSpielChequers, Malcolmxl5, Lightmouse, CarolinaSawDust, Rjc34, Ainlina, ClueBot, Sliderulex, DJSparky, Carriearchdale, XLinkBot, BodhisattvaBot, HexaChord, Addbot, Opus88888, Jonyshin, Luckasbot, Paraballo, KDS4444, Materialscientist, ArthurBot, LovesMacs, LilHelpa, Xqbot, Cantons-de-l'Est, Juscallmesteve, Niertap, Symplectic Map, I dream of horses, Baileyquarter, Mynster, Dolescum, ZxxZxxZ, Mariov0288, Tomásdearg92, USliferzon, ClueBot NG, KDS444, Widr, Theopolisme, Explodo-nerd, David.moreno72, Meeeeeeee39, Tentinator, Boo2blue, Niffy2000, Potchama and Anonymous: 147

- **Ammonal** *Source:* https://en.wikipedia.org/wiki/Ammonal?oldid=741820178 *Contributors:* JidGom, Riddley, DocWatson42, Knutux, Leandros, Nabla, Fernandojs, A2Kafir, InterruptorJones, Lectonar, Mac Davis, Thryduulf, Evan C, TotoBaggins, GraemeLeggett, Ian Dunster, Rangek, FlaBot, BjKa, YurikBot, Los688, KnightRider~enwiki, SmackBot, Krashlandon, J. Finkelstein, Hotspur23, Tintenammae, CBM, Nabokov, Chill doubt, Barek, .anacondabot, Gundato, Idioma-bot, Rei-bot, Sk741~enwiki, ViennaUK, Lightmouse, Moletrouser, A Georgian, Cngoulimis, Skyrocket654, Niceguyedc, Rickfive, Alexbot, Thewellman, Addbot, MartinezMD, Zorrobot, EVCM, Ulric1313, GrouchoBot, Haeinous, Tom.Reding, NitricAcidandTHC, Thedougler604, Helpful Pixie Bot, ChrisGualtieri, Mogism, Tommy Pinball, Monochrome Monitor, Dough34, Bender the Bot and Anonymous: 39

- **Armstrong's mixture** *Source:* https://en.wikipedia.org/wiki/Armstrong'{}s_mixture?oldid=741570714 *Contributors:* Jll, Ed g2s, Riddley, Darrien, Rick Burns, Canterbury Tail, Discospinster, Grutness, Bukvoed, Commando303, Firebug, Catsmeat, Physchim62, Edgar181, Gveret Tered, Christian75, Omerzu, NReitzel, Euclid1299, Fatpratmatt, Kavadi carrier, PrimusUnus, Idioma-bot, Broadbot, Kusk~enwiki, PL290, Addbot, EVCM, Materialscientist, ArthurBot, AbigailAbernathy, DASHBot, ClueBot NG, Helpful Pixie Bot, Cadillac000, Dacker1256, Grizzly510, GreenC bot and Anonymous: 19

- **Sprengel explosive** *Source:* https://en.wikipedia.org/wiki/Sprengel_explosive?oldid=636261134 *Contributors:* JakeVortex, Gbleem, Securiger, Lowellian, Longhair, JeremyA, Rjwilmsi, Shaddack, SmackBot, Reedy, Astrochemist, DerHexer, TXiKiBoT, Lamro, Sikboi, Addbot, Lightbot, AnomieBOT, Riventree and Anonymous: 3

- **ANFO** *Source:* https://en.wikipedia.org/wiki/ANFO?oldid=739713643 *Contributors:* Kpjas, Mav, Bryan Derksen, RTC, Fred Bauder, Isomorphic, Gbleem, Julesd, Mulad, Dcoetzee, AWhiteC, Stone, WhisperToMe, AnthonyQBachler, Riddley, Securiger, Centrx, DocWatson42, Ike~enwiki, Karn, Bkonrad, NeoJustin, Timbatron, Edcolins, OldakQuill, Discospinster, Rich Farmbrough, Hydrox, PatrikR, Nsaa, Jumbuck, Gene Nygaard, Evan C, Woohookitty, Xover, Before My Ken, WadeSimMiser, Lapsed Pacifist, Hbdragon88, GraemeLeggett, Pfalstad, Descendall, BD2412, Erikvanthienen, Jivecat, FlaBot, Chobot, YurikBot, NTBot~enwiki, Hellbus, Shaddack, Anomalocaris, Bachrach44, Millsey, Tachs, TransUtopian, Milliped, Petri Krohn, タチコマ robot, SmackBot, Reedy, Anastrophe, Eskimbot, Onebravemonkey, Edgar181, Gorman, Chris the speller, Thumperward, Hibernian, Fredvanner, Felipe La Rotta, Yaf, Ambix, Will Beback, Lambiam, John, Robofish, NongBot~enwiki, Hvn0413, D12000, Iridescent, Egor, Godgundam10, Fletcher, Srajan01, Christian75, ChrisIk02, Nabokov, Thijs!bot, CynicalMe, Nick Number, Gökhan, T96 grh, Father Goose, Miaers, KTo288, Afaber012, Holme053, JWhiteheadcc, SieBot, Galaplox, Ironman1104, ClueBot, Maxmc1027, Niceguyedc, Socrates2008, John Nevard, FOARP, Boleyn, SilvonenBot, Addbot, Dk pdx, Mentisock, LaaknorBot, Incredibleman007, Tide rolls, Lightbot, Cesiumfrog, Zorrobot, Hobbychemist, Yobot, Ptbotgourou, Librsh, Donfbreed, AnomieBOT, Archon 2488, 1exec1, EVCM, Quebec99, Jmundo, Champlax, GrouchoBot, JanDeFietser, Omnipaedista, Johnflan, Fixentries, Zacharysyoung, Cm2009, Weetoddid, Dnavirus, Rayshade, Miguel Escopeta, IVAN3MAN, Cnwilliams, Firsthuman, Kevintroy, RjwilmsiBot, VernoWhitney, NerdyScienceDude, GoingBatty, Joeseph0171, Dcirovic, Koryds2008, AvicBot, Shuipzv3, Redhanker, Ὁ οἶστρος, Sodmy, Beemmgee, 2tuntony, Socialservice, ClueBot NG, Biotechscientist, BarrelProof, Morgan Riley, Helpful Pixie Bot, HMSSolent, DanDan0101, Superdweezil, Tom Pippens, Safehaven86, WikiHannibal, MatsuRT, Cyberbot II, MyTuppence, Mysterious Whisper, Mogism, Locky153, Skinkworks, Absonant, SenfBaum, Narky Blert, DangerousJXD, Perapin, Donjuanmiguelacosta, TWaMoE, MickTheAwesomer, GreenC bot, Rhdzxjtsr and Anonymous: 163

- **Cheddite** *Source:* https://en.wikipedia.org/wiki/Cheddite?oldid=703415235 *Contributors:* Bryan Derksen, Heron, Rossami, Lee M, Securiger, Lowellian, Centrx, ChrisJ, Anthony Appleyard, SmackBot, Reedy, Krenn, Smokefoot, Hotspur23, Hqb, Cvf-ps, Addbot, Lightbot, Karanne, Dawzab, Erik9bot, FrescoBot, Miracle Pen, Lennard21, Rohan367, Backendgaming and Anonymous: 3

- **Oxyliquit** *Source:* https://en.wikipedia.org/wiki/Oxyliquit?oldid=740835380 *Contributors:* Patrick, Evanherk, Gbleem, Finlay McWalter, Naddy, Wolfkeeper, Leonard G., Degir6328, Giraffedata, Gene Nygaard, WadeSimMiser, Nukeqler, YurikBot, Gaius Cornelius, Shaddack, Redgolpe, SmackBot, Reedy, Weeniemann, Hgrosser, Rigadoun, Gil Gamesh, Van helsing, Ayecee, AlleborgoBot, Dusti, Addbot, Luckas-bot, Materialscientist, GliderMaven, Postlunarpaintings, EmausBot, ClueBot NG, Tideflat, ChrisGualtieri, Enterprisey, Dexbot, PaperKooper, Lugia2453, Doopadee, Jnsison94, Rodneykevins, School Friends of Karachi, Pglavey, Loxford7h, Bhutunpali, Rackcitybeach, Natiluvsnutella, Tahsin wsit, Mik757, Nagledagreat, OneFluidMovement, GreenC bot and Anonymous: 9

- **Panclastite** *Source:* https://en.wikipedia.org/wiki/Panclastite?oldid=638812040 *Contributors:* Mboverload, Shaddack, Arichnad, Betacommand, Colonies Chris, Nabokov, Chill doubt, Jfan00 IMG Alexbot, Addbot, D'ohBot, Oonissie, BattyBot, Monkbot and Anonymous: 3

48.3.2 Images

- **File:13-07-23-kienbaum-unterdruckkammer-33.jpg** *Source:* https://upload.wikimedia.org/wikipedia/commons/e/eb/13-07-23-kienbaum-unterdruckkammer-33.jpg *License:* CC BY 3.0 *Contributors:* Own work *Original artist:* Ralf Roletschek
- **File:2005fuel_import.PNG** *Source:* https://upload.wikimedia.org/wikipedia/commons/d/d4/2005fuel_import.PNG *License:* CC BY-SA 3.0 *Contributors:* Transferred from en.wikipedia to Commons by Stefan4 using CommonsHelper. *Original artist:* Anwar saadat at English Wikipedia
- **File:38_Special_-_SP_-_SB_-_1.jpg** *Source:* https://upload.wikimedia.org/wikipedia/commons/3/34/38_Special_-_SP_-_SB_-_1.jpg *License:* Public domain *Contributors:* This photo was taken by me with my camera. *Original artist:* Malis
- **File:38_special_FMJ_-_S&B_including_box.jpg** *Source:* https://upload.wikimedia.org/wikipedia/commons/5/5d/38_special_FMJ_-_S%26B_including_box.jpg *License:* CC BY 3.0 *Contributors:* My own camera *Original artist:* Me (Aida)
- **File:3rd_Battalion_3rd_Marines_controlled_detonation.jpg** *Source:* https://upload.wikimedia.org/wikipedia/commons/c/c8/3rd_Battalion_3rd_Marines_controlled_detonation.jpg *License:* Public domain *Contributors:* http://www.usmc.mil/unit/imef/Pages/OperationNewDawnpatrolsleadtocachefinds.aspx *Original artist:* Sgt. Mark Fayloga
- **File:40mm_table_tennis_ball_Celluloid.jpg** *Source:* https://upload.wikimedia.org/wikipedia/commons/c/cd/40mm_table_tennis_ball_Celluloid.jpg *License:* CC0 *Contributors:* Own work *Original artist:* Jü
- **File:45_ACP_-_FMJ_-_SB_-_2.jpg** *Source:* https://upload.wikimedia.org/wikipedia/commons/6/66/45_ACP_-_FMJ_-_SB_-_2.jpg *License:* Public domain *Contributors:* This photo was taken by me with my camera. *Original artist:* Malis
- **File:45_ACP_-_FMJ_-_SB_-_3.jpg** *Source:* https://upload.wikimedia.org/wikipedia/commons/4/43/45_ACP_-_FMJ_-_SB_-_3.jpg *License:* Public domain *Contributors:* This photo was taken by me with my camera. *Original artist:* Malis
- **File:7.62x25_-_FMJ_-_SB_-_1.jpg** *Source:* https://upload.wikimedia.org/wikipedia/commons/9/9f/7.62x25_-_FMJ_-_SB_-_1.jpg *License:* Public domain *Contributors:* This photo was taken by me with my camera. *Original artist:* Malis
- **File:9.2_inch_howitzer_shell_IWM.JPG** *Source:* https://upload.wikimedia.org/wikipedia/commons/a/a9/9.2_inch_howitzer_shell_IWM.JPG *License:* Attribution *Contributors:* Steve Johnson's cyber-heritage website http://www.cyber-heritage.com/imperial_war_museum/IMG_2584.html *Original artist:* Steve Johnson http://www.cyber-heritage.com
- **File:Acetone-peroxide-trimer-from-xtal-2009-3D-balls.png** *Source:* https://upload.wikimedia.org/wikipedia/commons/6/68/Acetone-peroxide-trimer-from-xtal-2009-3D-balls.png *License:* Public domain *Contributors:* Own work *Original artist:* Ben Mills
- **File:Acetone_Peroxide_Synthesis_V.2.svg** *Source:* https://upload.wikimedia.org/wikipedia/commons/c/c3/Acetone_Peroxide_Synthesis_V.2.svg *License:* CC0 *Contributors:* Own work *Original artist:* Jü
- **File:Acetone_peroxide.jpg** *Source:* https://upload.wikimedia.org/wikipedia/commons/b/bf/Acetone_peroxide.jpg *License:* Public domain *Contributors:* Own work *Original artist:* Spatula Tzar~commonswiki (talk)
- **File:Acetone_peroxide.svg** *Source:* https://upload.wikimedia.org/wikipedia/commons/7/73/Acetone_peroxide.svg *License:* Public domain *Contributors:* Own work *Original artist:* Benrr101
- **File:Aluminium_cylinder.jpg** *Source:* https://upload.wikimedia.org/wikipedia/commons/8/8a/Aluminium_cylinder.jpg *License:* CC BY-SA 3.0 *Contributors:* Own work *Original artist:*
- **File:Ambox_important.svg** *Source:* https://upload.wikimedia.org/wikipedia/commons/b/b4/Ambox_important.svg *License:* Public domain *Contributors:* Own work, based off of Image:Ambox scales.svg *Original artist:* Dsmurat (talk · contribs)
- **File:Ammonium_nitrate-fuel_oil_(ANFO)_explosive.jpg** *Source:* https://upload.wikimedia.org/wikipedia/commons/f/f8/Ammonium_nitrate-fuel_oil_%28ANFO%29_explosive.jpg *License:* CC BY-SA 3.0 *Contributors:* Own work *Original artist:* Firsthuman
- **File:Anfoa.jpg** *Source:* https://upload.wikimedia.org/wikipedia/commons/6/6e/Anfoa.jpg *License:* CC BY-SA 2.5 *Contributors:* Halen *Original artist:* Halen
- **File:Barometer_mercury_column_hg.jpg** *Source:* https://upload.wikimedia.org/wikipedia/commons/b/b9/Barometer_mercury_column_hg.jpg *License:* CC BY-SA 2.5 *Contributors:* Own work *Original artist:* Hannes Grobe 19:02, 3 September 2006 (UTC)
- **File:Barout_khaneh_near_Tehran_by_Eugène_Flandin.jpg** *Source:* https://upload.wikimedia.org/wikipedia/commons/9/93/Barout_khaneh_near_Tehran_by_Eug%C3%A8ne_Flandin.jpg *License:* Public domain *Contributors:* Voyage en Perse, avec Flandin, éd. Gide et Baudry, 1851 *Original artist:* Eugène Flandin
- **File:Benzinepomp002.jpg** *Source:* https://upload.wikimedia.org/wikipedia/commons/9/9c/Benzinepomp002.jpg *License:* Public domain *Contributors:* ? *Original artist:* ?
- **File:Black_Powder_Close_Up.jpg** *Source:* https://upload.wikimedia.org/wikipedia/commons/9/9c/Black_Powder_Close_Up.jpg *License:* Public domain *Contributors:* Own work *Original artist:* Mondebleu (talk) (Uploads)

- File:Bombing_up_106_Squadron_Lancaster_WWII_IWM_CH_12541.jpg *Source:* https://upload.wikimedia.org/wikipedia/commons/a/a3/Bombing_up_106_Squadron_Lancaster_WWII_IWM_CH_12541.jpg *License:* Public domain *Contributors:* This is photograph CH 12541 from the collections of the Imperial War Museums. *Original artist:* Bellamy W (F/O), Royal Air Force official photographer
- File:Booth_deringer.jpg *Source:* https://upload.wikimedia.org/wikipedia/commons/1/11/Booth_deringer.jpg *License:* Public domain *Contributors:* ? *Original artist:* ?
- File:British_20_mm_Oerlikon_shell_diagrams.jpg *Source:* https://upload.wikimedia.org/wikipedia/commons/a/a5/British_20_mm_Oerlikon_shell_diagrams.jpg *License:* Public domain *Contributors:* Downloaded from Steve Johnson's cyber-heritage page at http://web.ukonline.co.uk/stephen.johnson/arms/cnon20.jpg *Original artist:* Page layout changed to suit screen display by User:Rcbutcher.
- File:Bronze_cannon_of_1332.jpg *Source:* https://upload.wikimedia.org/wikipedia/commons/a/aa/Bronze_cannon_of_1332.jpg *License:* CC BY-SA 3.0 *Contributors:* Own work *Original artist:* BabelStone
- File:Burst_muzzle_loader_barrel.jpg *Source:* https://upload.wikimedia.org/wikipedia/commons/d/de/Burst_muzzle_loader_barrel.jpg *License:* CC BY-SA 3.0 *Contributors:* Photographed at Barocktage at Bückeburg Palace, Germany *Original artist:* Photographed by User:Bullenwächter
- File:Buying_fuelwood.jpeg *Source:* https://upload.wikimedia.org/wikipedia/commons/a/af/Buying_fuelwood.jpeg *License:* CC BY 2.5 *Contributors:* ? *Original artist:* ?
- File:Büchsenmeysterei_1531_CHF.jpg *Source:* https://upload.wikimedia.org/wikipedia/commons/b/b7/B%C3%BCchsenmeysterei_1531_CHF.jpg *License:* Public domain *Contributors:* Chemical Heritage Foundation *Original artist:* Anonymous
- File:C4_explosion.jpg *Source:* https://upload.wikimedia.org/wikipedia/commons/f/f9/C4_explosion.jpg *License:* Public domain *Contributors:* NIST, http://patapsco.nist.gov/ImageGallery/details.cfm?imageid=804 *Original artist:* Credit: NIST
- File:CANDU_fuel_bundles.jpg *Source:* https://upload.wikimedia.org/wikipedia/commons/5/57/CANDU_fuel_bundles.jpg *License:* Attribution *Contributors:* Originally uploaded to English Wikipedia by Dr. Jeremy Whitlock (User:Whitlock) of AECL. *Original artist:* AECL
- File:Charging_with_anfo.jpg *Source:* https://upload.wikimedia.org/wikipedia/commons/e/ee/Charging_with_anfo.jpg *License:* CC BY-SA 2.5 *Contributors:* Self-published work by Halen *Original artist:* Timo Halén (Halen)
- File:Chelyabinsk_meteor_event_consequences_in_Drama_Theatre.jpg *Source:* https://upload.wikimedia.org/wikipedia/commons/5/59/Chelyabinsk_meteor_event_consequences_in_Drama_Theatre.jpg *License:* CC BY-SA 3.0 *Contributors:* http://gallery.ru/watch?ph=z6Q-ewl8A *Original artist:* Nikita Plekhanov
- File:Chinese_rocket.png *Source:* https://upload.wikimedia.org/wikipedia/commons/5/5e/Chinese_rocket.png *License:* Public domain *Contributors:* http://history.msfc.nasa.gov/rocketry/03.html *Original artist:* NASA
- File:Coal_anthracite.jpg *Source:* https://upload.wikimedia.org/wikipedia/commons/7/72/Coal_anthracite.jpg *License:* Public domain *Contributors:* http://resourcescommittee.house.gov/subcommittees/emr/usgsweb/photogallery/images/Coal,%20anthracite_.jpg *Original artist:* ?
- File:Commons-logo.svg *Source:* https://upload.wikimedia.org/wikipedia/en/4/4a/Commons-logo.svg *License:* CC-BY-SA-3.0 *Contributors:* ? *Original artist:* ?
- File:Cougar_Hit_By_IED.jpg *Source:* https://upload.wikimedia.org/wikipedia/commons/b/b1/Cougar_Hit_By_IED.jpg *License:* Public domain *Contributors:* IraqSlogger, EUReferendum, Defense Industry Daily, Defense Department Contracts for 2,400 More MRAP Vehicles *Original artist:* U.S. Military Original uploader was IraqVet225 at en.wikipedia
- File:Crystal_energy.svg *Source:* https://upload.wikimedia.org/wikipedia/commons/1/14/Crystal_energy.svg *License:* LGPL *Contributors:* Own work conversion of Image:Crystal_128_energy.png *Original artist:* Dhatfield
- File:Cutaway_diagram_of_various_types_of_blasting_caps_and_detonators.svg *Source:* https://upload.wikimedia.org/wikipedia/commons/b/b7/Cutaway_diagram_of_various_types_of_blasting_caps_and_detonators.svg *License:* CC BY-SA 4.0 *Contributors:* Own work *Original artist:* raster: George William Herbert
- File:D-W002_Warnung_vor_explosionsgefaehrlichen_Stoffen_ty.svg *Source:* https://upload.wikimedia.org/wikipedia/commons/9/9f/D-W002_Warnung_vor_explosionsgefaehrlichen_Stoffen_ty.svg *License:* Public domain *Contributors:* drawn by Torsten Henning *Original artist:* Torsten Henning
- File:Dangclass1.svg *Source:* https://upload.wikimedia.org/wikipedia/commons/e/e7/Dangclass1.svg *License:* CC-BY-SA-3.0 *Contributors:* with Inkskape after Image:Dangclass1.gif by Kaverin *Original artist:* User:W!B:
- File:Dangclass5_1.png *Source:* https://upload.wikimedia.org/wikipedia/commons/6/68/Dangclass5_1.png *License:* CC-BY-SA-3.0 *Contributors:* ? *Original artist:* ?
- File:Dardanelles_Gun_Turkish_Bronze_15c.png *Source:* https://upload.wikimedia.org/wikipedia/commons/9/90/Dardanelles_Gun_Turkish_Bronze_15c.png *License:* Public domain *Contributors:* http://en.wikipedia.org/wiki/Image:Dardanelles_Gun_Turkish_Bronze_15c.png *Original artist:* en:User:The Land
- File:De_la_pirotechnia_1540_Title_Page_AQ1_(1).jpg *Source:* https://upload.wikimedia.org/wikipedia/commons/8/8d/De_la_pirotechnia_1540_Title_Page_AQ1_%281%29.jpg *License:* Public domain *Contributors:* Chemical Heritage Foundation *Original artist:* Vannoccio Biringucci
- File:Defense.gov_photo_essay_070901-F-3050V-503.jpg *Source:* https://upload.wikimedia.org/wikipedia/commons/2/2a/Defense.gov_photo_essay_070901-F-3050V-503.jpg *License:* Public domain *Contributors:*
  This Image was released by the United States Air Force with the ID 070901-F-3050V-503 <a class='external text' href='//commons.wikimedia.org/w/index.php?title=Category:Files_created_by_the_United_States_Air_Force_with_known_IDs,,&,.filefrom=070901-F-3050V-503#mw-category-media'>(next)</a>.
  This tag does not indicate the copyright status of the attached work. A normal copyright tag is still required. See Commons:Licensing for more information.
  Original artist: Master Sgt. Jim Varhegyi

48.3. TEXT AND IMAGE SOURCES, CONTRIBUTORS, AND LICENSES

- **File:Dnepr_rocket_lift-off_1.jpg** *Source:* https://upload.wikimedia.org/wikipedia/commons/4/47/Dnepr_rocket_lift-off_1.jpg *License:* CC BY 2.5 *Contributors:* ? *Original artist:* ?
- **File:EYE_Film_Institute_Netherlands_-_Nitrate_film_decay_-_3.JPG** *Source:* https://upload.wikimedia.org/wikipedia/commons/c/ce/EYE_Film_Institute_Netherlands_-_Nitrate_film_decay_-_3.JPG *License:* CC BY-SA 4.0 *Contributors:* Own work *Original artist:* Hansmuller
- **File:Edit-clear.svg** *Source:* https://upload.wikimedia.org/wikipedia/en/f/f2/Edit-clear.svg *License:* Public domain *Contributors:* The Tango! Desktop Project. *Original artist:*

    The people from the Tango! project. And according to the meta-data in the file, specifically: "Andreas Nilsson, and Jakub Steiner (although minimally)."
- **File:Edward_Teller_(1958)-LLNL.jpg** *Source:* https://upload.wikimedia.org/wikipedia/commons/c/cf/Edward_Teller_(1958)-LLNL.jpg *License:* Public domain *Contributors:* ? *Original artist:* ?
- **File:Eod2.jpg** *Source:* https://upload.wikimedia.org/wikipedia/commons/6/6d/Eod2.jpg *License:* Public domain *Contributors:* ? *Original artist:* ?
- **File:Essais_nucleaires_manif.jpg** *Source:* https://upload.wikimedia.org/wikipedia/commons/9/93/Essais_nucleaires_manif.jpg *License:* CC-BY-SA-3.0 *Contributors:* Community of the Ark of Lanza del Vasto. *Original artist:* Community of the Ark of Lanza del Vasto.
- **File:Explosions.jpg** *Source:* https://upload.wikimedia.org/wikipedia/commons/c/c7/Explosions.jpg *License:* Public domain *Contributors:* ? *Original artist:* ?
- **File:Extraction_of_oil.jpg** *Source:* https://upload.wikimedia.org/wikipedia/commons/b/ba/Extraction_of_oil.jpg *License:* Public domain *Contributors:* Угроза «финансового обрыва» и экономика РФ: сценарии развития *Original artist:* VOA
- **File:F1000016.JPG** *Source:* https://upload.wikimedia.org/wikipedia/commons/5/5a/F1000016.JPG *License:* Public domain *Contributors:* English Wikipedia *Original artist:* Eternalsleeper
- **File:Fat_man.jpg** *Source:* https://upload.wikimedia.org/wikipedia/commons/c/c2/Fat_man.jpg *License:* Public domain *Contributors:* U.S. Department of Defense *Original artist:* U.S. Department of Defense
- **File:Fission_bomb_assembly_methods.svg** *Source:* https://upload.wikimedia.org/wikipedia/commons/c/cb/Fission_bomb_assembly_methods.svg *License:* Public domain *Contributors:* Own work *Original artist:* Fastfission
- **File:Flag_of_IAEA.svg** *Source:* https://upload.wikimedia.org/wikipedia/commons/5/54/Flag_of_IAEA.svg *License:* Public domain *Contributors:* Flag code: [1] *Original artist:* IAEA
- **File:Flash_Powders.JPG** *Source:* https://upload.wikimedia.org/wikipedia/commons/5/5b/Flash_Powders.JPG *License:* CC BY 3.0 *Contributors:* Own work *Original artist:* DJSparky
- **File:Folder_Hexagonal_Icon.svg** *Source:* https://upload.wikimedia.org/wikipedia/en/4/48/Folder_Hexagonal_Icon.svg *License:* Cc-by-sa-3.0 *Contributors:* ? *Original artist:* ?
- **File:Fortin_La_Galera_01.jpg** *Source:* https://upload.wikimedia.org/wikipedia/commons/0/0f/Fortin_La_Galera_01.jpg *License:* CC0 *Contributors:* ? *Original artist:* ?
- **File:Free-to-read_lock_75.svg** *Source:* https://upload.wikimedia.org/wikipedia/commons/8/80/Free-to-read_lock_75.svg *License:* CC0 *Contributors:* Adapted from 9px|Open_Access_logo_PLoS_white_green.svg *Original artist:* This version:Trappist_the_monk (talk) (Uploads)
- **File:GHS-pictogram-exclam.svg** *Source:* https://upload.wikimedia.org/wikipedia/commons/c/c3/GHS-pictogram-exclam.svg *License:* Public domain *Contributors:* EPS file exclam.eps from UNECE web site converted with ImageMagick *convert* and with *potrace*, edited in *inkscape* *Original artist:* Unknown<a href='//www.wikidata.org/wiki/Q4233718' title='wikidata:Q4233718'><img alt='wikidata:Q4233718' src='https://upload.wikimedia.org/wikipedia/commons/thumb/f/ff/Wikidata-logo.svg/20px-Wikidata-logo.svg.png' width='20' height='11' srcset='https://upload.wikimedia.org/wikipedia/commons/thumb/f/ff/Wikidata-logo.svg/30px-Wikidata-logo.svg.png 1.5x, https://upload.wikimedia.org/wikipedia/commons/thumb/f/ff/Wikidata-logo.svg/40px-Wikidata-logo.svg.png 2x' data-file-width='1050' data-file-height='590' /></a>
- **File:GHS-pictogram-explos.svg** *Source:* https://upload.wikimedia.org/wikipedia/commons/4/4a/GHS-pictogram-explos.svg *License:* Public domain *Contributors:* EPS file explos.eps from UNECE web site converted with ImageMagick *convert* and with *potrace*, edited in *inkscape* *Original artist:* Unknown<a href='//www.wikidata.org/wiki/Q4233718' title='wikidata:Q4233718'><img alt='wikidata:Q4233718' src='https://upload.wikimedia.org/wikipedia/commons/thumb/f/ff/Wikidata-logo.svg/20px-Wikidata-logo.svg.png' width='20' height='11' srcset='https://upload.wikimedia.org/wikipedia/commons/thumb/f/ff/Wikidata-logo.svg/30px-Wikidata-logo.svg.png 1.5x, https://upload.wikimedia.org/wikipedia/commons/thumb/f/ff/Wikidata-logo.svg/40px-Wikidata-logo.svg.png 2x' data-file-width='1050' data-file-height='590' /></a>
- **File:GHS-pictogram-flamme.svg** *Source:* https://upload.wikimedia.org/wikipedia/commons/6/6d/GHS-pictogram-flamme.svg *License:* Public domain *Contributors:* EPS file flamme.eps from UNECE web site converted with ImageMagick *convert* and with *potrace*, edited and flame redrawn in *inkscape* *Original artist:* Unknown<a href='//www.wikidata.org/wiki/Q4233718' title='wikidata:Q4233718'><img alt='wikidata:Q4233718' src='https://upload.wikimedia.org/wikipedia/commons/thumb/f/ff/Wikidata-logo.svg/20px-Wikidata-logo.svg.png' width='20' height='11' srcset='https://upload.wikimedia.org/wikipedia/commons/thumb/f/ff/Wikidata-logo.svg/30px-Wikidata-logo.svg.png 1.5x, https://upload.wikimedia.org/wikipedia/commons/thumb/f/ff/Wikidata-logo.svg/40px-Wikidata-logo.svg.png 2x' data-file-width='1050' data-file-height='590' /></a>
- **File:GHS-pictogram-rondflam.svg** *Source:* https://upload.wikimedia.org/wikipedia/commons/e/e5/GHS-pictogram-rondflam.svg *License:* Public domain *Contributors:* EPS file rondflam.eps from UNECE web site converted with ImageMagick *convert* and with *potrace*, edited and flame redrawn in *inkscape* *Original artist:* Unknown<a href='//www.wikidata.org/wiki/Q4233718' title='wikidata:Q4233718'><img alt='wikidata:Q4233718' src='https://upload.wikimedia.org/wikipedia/commons/thumb/f/ff/Wikidata-logo.svg/20px-Wikidata-logo.svg.png' width='20' height='11' srcset='https://upload.wikimedia.org/wikipedia/commons/thumb/f/ff/Wikidata-logo.svg/30px-Wikidata-logo.svg.png 1.5x, https://upload.wikimedia.org/wikipedia/commons/thumb/f/ff/Wikidata-logo.svg/40px-Wikidata-logo.svg.png 2x' data-file-width='1050' data-file-height='590' /></a>

- File:Gurney-Asymmetrical-Sandwich.png *Source:* https://upload.wikimedia.org/wikipedia/commons/a/a2/Gurney-Asymmetrical-Sandwich.png *License:* CC BY-SA 3.0 *Contributors:* Own work *Original artist:* Georgewilliamherbert

- File:Gurney-Cylindrical-Implosion.png *Source:* https://upload.wikimedia.org/wikipedia/commons/d/d2/Gurney-Cylindrical-Implosion.png *License:* CC BY-SA 3.0 *Contributors:* Own work *Original artist:* Georgewilliamherbert

- File:Gurney-Cylindrical.png *Source:* https://upload.wikimedia.org/wikipedia/commons/5/53/Gurney-Cylindrical.png *License:* CC BY-SA 3.0 *Contributors:* Own work *Original artist:* Georgewilliamherbert

- File:Gurney-Effective-Volume.png *Source:* https://upload.wikimedia.org/wikipedia/commons/6/6a/Gurney-Effective-Volume.png *License:* CC BY-SA 3.0 *Contributors:* Own work *Original artist:* Georgewilliamherbert

- File:Gurney-Infinitely-Tamped-Sandwich.png *Source:* https://upload.wikimedia.org/wikipedia/commons/5/55/Gurney-Infinitely-Tamped-Sandwich.png *License:* CC BY-SA 3.0 *Contributors:* Own work *Original artist:* Georgewilliamherbert

- File:Gurney-Open-Faced-Sandwich.png *Source:* https://upload.wikimedia.org/wikipedia/commons/5/5f/Gurney-Open-Faced-Sandwich.png *License:* CC BY-SA 3.0 *Contributors:* Own work *Original artist:* Georgewilliamherbert

- File:Gurney-Spherical-Implosion.png *Source:* https://upload.wikimedia.org/wikipedia/commons/5/5c/Gurney-Spherical-Implosion.png *License:* CC BY-SA 3.0 *Contributors:* Own work *Original artist:* Georgewilliamherbert

- File:Gurney-Spherical.png *Source:* https://upload.wikimedia.org/wikipedia/commons/a/a9/Gurney-Spherical.png *License:* CC BY-SA 3.0 *Contributors:* Own work *Original artist:* Georgewilliamherbert

- File:Gurney-Symmetrical-Sandwich.png *Source:* https://upload.wikimedia.org/wikipedia/commons/7/71/Gurney-Symmetrical-Sandwich.png *License:* CC BY-SA 3.0 *Contributors:* Own work *Original artist:* Georgewilliamherbert

- File:HMX-3D-balls.png *Source:* https://upload.wikimedia.org/wikipedia/commons/2/21/HMX-3D-balls.png *License:* Public domain *Contributors:* ? *Original artist:* ?

- File:HMX.png *Source:* https://upload.wikimedia.org/wikipedia/commons/0/0b/HMX.png *License:* Public domain *Contributors:* http://en.wikipedia.org/wiki/Image:HMX.png *Original artist:* Edgar181

- File:Hagley_Mill_Equipment.jpg *Source:* https://upload.wikimedia.org/wikipedia/commons/2/22/Hagley_Mill_Equipment.jpg *License:* CC-BY-SA-3.0 *Contributors:* Own work *Original artist:* Ukexpat

- File:Handling_Explosives_in_Underground_Mines.webm *Source:* https://upload.wikimedia.org/wikipedia/commons/6/6a/Handling_Explosives_in_Underground_Mines.webm *License:* Public domain *Contributors:* NIOSH YouTube Channel *Original artist:* National Institute for Occupational Safety and Health

- File:Hazard_E.svg *Source:* https://upload.wikimedia.org/wikipedia/commons/b/bb/Hazard_E.svg *License:* Public domain *Contributors:* Converted from EPS file at http://forum.cptec.org/index.php?showtopic=368 *Original artist:* ?

- File:Hazard_N.svg *Source:* https://upload.wikimedia.org/wikipedia/commons/6/6a/Hazard_N.svg *License:* Public domain *Contributors:* Converted from EPS file at http://forum.cptec.org/index.php?showtopic=368 *Original artist:* See historic

- File:Hazard_T.svg *Source:* https://upload.wikimedia.org/wikipedia/commons/3/39/Hazard_T.svg *License:* Public domain *Contributors:* ? *Original artist:* ?

- File:Hazard_TT.svg *Source:* https://upload.wikimedia.org/wikipedia/commons/8/86/Hazard_TT.svg *License:* Public domain *Contributors:* ? *Original artist:* ?

- File:Helmet_logo_for_Underwater_Diving_portal.png *Source:* https://upload.wikimedia.org/wikipedia/commons/5/5e/Helmet_logo_for_Underwater_Diving_portal.png *License:* Public domain *Contributors:* This file was derived from Kask-nurka.jpg: <a href='//commons.wikimedia.org/wiki/File:Kask-nurka.jpg' class='image'><img alt='Kask-nurka.jpg' src='https://upload.wikimedia.org/wikipedia/commons/thumb/0/0a/Kask-nurka.jpg/50px-Kask-nurka.jpg' width='50' height='70' srcset='https://upload.wikimedia.org/wikipedia/commons/thumb/0/0a/Kask-nurka.jpg/75px-Kask-nurka.jpg 1.5x, https://upload.wikimedia.org/wikipedia/commons/thumb/0/0a/Kask-nurka.jpg/100px-Kask-nurka.jpg 2x' data-file-width='981' data-file-height='1371' /></a>
  Original artist: Kask-nurka.jpg: User:Julo

- File:Home-made_explosives_packed_in_oil_drums_being_dealt_with_by_EOD_Operator._MOD_45159058.jpg *Source:* https://upload.wikimedia.org/wikipedia/commons/6/67/Home-made_explosives_packed_in_oil_drums_being_dealt_with_by_EOD_Operator._MOD_45159058.jpg *License:* OGL *Contributors:*
  Photo http://www.defenceimagery.mod.uk/fotoweb/fwbin/download.dll/45153802.jpg *Original artist:* Unknown<a href='//www.wikidata.org/wiki/Q4233718' title='wikidata:Q4233718'><img alt='wikidata:Q4233718' src='https://upload.wikimedia.org/wikipedia/commons/thumb/f/ff/Wikidata-logo.svg/20px-Wikidata-logo.svg.png' width='20' height='11' srcset='https://upload.wikimedia.org/wikipedia/commons/thumb/f/ff/Wikidata-logo.svg/30px-Wikidata-logo.svg.png 1.5x, https://upload.wikimedia.org/wikipedia/commons/thumb/f/ff/Wikidata-logo.svg/40px-Wikidata-logo.svg.png 2x' data-file-width='1050' data-file-height='590' /></a>

- File:IDF-D9-Zachi-Evenor-001.jpg *Source:* https://upload.wikimedia.org/wikipedia/commons/f/f2/IDF-D9-Zachi-Evenor-001.jpg *License:* CC BY 3.0 *Contributors:* Flickr: https://www.flickr.com/photos/zachievenor/6969547720/in/photostream/ *Original artist:* Zachi Evenor, Israel

- File:IED_Baghdad_from_munitions.jpg *Source:* https://upload.wikimedia.org/wikipedia/commons/a/a5/IED_Baghdad_from_munitions.jpg *License:* Public domain *Contributors:* ? *Original artist:* ?

- File:IED_Controlled_Explosion.jpg *Source:* https://upload.wikimedia.org/wikipedia/commons/9/96/IED_Controlled_Explosion.jpg *License:* Public domain *Contributors:* Transferred from en.wikipedia to Commons by Sreejithk2000 using CommonsHelper. *Original artist:* Jumping cheese at English Wikipedia

48.3. TEXT AND IMAGE SOURCES, CONTRIBUTORS, AND LICENSES

- File:IED_detonator.jpg *Source:* https://upload.wikimedia.org/wikipedia/commons/a/a5/IED_detonator.jpg *License:* Public domain *Contributors:* U.S. Dept. of Defense here. *Original artist:* Lance Cpl. Bobby J. Segovia
- File:Ibn_Ghanims_gun.jpg *Source:* https://upload.wikimedia.org/wikipedia/commons/3/39/Ibn_Ghanims_gun.jpg *License:* CC BY-SA 3.0 *Contributors:* Own work *Original artist:* Yakumaku
- File:Improvised_explosive_device_explosively_formed_penetrator_Iraq.jpg *Source:* https://upload.wikimedia.org/wikipedia/commons/b/be/Improvised_explosive_device_explosively_formed_penetrator_Iraq.jpg *License:* Public domain *Contributors:* Transferred from en.wikipedia to Commons. *Original artist:* StuCPO at English Wikipedia
- File:Inspection_of_IED_(Improvised_Explosive_Device)_by_X-ray.jpg *Source:* https://upload.wikimedia.org/wikipedia/commons/a/ae/Inspection_of_IED_%28Improvised_Explosive_Device%29_by_X-ray.jpg *License:* CC BY-SA 3.0 *Contributors:* Own work *Original artist:* RadXman
- File:Iraq_carbomb.jpg *Source:* https://upload.wikimedia.org/wikipedia/commons/4/44/Iraq_carbomb.jpg *License:* Public domain *Contributors:* ? *Original artist:* ?
- File:Irvinepowderhouse2.JPG *Source:* https://upload.wikimedia.org/wikipedia/commons/b/b7/Irvinepowderhouse2.JPG *License:* Public domain *Contributors:* Transferred from en.wikipedia *Original artist:* Rosser1954 at en.wikipedia
- File:J._C._Stövesandt_1748_Deutliche_Anweisung_zur_Feuerwerkerey.jpg *Source:* https://upload.wikimedia.org/wikipedia/commons/b/b9/J._C._St%C3%B6vesandt_1748_Deutliche_Anweisung_zur_Feuerwerkerey.jpg *License:* Public domain *Contributors:* Chemical Heritage Foundation *Original artist:* Stövesandt, J. C.
- File:KatyushaMusee.jpg *Source:* https://upload.wikimedia.org/wikipedia/commons/9/9d/KatyushaMusee.jpg *License:* Public domain *Contributors:* Taken by me in Paris. *Original artist:* User:Ben_pcc
- File:Large_bonfire.jpg *Source:* https://upload.wikimedia.org/wikipedia/commons/3/36/Large_bonfire.jpg *License:* CC-BY-SA-3.0 *Contributors:* Originally uploaded to the English Wikipedia here by the author *Original artist:* Fir0002
- File:Light_box_displaying_a_nitrate_photograph_negative_panorama_suffering_from_deterioration.jpg *Source:* https://upload.wikimedia.org/wikipedia/commons/2/26/Light_box_displaying_a_nitrate_photograph_negative_panorama_suffering_from_deterioration.jpg *License:* CC BY 2.0 *Contributors:* http://www.flickr.com/photos/lac-bac/5861164524/sizes/o/in/photostream/ *Original artist:* Library and Archives Canada
- File:Log_in_fireplace.jpg *Source:* https://upload.wikimedia.org/wikipedia/commons/9/93/Log_in_fireplace.jpg *License:* GFDL 1.2 *Contributors:* Own work *Original artist:*
fir0002 | flagstaffotos.com.au
- File:Martello_Tower_barrels.jpg *Source:* https://upload.wikimedia.org/wikipedia/commons/9/98/Martello_Tower_barrels.jpg *License:* Public domain *Contributors:* Own work (Original text: *I (Grmike (talk)) created this work entirely by myself.*) *Original artist:* Grmike at English Wikipedia
- File:Meister_der_Shâh-Jahân-Nâma-Memoiren_001.jpg *Source:* https://upload.wikimedia.org/wikipedia/commons/9/93/Meister_der_Sh%C3%A2h-Jah%C3%A2n-N%C3%A2ma-Memoiren_001.jpg *License:* Public domain *Contributors:* The Yorck Project: *10.000 Meisterwerke der Malerei*. DVD-ROM, 2002. ISBN 3936122202. Distributed by DIRECTMEDIA Publishing GmbH. *Original artist:* Meister der Shâh-Jahân-Nâma-Memoiren
- File:Merge-arrow.svg *Source:* https://upload.wikimedia.org/wikipedia/commons/a/aa/Merge-arrow.svg *License:* Public domain *Contributors:* ? *Original artist:* ?
- File:Mergefrom.svg *Source:* https://upload.wikimedia.org/wikipedia/commons/0/0f/Mergefrom.svg *License:* Public domain *Contributors:* ? *Original artist:* ?
- File:Ming_matchlocks.jpg *Source:* https://upload.wikimedia.org/wikipedia/commons/5/50/Ming_matchlocks.jpg *License:* Public domain *Contributors:* ? *Original artist:* ?
- File:Môko_Shûrai_Ekotoba.jpg *Source:* https://upload.wikimedia.org/wikipedia/commons/1/19/M%C5%8Dko_Sh%C5%ABrai_Ekotoba.jpg *License:* Public domain *Contributors:* 蒙古襲来絵詞 *Original artist:* 竹崎季長
- File:NNSA-NSO-787.jpg *Source:* https://upload.wikimedia.org/wikipedia/commons/e/eb/NNSA-NSO-787.jpg *License:* Public domain *Contributors:* This image is available from the National Nuclear Security Administration Nevada Site Office Photo Library under ID 787. *Original artist:* National Nuclear Security Administration / Nevada Site Office
- File:NTS_-_BEEF_-_WATUSI.jpg *Source:* https://upload.wikimedia.org/wikipedia/commons/3/31/NTS_-_BEEF_-_WATUSI.jpg *License:* Public domain *Contributors:* Nevada National Security Site Tour Booklet, part 2 *Original artist:* National Nuclear Security Administration / Nevada Site Office
- File:Nagasakibomb.jpg *Source:* https://upload.wikimedia.org/wikipedia/commons/e/e0/Nagasakibomb.jpg *License:* Public domain *Contributors:* http://www.archives.gov/research/military/ww2/photos/images/ww2-163.jpg National Archives image (208-N-43888) *Original artist:* Charles Levy from one of the B-29 Superfortresses used in the attack.
- File:Nalleja.jpg *Source:* https://upload.wikimedia.org/wikipedia/commons/8/84/Nalleja.jpg *License:* CC BY-SA 2.5 *Contributors:* Own work *Original artist:* Timo Halén
- File:Nirtoglycerin_3D_BallStick.png *Source:* https://upload.wikimedia.org/wikipedia/commons/1/1f/Nitrogylcerin_%283D_ball-and-stick_model%29.png *License:* Public domain *Contributors:* Own work *Original artist:* Woodenchemist
- File:Nitrocellulose-2D-skeletal.png *Source:* https://upload.wikimedia.org/wikipedia/commons/8/83/Nitrocellulose-2D-skeletal.png *License:* Public domain *Contributors:* ? *Original artist:* ?

- File:Nitrocellulose-3D-balls.png Source: https://upload.wikimedia.org/wikipedia/commons/e/ec/Nitrocellulose-3D-balls.png License: Public domain Contributors: ? Original artist: ?
- File:Nitrocellulose_01.JPG Source: https://upload.wikimedia.org/wikipedia/commons/4/4a/Nitrocellulose_01.JPG License: CC BY 4.0 Contributors: Own work Original artist: Aleksander Sobolewski
- File:Nitrocellulose_02.ogv Source: https://upload.wikimedia.org/wikipedia/commons/9/9f/Nitrocellulose_02.ogv License: CC BY 4.0 Contributors: Own work Original artist: Aleksander Sobolewski
- File:Nitrocellulose_hexanitrate.jpg Source: https://upload.wikimedia.org/wikipedia/commons/3/3e/Nitrocellulose_hexanitrate.jpg License: CC-BY-SA-3.0 Contributors: ? Original artist: ?
- File:Nitroglycerin-3D-vdW.png Source: https://upload.wikimedia.org/wikipedia/commons/c/cd/Nitroglycerin-3D-vdW.png License: Public domain Contributors: ? Original artist: ?
- File:Nitroglycerin.svg Source: https://upload.wikimedia.org/wikipedia/commons/a/a7/Nitroglycerin.svg License: Public domain Contributors: Own work Original artist: Mrgreen71
- File:Nitroglycerin_Synthesis_V.1.svg Source: https://upload.wikimedia.org/wikipedia/commons/6/6c/Nitroglycerin_Synthesis_V.1.svg License: Public domain Contributors: Own work Original artist: Jü
- File:Nitropenta_synthesis.svg Source: https://upload.wikimedia.org/wikipedia/commons/8/8c/Nitropenta_synthesis.svg License: Public domain Contributors: Own work Original artist: Codc (<a href='//commons.wikimedia.org/wiki/User_talk:Codc' title='User talk:Codc'>talk</a>)
- File:Nobel_patent.jpg Source: https://upload.wikimedia.org/wikipedia/commons/6/6c/Nobel_patent.jpg License: Public domain Contributors: http://www.statensarkiv.se/default.aspx?id=12231 Original artist: Alfred Nobel
- File:Nuclear_Weapon.ogg Source: https://upload.wikimedia.org/wikipedia/commons/a/ab/Nuclear_Weapon.ogg License: GFDL Contributors:
- Derivative of Nuclear Weapon Original artist: Speaker: Markkasan
  Authors of the article
- File:Nuclear_fuel_pellets.jpeg Source: https://upload.wikimedia.org/wikipedia/commons/a/ae/Nuclear_fuel_pellets.jpeg License: Public domain Contributors: ? Original artist: ?
- File:Operation_Castle_-_Romeo_001.jpg Source: https://upload.wikimedia.org/wikipedia/commons/a/a7/Operation_Castle_-_Romeo_001.jpg License: Public domain Contributors: This image is available from the National Nuclear Security Administration Nevada Site Office Photo Library under number XX-33. Original artist: United States Department of Energy
- File:Operation_Upshot-Knothole_-_Badger_001.jpg Source: https://upload.wikimedia.org/wikipedia/commons/7/79/Operation_Upshot-Knothole_-_Badger_001.jpg License: Public domain Contributors: This image is available from the National Nuclear Security Administration Nevada Site Office Photo Library under number XX-34. Original artist: Photo courtesy of National Nuclear Security Administration / Nevada Site Office
- File:PETN-from-xtal-2006-3D-balls-B.png Source: https://upload.wikimedia.org/wikipedia/commons/6/6c/PETN-from-xtal-2006-3D-balls-B.png License: Public domain Contributors: Own work Original artist: Ben Mills
- File:PETN.svg Source: https://upload.wikimedia.org/wikipedia/commons/8/88/PETN.svg License: Public domain Contributors: Own work Original artist: Bangin
- File:Pentaerythritol_tetranitrate_04.JPG Source: https://upload.wikimedia.org/wikipedia/commons/e/ec/Pentaerythritol_tetranitrate_04.JPG License: CC BY 4.0 Contributors: Own work Original artist: Aleksander Sobolewski
- File:Pentryt.jpg Source: https://upload.wikimedia.org/wikipedia/commons/5/55/Pentryt.jpg License: CC BY 4.0 Contributors: Own work Original artist: Aleksander Sobolewski
- File:Photography_of_bow_shock_waves_around_a_brass_bullet,_1888.jpg Source: https://upload.wikimedia.org/wikipedia/commons/0/09/Photography_of_bow_shock_waves_around_a_brass_bullet%2C_1888.jpg License: Public domain Contributors: Scan from book (now lost) Original artist: Ernst Mach (1838–1916)
- File:Pistolet_à_percussion_inversée_IMG_3074.jpg Source: https://upload.wikimedia.org/wikipedia/commons/c/c9/Pistolet_%C3%A0_percussion_invers%C3%A9e_IMG_3074.jpg License: CC BY-SA 2.0 fr Contributors: Own work Original artist: Rama
- File:PonceauMembrane.png Source: https://upload.wikimedia.org/wikipedia/commons/e/ec/PonceauMembrane.png License: CC BY-SA 3.0 Contributors: Own work Original artist: Argymeg
- File:Portal-puzzle.svg Source: https://upload.wikimedia.org/wikipedia/en/f/fd/Portal-puzzle.svg License: Public domain Contributors: ? Original artist: ?
- File:Powder_Samples.jpg Source: https://upload.wikimedia.org/wikipedia/commons/1/1e/Powder_Samples.jpg License: CC-BY-SA-3.0 Contributors: Own work Original artist: Arthurrh
- File:Pressure_exerted_by_collisions.svg Source: https://upload.wikimedia.org/wikipedia/commons/9/94/Pressure_exerted_by_collisions.svg License: CC BY-SA 3.0 Contributors: Own work, see http://www.becarlson.com/ Original artist: Becarlson
- File:Pressure_force_area.svg Source: https://upload.wikimedia.org/wikipedia/commons/f/ff/Pressure_force_area.svg License: CC BY-SA 3.0 Contributors: Own work Original artist: Klaus-Dieter Keller
- File:Pressure_plot.png Source: https://upload.wikimedia.org/wikipedia/commons/4/40/Pressure_plot.png License: Public domain Contributors: self-made in en:Inkscape. (The SVG version of the file is here.) Original artist: -- Myth (Talk) 04:54, 9 March 2007 (UTC)
- File:Propane_tank_20lb.jpg Source: https://upload.wikimedia.org/wikipedia/commons/f/fe/Propane_tank_20lb.jpg License: CC BY-SA 3.0 Contributors: Own work Original artist: Hustvedt

48.3. TEXT AND IMAGE SOURCES, CONTRIBUTORS, AND LICENSES

- **File:Question_book-new.svg** *Source:* https://upload.wikimedia.org/wikipedia/en/9/99/Question_book-new.svg *License:* Cc-by-sa-3.0 *Contributors:*
  Created from scratch in Adobe Illustrator. Based on Image:Question book.png created by User:Equazcion *Original artist:*
  Tkgd2007

- **File:RDX.svg** *Source:* https://upload.wikimedia.org/wikipedia/commons/8/8c/RDX.svg *License:* Public domain *Contributors:* Own work *Original artist:* Snubcube (<a href='//commons.wikimedia.org/wiki/User_talk:Snubcube' title='User talk:Snubcube'>talk</a>)

- **File:RDX_3D_BallStick.png** *Source:* https://upload.wikimedia.org/wikipedia/commons/7/77/RDX_3D_BallStick.png *License:* Public domain *Contributors:* Own work *Original artist:* Woodenchemist

- **File:Radioactive.svg** *Source:* https://upload.wikimedia.org/wikipedia/commons/b/b5/Radioactive.svg *License:* Public domain *Contributors:* Created by Cary Bass using Adobe Illustrator on January 19, 2006. *Original artist:* Cary Bass

- **File:Rael_Nuclear_use_locations_world_map.png** *Source:* https://upload.wikimedia.org/wikipedia/commons/a/a1/Rael_Nuclear_use_locations_world_map.png *License:* CC BY-SA 3.0 *Contributors:* in Paint
  Previously published: 25-07-2012 *Original artist:* Palli3000

- **File:Rocket_warfare.jpg** *Source:* https://upload.wikimedia.org/wikipedia/commons/c/c6/Rocket_warfare.jpg *License:* Public domain *Contributors:* nasa.gov "Reproduced from a painting by Charles Hubbell and presented here courtesy of TRW Inc. and Western Reserve Historical Society, Cleveland, Ohio" *Original artist:* Charles H. Hubbell (1898-1971)

- **File:SS-24_silo_destruction.jpg** *Source:* https://upload.wikimedia.org/wikipedia/commons/9/9c/SS-24_silo_destruction.jpg *License:* Public domain *Contributors:* ? *Original artist:* ?

- **File:Schlierenfoto_Mach_1-2_Pfeilflügel_-_NASA.jpg** *Source:* https://upload.wikimedia.org/wikipedia/commons/7/7b/Schlierenfoto_Mach_1-2_Pfeilfl%C3%BCgel_-_NASA.jpg *License:* Public domain *Contributors:* ? *Original artist:* NASA

- **File:Sedan_Plowshare_Crater.jpg** *Source:* https://upload.wikimedia.org/wikipedia/commons/b/b6/Sedan_Plowshare_Crater.jpg *License:* Public domain *Contributors:* This image is available from the National Nuclear Security Administration Nevada Site Office Photo Library under number NF-12187. *Original artist:* Federal Government of the United States

- **File:Sellier_&_Bellot_logo.png** *Source:* https://upload.wikimedia.org/wikipedia/en/5/5b/Sellier_%26_Bellot_logo.png *License:* Fair use *Contributors:*
  The logo is from the http://www.fs.cvut.cz/cz/u218/obor/industry/clikmapa/region/logo/jihcech/sellier.jpg website. http://www.fs.cvut.cz/cz/u218/obor/industry/clikmapa/region/logo/jihcech/sellier.jpg *Original artist:* ?

- **File:Size0-army_mil-44434-2009-07-10-090719.jpg** *Source:* https://upload.wikimedia.org/wikipedia/commons/1/1a/Size0-army_mil-44434-2009-07-10-090719.jpg *License:* Public domain *Contributors:* http://www.army.mil/-images/2009/07/09/44434/index.html *Original artist:* United States Army

- **File:Sound-icon.svg** *Source:* https://upload.wikimedia.org/wikipedia/commons/4/47/Sound-icon.svg *License:* LGPL *Contributors:* Derivative work from Silsor's versio *Original artist:* Crystal SVG icon set

- **File:SpongeDiver.jpg** *Source:* https://upload.wikimedia.org/wikipedia/commons/8/81/SpongeDiver.jpg *License:* Public domain *Contributors:* Own work *Original artist:* Bryan Shrode

- **File:Start_of_Tet_Offensive.png** *Source:* https://upload.wikimedia.org/wikipedia/commons/e/ed/Start_of_Tet_Offensive.png *License:* CC BY-SA 4.0 *Contributors:* Own work *Original artist:* Icemanwcs

- **File:Supersonic-bullet-shadowgram-Settles.tif** *Source:* https://upload.wikimedia.org/wikipedia/commons/8/89/Supersonic-bullet-shadowgram-Settles.tif *License:* CC BY-SA 3.0 *Contributors:* Own work *Original artist:* Settles1

- **File:Symbol_book_class2.svg** *Source:* https://upload.wikimedia.org/wikipedia/commons/8/89/Symbol_book_class2.svg *License:* CC BY-SA 2.5 *Contributors:* Mad by Lokal_Profil by combining: *Original artist:* Lokal_Profil

- **File:Symbol_list_class.svg** *Source:* https://upload.wikimedia.org/wikipedia/en/d/db/Symbol_list_class.svg *License:* Public domain *Contributors:* ? *Original artist:* ?

- **File:TNT-from-xtal-1982-3D-balls.png** *Source:* https://upload.wikimedia.org/wikipedia/commons/2/24/TNT-from-xtal-1982-3D-balls.png *License:* Public domain *Contributors:* Own work *Original artist:* Ben Mills

- **File:TNT_Allocations_Germany.gif** *Source:* https://upload.wikimedia.org/wikipedia/commons/d/db/TNT_Allocations_Germany.gif *License:* Public domain *Contributors:* http://www.sturmvogel.orbat.com/ussbsappd.html *Original artist:* The U.S. Strategic Bombing Survey: European Theater of Operations

- **File:TNT_detonation_on_Kahoolawe_Island_during_Operation_Sailoir_Hat,_sjot_Bravo,_1965.jpg** *Source:* https://upload.wikimedia.org/wikipedia/commons/e/ef/TNT_detonation_on_Kahoolawe_Island_during_Operation_Sailoir_Hat%2C_sjot_Bravo%2C_1965.jpg *License:* Public domain *Contributors:* Naval Historical Center / http://www.history.navy.mil/photos/events/ev-1960s/ev-1965/op-sa-ht.htm *Original artist:* US Navy Employee

- **File:Teller-Ulam_device_3D.svg** *Source:* https://upload.wikimedia.org/wikipedia/commons/c/c1/Teller-Ulam_device_3D.svg *License:* Public domain *Contributors:* ? *Original artist:* ?

- **File:Tetracyanoquinodimethane_Formula_V.1.svg** *Source:* https://upload.wikimedia.org/wikipedia/commons/6/67/Tetracyanoquinodimethane_Formula_V.1.svg *License:* CC0 *Contributors:* Own work *Original artist:* Jü

- **File:Tetrameric_Acetone_Peroxide_01.JPG** *Source:* https://upload.wikimedia.org/wikipedia/commons/b/b1/Tetrameric_Acetone_Peroxide_01.JPG *License:* CC BY 4.0 *Contributors:* Own work *Original artist:* Aleksander Sobolewski

- File:Text_document_with_red_question_mark.svg *Source:* https://upload.wikimedia.org/wikipedia/commons/a/a4/Text_document_with_red_question_mark.svg *License:* Public domain *Contributors:* Created by bdesham with Inkscape; based upon Text-x-generic.svg from the Tango project. *Original artist:* Benjamin D. Esham (bdesham)

- File:Transonic_flow_patterns.svg *Source:* https://upload.wikimedia.org/wikipedia/commons/6/6d/Transonic_flow_patterns.svg *License:* Public domain *Contributors:* Airplane Flying Handbook. U.S. Government Printing Office, Washington D.C.: U.S. Federal Aviation Administration, p. 15-7. FAA-8083-3A. *Original artist:* U.S. Federal Aviation Administration

- File:Trident_C-4_montage.jpg *Source:* https://upload.wikimedia.org/wikipedia/commons/7/7f/Trident_C-4_montage.jpg *License:* Public domain *Contributors:* ? *Original artist:* ?

- File:Trinitrotoluen.JPG *Source:* https://upload.wikimedia.org/wikipedia/commons/9/9d/Trinitrotoluen.JPG *License:* CC BY-SA 3.0 *Contributors:* Own work *Original artist:* Daniel Grohmann

- File:Trinitrotoluene.svg *Source:* https://upload.wikimedia.org/wikipedia/commons/c/c4/Trinitrotoluene.svg *License:* Public domain *Contributors:* ? *Original artist:* ?

- File:Trinity_explosion_film_strip.jpg *Source:* https://upload.wikimedia.org/wikipedia/commons/a/ab/Trinity_explosion_film_strip.jpg *License:* Public domain *Contributors:* [1] *Original artist:* Berlyn Brixner.

- File:Tu_braunschweig_750_grad_ofen.jpg *Source:* https://upload.wikimedia.org/wikipedia/commons/4/48/Tu_braunschweig_750_grad_ofen.jpg *License:* CC BY 3.0 *Contributors:* Own work *Original artist:* Achim Hering

- File:Tu_braunschweig_b1_brandschacht.jpg *Source:* https://upload.wikimedia.org/wikipedia/commons/5/5f/Tu_braunschweig_b1_brandschacht.jpg *License:* CC BY 3.0 *Contributors:* Own work *Original artist:* Achim Hering

- File:Tu_braunschweig_b1_ofen_gestell.jpg *Source:* https://upload.wikimedia.org/wikipedia/commons/d/d8/Tu_braunschweig_b1_ofen_gestell.jpg *License:* CC BY 3.0 *Contributors:* Own work *Original artist:* Achim Hering

- File:Tání_TNT_při_81_°C.JPG *Source:* https://upload.wikimedia.org/wikipedia/commons/5/51/T%C3%A1n%C3%AD_TNT_p%C5%99i_81_%C2%B0C.JPG *License:* CC BY-SA 3.0 *Contributors:* Own work *Original artist:* Daniel Grohmann

- File:USMC-100414-M-5241M-001.jpg *Source:* https://upload.wikimedia.org/wikipedia/commons/4/4c/USMC-100414-M-5241M-001.jpg *License:* Public domain *Contributors:*
  This Image was released by the United States Marine Corps with the ID 100414-M-5241M-001 <a class='external text' href='//commons.wikimedia.org/w/index.php?title=Category:Files_created_by_the_United_States_Marine_Corps_with_known_IDs,,&,,filefrom=100414-M-5241M-001#mw-category-media'>(next)</a>.
  This tag does not indicate the copyright status of the attached work. A normal copyright tag is still required. See Commons:Licensing for more information.
  Original artist: ?

- File:US_Navy_111213-N-BA263-596_Composition_C-4_demolition_charges_await_use_as_explosive_ordnance_disposal_technicians_assigned_to_Commander,_Task_Grou.jpg *Source:* https://upload.wikimedia.org/wikipedia/commons/f/fe/US_Navy_111213-N-BA263-596_Composition_C-4_demolition_charges_await_use_as_explosive_ordnance_disposal_technicians_assigned_to_Commander%2C_Task_Grou.jpg *License:* Public domain *Contributors:*
  This Image was released by the United States Navy with the ID 111213-N-BA263-596 <a class='external text' href='//commons.wikimedia.org/w/index.php?title=Category:Files_created_by_the_United_States_Navy_with_known_IDs,,&,,filefrom=111213-N-BA263-596#mw-category-media'>(next)</a>.
  This tag does not indicate the copyright status of the attached work. A normal copyright tag is still required. See Commons:Licensing for more information.
  Original artist: U.S. Navy photo by Chief Mass Communication Specialist Kathryn Whittenberger

- File:US_and_USSR_nuclear_stockpiles.svg *Source:* https://upload.wikimedia.org/wikipedia/commons/b/bb/US_and_USSR_nuclear_stockpiles.svg *License:* Public domain *Contributors:* Own work Source data from: Robert S. Norris and Hans M. Kristensen, "Global nuclear stockpiles, 1945-2006," *Bulletin of the Atomic Scientists* 62, no. 4 (July/August 2006), 64-66. Online at http://thebulletin.metapress.com/content/c4120650912x74k7/fulltext.pdf *Original artist:* Created by User:Fastfission first by mapping the lines using OpenOffice.org's Calc program, then exporting a graph to SVG, and the performing substantial aesthetic modifications in Inkscape.

- File:W87_MX_Missile_schematic.jpg *Source:* https://upload.wikimedia.org/wikipedia/commons/7/7c/W87_MX_Missile_schematic.jpg *License:* Public domain *Contributors:* ? *Original artist:* ?

- File:Wheelbarrow_bomb_disposal_device_being_operated_by_a_team_from_321_EOD_MOD_45159057.jpg *Source:* https://upload.wikimedia.org/wikipedia/commons/a/a4/Wheelbarrow_bomb_disposal_device_being_operated_by_a_team_from_321_EOD_MOD_45159057.jpg *License:* OGL *Contributors:*
  Photo http://www.defenceimagery.mod.uk/fotoweb/fwbin/download.dll/45153802.jpg *Original artist:* Unknown<a href='//www.wikidata.org/wiki/Q4233718' title='wikidata:Q4233718'><img alt='wikidata:Q4233718' src='https://upload.wikimedia.org/wikipedia/commons/thumb/f/ff/Wikidata-logo.svg/20px-Wikidata-logo.svg.png' width='20' height='11' srcset='https://upload.wikimedia.org/wikipedia/commons/thumb/f/ff/Wikidata-logo.svg/30px-Wikidata-logo.svg.png 1.5x, https://upload.wikimedia.org/wikipedia/commons/thumb/f/ff/Wikidata-logo.svg/40px-Wikidata-logo.svg.png 2x' data-file-width='1050' data-file-height='590' /></a>

- File:Wiki_letter_w_cropped.svg *Source:* https://upload.wikimedia.org/wikipedia/commons/1/1c/Wiki_letter_w_cropped.svg *License:* CC-BY-SA-3.0 *Contributors:* This file was derived from Wiki letter w.svg: <a href='//commons.wikimedia.org/wiki/File:Wiki_letter_w.svg' class='image'><img alt='Wiki letter w.svg' src='https://upload.wikimedia.org/wikipedia/commons/thumb/6/6c/Wiki_letter_w.svg/50px-Wiki_letter_w.svg.png' width='50' height='50' srcset='https://upload.wikimedia.org/wikipedia/commons/thumb/6/6c/Wiki_letter_w.svg/75px-Wiki_letter_w.svg.png 1.5x, https://upload.wikimedia.org/wikipedia/commons/thumb/6/6c/Wiki_letter_w.svg/100px-Wiki_letter_w.svg.png 2x' data-file-width='44' data-file-height='44' /></a>
  Original artist: Derivative work by Thumperward

- **File:Wikinews-logo.svg** *Source:* https://upload.wikimedia.org/wikipedia/commons/2/24/Wikinews-logo.svg *License:* CC BY-SA 3.0 *Contributors:* This is a cropped version of Image:Wikinews-logo-en.png. *Original artist:* Vectorized by Simon 01:05, 2 August 2006 (UTC) Updated by Time3000 17 April 2007 to use official Wikinews colours and appear correctly on dark backgrounds. Originally uploaded by Simon.
- **File:Wikiquote-logo.svg** *Source:* https://upload.wikimedia.org/wikipedia/commons/f/fa/Wikiquote-logo.svg *License:* Public domain *Contributors:* Own work *Original artist:* Rei-artur
- **File:Wikisource-logo.svg** *Source:* https://upload.wikimedia.org/wikipedia/commons/4/4c/Wikisource-logo.svg *License:* CC BY-SA 3.0 *Contributors:* Rei-artur *Original artist:* Nicholas Moreau
- **File:Wiktionary-logo-v2.svg** *Source:* https://upload.wikimedia.org/wikipedia/commons/0/06/Wiktionary-logo-v2.svg *License:* CC BY-SA 4.0 *Contributors:* Own work *Original artist:* Dan Polansky based on work currently attributed to Wikimedia Foundation but originally created by Smurrayinchester
- **File:Women_Strike_for_Peace_NYWTS.jpg** *Source:* https://upload.wikimedia.org/wikipedia/commons/8/88/Women_Strike_for_Peace_NYWTS.jpg *License:* Public domain *Contributors:* Library of Congress Prints and Photographs Division. New York World-Telegram and the Sun Newspaper Photograph Collection. http://hdl.loc.gov/loc.pnp/cph.3c28465 *Original artist:* New York World-Telegram and the Sun staff photographer: Stanziola, Phil, photographer.
- **File:X_mark.svg** *Source:* https://upload.wikimedia.org/wikipedia/commons/a/a2/X_mark.svg *License:* Public domain *Contributors:* Own work *Original artist:* User:Gmaxwell
- **File:Yes_check.svg** *Source:* https://upload.wikimedia.org/wikipedia/en/f/fb/Yes_check.svg *License:* PD *Contributors:* ? *Original artist:* ?
- **File:Yuan_chinese_gun.jpg** *Source:* https://upload.wikimedia.org/wikipedia/commons/c/cf/Yuan_chinese_gun.jpg *License:* CC BY-SA 3.0 *Contributors:* Own work *Original artist:* Ytrottier

48.3.3 Content license

- Creative Commons Attribution-Share Alike 3.0

Made in the USA
Las Vegas, NV
31 December 2023

83750690R00136